The Native Ground

EARLY AMERICAN STUDIES

Daniel K. Richter and Kathleen M. Brown, Series Editors

Exploring neglected aspects of our colonial, revolutionary, and early national history and culture, Early American Studies reinterprets familiar themes and events in fresh ways. Interdisciplinary in character, and with a special emphasis on the period from about 1600 to 1850, the series is published in partnership with the McNeil Center for Early American Studies.

A complete list of books in the series is available from the publisher.

The Native Ground

Indians and Colonists in the Heart of the Continent

Kathleen DuVal

PENN

University of Pennsylvania Press
Philadelphia

10   9   8   7   6   5   4   3   2   1

Published by
University of Pennsylvania Press
Philadelphia, Pennsylvania 19104-4112

Library of Congress Cataloging-in-Publication Data

DuVal, Kathleen.
    The native ground : Indians and colonists in the heart of the continent / Kathleen DuVal.
       p.   cm.—(Early American studies)
    Includes bibliographic references and index.
    ISBN-13: 978-0-8122-3918-8 (acid-free paper)
    ISBN-10: 0-8122-3918-0 (acid-free paper)
    1. Indians of North America—Arkansas River Valley—History.   2. Indians of North
America—First contact with Europeans—Arkansas River Valley.   3. Colonists—Arkansas
River Valley—History.   4. Arkansas River Valley—Ethnic relations.   5. Arkansas River
Valley—History.   I. Title.   II. Series.
E78.A8D88   2006
976.7'300497—dc22   2005058589

to My Family

Contents

Illustrations

Figures

Maps

Introduction

In the summer of 1673, a Quapaw Indian spotted two canoes full of Frenchmen descending the broad, brown waterway that Algonquian speakers named the *Mississippi*, the "Big River." When the people of Kappa, the northernmost Quapaw town, heard the news, they prepared to welcome the newcomers. Several Quapaws paddled their own canoes into the river, and one held aloft a *calumet*, a peace pipe. As the Quapaws hoped, this sign of peaceful intentions, recognized by native peoples across North America, allayed the fears of their French visitors—Quebec merchant Louis Jolliet, Jesuit priest Jacques Marquette, and their handful of companions. As his canoe pulled up beside the Frenchmen, the man holding the calumet sang a song of welcome. He handed them the pipe, with some cornbread and *sagamité*, corn porridge. After the visitors had smoked and eaten, the Quapaws led them to Kappa, on the banks of the Mississippi some twenty-five miles north of the mouth of the Arkansas River. There, under persimmon and plum trees, the women prepared a place for the visitors to sit among the town's elders, on fine rush mats, surrounded by the warriors. The rest of the men and women of Kappa sat in an outer circle. One of the young men of the town translated for Marquette through an Algonquian language that both of them knew.[1]

The Quapaws' message was clear. They wanted an alliance with the French. From neighbors to the east, the Quapaws had learned of Europeans and the powerful munitions that they traded and gave to their Indian allies. But, as the Quapaw elders explained to their visitors, enemies had "prevented them from becoming acquainted with the Europeans, and from carrying on any trade with them." The Quapaws hoped that Jolliet and Marquette would be the first of many French visitors who would prove steady allies and provide useful goods.

The Quapaws were purposefully shaping the newcomers' understandings of the North American mid-continent and the people who lived there. While the Quapaws demonstrated that they were generous and friendly, they portrayed their enemies as aggressive and dangerous. When the visitors

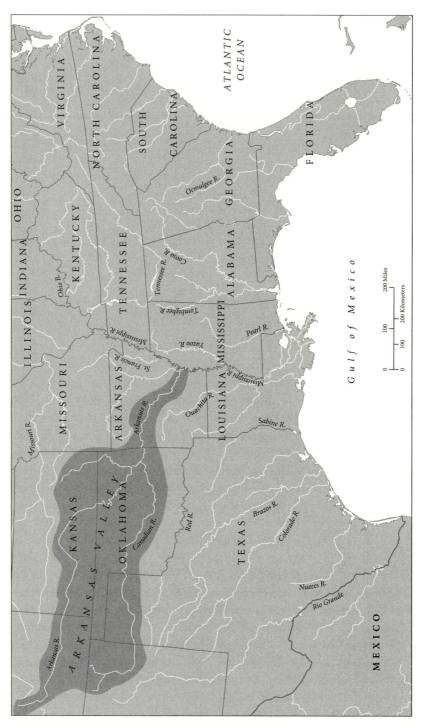

Map 1. The heart of the continent.

mentioned that they intended to continue following the Mississippi to the sea, the Quapaws knew that such a trip would give their rivals, the Tunicas, Yazoos, and Koroas, the opportunity to influence French perceptions and to forge their own exclusive alliance with the visitors. Therefore, the Quapaws warned their guests that the trip would be extremely dangerous because the Indians to the south "had guns and were very warlike." Swayed by the warning, Jolliet and Marquette turned back toward Canada, where they would convey the Quapaws' description of the remainder of the route to the Gulf of Mexico, without having seen it themselves.

While Jolliet and Marquette believed that they were establishing contact with the native people of this region, the Quapaws' situation was a bit more complicated than they revealed. They were particularly interested in shaping French impressions of and involvement in the region because they themselves had only recently settled there. Apparently, some decades earlier, Iroquoian-speakers had used Dutch weapons to raid Indians to their west, compelling several Dhegiha Siouan peoples—the Quapaws, Osages, Omahas, Poncas, and Kansas—to move west of the Mississippi River. Most had headed northwest from the mouth of the Ohio, but the Quapaws had settled farther south, near the juncture of the Arkansas and Mississippi rivers. Here, they faced new challenges from native peoples with longer histories in the region who contested the Quapaws' right to be there. The Tunicas, Yazoos, and Koroas to the south and Caddoan-speaking peoples to the west attacked the newcomers for positioning themselves in territory that the older residents still considered their own. Surrounded by rivals, the Quapaws had no access to the English and Dutch arms trade in the East or the Spanish posts in the West and saw the French visitors as their opportunity to shift local power relations in their favor.[2]

*   *   *

The meeting between the Quapaws and this French party was only one of countless encounters wherein one people attempted to shape another's interpretation of the mid-continent, the region along the central Mississippi River and its western tributaries, the Missouri, St. Francis, White, Arkansas, Ouachita, and Red Rivers. This book particularly centers on the Arkansas River Valley because of its sustained Indian and European diversity. This complicated and contested region experienced waves of successive migrations of Indians and Europeans, from millennia B.C. through the early nineteenth century. At various times, Mississippian chiefdoms, a variety of

Caddoan-speakers, Illinois peoples, Quapaws, Osages, Shawnees, Miamis, and Cherokees called the Arkansas Valley home. France, Spain, Britain, and the United States all attempted to make the region and its peoples part of their empires. Surrounded by numerous and changing potential allies and enemies, the various peoples of the region confronted a constant problem in trying to establish a stable set of relations that would secure their rights to live, hunt, farm, and trade in the heart of the continent.

In their negotiations, Indians and Europeans alike sought to control the culture of diplomacy and trade and to define themselves and others in ways that forwarded their own interests. Both Indians and Europeans purposefully constructed and advanced notions of *us* and *them*, but these categories were never as simple as *Indians* and *Europeans*. Because their lives and livelihoods depended on making distinctions, all were mindful of the differences between, for example, the French and the English, and the Osages and the Shawnees. When new Indians or Europeans arrived, they found themselves recruited by those already there, who sought to teach newcomers their interpretation of the history, customs, and peoples of the region. Which people's vision prevailed depended on their powers of persuasion—verbal, economic, and military.

In the heart of the North American continent, far from centers of European population and power, Indians were more often able to determine the form and content of inter-cultural relations than were their European would-be colonizers. As a whole, Indians outnumbered non-Indians, and every Indian group outnumbered every non-Indian group until at least 1815. Besides their numbers, Indians took advantage of Europeans' lack of information about the region and its peoples to shape their understandings and actions, as the Quapaws did with Jolliet and Marquette in 1673.

Historian Richard White has labeled the colonial Great Lakes region a "middle ground" in which, because no Indians or Europeans could control their neighbors, all had to accommodate the others, together forging new shared meanings and practices, often based on "creative misunderstandings" that allowed Indians and Europeans to hide some of their more incompatible goals and intentions from one another. An aggregation of ethnically and linguistically diverse refugees populated the Great Lakes. Although they based their alliance on their own older beliefs and practices, they needed the "glue" of French mediation and authority to bind them together. In direct contrast, the Arkansas Valley was home to a few large and relatively cohesive tribes from the time the French arrived through the early nineteenth century.[3]

Since the publication of White's masterful book, historians of colonial interactions have tended to assume that Native Americans *wanted* to construct middle grounds with Europeans. In reality, only relatively weak people desired the kind of compromises inherent in a middle ground. Cohesive native peoples preferred to maintain their own sovereign identities and make independent decisions regarding the ways they ran their societies and the uses to which they put their land and resources. And they wanted to set the terms of engagement with neighboring peoples. For Mississippians, Quapaws, Osages, French settlers, Cherokees, and eventually Anglo-Americans, the Arkansas Valley was not a middle ground but each group's claimed native ground. Each people in the Arkansas Valley, no matter how long it had been in the region, portrayed itself as native and thus deserving of a place on the land. So who were the true natives? That question framed the region's history for two centuries. The term *native ground* reflects the diverse and contradictory answers to this question as well as the fact that Native Americans, not Europeans, controlled the Arkansas Valley.

Calling the pre-nineteenth-century Arkansas Valley a native ground should in no way imply that native peoples always respected one another's conceptions of sovereignty, land rights, and relations with others. As the Quapaws' meeting with Jolliet and Marquette attests, Indians often used Europeans and their weapons to gain advantages over other Indians. When Indians lost ground, as the Tunicas did in the sixteenth century, Caddoan-speakers did in the eighteenth century, and the Osages did in the early nineteenth century, they lost it to other Indians. Only in the 1820s did Anglo-American settlers outnumber and overwhelm Arkansas Valley Indians.

*   *   *

In the Arkansas Valley from the sixteenth through the early nineteenth centuries, European colonialism met neither accommodation nor resistance but incorporation. Rather than being colonized, Indians drew a successive series of European empires into local patterns of land and resource allocation, sustenance, goods exchange, gender relations, diplomacy, and warfare. Dependency theory argues that Europeans drew colonized places into the global market, benefiting core regions while making colonized peoples dependent on European goods and unable to control their economies and ultimately their political and social systems. This model does not fit the Arkansas Valley because it exaggerates both pre-colonial economic isolation and European colonial control. Before Europeans arrived, the people of the Arkansas Valley already participated in a continental system in which they exchanged necessities and luxury goods and at times altered production to meet demand of their exchange partners. Tenth-century Arkansas Valley farmers who acquired hoes from the Mill Creek hoe-blade industry across the Mississippi depended on exchange in much the same way that their descendants did. Mill Creek hoes, French guns, and British cloth had value and meaning, but Indians of the Arkansas Valley could have adjusted to life without them. The region was made more cosmopolitan for its trade connections but not controlled by them.[4]

The Arkansas Valley was remarkably diverse, creating countless opportunities for negotiations over the various groups' identities and relations with one another. As a place where Indians and Europeans from East and West met, this area provides a link between the colonial-era Southeast and Southwest, whose historiographies have been quite separate. In the Arkansas Valley, a score of indigenous cultures vied for dominance with each other and with diverse, but much less populous, European groups. Its history helps to reveal the diversity of native societies, as well as the tenuous nature of European colonization across the North American continent. The region's native peoples demonstrate that there was no single native way. Nor was there a single European way, for European colonists were no more monolithic than Indians. Settlers, traders, adventure-seekers, priests, soldiers, bureaucrats, and wives came from Europe and other colonies with a variety of motives and ambitions, often in conflict with those of other Europeans.

Because of their diversity and small numbers, Europeans could not establish themselves in the Arkansas Valley alone. Rather, they molded their economic, political, and social policies to Indian desires and demands. The French and Spanish *tried* to construct the exploitative exchange relations that theorists would later call dependency, and they succeeded in brutally exploiting other places, but they failed in the Arkansas Valley. Only a few individual traders over the course of centuries became wealthy. Most simply earned a subsistence by adapting to Indian desires and policies. For their part, colonial governments not only failed to profit from their relationships in the Arkansas Valley, they had to pay dearly for them. If the purpose of overseas empires was increasing the home country's power and wealth by extracting the resources of another land, the mid-continent never fit the bill. Lower Louisiana, with its guardianship of the Mississippi River and its commerce and eventual plantation economy, contributed somewhat to French and Spanish imperial aims, but most of the Louisiana colony proved a financial loss. In fact, before the nineteenth century, colonial efforts across most of the North American West resembled the Arkansas Valley more than they did the eastern seaboard.[5]

*   *   *

Throughout the colonial period, Indians retained sovereignty over the Arkansas Valley. Europeans distinguished between two kinds of sovereignty: property and authority. Individuals or families might own property in land and goods, but their monarch retained authority over all property and subjects within the realm. How much control this authority conveyed was, naturally, a long-standing subject of debate. Employing various justifications—including arguing that lands were vacant, that non-Christians had no right to hold land, or that it was surrendered by Indians willingly or after losing a just war—Europeans attempted to establish both types of sovereignty over the "New World."[6]

From these attempts stemmed a common misperception, which continues today, that pre-colonial and colonial-era Indians had no concept of property rights. It is true that Indians did not own *private* property, but the general concepts of both property and authority were not alien to them. Property rights simply grant the ownership of certain resources and do not have to include private property. Also, property can be owned by groups, not just individuals. Europeans, especially the English, tended to define America as *res nullius*, "no one's property," when in fact various groups managed resources as distinct common property, where certain peoples held rights and excluded other peoples. The fact that this exclusion sometimes required force reveals that such rights were, unsurprisingly, contested.[7]

Indians of the Arkansas Valley held sovereignty according to both their own and European definitions. They exercised property rights over most of the region's land and resources and contested control with one another. They wielded authority over the small amounts of land that Europeans held, deciding whether to allow a European the use of a particular piece of land for a military post, farm, or village within their jurisdiction. For example, in the late seventeenth century, the French negotiated with the Quapaw Indians the right to establish a fort at the mouth of the Arkansas River in return for alliance and gifts. But the Quapaws retained the right to manage the surrounding lands, living and hunting on them as they wished and controlling the access of other native and European outsiders. Europeans claimed sovereignty against other Europeans, often successfully, writing their own names across maps of North America, but they were not able to enforce those claims on Indians. In fact, they used Indians to ward off other European claims.

Which European power negotiated and allied with which Indians often determined which Europeans could claim a territory. Europeans gained their sovereignty vis-à-vis one another in part by piggy-backing on Indians' sovereignty. Colonial administrators generally delineated the boundaries of their empires by referring to the native peoples with whom they had forged alliances. French administrators referred to the land "aux Arkansas"—at the home of the Arkansas (one name for the Quapaw Indians). This phenomenon pervaded early colonial thinking and continued to inform colonial geographies even after Indians had lost their lands. Of course, this type of claim implied recognition of Indian sovereignty.[8]

The European use of alliances to establish colonial claims reflected a native reality—connections conferred power, and isolation could bring disaster. Often, what Indians found most interesting about Europeans was their connection to the manufacturing centers of Europe. Two of the central peoples of this study, Osages and Quapaws, employed connections for their own benefit in quite different ways. The Osages took advantage of French exchange to build their own trading empire, expanding onto new lands and casting out native rivals. In contrast, the Quapaws built alliances with a wide variety of Indian and European peoples in order to increase their own stability in a contested place. In the process, they became the people to whom newcomers had to go for the ceremonies that would establish legitimate rights to local land and resources. Rather than weakness, interdependence was a form of power. A people with no links of interdependence could be in trouble, as Europeans quickly discovered.

* * *

In suggesting that native peoples in the Arkansas Valley retained power over the land and over their interactions with Europeans, I do not mean to retreat into an older perception of Indians as timeless and unchanging. Neither do I suggest that European empires had no effect. On the contrary, Indians and their homeland changed dramatically over these centuries. The diseases that struck the continent in the 1500s and continued to hit Indian populations in waves for the next three centuries transformed the Americas. But Europeans did not control disease, and it did not doom Indian occupation of the Americas. Surviving Indians whose communities had been devastated had to respond, changing their living arrangements and at times even their cosmologic understandings of the world, but they did not give up their world. They formed new societies, melding aspects of older ones. Native peoples coped with traumatic changes in creative ways that, paradoxically, served to reconstitute *native* concepts of order, geography, and human relations. Imperial competition, gunpowder, and steel were also unprecedented in native experience. But Arkansas Valley Indians directed the course of change and held more control over the methods and volume of goods exchange than did Europeans.[9]

* * *

The Arkansas Valley provides a rare view into a world largely governed by native terms of organization and epistemology. Rather than the concepts of individual land ownership that Anglo-Americans would introduce in the nineteenth century, earlier residents defined the region in relational terms. Politics involved establishing friendly and reciprocal relations and negotiating the responsibilities of friendship. Newcomers had to accept defined places in a hierarchic system of real and fictive kinship, becoming part of familial networks and responsibilities, affecting everything from trade to land use. Most Indians in this era were comfortable with multiple layers of land rights. One group might have the exclusive right to farm a region, others could hunt there seasonally, and still others had no rights there at all. These ways in which Indians defined the land in turn shaped European divisions. For example, eighteenth-century Indians and Europeans grudgingly respected the Osage ability to defend their well-defined hunting territory against rival hunters and anyone attempting to trade with those hunters. In contrast, Indians paid no serious attention to French or Spanish admonitions to prevent British traders from operating west of the Mississippi. Native Americans did not consider their homelands part of European empires, and a local French commander with a handful of soldiers knew well the vacuity of colonial claims.

For historians, the concept of *borderlands* has yielded important insights into both European-American ways of defining and conquering new lands and Native American understandings of and reactions to those processes. However, seeing the Americas as places where whites gradually imposed borders can obscure the fact that Indians constructed and contested their own borders, geographic and metaphoric, long before Europeans arrived. For example, by the time Hernando de Soto visited the Arkansas Valley in the

1540s, the border between the Mississippian chiefdoms of Casqui and Pacaha was so stark and mutually recognized that neither of their chiefs had ever crossed it. Without the power to enforce their own sovereignty in the Arkansas Valley, Europeans settled for simply carving out rights within native notions of layered occupations. The United States was not the first political entity to enforce borders in the Arkansas Valley, just the first non-Indian one.[10]

This story of one contingent place contributes to a reorientation in thinking about colonialism itself. Early American history is too rich for the old narrative that presumes the inevitability of European colonial success. That colonial narrative implicitly assigns an exotic status to native peoples while too easily identifying with (even if criticizing) European rationales. My work seeks, in effect, to exoticize the Europeans and show how Indians incorporated them into their native-dominated, if contested and unstable, world.[11]

This reorientation turns well-known concepts of colonialism on their heads. Like *borderland,* the word *native* becomes slippery as new groups—including Quapaws, French, Africans, Osages, and Cherokees—settled in the valley and raised subsequent generations. When newcomers arrived, previous residents sought to establish themselves as the "natives" in hopes of persuading others that they were authorities on the region with a right to live there and to direct its future. *Warlike* takes on new shades of meaning when Mississippian peoples used it for their enemies and Quapaws applied it to Tunicas, as does *savage* when employed by Cherokees talking about Osages. Even the "Indians" and "Colonists" of my book's title set up a false dichotomy because Indians controlled the destiny of European immigrants, and successful expansionists were usually Indian.

However, in the nineteenth century, the most successful expansionists were of European descent. These immigrants from the British colonies moved west across the Mississippi River for much the same reasons as earlier newcomers—economic opportunities, freedom from subordination, and the land that could provide both. But in contrast to earlier newcomers, most of these settlers did not forge ties of trade or alliance with previous residents. They wanted the land for themselves, and their unprecedented large numbers and their ties to the military and economic might of the United States allowed them to resist incorporation into local ways. They rewrote history, as others had before them, this time making the mid-continent their exclusive native ground.

The Anglo-Americans who moved to the Arkansas Valley in the 1820s were unprecedented not only in their numbers but also in their refusal to negotiate ways of sharing the land. Before the nineteenth century, each people in the Arkansas Valley tended to believe in its own *cultural* superiority. The people of the Mississippian town of Pacaha thought they were wiser than their neighbors in Casqui. Colonial administrators considered *voyageurs* (independent French traders) as "the scum of the posts."[12] The Spanish believed they were better organized than the French. Eighteenth-century Osages considered their men stronger warriors than the British.

In contrast, during the early nineteenth century, Anglo-Americans came west with a developing ideology of their own *innate, biological* superiority. Negating the old ways, they initiated a future in which one people would claim exclusive ownership of the mid-continent. After the War of 1812, these settlers came in numbers large enough to overwhelm the region's inhabitants. They came seeking individual and family independence, but it was their ties to the East that granted them the military and economic power to reject the earlier patterns of cross-cultural relationships. As citizens in the American republic, they persuaded the federal government to muster its resources on behalf of their dreams of landholding and citizenship.

*   *   *

Yet, as certain as these nineteenth-century colonizers were of the permanence and justness of their dominance, they proved historically contingent too, as subsequent generations of Quapaws, Osages, and Cherokees have in no way disappeared, physically or culturally. Not an exclusively white man's country after all, the Arkansas Valley, like the United States generally, continues to debate, negotiate, and litigate over issues of land and culture. Today, Indian rights to host and profit from gaming on their reservations stand as a new kind of layered occupation of American land.

It is tempting to let the tragic Indian removals of the 1820s and 1830s and the rise of the cotton South obscure the centuries in which Indians dominated the region. Of course, if we look for signs of Indians' losing ground, we can discover declension—devastating population loss due to disease, the decline of women's economic and political power, the increasing importance of European symbols of authority such as medals, the eventual loss of land. But if we look more closely and lay aside the well-known story line of colonialism in general and nineteenth-century United States expansion in particular, the picture changes. Even historians who study the colonized may, in their search for resistance to colonialism, miss occasions when "colonization" was a claim at which the "colonized" would have scoffed. Of course, in certain places at certain times colonization meant brutal control, and armed rebellion or more subtle forms of resistance were the only ways to fight it. But in most places, natives and newcomers together constructed their relations. And in the Arkansas Valley, native peoples did not simply affect Europeans. For nearly three centuries after Hernando de Soto's visit, Indians remained the primary agents; they called the shots.

The story of colonial America is not European triumphalism and the imminent emergence of the American nation-state. Nor is it evil colonialism versus righteous but futile resistance. Such simplifications belittle three centuries of interaction and negotiation over space and culture among a large variety of peoples. Like early American history in general, this study concerns groups of people negotiating and fighting over the present and future (and sometimes the history) of the continent.

*   *   *

Europeans recorded most of the sources for this study. Even oral histories that involve the colonial past were transcribed by anthropologists who were either not Indian or not of the tribe telling the oral history. However, by examining a variety of sources over a multi-century time period, I have attempted to correct for the individual biases of particular observers and the cultural biases associated with particular eras. Long letters from bored commandants exiled to a place that they saw as the end of the world—these serve as extremely useful accounts of Indian activities and rhetoric. Similarly, archaeology, travelers' and missionaries' accounts, and the smatterings of available oral history all have their shortcomings, but together, I think, provide enough of a picture of the native Arkansas Valley to illustrate the nature of cross-cultural interactions there, particularly when observed with the tools of ethnohistory. Throughout, translations from French and Spanish are mine unless otherwise noted.

Chapter 1
A Bordered Land, to 1540

The Arkansas River begins in the West, high up in the Rocky Mountains. For hundreds of miles, it crosses dry plains and prairies, now the states of Kansas and north-central Oklahoma. In the central Arkansas Valley, the channel narrows to cut between the blue-green Boston Range of the Ozark Mountains and the rolling green Ouachita Mountains, now eastern Oklahoma and western Arkansas. Finally, in the marshy lower Arkansas Valley, smaller creeks and ox-bow lakes merge with the main stream, as it winds along the lowlands to the Mississippi. The White River flows sharply southeast to meet the Arkansas's mouth. Other deltas lie to the north and south, all part of the lower Mississippi Alluvial Valley. The St. Francis River enters the Mississippi at the current state border of Arkansas and Missouri. Farther north, the Missouri River runs roughly parallel to the Arkansas River from the Rockies to the Mississippi. The Ouachita River crosses southern Arkansas and northeastern Louisiana, and the Red River lies farthest south. Across the Mississippi, the Ohio River, and from it the Wabash, Cumberland, and Tennessee rivers, connect the Mississippi to the eastern half of the continent.

Archaeological evidence indicates that at least 10,000 years ago people lived along the Arkansas River and in surrounding hills and mountains. It is difficult to reconstruct the history of people who left no written or oral records. Still, archaeological findings combined with written accounts from the Hernando de Soto and Francisco Vázquez de Coronado expeditions of 1541 reveal some of the ways the native peoples of earlier centuries lived and interacted with one another and make it possible to imagine how those practices developed. Historians of the colonial period often assume that Europeans brought unprecedented change. In reality, change and cross-cultural exchange are as old as human residence in the Americas.

* * *

We do not know why the first people settled in the mid-continent. They may have come to hunt the region's giant bison, mammoth, mastodon, and deer.

The earliest settlers may also have come for reasons we can only imagine, pushed by conflict or overpopulation wherever they had lived before or pulled by prophecies or charismatic leaders. Whatever their reasons for coming, by 7000 B.C. their population had grown through immigration and natural increase. The region certainly abounded in natural resources. For food and apparel, the upper Arkansas Valley provided bison, which wandered eastward from the Plains in the hot summer to cool themselves in the shaded woods of the central valley. In the mountains and valleys, deer, elk, turkeys, beavers, bears, wildcats, woodchucks, foxes, squirrels, rabbits, opossums, muskrats, and raccoons fed the central valley's people. In fields and forests, people found hickory nuts, acorns, black walnuts, pecans, poke, lamb's-quarter, wild potatoes, sunflower seeds, mulberries, Jerusalem artichokes, and wild onions. The river and the lower valley's swamps provided fish, mussels, turtles, and frogs. Ducks and geese migrated along the marshlands of the Mississippi flyway. People established hundreds of settlements, from the Mississippi to the Plains, and from the Ozark Mountains north of the Arkansas to the Ouachita Mountains in the south.[1]

As the population increased, different groups of people began encountering one another more often as they visited seasonal resource bases. Fall and winter ranges for hunting began to overlap. If one band burned brush at the edge of a forest to clear space for plants that deer liked to eat, those hunters would have been frustrated to find others killing deer that their own practices had lured there. Seasonal harvests probably brought groups into contact and potential conflict. Discovering that another group had picked clean one's summer blackberry, raspberry, dewberry, or muscadine patch must have been particularly disappointing. Arkansas Valley persimmons grow and ripen in the summer and fall, staying unbearably tart until first frost opens a short window for harvesting the sweet fruit before it rots on the ground. Bands who knew the place and time for the persimmon harvest had to determine how to share or win the fruit. High-quality chert for knife and spear blades pervades mountains above the central Arkansas Valley but is hard to find farther downriver. When the land became warmer and drier after about 6000 B.C., people began to cluster near the region's rivers, bringing them into closer contact. Living, hunting, harvesting, and quarrying at the same places and times created the potential for conflict among groups of people and the need for establishing ways of communicating and negotiating with neighbors, ways that were established and surely repeatedly transformed over the millennia before A.D. 1500. Thus, borders and land use rights were negotiated.[2]

North Americans developed common methods of establishing and maintaining connections across cultural and spatial borders. The centerpiece of native North American interactions was exchange. By no means sporadic or inconsequential, exchange was regular, formalized, and ritualized. Friendly peoples exchanged food, raw materials, manufactured goods, news, marriage partners, religious practices, technological innovations, and philosophical, economic, political, and diplomatic ideas. In contrast, enemies refused to exchange in mutually beneficial ways but rather raided one another for non-consensual and non-reciprocal exchange items, including captives. And enemies and friends were not permanent categories. A peace ceremony could transform enemies into friends, and a surprise raid or unresolved murder could do the opposite.[3]

By the time that Europeans arrived, certain cross-cultural practices were so widespread that it is reasonable to surmise that they developed during these earlier millennia of interaction. One of the earliest needs must have been to establish friendly intentions with those speaking a different language and practicing inscrutable customs. Experiments with sharing food and a smoke, singing songs that the singers hoped sounded friendly, and giving gifts probably grew in complexity and standardization through repetition. Residents surely instructed newcomers in the methods of diplomacy. As societies rubbed against one another across the continent, North Americans generally came to recognize distinct signs as proposals for communication or for combat. Leaders, negotiators, and guests probably gave one another blankets, skins, fish, venison, and even sexual partners as signs of good will for centuries before their descendants gave similar goods to Europeans.[4]

As natives of the mid-continent walked and canoed to and from perennial food-gathering and hunting sites, these paths became routes of trade as well. A need for allies and a desire for a variety of foods, tools, apparel, and information must have brought representatives from various peoples into exchange relationships that transformed initial gift exchanges into perpetual, reciprocal trading partnerships. People living near the mountains would have found it convenient to give their local ores to a riverside people in exchange for feathers and dried fish, and a trade in food could insure against times of famine. In addition to efficiency, regional specialization furthered communication and mutual reliance, reducing violent clashes over resources or territory.[5]

Trade both lessened conflict over borders and made them more evident. If one group became known as a purveyor of quartz, for example, its geographic borders and identity became more distinct. This group became identified as the people whose lands included the quarries and who operated as quartz miners and processors.

Desire for goods was part of the reason for trade, but power probably played an even greater role, especially over time. North Americans came to believe that power resulted from extensive connections. A wide network of diplomatic exchange brought in powerful goods and knowledge and could potentially raise allied armies in times of war. Self-sufficiency—material or spiritual—was anathema to most North Americans. The common conception of Indians as isolated before colonization and then "dependent" once tempted by European goods is grossly inaccurate. To be isolated was always to court disaster.

Perhaps through contact with neighbors who had trade connections in the opposite direction, exchange routes expanded. Seashells from the Gulf of Mexico and copper from the Great Lakes reached the Arkansas Valley by 3000 B.C. Arkansas Valley residents probably received copper and shells in exchange for chert, quartz, deerskins, mussels, and freshwater pearls. Some traders traveled long distances, but most goods probably spread through reciprocal trades from society to society, as local traders exchanged both exotic and indigenous goods. Local and long-distance trade passing through the Arkansas Valley eventually included, at various times, stone axe heads and spear blades, cloth woven from plant fibers and animal hairs and colored with plant dyes, finely crafted wooden bowls, cane baskets, conch shell cups, rattles made by sealing pebbles in turtle shells, ceramic figurines, animal skins and furs, dried meat and fish, corn, beans, salt, engraved and polished beads, necklaces and breastplates made of copper and shell, carved stone animal pendants, raw materials such as North Carolina mica and obsidian from the West, and human exchanges, including marriage partners and captives.[6]

Over time the network stretched from the Great Lakes, down the Mississippi, out the Arkansas, Missouri, and Red rivers to the Plains and the Rockies, up the Ohio and Tennessee rivers to the Appalachians, and across the Southeast. It spanned thousands of square miles and reached, at the least, hundreds of thousands of people. The large volume of goods, including many of heavy stone, required the dugout canoes that European explorers saw in the sixteenth century. The largest canoes could carry scores of people and probably hundreds of pounds of goods up and down the rivers of the Mississippi basin and possibly around the Gulf. As they were to do with Europeans in later centuries, Indians exchanged goods that they wanted and needed.[7]

By 1500 B.C., the region that is now northern Louisiana began to manu-facture goods on a large scale. Archaeologists have given this society the un-fortunate name of Poverty Point (certainly not what its people called their home). In response to this new society's demand for raw materials, people living in the mountains around the Arkansas Valley became some of the largest exporters of minerals in North America. The Ozarks provided chert for blades and dart points and red and black iron oxide ores, which were ground into a powder to color tattoos or to mix with grease for body paint. The Ouachita Mountains south of the Arkansas yielded sandstones, various iron oxides, and bauxite. People of both mountain ranges mined vast amounts of silvery galena to make decorative sparkles and silvery paint. Arkansas Valley miners distributed quartz crystals, prisms, and pyramids in a variety of shapes and colors—clear, white, rose, purple, smoky gray, black, and dark red. Goods traveled back and forth on the path later called the Natchitoches Trail.[8]

In addition to goods, people also made exchanges that were less tangible and harder to reconstruct from archaeological remains. Because groups spoke different languages, some individuals learned other languages, thereby facilitating exchange of information. They may also have exchanged craft-workers, students, apprentices, and items that have not occurred to us. Commonalities across contemporary cultures reveal that cross-cultural con-versation spread ideas about technology. Neighbors shared information about what plants could be eaten and how they tasted best. Innovative fisher-men showed others how to construct sturdy nets and to bait multiple hooks on trotlines. An arrow in the body was an abrupt and painful way to learn of one's neighbor's technological innovation. Due to their evident utility for hunting and warfare, the bow and arrow were ubiquitous by the eighth cen-tury, and manufacturers adapted bow technology to create a new drill for bead-making.[9]

Similarly, over thousands of years, the ancestors of the women whom Europeans observed farming in the colonial period developed new ways of preparing food. Several thousand years B.C., women who had previously simply cooked directly in or over a fire began to heat stones and drop them into wooden containers filled with water to boil vegetables and meat prod-ucts. The use of cooking stones spread, but using them was a laborious busi-ness, requiring the cook repeatedly to heat and add stones. By 1300 B.C. in the lower Mississippi River bottoms, women adopted a new kind of vessel, coiled pots. Baking the clay made the vessels sturdy and fireproof so that they could sit directly in the fire for boiling or roasting foods, but they cracked at high temperatures. With countless trials and errors and advice from other experimenters, potters developed methods of tempering clay to prevent cracking by adding plant fibers, sand, or finely ground minerals.[10]

As ceramics and ideas about their manufacture spread, so did a new technology that would have even more significant effects, agriculture. First, gourds and advice on growing them reached the Arkansas Valley. By 2000 B.C., women in the Mississippi Valley began to apply domesticating techniques, gathering and replanting seeds and weeding around them, to local plants—greens, sunflowers, and possibly tobacco. They found that the rivers of the mid-continent provided annual floods that replenished the soil, making their banks ideal for hoe agriculture. And they learned plant selection. Farmers extracted and planted seeds from the largest gourds in order to grow large containers. They chose seeds from the fleshiest squashes to cultivate better food. They planted the largest sunflower seeds for plentiful oil and eating.[11]

In the early centuries of the first millennium A.D., farmers in the mid-continent added corn, a crop developed in Mexico that spread to the Southwest before the turn of the millennium. Across the Americas, farmers gradually expanded corn production and developed different varieties to increase kernel and cob size and yields and to fit regional water and sunlight conditions. Farmers learned that reused fields declined in productivity over the years and, in response, developed methods of renewing depleted fields. Each spring, they burned the previous year's debris and tilled the ashes into the soil. Cooks developed ways of preparing corn, including grits and cornbread, sometimes flavored with persimmons and other dried fruit.[12]

Manufacturing and using new inventions in turn necessitated new trade goods, such as the strong and supple wood of the Osage Orange tree, which made an excellent bow. Cornstalks supported a new crop, beans, which complemented the nutritional value of corn by completing its protein and warding off pellagra, for which purpose North Americans also began to trade lime to cook with corn to make hominy. Squash plants provided weed control and additional vitamins and flavor. Field agriculture spawned at least one strikingly centralized manufacturing and distribution process, the great Mill Creek hoe and spade industry. Beginning around A.D. 700, miners quarried the hills of southern Illinois for stone to craft into hoe and spade blades, which they exported up and down the Mississippi to farmers throughout central and southeastern North America, as far northeast as Lake Erie and as far west as the eastern Plains. Farmers strapped the blades onto wooden handles, used them to cultivate and harvest their crops, sharpened them when they became dull, and carefully stored them in pits during the winter. Strong and well-crafted, these hoes and spades edged out older shell and limestone hoes and established for the Mill Creek people a monopoly and a reputation as the manufacturers of hoes and spades. Within other societies, possession of a Mill Creek hoe may have signified status and power over agricultural distribution.[13]

One of the most commonly exchanged articles served ritual and diplomacy as well as pleasure, the pipe. When the French first came to the Mississippi Valley, nearly every Indian they met knew the calumet—a feathered shaft attached to a pipe bowl—as a symbol with so much symbolic power that Europeans began to carry their own to use for the same purpose, either making peace or sealing an alliance against a common enemy. The thousands of pipes found in ancient remains across the region reveal that the pipe became an important cross-cultural symbol in the Arkansas Valley by at least A.D. 1500. If the visitors brought the calumet, they may have expected that their generosity in leaving the beautiful symbol behind would commemorate the alliance for years to come.[14]

None of this is to say that exchange continuously increased in variety and volume from 8000 B.C. until the sixteenth century. In reality, trade ebbed and flowed in different places, as societies rose and fell and as culture and politics changed. For example, when the Poverty Point culture declined around 700 B.C., demand for Ozark and Ouachita Mountain natural resources fell. Goods likely served many and changing purposes, including utility, fashion, prestige, and spirituality. Scarcity and distance increased the goods' value. Much of the jewelry and decorative objects that archeologists have uncovered in the South is copper, far from the Great Lakes copper mines. In contrast, in the northern Mississippi Valley far from the sea, artifacts are more often of shell. In many archaeological sites in the Arkansas Valley, halfway between, both copper and shell abound.[15]

Long before the sixteenth century, standardized practices of cross-cultural relations had spread widely, including the link between diplomacy and exchange. It seems likely that people quickly found that, when they lived in proximity to other peoples, stable trading and gifting relationships could maintain peace along their borders. For Arkansas Valley residents and their neighbors, exchange both reflected and proved friendly intentions, and friendly relations involved goods exchange. By de Soto's and Coronado's 1541 visits, sharing food and gifts clearly expressed friendship between distinct peoples, an especially important function when language differences complicated spoken communication. Visitors gave presents to express their friendship and their gratitude for the hospitality.[16]

At some point in the evolution of diplomacy in North America, cross-cultural negotiation became a generally male role, while the material aspects of hosting became female. Probably this trend grew out of women's responsibility for growing and gathering plant foods and for preparing all food. In addition, because men's hunting and warfare took them farther afield, men were often the first to meet a new people away from home. Thus, men became the most natural diplomats when receiving at home. Perhaps because symmetry is useful to diplomacy, this form of gendered diplomatic practices became standard throughout the region, although women served as diplomatic chiefs in some societies. However, it is also possible that diplomacy was initially a female responsibility, at least in matrilineal societies, and that at some point male chiefs began to appropriate this role.[17]

Because of the nature of archaeological evidence, goods exchange is the most apparent diplomatic technique employed in early North American foreign relations, but negotiators surely practiced other methods as well. Some clues come from de Soto's 1541 travels in Casqui and Pacaha, near the St. Francis River, north of the Arkansas. Archaeologists have labeled these societies Mississippian chiefdoms, defined as hierarchic, kin-based societies with relatively high population densities. When the chief of Casqui offered de Soto one of his daughters to "unite his blood with that of so great a lord," he was following an ancient practice of sealing cross-cultural alliances. Competitive games may also have channeled and deflected group violence. Chunkey, a game that survived into the twentieth century, involved rolling a stone and trying to toss a spear to the place the stone would stop, with spectators betting on the outcome. Archaeologists have found thousands of these stones throughout the Mississippi basin. If diplomacy and games failed to maintain friendship, societies could suspend peaceful exchange relations and instead fight and raid. The sixteenth-century relationship between two neighboring chiefdoms, Casqui and Pacaha, illustrates the connection between exchange and friendship. Casqui had peaceful exchange relations with other peoples, but its only contact with Pacaha was in war, each side raiding the other for goods and slaves.[18]

*   *   *

Centuries of exchange between bordering peoples encouraged social changes, the most dramatic of which probably stemmed from agriculture. The introduction and expansion of field agriculture meant that by A.D. 700, people in the central and lower Arkansas Valley usually raised more than

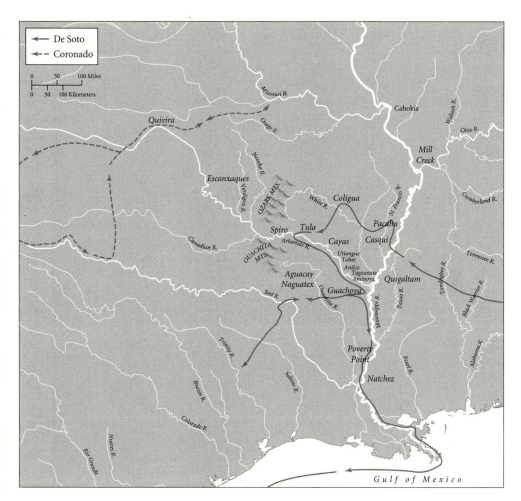

Map 2. Arkansas Valley, to 1500s.

they needed. Crops provided them with reliable food in the summer and early fall, when game was harder to find in the deciduous forests, the water was too low for good fishing, and most of the waterfowl had flown north. For security in the winter and spring, they dried and stored the produce of the summer and fall. Tied down to their crops and storehouses, they depended on traders to exchange their goods and on neighbors when they faced the periodic environmental disasters that all farmers understand— floods, storms, droughts, and pests.[19]

Growing population, declining seasonal migration, and increasing dependence on larger groups of people also changed the nature of societies and the borders between them. While traditional methods of sharing and dividing lands for hunting and gathering continued in some places, many peoples began to form more centralized social structures. Beginning around A.D. 700 in what archaeologists have labeled the Mississippian period, independent groups began to store food and conduct planting and harvesting rituals and festivals together as well as to provide for mutual protection against common enemies. They built towns near good agricultural land, usually beside rivers and lakes for water, fish, waterfowl, and mud for pottery and earthworks. Centralization spread. Societies might band together in desired locations, take over other societies, or centralize in response to an enemy's centralization. While centralized societies had previously existed, the Mississippian chiefdoms were probably unprecedented in number and density. Thousands of people settled in or near towns in the Mississippi Valley and the Southeast, including (in the names used today) Etowah in the Appalachians, Cahokia across the Mississippi from present-day St. Louis, Toltec near present-day Little Rock, Spiro higher up the Arkansas River near the state border of Oklahoma and Arkansas, and, by A.D. 1500, Natchez on the lower Mississippi. Over time, some chiefdoms fell as others took their places.[20]

In an era of distinct chiefdoms, new boundaries and identities developed. Particular pottery styles, for example, were associated with the potters of particular places. We do not even know what most of these peoples called themselves, but we can imagine a Cahokian pleased to acquire a highly-polished fiery red funnel whose color, shape, and fabric-impressed pattern marked it as the work of Zebree, on the St. Francis River. Mississippian mound complexes in the lower Mississippi alluvial plain, including the lower Arkansas and St. Francis valleys, served as civic and ceremonial centers for people living on farmsteads nearby. In the central Arkansas Valley, people also adopted agriculture and built some mounds, but they lived more dispersed over the land, with smaller town centers serving smaller numbers of people. They farmed, hunted, gathered, and traded mineral resources to friendly neighbors.[21]

The Arkansas Valley rapidly became an important Mississippian trade route. The lower valley mound center that archaeologists call Toltec was founded around A.D. 700, with a plaza, nearly twenty mound sites for important buildings, and at least one burial mound. Large quantities of minerals, copper, and shell found there suggest that Toltec was an important link in trade among various communities from the Ozarks in the north to the Ouachitas and Red River in the south.[22]

After 1200, Spiro, Toltec's neighbor to the west, replaced the older ceremonial center as the hub of trade on the Arkansas River. Under Spiro's influence, the Arkansas River Valley became the main trade route that connected the Plains to the Mississippi River, whence native traders' networks stretched east to connect all the great Mississippian chiefdoms of North America. The tremendous quantities of exotic goods that archaeologists have found at Spiro—and of Spiroan goods found elsewhere—reveal the large volume of trade. Spiroans imported thousands of pounds of finished goods and raw materials, which they manufactured into such specialty items as copper-covered cedar masks with teeth made of mother-of-pearl. Their highly productive textile manufacturers spun animal hair and bark threads into cord, which they wove with turkey, Canadian goose, and swan feathers into blankets and garments. They made beads of polished stone, bone, wood, and copper in all shapes, some dyed or carved. These Spiro-manufactured goods appear at Cahokia, exchanged for Cahokian shell and copper artwork and pottery (which probably contained food, salt, and seeds), Mill Creek hoes and axes, and necklaces and vessels made across the Mississippi Valley and the Appalachians, all of which appear in Spiro excavations. Spiroans altered their imports for their own purposes, for example refitting a Cahokian statue into a large pipe. Starting around A.D. 1400, Spiroans traded eastern goods farther southwest for cotton cloth, pottery, Osage Orange bows from Texas, and bison hides and meat from the Plains, some of which they sent back east. In fact, it appears that Indians living on the edge of the Plains responded to Mississippian demand by hunting more bison, which they sent east through Spiro. Spiroans also apparently distributed information, in part by engraving and embossing imported conch shells and copper with pictorial representations.[23]

Although governance is more difficult to infer than residential patterns or technology, early European explorers' accounts suggest that hereditary chiefs ruled at least some Mississippians. Long-distance exchange probably helped some traders or other individuals to gain power. A person with access to exotic trade goods could use them to gain favors and allegiance, and cross-cultural connections could help to prevent war and encourage trade, thus increasing the individual's utility to his or her people. At various times, a supreme or paramount chief united several chiefdoms into a larger one, including Pacaha, Casqui, Quiguate, Coligua, Utiangue, Guachoya, Anilco, Aminoya, and Tagoanate—all lower Arkansas Valley chiefdoms that de Soto visited in the early 1540s.[24]

Mississippian chiefdoms varied in their social structures and governance. Archaeologists have found evidence that Mississippians could be brutal. A copper plate from Spiro depicts a person holding a war club in the right hand with a severed head in the left. It is unclear whether this scene of violence portrayed warfare or intra-societal authority. In any case, the vast amounts of war clubs found reflect their importance as war symbols, and thus the centrality of war. Bodies buried with unusual amounts of goods and sometimes with people, who may have been killed to be buried with the deceased noble, suggest a powerfully-enforced hierarchic social system. After A.D. 1400, Spiro may even have become more stratified, as evidenced by a sharp increase in burial differentiation. But other towns, such as those that archaeologists identify as Pacahan, do not have highly differentiated burials or obvious authority symbols. In many places, those who used their access to trade goods as a means of acquiring prestige or influence found themselves involved in a system of reciprocity, in which they became responsible for distributing gifts and ensuring the subsistence of their people.[25]

Political differences likely influenced people's perceptions of themselves and others, some valuing a centralized, well-ordered society and others a more egalitarian one. Of course the subtleties of identity and power are difficult to glean from archaeology and explorers' erratic and confused accounts. Archaeologist George Sabo III has suggested that, while Mississippian societies were hierarchic, they may not have competed for conquest and control of people and their resources, as Europeans did, but rather for prestige, through forging kinship connections and acquiring reputations for generosity and supernatural power.[26]

Religious practices and beliefs are even more difficult to ascertain. Historical accounts suggest that people expected their priests to prevent natural disasters and to provide supernatural assistance in battle. Some chiefs combined the role of chief and priest into a powerful being, such as the Natchez Sun. Most of their religions likely were inclusivist, willing to incorporate new religious ideas and practices into those they already had. This tendency added a religious dimension to connections with other peoples. And the belief that

Figure 1. Effigy from Spiro Mound. This stone pipe reveals much about Spiro culture. Note the careful workmanship, the earspools, and the subject matter— probably a decapitation. Courtesy National Museum of the American Indian, Smithsonian Institution, Washington, D.C.

all people and animals had a spiritual nature, potentially friendly or hostile, kept them wary at first meetings until discovering a newcomer's true nature.[27]

These centuries set patterns that would continue into later times. Inclusivism would color how natives dealt with newcomers who brought new customs and beliefs. Diversity would continue to demand that different kinds of people figure out ways of living together, and some forms of diplomacy, exchange, and conflict would last. Incorporating alien peoples proved to be an effective means of maintaining and increasing power, and societies of the Arkansas Valley would continue to do so on individual and societal levels. And, as in the past, change would be part of life.

*   *   *

In the thirteenth and fourteenth centuries, those chiefdoms near the Mississippi experienced another round of dramatic changes. Cahokia, the largest polity on the Mississippi, declined. Perhaps its leaders had tried to gain too much power and either pushed their people into rebellion or provoked infighting among the towns within their sphere. Or perhaps the leaders and social structure had proved incapable of providing for the people in a time of declining food productivity. The destabilization and population movements caused by the fall of Cahokia seem to have increased warfare throughout neighboring regions. The lower Arkansas Valley's independent chiefdoms apparently felt a growing need for protection from one another. People increasingly farmed on their towns' outskirts only during the day and lived inside fortified towns, such as those in the chiefdoms of Guachoya and Anilco at the Arkansas River's mouth and Pacaha and Casqui between the Arkansas and the St. Francis. Borders between peoples increased in importance as neighbors seemed more unified and dangerous. The "Little Ice Age" of the mid-fourteenth century only increased these centralization trends near the Mississippi, as crop yields shrank and protecting food storage areas became more important. Some smaller chiefdoms combined for mutual protection or became vassals of other chiefdoms, such as Pacaha.[28]

Thus, while the grandeur of the sixteenth-century chiefdoms along the Mississippi impressed the Spaniards, their inhabitants may have seen their recent history as a declension. The Spaniards saw palisades and moats as signs of civilization, but in reality, more peaceful times when families could live on their own farms had given way to an era of war in which they had to live in fortified town centers under their local chiefs' protection, and perhaps authority. Elaborate continental trade links of earlier centuries weakened as people withdrew into fortified centers. Traders continued to cross the region, protected by their usefulness, but they may have found themselves caught between warring peoples more often than they wished.[29]

Fourteenth- and fifteenth-century changes sparked opposite trends to the west, in the central Arkansas Valley. Spiro at first responded to the fall of Cahokia by trading more with the Red River Valley, but the changed market and declining agriculture decreased the food surplus. Around the turn of the sixteenth century, as trading opportunities lessened, the weather worsened, and the Spiro elite proved themselves unable to control either, Spiroans gradually abandoned their mounds. It is possible that after the 1520s, European diseases spread north from Mexico and accelerated these trends. In any case, the descendants of Spiro began to adopt the patterns of their neighbors to the west, spending long periods of the year hunting on the Plains.[30]

Thus, as chiefdoms near the Mississippi centralized, borders between regions and peoples in the lands closer to the Plains became less rigid. These Plains-hunting peoples lived in smaller, more mobile bands than their ancestors and may have begun to think of themselves and their homelands in more localized ways than when they had been the major Plains-Mississippian trading entrepôt. By 1540, tens of thousands of descendants of Spiro and their upstream neighbors were living in dense but dispersed seasonal communities in the central Arkansas Valley. Early Spanish accounts record their names as Cayas, Tula, Quivira, and the "Great Settlement." Most spent the summer and fall in rural communities on river valleys beside their agricultural plots. In the winter, they headed for the Plains farther out the Arkansas River, where the men hunted bison and the women dressed the skins. Most were probably ancestors of Caddoan-speaking peoples: Taovayas, Iscanis, Guichitas, Tawakonis, and Panis Noirs of the seventeenth century and the Wichita (Kitikitish), Caddo, and Pawnee confederacies of more recent times.[31]

In the sixteenth-century central and upper valley, each settlement ruled itself, spoke its own dialect or language, and probably had independent governance, religious beliefs and practices, and social structure. Sometimes they allied or warred with one another, and they often fought or traded with bands of Teyas (who lived to their southwest and probably also spoke a Caddoan language) and with Athapaskan-speaking Querechos (ancestors of the Apaches and Navajos). Quivira and Cayas traded such goods as bison products, painted deer hides, and salt down the Arkansas River to the Mississippi Valley and corn to people farther west, but not with the centralization and volume that thirteenth-century Spiro had.[32]

Thus, when sixteenth-century Spaniards approached the Arkansas Valley—Hernando de Soto from the east and Francisco Vázquez de Coronado from the west—they found two quite different worlds, much more different from each other than they would have been two centuries earlier. Near the Mississippi, chiefdoms had hardened their borders, centralizing how they lived and leaving nearly-empty border zones between provinces. In contrast, people upriver, nearer the Plains, lived more spread out than they had in the past. But even they still defined lands and resources as belonging to one group or another.[33]

*   *   *

Contrary to assumptions that only Europeans drew borders, Indians across the continent defined, defended, and disputed geographic and metaphoric borders long before Europeans arrived. Some lands, and all of the rights on them, fell under the exclusive sovereignty of one people, as a Mississippian chiefdom's towns and agricultural plots belonged to its people. Borderlands between chiefdoms were generally open to anyone who wanted to hunt, fish, or gather, although in years of scarcity, they might run into others who contested the border zone. Indians had developed recognized methods of dealing across borders, thereby establishing the networks of exchange and diplomacy that, ideally at least, increased security and well-being.[34]

In the coming centuries, Europeans would define the heart of the continent as a far periphery of the cores of their empires—Paris, London, Seville. It would be the far northern edge of New Spain in the sixteenth century, the wilds of Louisiana in the seventeenth and eighteenth, and the United States frontier for the first decades of the nineteenth. At various times, it would lie on the border of empires—New France and New Spain, New Spain and the British colonies, New Spain and the expanding United States. But the region was native ground to its people. It had its own cores and peripheries, borders and borderlands. Its diverse Indians continued to define and negotiate over land in their own ways despite becoming part of the colonial world. Indeed, Indian ways of defining and dividing the region and conducting cross-cultural interactions would prove more effectual than European ways for centuries to come. And, as in the past, people would continue to contest and alter ways of living there.

Chapter 2
Hosting Strangers, 1541–1650

On a sunny morning in late June 1541, the town of Pacaha was bustling. In fields outside the town walls, women used their imported stone hoes to weed and break up the ground around the new corn and bean shoots, while other Pacahans collected the rabbits caught in the snares dispersed throughout the cornfields. A canal brought water from the nearby Mississippi River to the moat that surrounded Pacaha on three sides, 100 feet wide, by one visitor's estimation. A palisade of tall mortared posts enclosed the town's fourth side. The broad hill that the town sat upon granted protection from flood waters and a long-distance view of the plain below. Atop the main hill rose several large mounds, on which sat many of its homes and public buildings.[1]

In the moat and canal, fishermen had cast their nets and were bringing in bass and catfish. Other Pacahans had gathered clay from the edge of the canal and were carrying it in large baskets along the road that led up to the town. In one of the town's hundreds of wooden buildings, women picked out the pebbles and grass from the clay, sifted out any smaller debris, worked it with their hands into long coils, and built the coils into jars, bowls, and pitchers. Nearby, other women etched, rubbed, and painted elaborate designs on their vessels. In another building, men worked local and imported flinty chert into sharp arrowheads, which they bound to cane shafts. Near the canals, builders used torches and stone tools to carve out and shape twenty- to thirty-foot trees into boats. Skill and industry in boat-building and weapon-making had helped Pacaha to become a dominant chiefdom during the waves of dramatic change that racked the region in the previous centuries and to extend its influence over other towns on both sides of the Mississippi.

Traders from the West walked past the fishermen and clay collectors to arrive at the town's gate. They stated their business to the sentries and proceeded to the main plaza, hoping to find Pacahan partners as well as traders from the East with whom they could exchange their salt, bison hides, and wildcat furs for corn and beans from last year's harvest, dried fish, shell beads, and freshwater pearls. At one end of the plaza, a priest was tending to temple business. On top of the largest of the platform mounds, the chiefdom's young chief, called simply Pacaha, strolled around his spacious residence. His dominion included not only this town but scores of nearby towns inhabited by tens of thousands of people. At the top of one of the palisade's towers, a lookout surveyed the countryside. To the east, the Mississippi River rolled along, sparkling brown in the late spring sun. To the west, the flat bottom lands were interrupted by a single long ridge.

Suddenly, the lookout glimpsed an alarming sight: an army approaching from the south. Five thousand warriors wore tall plumes and carried bows and arrows. The lookout recognized them as soldiers of Casqui, the chiefdom just to the south. Worn out by war with Pacaha that had lasted for generations, the Casquis had been losing ground. The last thing the people of Pacaha expected was an army of Casquis advancing on their own capital. What inspired this audacity? The answer marched in front of the Casquis: hundreds of warriors carrying gleaming spears and clanking swords, with crossbows strapped across their backs, some clad from head to toe in a gray metal that reflected the sun. Alongside them, other warriors in similar attire rode fearsome beasts, even taller than bison. In front walked dogs, bigger than the Pacahans had ever seen, snarling and baring their frightful teeth. The Casquis had found an ally—the Spanish conquistadors led by Hernando de Soto.[2]

The chief of Pacaha could more easily deduce the reason for Casqui's boldness than the answers to his next logical questions: who were these new warriors with their strange implements, and how should he deal with them? The chiefs of Pacaha and Casqui, like sixteenth-century people across the Americas, had to figure out how to understand and interact with Europeans. In the mid-continent, Spaniards appeared as roving outlaws, different from normal visitors—traders, friendly diplomats, and enemy warriors. These men seemed to have no home and no clear identity or intent. While wary, native peoples generally attempted to fit the Spaniards into traditional frameworks, to negotiate with them according to established customs, and to use them for local purposes, including fighting one another. Whether they could succeed was another question.

Guns and horses were new to the Arkansas Valley, but negotiating with outsiders and adapting to changes were not. Rather than a first cross-cultural encounter, the Arkansas Valley's introduction to Europeans was one in a long line of encounters with foreign cultures that brought fresh ideas, technologies,

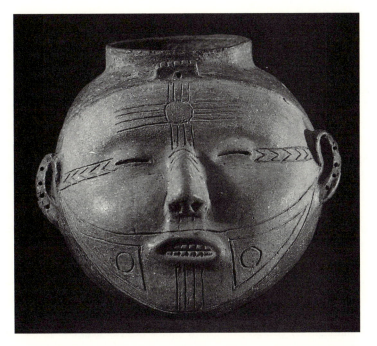

Figure 2. Mississippian head pot from Bradley. Bradley is a Mississippian site that was probably the town of Pacaha. Note the facial tattoos, especially the cross symbol on the forehead, representing the four directions of the earth in harmony with one another and the upper world. Courtesy University of Arkansas Museum, Fayetteville.

dangers, and opportunities. Coastal Native Americans, who usually glimpsed Europeans' ships before catching sight of the men themselves, were shocked to see iron-clad figures emerge from "floating islands." Many suspected that these visitors were as otherworldly as they were unprecedented, although they soon came to think differently. But the people of the mid-continent did not see Spanish ships. While they rightly suspected that these newcomers had access to knowledge and power from another place, these Indians knew the visitors were human. As strange as the newcomers looked, sounded, and acted, Arkansas Valley people strove to fit them into older understandings and practices.[3]

* * *

The 1541–1543 expeditions of de Soto and Francisco Vázquez de Coronado provide us with our earliest documentary accounts of the Arkansas Valley.

While richer in human detail than archaeological records, the accounts have their own pitfalls. Translations from native languages to Spanish could distort meaning. As with all European sources, there was much of Indians' worlds that the explorers did not see or saw without understanding. Other problems arise in the recording of the accounts. All of the de Soto accounts were written after the expedition returned, so none are true journals. It appears that one participant, Luis Hernández de Biedma, the expedition's factor, wrote one of the extant accounts. The other three were compiled by non-participants, who claimed to draw their information from some combination of interviews and written accounts that no longer exist. Garcilaso de la Vega, the son of an Incan woman and Spanish man, wrote the most detailed account. Some of his colorful stories reflect his knowledge of Peru, his image of great American empires' nobly confronting Spanish conquistadors, and substantial reliance on contemporary literary tropes. Similarly, no diaries exist for Coronado's trip. However, several letters written during the expedition survive, and three participants wrote full-length accounts of the expedition after returning home. Several participants testified during inquiries into atrocities committed by the Coronado expedition, but they surely shaped their versions in light of threatened punishment. For all of the accounts, the need to sell books, justify deaths and expenses, advocate further expeditions, and vilify or glorify Spaniards or Indians influenced what their authors omitted or included.[4]

These written accounts tell stories, which grant a sense of intimacy with the people of that time and place, but explorers' tales are a dangerous source. For example, Pedro de Castañeda de Náxera, a Coronado expedition participant, told of a woman who grew up on the eastern edge of the Plains and was enslaved at one of the Tiguex pueblos in the Rio Grande Valley. In the spring of 1541, a man named Juan de Zaldívar acquired her from the pueblo. With Zaldívar, Coronado, and an army of Spaniards and Mexican Indians, she walked across the Plains until they reached her people's hunting lands, where she seized her opportunity to escape. After wandering for more than a week, she failed to find her people, instead encountering the remnants of de Soto's expedition. To her dismay, these men enslaved her too. They forced her to walk down the Arkansas River with their other Indian slaves, guides, and interpreters, who hailed from as far away as southern Florida. In the summer of 1543, their boats carried her down the Mississippi and either left her at the mouth of that river, hundreds of miles from her home, or took her to another continent.[5]

It is possible that the Teya woman's capture by de Soto's men is a fiction that Castañeda constructed in order to dramatize to Spanish readers how close the two expeditions came to each other without meeting. None of the de Soto accounts mentions her, although de Soto often asked Indians whether they had heard of another European expedition. The Teya woman's story is just that—an intriguing human story that may have happened, but likely did not. Readers should regard the individuals and stories in this chapter not as replications of the places that the expeditions visited but as impressionistic and at times even metaphoric portraits of the sixteenth-century Arkansas Valley. They are infinitely better than nothing.

De Soto and his men lied, murdered, stole, and swindled their way to the mid-continent, and tales of their brutality probably preceded them. However, by the time de Soto crossed the Mississippi and entered Casqui chiefdom, he was a less threatening invader than he had been when he landed at Tampa Bay in 1539. Many of the men who landed in Florida had died, as had most of their horses. The soldiers had likely shed some of their heavy, hot armor during their march across the Southeast. Thus, the Indians of the Arkansas Valley held the upper hand, both collectively (although they were unlikely to act together) and as individual societies, each of which outnumbered the expeditionary force.[6]

De Soto's model of Indian relations came from successes farther south. As every would-be conquistador knew, Hernán Cortés had used native alliances to bring down Montezuma's empire. The great advantage that Cortés had when he entered the Valley of Mexico in 1520 was that almost everyone despised Montezuma's Mexica people for their imperial ways. In Peru, Francisco Pizarro had stumbled upon the double opportunity of an epidemic (spread south from Mexico) and an Incan civil war. The turmoil allowed him to play each side against the other. As one of Pizarro's top commanders, de Soto had observed how that conqueror shifted the odds in favor of the outnumbered Spanish, including Pizarro's surprise capture of the Inca himself, which gave the Spanish a military advantage over his astonished and leaderless warriors. De Soto hoped that Florida would prove to be his Mexico or Peru.[7]

De Soto's greatest disadvantage was lack of information. Montezuma's enemies had purposefully given Cortés a clear picture of Mexica wealth, potential allies, and the geography of central Mexico. The clarity and forcefulness of their message drew Cortés into alliances with them against their common enemy (and deflected Spanish violence away from themselves). In contrast, in the lower Arkansas Valley, diverse Indian agendas made information confusing, inconsistent, and unreliable. One people's descriptions of their region and their neighbors usually proved the opposite of what other informants said, and often both bore little relation to reality. For example, Indians captured outside the town of Pacaha encouraged the Spanish to visit a land of "large villages" to the northwest, which turned out to be "an uninhabited land of very great swampy lakes."[8] Northwest of Pacaha, the Spaniards asked some Quiguate Indians about areas that might have gold, silver, and guides who could escort them to the Pacific. The Quiguates suggested their neighbors the Coliguas. But, according to one account, other Indians on the road advised the Spanish to avoid the people of Coligua because they fired poison arrows. Deciding to take a chance, the Spaniards traveled to Coligua, where they found neither poison arrows, precious metals, nor information regarding the ocean, only a suggestion that they try going south.[9]

Indians used the ignorance and vulnerability of their "discoverers" to shape de Soto's mission to their own ends. Isolated and ignorant, the Spanish could never be certain whether things were as they saw them or had been manipulated by Indian direction-givers and guides. In this kaleidoscopic world, de Soto and his men found little success. Explorers needed to know passable roads, the opportunities of finding food, and information on the peoples they might encounter, whether they be potential friends or certain enemies. Lack of information could prove deadly. De Soto's troops spent one long and disastrous day in March 1542 looking for a place to ford a lake that emptied into the Arkansas River. One Spaniard drowned in an attempt to cross before two passing Indians showed them a better crossing place.[10]

Indians were de Soto's only source of information on the history and current status of cross-cultural relations. Leaders who wanted to persuade the Spaniards to fight on their side or not to ally with their enemies portrayed their neighbors as hostile people with no riches or food to share. When the Spaniards stayed too long and ate too much food, their hosts steered them *toward* their enemies, whom they described as friendly and wealthy people, and away from their friends, whom they portrayed as ruthless, poor, or both. For example, descending the Arkansas River in the winter of 1541, de Soto's men captured two Indians to ask how far they were from the Utiangue chiefdom. The captives replied that it was about a week away. Unsolicited, they also mentioned that another chiefdom at about the same distance was "plentifully abounding in maize and of much population." Because, as the Spanish later discovered, Utiangue also abounded in corn, it seems likely that the captives hailed from there and wanted to steer the clearly dangerous and hungry visitors away from their home.[11]

De Soto's expedition depended on Indians for its success and even survival. Only the region's people could provide information, food, and safe water, to say nothing of the prizes that Spaniards had come seeking: gold and silver in the short run and tribute from *encomiendas* (feudal-like estates). By a great stroke of luck, the expedition had found an interpreter about a week after landing at Tampa Bay in 1539. Stranded by the disastrous Pánfilo de Narváez expedition, which had also left Alvar Núñez Cabeza de Vaca to wander along the Gulf Coast, Juan Ortiz had been held captive at Ucita for twelve years. Having learned that town's Timucuan language, Ortiz could translate between the Spaniards and the Indians who spoke that language. For the next location, the Spanish simply had to find someone who could speak both Ortiz's Timucuan language and the language of the new place. Throughout the journey, as long as the Spanish could find an interpreter for a new language, they could communicate through a string of interpreters, ending with Ortiz's Spanish. Still, with each addition, misunderstandings increased, and the Spaniards became more dependent on their native interpreters.[12]

While Montezuma's empire had terrorized the peoples of central Mexico, power in the North American mid-continent was not centralized. Chief Casqui wanted to defeat Pacaha. In a similar situation, the chief of nearby Guachoya chiefdom wanted Spanish assistance against his enemy, Anilco, but had no serious quarrel with either Pacaha or Casqui. None of the chiefs was eager to fight in another's battles. Most were fighting several different, unallied enemies. As one Spanish account put it, "nearly all the provinces the Spaniards traversed were at war with one another." Occasionally armies fought major battles, but much more often enemies crossed into one another's lands to launch small-scale surprise attacks to take captives and spoils and to instill fear. Always anticipating either an attack or an opportunity to surprise an enemy, most residents of the lower Arkansas Valley traveled "with their weapons constantly in readiness, because they are nowhere safe from their enemies" (although the Spaniards themselves may have increased the natives' state of preparedness).[13] With no common enemy, de Soto could not instigate a common fight. In addition, in no place did de Soto find the riches that Cortés had discovered. Rumors of wealth in far-off chiefdoms kept him searching, unwilling to commit to large-scale war against any people who had no gold or silver.

The search had led de Soto to the chiefdom of Casqui in June 1541. There, de Soto's Iberians, Africans, and southeastern Indians had arrived not as a conquering army, but as thieves, stealing food and blankets from one of the outlying towns. Instead of trying to punish them, the Casqui chief had recognized an opportunity to gain an advantage over his rival Pacaha. Entering into diplomatic relations with the Spaniards, he hoped to build a connection that would both divert their violence and theft and turn their numbers, armor, steel weapons, and powerful steeds against Pacaha.

Chief Casqui and his nobles processed out of their main town to welcome the Spaniards, courting their friendship with gifts and speeches. Because no Spaniards recorded the proceedings that day, we cannot know what Chief Casqui and his fellow lords said, but participants recalled that they flattered de Soto and his men. According to André de Burgos, who published an account from the notes of a Portuguese "gentleman of Elvas" who accompanied the expedition, the chief said something like: "Very lofty, powerful, and illustrious Lord: May the coming of Your Lordship be very propitious." Although, he conceded, "you entered my land killing and making captive the inhabitants of it and my vassals, I resolved to conform my will to yours, and . . . to consider as good all that your Lordship might do." The Casquis assured de Soto that they did not desire war with the Spanish but rather wanted to assist their mission. To supplement the words, the chief offered the visitors much-needed food to fill their empty stomachs, clothing to replace their tatters, and a place to lodge in his palace.[14]

Knowing that the Spanish had never visited his land, Chief Casqui took advantage of their ignorance to shape their understandings of the place and its peoples. With his gifts and friendly words, the chief demonstrated his people's benevolence and generosity, while urging war against Pacaha. He persuaded de Soto that accepting friendship from his people and joining them against the wealthy Pacahans would be the Spaniard's wisest path to procure the gold he coveted. The chief must have noticed that, despite the newcomers' armaments and bravura, there were only a few hundred of them in a native land populated by tens of thousands. Surely they needed allies too.

As Chief Casqui predicted, his hospitality and words of peace delighted the weary Spaniards. While Casqui desired de Soto's friendship, de Soto needed Casqui's. Despite their impressive appearance, de Soto's troops could not fight all of the region's people. Fifty years earlier, Columbus had happened upon the Americas in his attempt to recruit Asian assistance and resources for the Spanish conflict with the Islamic empires. But once in the Americas, Spaniards found themselves being recruited into American conflicts. When de Soto's forces had recuperated from their travels, the new allies advanced on Pacaha, the Spanish in search of gold and the Casquis seeking to overthrow their rival.[15]

When the chief of Pacaha saw the armies approaching, he decided to flee, then contemplate how to react from a position of safety. While Pacaha's palisade and moat could repel small groups of invaders, Pacahans had a stronger defensive site on an island fortified by two log palisades and thick trees and brambles extending to the shore. The chief led some 5,000 of his people, including the warriors, out the back gate of the town to the island, while others dispersed into the woods. The Casquis captured all the Pacahans they could find, and they and the Spaniards plundered the town. Although the Casquis won a significant victory and both Casquis and Spaniards found valuable bison hides and wildcat furs, the Spaniards discovered no gold.[16]

The Pacahans, however, were not conquered. Because he did not face multiple, united enemies, Chief Pacaha accomplished what Montezuma could not. He persuaded the Spanish invaders that alliance with his people would be more advantageous than enmity. At first, with thousands of combined Spanish and Casqui warriors descending on his town, Chief Pacaha did not have the luxury to court de Soto. But he took his first opportunity to employ Chief Casqui's methods. While Chief Casqui was away with his army, Chief Pacaha and his entourage returned to their town with great ceremony. The chief presented gifts to de Soto and declared that he had forgiven him for the "damage" he had done. Angry at Chief Casqui for his failure to rout the Pacahans from their fortified island and eager to make a more powerful friend, de Soto agreed to peace. With no allies besides Casqui, the odds stacked up against de Soto, so he decided to befriend both and thus avoid a dangerous and unfruitful war. When Chief Casqui returned, he was disappointed to discover that being the Spaniards' first friend in a conflict did not make him their best friend, but power politics dictated both the newcomers' and the older residents' choice of allies.[17]

The chiefdoms of Anilco and Guachoya also recruited de Soto. These were two other chiefdoms, probably just north and south of the Arkansas River's mouth, that also had emerged stronger during the previous centuries' process of centralization. In the spring of 1542, the chief of Anilco, a heavily-populated chiefdom, sent his armed warriors to surround his main town and a diplomat to confer with the Spaniards while the rest of the people escaped with the town's provisions and valuables. When the Spaniards approached the Guachoya chiefdom, its people too fled with all they could carry, but the chief's interest in the Spaniards increased once he heard of their hostilities with Anilco, and he returned with gifts to attempt an alliance.[18]

One people whose enmity might have united the other residents of the lower Arkansas Valley with the Spanish were the Tulas, who lived farther up the Arkansas River, possibly in the mountains above the old town-center of Spiro. But de Soto's information-gathering methods and burgeoning reputation as dangerous and deceitful precluded a joint anti-Tula war. When a Caya chief and several of his people found themselves captured by de Soto in the central Arkansas Valley (between present-day Little Rock and Fort Smith) in the fall of 1541, they did not urge a joint war against their enemies the Tulas. Rather, they praised Tula as "the best populated land thereabout," which, they promised, he would find "well-provisioned."[19]

The Cayas neglected to mention that the Tulas were the most feared people in the Arkansas Valley. The Spaniards would learn the hard way that the Tulas' reputation for "ferocity and inhumanity" had led other Arkansas Valley peoples to be, as one chronicler put it, "disturbed simply by hearing the name of Tula," so much that "they frighten the children with it to make them hush when they cry." According to one account, in towns that the Spaniards visited later, children would play at fighting battles against one another. When a Tula boy whom the Spanish had captured joined the game, he led his team's charge, yelling "Tula!" So fearsome was the sight and sound that he frightened the other side into retreat. The adults observing the game explained that Tula warriors did the same in real battles, scattering rivals who knew "they were extremely cruel to their enemies and never took them alive." But de Soto learned this lesson too late, after he and his men marched blissfully unaware into Tula territory. In the face of astonishing "ferocity," the Spanish retreated, and even when they won a later battle, they gained only a few bison hides and no useful information. The Tulas insisted that they "knew of not one large village" to the west but that the Spanish could find large towns to the east, southeast, and northwest. In other words, they advised going anywhere but farther into Tula.[20]

Even the Tulas, widely despised and feared, did not pose enough of a threat to bring enemies together against them. Most simply kept in mind where and who the Tulas were and avoided any contact that would anger them. As crude as Spanish diplomacy was in the Arkansas Valley, Tulan diplomacy was perhaps even more basic. Their policy of cross-cultural relations seems to have been simply to terrify any neighbors who came too close. The policy worked, as far as it went. No one invaded them, and probably no one traded with them either. They lacked the economic and diplomatic connections that increased the security of other societies but compensated by developing a fearsome reputation and, perhaps more importantly, not encroaching on their neighbors. Unlike Montezuma's people, they were no empire. They demanded, albeit in not very diplomatic terms, something that their neighbors could easily provide—to be left alone.

Mississippians defined all aspects of the world as potentially hostile or friendly. The trick lay in converting potentially hostile people, animals, and forces into useful ones. This was a dangerous business. A common lower Arkansas Valley motif portrayed a winged serpent, signifying the fusing of the lower world (the serpent) and the upper (the wings). The winged serpent transformed divergent and powerful forces into a harmonious whole, but combining alien elements incorrectly could bring disaster. These new Europeans, with their technologies and spirits, could prove either dangerous or useful. The people they met tried to feel them out and put them to use, usually through reciprocity, offering what they had and hoping to receive beneficial relations, goods, and services in return. But the Spaniards came with nothing to give, except possibly military assistance. They must have resembled the Tulas in their lack of useful connections. Whatever appealing trade goods Europe had to offer, these Spaniards had little left by the time they reached the mid-continent. They seemed unconnected and friendless, and, unlike the Tulas, they did intrude.[21]

Weaker in numbers, Spaniards hoped to inspire fear with their signs of otherness—especially horses and armor. Guns were not yet as impressive as they would be in coming centuries because the soldiers had little practice using them, they were heavy and inaccurate, they were likely to misfire, they never worked in the rain, and the powder that de Soto had brought was nearly gone by 1541. According to Garcilaso, the Indians not only did not fear the guns but "were contemptuous and made fun of them" (at least once their ears stopped ringing from the first shot). Horses were more effective. Castañeda, a participant in the Coronado expedition, recalled that they had the power to "instill the greatest fear in the enemy."[22]

In addition to their material signs of strength, the Spanish hoped to awe and proselytize Indians with displays of spiritual power and supernatural knowledge. When, at the start of their negotiations, Pacaha sent a surrogate to meet with de Soto, the Spaniard must have found out from some Indian source that this was not the real chief. Declaring his knowledge, de Soto attempted to persuade the Pacahans that "they could do nothing that he did not know before they thought of it." As de Soto probably learned from his research, explorers from Columbus to Cabeza de Vaca had conveyed the perception of supernatural powers in order to instill awe and compliance in potential allies and rivals.[23]

Indeed, most people in the Arkansas Valley hesitated to dismiss the newcomers' claims. New technologies could indicate access to spiritual power. A leader who, like Chief Casqui, felt in need of an influx of strength found Christian symbols appealing and may have wanted to incorporate them into his spiritual arsenal. When de Soto first visited Casqui, the Spaniard explained how his god had suffered on a cross. After hearing this sacred story, the chief directed Casqui builders to construct a wooden cross and erect it atop the tallest of the town's mounds. Each of the Spaniards knelt before the cross, and the people of Casqui did the same.[24]

The Spaniards attributed the Casquis' interest in the cross to the power of the Christian god, and it is likely that were partly right. Suspecting that the Spanish were a powerful people, the Casquis wanted to draw on the newcomers' material and spiritual might. Losing ground against Pacaha and suffering a drought, the Casquis may have begun to question their priests' effectiveness, or at least figured that adding to their spiritual power could only help. And the cross resonated with a similar symbol in Mississippian cosmology, which represented the four directions of the earth in harmony with one another and the upper world. Indeed, it apparently did soon rain. On a more political level, the Casquis surely also knew that honoring another people's god could help to seal their friendship.[25]

After drawing on Spanish spiritual power, the Casquis sought to diminish that of the Pacahas. In Garcilaso's telling, which seems to fit with Mississippian beliefs about the sacred power of ancestors, generations of defeat made the Casquis' pillaging of Pacaha's main town particularly vindictive. Knowing that the temple was the town's most sacred place, filled with spiritual symbols and housing the bodies of Pacaha's prestigious ancestors, Casqui warriors reportedly plundered the goods and opened the wooden sepulchers to throw the human remains on the floor. They took down the heads of defeated Casqui warriors that they found mounted on posts around the temple and replaced them with freshly-killed and de-bodied Pacahan heads.[26]

For the Casquis, spirituality was both a powerful force and a political tool. Destroying the temple was surely intended both to weaken the Pacahans and to frighten them with Casqui ruthlessness. Similarly, Chief Casqui seems to have been both truly impressed with Christianity's power and willing to use his knowledge of Christianity to manipulate the Spanish. The chief tried to prevent a Pacaha-Spanish alliance by calling on Spanish sacred symbols. One of the Casquis apparently warned the Casqui chief of the negotiations between de Soto and Pacaha. The Casqui chief rushed back with fifty Indians "in very fine array" and bearing gifts to heal the damage. Chief Casqui chided de Soto for breaking the bonds of a mutually understood friendship, saying "How, my lord, is it possible that having given me the promise of amity, without my having done you any damage or given any occasion, you wish to destroy me, your friend and brother?"

Seeing that the Pacahans had now painted crosses on their foreheads, Casqui accused de Soto: "You gave me the cross to defend myself from my enemies, and with that same [cross] you wish to destroy me." Drawing on de Soto's source of spiritual power, he recalled that "the women and boys and all those of my land knelt down to it to ask for rain from the God who you said suffered on it, and he heard us and gave it to us in great abundance and saved our cornfields and seed beds; now that we have more faith in it and in your friendship, you wish to destroy those children and women who love you and your God so much." Chief Casqui accused de Soto of choosing to "offend your own God and us, when on his behalf, you assured us in his name and received us as friends." While the interpreters or the Spanish who told or recorded this account may have exaggerated Casqui's declarations of faith, it is easy to believe that the chief accused de Soto of treachery, citing their ritual on the mound as having sealed their friendship.[27]

Chief Casqui's argument worked. Sacred Christian symbols held tremendous significance for the Spanish, who could by no means ignore this appeal. Moved by the chief's terms, de Soto agreed that he and his men had indeed not "come to destroy you, but rather to make you know and understand the cross and our God, as you say." De Soto asserted that it had just been a misunderstanding, and indeed that his god "commands that we love you like a brother, and that we do things for you, because you and your people are our brothers." Yet de Soto was a crafty invader above all. Still believing that Pacaha was a more valuable friend than Casqui, de Soto purposefully chided Chief Casqui in his rival's presence for previously leaving the town.[28]

*   *   *

On the surface, it was easy for Spaniards and Indians to overlook their differences. They could agree on gifts as signs of surrender or friendship. When Indians presented corn, fish, skins, blankets, female companions, and male and female slaves, the Spanish understood them as signs of friendship. For their part, the Spanish arrived in the Americas with their own traditions of reciprocal and obligatory gift-giving. As historian Natalie Zemon Davis has shown for early modern France, gift economies can coexist with market economies. While prices dominate exchange in some sectors, gifts, with their attendant expectations of reciprocity, can govern others.[29]

In Europe, as in North America, gifts could ease relations both within societies and in diplomatic negotiations among Europeans. Noblesse oblige of rulers to their peoples and expedition leaders' obligations to share spoils (if not quite evenly) with soldiers in their parties are not the same as Native American reciprocative responsibilities, but these European practices gave Spaniards some context for Native American expectations. Similarly, diplomacy was an individualized negotiation in both traditions. For Mississippian chiefs and for European monarchs, alliances were based on friendships between leaders, who either personally or through representatives negotiated their relations. Thus, friendship was a natural trope for European negotiators to adopt in relating to Indians. Like Indians, Europeans also believed that friendship, and the trust it implied, facilitated trade. War usually meant an end to legitimate international trade.[30]

But outward signs of agreement could conceal more complicated realities. Much of the time the Spanish could not discern the truth. The fact that Indian warfare centered on surprise attacks and ambushes rather than field encounters made duplicitous diplomacy a part of good strategy. Throughout the Arkansas Valley, each group attempted to portray a simplified world, where everyone was a friend or enemy. But friends were seldom as trustworthy as they portrayed themselves, and all parties tried to mold the obligations of friendship. Chief Casqui, like many other chiefs, tried to persuade the Spanish that friendship required fighting the chief's enemies. Elaborate welcoming ceremonies and generous gifts in part were meant to inspire awe in visitors but also could serve more immediate purposes. At the same time that leaders came forward from their towns to meet the Spanish with the traditional greetings, gifts, and pledges of friendship, their people were usually sneaking their food supplies and children out the back gate to make them safe from the ravenous Spaniards. Also, a first meeting was a perfect time to scope out the visitors' intentions and force. When the Spanish settled down for the winter of 1541–1542 at Utiangue, probably on the Arkansas River near present-day Little Rock, its chief sent a delegation with what the Spaniards later viewed as a "false message" of friendship, so that the delegates could spy on the Spanish.[31]

As murky as the sources are, it is clear that the Spanish were wearing out their welcome. They intruded and demanded what Indians could not provide—gold and unreasonable amounts of food. While most leaders initially worked to incorporate the Spanish into existing practices and policies, by the end of 1542, it appears that most had begun to identify them as a dangerous enemy. As tense as the lower Arkansas Valley had become by the sixteenth century, most people knew who and where their enemies were. The people of the Arkansas Valley had tried to fit the Spaniards into older ways of diplomacy, but they had proved volatile and unpredictable. They pledged friendship and believed they were peace-makers, yet their words and cere-monial acts seemed to mean nothing to them. They failed to understand their weak position, instead lecturing more powerful lords. Another source of conflict could have been rape, which might have angered Indians without being recorded in Spanish accounts.[32]

The Spaniards' confusion only increased as they lingered in the Arkansas Valley. Their interpreter, Juan Ortiz, died at Utiangue in the winter of 1541–1542. A young man whom they had captured in Cofitachequi (South Carolina) had learned some Spanish and took on Ortiz's role. However, as the Spanish lamented, "to learn from the Indians what [Ortiz] stated in four words, with the youth the whole day was needed; and most of the time he understood just the opposite of what was asked." With the loss of their trans-lator and some 200 of their soldiers, the Spaniards were visibly less powerful than they had been when they crossed the Mississippi. The damage that the Spanish wrought wherever they went began to outweigh the opportunities that they could provide.[33]

As Indian interest in the Spanish diminished and hostility to them grew, some former enemies began to define the Spanish as a common enemy and to forge an anti-Spanish coalition. It appears that the leader of this coalition was the chief of Quigaltam, a chiefdom on the east bank of the Mississippi with more than 500 houses in its principal town. De Soto never impressed this chief. In the spring of 1542, he received a Spanish messenger, who invited the chief to visit de Soto at Guachoya and conveyed de Soto's message that he "was the son of the sun and that wherever he went all obeyed him and did him service." Calling the Spaniard's bluff, the chief of Quigaltam sent the messenger back to say that if de Soto was indeed the son of the sun, "let him dry up the great river and he would believe him. With respect to the rest, he was not accustomed to visit any one." On the contrary, the chief declared, all those that he knew "visited and served him and obeyed him and paid him tribute, either by force or of their own volition." The chief assured de Soto that "if he came in peace" to Quigaltam, the chief "would welcome him with special good will," but "if he came in war," the chief would fight back, "for not for him or any other would he move one foot backward." De Soto would have to prove his omniscience and omnipotence before the chief of Quigaltam would believe any of it. De Soto badly wanted to punish what he saw as inso-lence, but he was outnumbered and, as one account put it, "his strength was now no longer so great that he did not need to take advantage of cunning rather than force." Indeed, in his winter quarters for 1542–1543, he refrained from repairing some openings in the stockade "in order that the Indians might not think he feared them."[34]

Natives of the lower Arkansas Valley were slowly concluding that the Spanish posed a greater threat than did any of their neighbors. Unlike the perfect combination of the winged serpent, the Spaniards had proved dangerous to the people who attempted to unite with them. The confused nature of Spanish accounts makes it impossible to know the extent of the anti-Spanish coalition-building. It seems clear that Indians debated how to deal with the interlopers. Some wanted to expel them from the region, but others had heard de Soto describe his desire to settle the Mississippi Valley with *encomiendas*. They hoped to destroy the expedition and thereby prevent it from returning with more troops and settlers. Thus, in the spring of 1542, the chief of Guachoya declined to give de Soto information on getting to the Gulf of Mexico. According to one of the participants in the expedition, de Soto, "from seeing himself cut off and seeing that not one thing could be done according to his purpose, was afflicted with sickness and died." Lost in a land controlled by people growing to despise him, de Soto perished for lack of information.[35]

De Soto's men decided to keep his death a secret, figuring that their hosts and other Indians would be more emboldened to attack a leaderless crew. In addition, they had previously implied that Spaniards were immortal, although there is no evidence that Indians had ever believed them. The new leader, Luis de Moscoso de Alvarado, had his men sneak de Soto's body out of the gates of the town one night for burial. But some Guachoyas soon discovered the disturbed ground and began to ask where de Soto had gone. On Moscoso's orders, several Spaniards again crept out at night, disinterred the body, took it out in a canoe, and threw it into the river, either the Mississippi or the Arkansas.[36]

After de Soto's death, Moscoso found himself no better informed about people or food sources along the Mississippi River south of Quigualtam or how far it was to the sea. When the chief of Guachoya revealed that he knew de Soto was dead, Moscoso decided it was time to leave. Instead of attempting to descend the unfamiliar Mississippi, he pressed southwest toward New Spain by land. But this plan too depended on provisions and directions from the peoples through whose lands the Spaniards would pass. Finding little assistance, they marched in circles for some 500 miles before giving up and returning to the Mississippi. The Spaniards settled for the winter of 1542–1543 at

Aminoya, probably on the Mississippi a few miles north of Anilco, to build boats for escaping down the Mississippi.[37]

Again, truth fragmented for the Spaniards. As they grew convinced of a conspiracy against them, their accounts become confused by anxiety and paranoia. The chiefs of Anilco, Guachoya, and Tagoanate (the next chiefdom to the north) brought canoes full of ropes and blankets for the Spanish to make into sails. One of the expedition's chroniclers interpreted their generosity as part of his god's plan, saying "it surely seems that it was God's will to protect them in so great need, disposing the Indians to bring them." But the chiefs may have wanted to either speed the Spaniards on their way or disguise the impending attack.[38]

The Indians of the lower Arkansas and middle Mississippi had learned some lessons about the Spanish. They were undependable allies. De Soto and Moscoso were not as powerful, wise, or immortal as they claimed. The Spanish were more trouble than they were worth. Still, it was a long path from agreeing that the Spanish were unwelcome to joining with former enemies to expel them. Any unifying must have required remarkable efforts of diplomacy. We can only imagine scenes in which emissaries of Quigualtam arrived at Anilco, presented baskets of pecans and armloads of copper masks in return for an elaborate meal, before they settled down to negotiate their new relationship and their war plan. The fact that the Spanish learned of the plots indicates that the effort was not universally successful, and among those who joined there was much debate as to strategy. Local rivalries surely played a role in deciding whether it was preferable to send the Spaniards on their way or to try to kill them all. Some people probably still feared their native neighbors more, and others played both sides, joining the coalition while also trying to take advantage of the Spaniards. Or perhaps there was no coalition, only separate peoples growing tired of the Spanish.

The chief of Quigualtam clearly threatened the Spaniards. Through a messenger, he threatened to "kill them all in one battle . . . and put a stop to the evil lives they were leading, lost in foreign lands, robbing and killing like highwaymen and vagabonds." He told them that he had "sworn by the Sun and Moon not to make friends with them as the other [chiefs] had done through whose lands they had passed, but he would kill them and hang them from the trees." To stop their terrorizing and prevent them from returning with reinforcements, the chief apparently sent ambassadors to his neighboring chiefs, telling them of his plan and saying, in Garcilaso's imagined reconstruction, "since the danger he feared and wished to guard against was common to all of them, he begged and exhorted them that, abandoning their hostilities and the past anger that had always existed among them, they unite all together and with one accord to forestall and prevent the evil that might befall them if foreigners should come to take away their lands, women, and children, making them slaves and tributaries."[39]

The Spaniards depended for much of their information on torture, a particularly unreliable method. One captive alleged that some twenty chiefs—including those of Anilco, Guachoya, and Tagoanate—were plotting against the Spaniards. From another tortured captive, the Spanish inferred that the Quigaltam chief planned to use the signs of friendship to destroy the Spanish. According to this testimony, the conspirators would send gifts to them every day, beginning three days before the planned day of the attack. These embassies would serve three purposes: confirming their conspiracy to one another, keeping the Spanish off their guard, and secretly spreading the word to Indian slaves held within the Spanish encampment. On the fourth day, the slaves and gift-bearers would steal the Spanish weapons and set fire to the houses. When the chiefs and warriors gathered outside saw the fires, they would rush in to destroy the Spaniards.[40]

On the appointed first day of the conspiracy, indeed, thirty Guachoya Indians bearing gifts arrived at Aminoya, confirming to Moscoso the rumors he had received. And yet, we do not know if Moscoso had this information ahead of time or if those who told the tale later molded the spotty and con-tradictory evidence into a neat plot. In any case, Moscoso panicked. He cut off their right hands and sent the emissaries back to Guachoya. Assuring Moscoso of his loyalty, Chief Guachoya persuaded the confused and fright-ened Spaniard that it was in fact Anilco and Tagoanate who were plotting. Under torture, some Anilco and Tagoanate Indians admitted their involve-ment. Moscoso handed the Anilcos over to Chief Guachoya to be killed, cut off the noses and right hands of the Tagoanates, and prayed for the swift construction of his boats.[41]

The vessels finally ready in the summer of 1543, the remaining Spaniards hurriedly abandoned Aminoya. They sailed down the Mississippi past Guachoya, where people on shore offered to fight with them against Quigual-tam. By this time, Moscoso could not distinguish truth from deception or friends from enemies, so the Spaniards sailed on. All seemed fine at first, but at dawn of their second day, nearly 100 large boats came into sight ahead, spread out across the broad Mississippi as far as Spanish eyes could see. Each boat held as many as eighty warriors and oarsmen, plus a headman in color-ful plumes. According to the interpreters, as the Indians rowed, they sang of "their own strength and bravery," warning the Spaniards that "it would do them no good to flee from the country, for all of them would soon die in the water" and that they would become "food for the fishes and marine animals, and thus their iniquities and the vexation that they were giving the whole world would be ended."[42]

Finally, one of the boats pulled up to Moscoso. A spokesman declared that Quigualtam was not the Spaniards' enemy. With a shaking voice, Moscoso answered that he "appreciated his friendship highly." Almost immediately, a volley of arrows sprang from the boats, covering the Spanish boats and wounding many men and horses. The Indians' oars moved them so swiftly and accurately through the water that Spanish swords could never reach them. Frustrated, fifteen Spaniards pursued their attackers in the four or five canoes that the boats had been towing. The Indians simply encircled and overturned these small canoes. Some Spaniards sank in their heavy armor. Those who tried to hold onto a canoe or swim were struck over the head with oars and clubs. Only four made it back to the boats.

For the next two weeks, the Indians followed, shooting arrows and once boarding a boat and carrying away an Indian woman. At one point, when some of the Spaniards attempted to get provisions from a town on the shore, Indians attacked by water and land. The Spaniards had to abandon their remaining horses, which they had taken ashore. According to Garcilaso, the Indians shot the horses as if they were deer, "with extreme joy and satisfaction." Unlike later Plains Indians who would adopt the horse to increase their own mobility, these people rejected Spaniards *and* their accessories. They harassed the Spaniards most of the way to the sea, killing scores and leaving the rest wounded and hungry.[43]

When at first de Soto and his men seemed to offer an opportunity to shift the balance in favor of one warring society or another, chiefs shaped the Spaniards' perceptions of the region, giving versions so varied that the newcomers could not achieve their goals or even find their way home. But this confusion was clarity itself compared to what happened once the Arkansas Valley's residents realized the Spanish were more trouble than they were worth. Then the only discernable truth was that at least some of these people wanted no more to do with Spaniards.

*   *   *

Indians farther up the Arkansas River would confuse a different group of Spaniards, every bit as committed to gold and bullying as de Soto's men. At the same time that the Indians of the lower Arkansas plotted to expel

Spaniards, a man from the Arkansas River was inviting Coronado and his army to come farther into North America. The man enticed Coronado to extend his journey, which had begun in Mexico City and brought him to the pueblos of New Mexico, by another 600 miles across the Plains to the Arkansas Valley. Like that of the Teya woman discussed earlier, much of this Indian's history involves conjecture, and much is entirely unknown. Like hers, his name is forgotten—Coronado called him El Turco, perhaps because Coronado thought his hairstyle, clothes, or face looked Turkish. Maybe, as Jane MacLaren Walsh has suggested, Coronado and his men only later referred to the man as El Turco because they believed he had lied to them, as they assumed Turks naturally did.[44]

El Turco probably grew up along the Arkansas River in present-day Kansas or Oklahoma, learning to hunt turkey and deer under the oaks and dogwoods close to home and bison on the eastern edge of the Plains. By 1540, he had traveled widely, visiting chiefdoms near the Mississippi, the pueblos of the Southwest, and the Plains in between. In his travels, El Turco had learned some of the Mexica language of Nahuatl and a Plains sign language, which he used to communicate with the peoples whom he visited. He may have been a trader, carrying the products of his people's bison hunt along the Arkansas River and the Plains trade routes to acquire cotton cloth and turquoise at the pueblos and quartz near the Mississippi. He may even have carried some of the very hides that chiefs of the lower Arkansas gave to de Soto. He may have been a slave, captured like the Teya woman by his people's enemies and passed along the same trading networks that hides, shells, and copper traveled.[45]

What is clear is that El Turco took advantage of Spanish vulnerability. While multiple sources of information confused and afflicted the de Soto expedition, one man manipulated Coronado's experiences. At Pecos pueblo, near what would later be the city of Santa Fe, El Turco met members of Coronado's exploring party and apparently decided that they could aid him in some way. Perhaps he, like Chief Casqui, hoped that the more than 1,000 men and women that Coronado brought could change the balance of power in his people's favor. Or, if El Turco was being held captive by the people of Pecos, maybe he wanted an excuse to go home. If a trader, he may simply have preferred crossing the Plains with an army to walking unprotected past Querecho bands. Or he may have been assisting Pecos by drawing away the disruptive Spaniards. For whatever reasons, El Turco invited Coronado to come east with him to a land he called Quivira. He described the splendor of its cities, larger and better-constructed than the southwestern pueblos. As they listened, the Spaniards' imagination and desire translated El Turco's hand signals and Nahuatl into the words they longed to hear—gold and silver. In their interpretation, the lords of Quivira ruled over a "rich country abounding in gold" and ate from golden and silver vessels. This vision captured the Spaniards, disappointed that they had found nŏ gold or silver in the pueblos, despite Coronado's hopes that these were the cities of Cíbola of which Cabeza de Vaca had heard tales. Perhaps El Turco's Quiviran cities were the real thing.[46]

If Coronado and his men had not been bedazzled by dreams of riches, they would have seen warning signs before committing themselves to El Turco's plan. In his first conversation with the Spaniards, El Turco told the captain of artillery, Hernando de Alvarado, that he had come to the pueblos with a "bracelet and other gold pieces" from Quivira but that a chief of Pecos, whom the Spaniards called Bigotes for his "long mustaches," had taken them from him. If Alvarado could retrieve this jewelry from Bigotes, it would serve as proof of El Turco's tales of gold. When questioned, Chief Bigotes told the Spaniards that El Turco was lying about both the jewelry and Quivira's wealth. Unsurprisingly, El Turco's version proved more seductive than that of Bigotes. Deciding that Bigotes must be the one lying, the Spanish tortured him with their giant dogs. When supplies from New Spain failed to appear, food and clothing shortages caused armed conflict between the Spaniards and their hosts at several pueblos that winter. Although their arms and ruthlessness prevailed in these conflicts, the Spanish felt reluctant to remain in a hostile place that apparently contained no riches. Even though the jewelry never surfaced, El Turco's plan began to look even more appealing.[47]

In contrast, the winter of 1540–1541 diminished the Spaniards' appeal in the eyes of El Turco. To impress him with Spanish ferocity, Coronado's men made sure that El Turco and another Quiviran, Ysopete, observed the Spanish destroy Tiguex and surrounding pueblos and kill hundreds of their people, burning many of them alive. Growing reluctance to expose his homeland to these violent intruders may explain the strange journey on which El Turco led the Spanish.[48]

On April 23, 1541, Coronado and his army—some 300 Spanish cavalry, 1,000 native Mexican infantry, uncounted Spanish and Mexican wives, and several hundred male and female servants and slaves—followed El Turco toward the heart of the continent. Once they left the pueblos, they were at El Turco's mercy. If de Soto's men felt confused and vulnerable on the lower Arkansas, the western Plains were almost incomprehensible. Once on the Plains, every direction looked the same. As one of Coronado's men put it,

Figure 3. Spanish drawing of a bison, 1554. This may be the first European depiction of the American bison. Having never seen one, the artist used contemporary descriptions to imagine the fascinating beast. From Francisco López de Gómara, *La historia general de las Indias* (Anvers, 1554). Courtesy DeGolyer Library, Southern Methodist University.

"wherever a man stands he is surrounded by the sky." This situation incapacitated and frightened the explorers. The only landmarks, a few tree-lined rivers, were invisible until one was right upon them, and they immediately disappeared upon leaving them. Even determining the direction from which the party had come was difficult, as the 5,000 combined people, horses, mules, and sheep "left no more traces when they got through there than if no one had passed over." In desperate efforts to keep from losing their rear guard, the army left stacks of bones and bison dung as markers.[49]

Bison dung may have assisted navigation, but the dizzying herds themselves impeded it. Members of the expedition described bison as the "most monstrous beasts ever seen or read about" and as numerous on the Plains as "the fish in the sea." Besides killing several horses and wounding many men, the bison also had the frightening power to lure men to their death. The army had to hunt bison, the only source of sustenance that they could see on the Plains, but hunters who followed prey could lose sight and sound of their compadres, seeing only level grassland in all directions and no tracks to follow back. Whenever the soldiers discovered that someone was missing, they blew horns, beat drums, fired guns in the air, and built bonfires. Still, some hunters remained lost for days, and at least one man never found his way back. Adrift in these unknown and unreadable lands, the Spaniards blindly followed their guide.[50]

The first groups that they met on the Plains seemed to confirm El Turco's story. A band of Querechos spoke to El Turco, who was leading the army. Turning to Coronado, El Turco translated the Querechos' words and hand signs as "lavish reports of settlements all east of our present location." Before long, the Spanish realized what El Turco surely already knew, that using the travel promoter as the interpreter gave that person tremendous power. De Soto could generally assume that Juan Ortiz's motives paralleled those of his countrymen. Coronado had no such assurance.[51]

El Turco's monopoly on information did not last long. First, the Spanish became able to deduce some information for themselves. They could see that, although they had been traveling for weeks, the Plains still seemed to stretch on forever. They knew their bellies were uncomfortable from eating only bison, although they recalled that El Turco had described plentiful corn grown along the journey. Surely he had planned to follow river banks, with their clearer paths, larger populations, and more abundant provisions. After observing Spanish violence the previous winter, El Turco seems to have formed a new plan, to get them lost. Deposed in 1546 to explain this disastrous mission, First Officer Don García López de Cárdenas claimed that, under questioning and presumably torture, El Turco declared that his purpose was, through hunger and thirst, "to kill them all so that they would not go to his country."[52] Another account held that El Turco admitted that the people of Pecos had asked him to "lead them astray on the Plains," "believing that they would not know how to hunt or survive without maize."[53] El Turco's hand signals and Nahuatl could be hard to interpret, but the Spaniards became convinced that he was plotting to kill them.

When the Spanish began to doubt their guide and seek other sources of information, they turned to Ysopete, the other Arkansas Valley native who had joined them at Pecos. Like El Turco, Ysopete demonstrates the extensive range of Arkansas Valley connections and suggests that de Soto could have found information about the West if the people he met had been willing to give it. In response to Coronado's questioning, Ysopete said that Quivira was indeed a permanent set of towns, as El Turco had described, with a large population, agriculture, and a centralized government. After that, his and El Turco's stories diverged. According to Ysopete, Quivira's houses were straw, not stone, and it was farther than El Turco had said, in a different direction. In response, El Turco called Ysopete "a scoundrel who did not know what he was talking about." Deciding that his food sources were too undependable, Coronado sent the bulk of his army back to the pueblos and continued on with only thirty horsemen, with Ysopete guiding and El Turco in chains in the back.[54]

With Ysopete interpreting, people they met began to tell a different story. Teya bands swore that Quivira had no stone houses and little corn. Upon reaching what archaeologists believe was the Arkansas River, the Spaniards met some hunters who ran away at the sight of them. When Ysopete spoke in their language, they returned and escorted the Spaniards to the place that Ysopete called Quivira. These Quivirans welcomed the Spaniards to their towns in present-day Kansas or Oklahoma, some 400 miles west of Pacaha, Casqui, and the rambling de Soto. But they failed to give the Spaniards what they wanted most. Although the Spaniards admitted that the chiefdom was "well settled," with better houses and agriculture than those they had seen thus far, the two dozen towns were not the lavish cities with multi-storied stone houses, wealthy lords, and gold and silver vessels that they had inferred from El Turco's hand signs. They found no gold nor silver "nor information of any." A few Quivirans wore copper collars but only said they were from "farther on." Others showed bits of something that looked like gold, but Coronado suspected that Mexican Indians in his own army had brought it from New Spain and given it to the Quivirans who gave it to him. It is possible that, behind Coronado's back, the Quivirans and Mexican Indians had been conducting their own diplomacy. Besides this tantalizing glimpse, it is impossible to determine whether Quivirans and other North Americans saw the black, white, and Indian travelers as equally "Spanish" or as representatives of various societies.[55]

When Coronado asked various Quivirans about settlements to the east, they either claimed ignorance or said that the Plains ended but that the people farther east only hunted and had no agriculture or great cities. Part of the problem was language—each town spoke a different one. Ysopete was now the only translator, and he did not speak Spanish or Nahuatl. Many misunderstandings arose. Somehow Coronado got the impression that a chief in one of Quivira's towns was a Spaniard, left behind when Cabeza de Vaca passed through. Eager for direct communication, Coronado wrote him a letter. Being neither Spanish nor from a culture with a written language, the chief must have been perplexed when the paper with its strange markings was laid into his hands. Frustrated in their attempts to communicate or find riches or cities, the Spanish killed El Turco.[56]

The motives and strategies of El Turco and Ysopete are murky. While Ysopete identified himself as Quiviran, it is less clear that the "Quivira" that Coronado visited was El Turco's homeland. In some accounts, he refers to "Harahey" as his home, a place probably farther up the Arkansas River and inhabited by ancestors of the Pawnees. Or El Turco may have come from a Mississippian town and successfully diverted the invaders from his home, a theory that would explain the disparity between El Turco's descriptions of "Quivira" and the reality of the place to which Ysopete led them.

While de Soto's hosts grew to disbelieve his claims to spiritual power, Coronado and his men came to see El Turco in increasingly supernatural terms. To them, only the devil could grant an individual the power that El Turco had to lead them so far astray. A Spaniard named Cervantes who was guarding El Turco during the siege of Tiguex swore that he saw El Turco talking with the devil. During the battle, he told Cervantes that the people of Tiguex had killed five Spaniards. When Cervantes asked how he could know this fact, which turned out to be true, El Turco replied that he "knew it already and that he needed no one to tell it to him."[57] If Cervantes's tale is true, El Turco, like de Soto, claimed knowledge beyond normal capabilities in order to increase his usefulness as a friend and fearsomeness as an enemy. On the other hand, Cervantes's tale may have emerged after El Turco's death, as a witchcraft accusation. In either case, it seemed to the Spanish that El Turco had bewitched them. Recalling El Turco's deceitful temptations, one of the mission's chroniclers recalled that "it looked as if the devil had spoken through him."[58] In the Spanish telling, El Turco's spotty Nahuatl and mute hand signals became discourse so dexterous and effective that it must have had supernatural assistance.

For their part, the Quivirans must have seen the Spaniards as poor and ignorant. Like de Soto, Coronado found that his lack of connections to sources of goods or power made him largely useless. The only resource that the Spaniards found in Quivira was aid in returning west. The Quivirans gladly provided them with fresh and dried corn and five or six Quiviran guides, who led them back up the Arkansas River and along a better road to the Teyas, who in turn showed them an easier and more direct route back to the pueblos. Like their neighbors downriver, the Quivirans did not regret the departure of their inarticulate, disconcerting guests.[59]

*   *   *

Initially hopeful about what the other offered, Spaniards and Arkansas Valley natives grew disillusioned with one another. Still, for some Spaniards, hope lingered after 1541. Despite their wasted time, disappointment, and suspicions of devilry, some Spaniards believed that they simply had failed to look hard enough. Several of Coronado's men departed with the nagging feeling that Quivira's riches lay just beyond the towns that they had searched. During the journey back to the pueblos, the Teyan guides fueled this suspicion with tales of chiefdoms to the east with "large settlements and mighty rivers," probably referring to Mississippian towns.[60] Back at the pueblos in the fall of 1541, Spanish regrets grew. Some spoke with a Quiviran named Xabe, who expressed surprise that the Spaniards had failed to find gold and silver and declared that they must not have gone far enough.[61]

Uneasily ensconced in Tiguex for another long winter (1541–1542), Coronado's forces mulled over the disappointments of Quivira. As they sat around their fires and relived the summer's events, several found themselves "not satisfied to think that there was no gold" and decided "that it was to be found inland," not far from Quivira. They remembered that, although the Quivirans claimed to have no gold, "they knew what it was and they had a name for it, calling it *acochis*."[62] Nurturing such suspicions, many hoped to return to Quivira in the spring to continue searching for gold and other resources. However, Coronado suffered a horse-riding accident during the winter and decided to cut his losses, return to New Spain, and perhaps come back with more forces.[63]

De Soto's failed expedition sparked similar yearnings. While those who escaped down the Mississippi hoped never to see their adversaries or that land again, people at home who heard their tales of bountiful, developed lands imagined untapped resources. The Incan-Spanish historian Garcilaso de la Vega lamented that the explorers "did not consider that, if [gold and silver] had not been found, it was because these Indians do not seek these metals or value them." Just because they did not use gold and silver for buying and selling, he instructed his readers, "it is not to be assumed that there is none in La Florida. If a search should be made, mines of gold and silver would be found, just as new ones are discovered every day in México and El

Perú." Besides precious metals, the Arkansas Valley would provide "fertile and abundant" lands, "sufficient to lay the foundations of an empire." There, Spaniards could grow "fruits, vegetables, grains, and cattle," find pearls, produce silk, and, of course, "remove from the power of our enemy [the devil] so great a number of souls as he has blinded with idolatry."[64]

The Valley apparently had no regrets at the Spaniards' departure. Initially, many of its residents had considered de Soto's expedition a powerful addition to their friends and had enthusiastically recruited its members. Similarly, El Turco had drawn Coronado's men to his assistance, although the Quivirans, with fewer reasons to fight their neighbors, had less interest in a Spanish alliance. But the newcomers violated the obligations of guests. They overstepped their prerogatives, overstayed their welcome, and gave nothing in return. They took leaders and others captive, forcibly appropriated Indian possessions, killed when it suited them, and demonstrated an annoying obsession with shiny metals.[65]

De Soto and Coronado are shocking in their violence. Perhaps being outnumbered and afraid made them some of the most instinctively violent people around. Violence was nothing new in the Arkansas Valley, but Indians had established elaborate methods of befriending and exchanging with neighboring peoples in order to discourage conflict over land and resources, or perhaps in some cases to give leaders a monopoly on violence. These methods generally worked. Acting with more frequent and less predictable violence, demanding what they could not have, and failing to forge strong connections, the Spaniards threatened to disrupt the tenuous balance.

When Spaniards returned over the following century, the peoples of the Arkansas Valley had learned not to welcome them as before. In the spring of 1542, six men from Coronado's expedition set off for Quivira again rather than returning to New Spain. These were Fray Juan de Padilla, a Portuguese soldier named Campo, a mestizo soldier, and three men training to become friars—a free black man and two Indians from New Spain named Lucas and Sebastian. A few months later, Campo, Lucas, and Sebastian appeared in New Spain, explaining that the Quivirans had killed their companions. Apparently, the Quivirans' experience with Coronado had taught them to trust no "Spaniards," whatever their vocation, color, or origin. Quivirans also destroyed a party of thirty men who came north in 1593 seeking riches, according to Jusepe Gutiérrez, an Indian from the northern Mexico pueblo of Culhuacán, who escaped.[66]

These tales simply excited more interest, this time in Juan de Oñate, whose father had fought with Cortés in Mexico and whose wife, Doña Isabel de Tolosa, was the granddaughter of Cortés and the great-granddaughter of Montezuma. Oñate settled a small colony in New Mexico in 1598 but longed to find a source of more immediate wealth. Gutiérrez led Oñate across the Plains in June 1601 with some eighty soldiers, two friars, many servants and slaves, and hundreds of horses and mules to carry the equipment, which included four pieces of artillery. After some 200 leagues, they came upon an encampment of people whom they could not identify from previous accounts. The Spanish participants later estimated their numbers as more than 200,000. They called these new people Escanxaques because their first action was to give the Spanish a sign of peaceful greeting by stretching their hands toward the sun and saying "escanxaque."[67]

As Apache interpreters translated these people's words into their own language for Gutiérrez, who translated into Spanish, the Escanxaques described their lands, their large numbers, their neighbors, and their desire "to be friends." When the Spanish asked them if they knew the fate of the 1593 expedition, they described in graphic terms how their enemies in the "Great Settlement" had killed and burned the Spaniards. Two or three days downriver from where Oñate met the Escanxaques, this Great Settlement appears to be Coronado's "Quivira." The Escanxaques warned Oñate and his men to take care "lest these people, who were very numerous, burn them as they had the others." They advised fighting them, with Escanxaque assistance. Perhaps newcomers to the region, the Escanxaques sought Spanish military assistance, as other Arkansas Valley residents had in the past. When Oñate refused their offer and insisted on going alone, hoping to find better information through peaceful contact, the Escanxaques cautioned them "not to trust these people." Hoping to cause friction between Oñate's forces and the Great Settlement, about 100 Escanxaques followed behind, repeatedly sending representatives to tell the Spanish they were "coming close to their enemies, whom they wanted to fight, and to help the Spaniards."

When the Spanish reached the settlement, its people declared their friendship and invited the visitors into their town. They asked Oñate to dismiss the Escanxaque escort "since they were their enemies." Before he could attempt such a thorny assignment, nearly 1,000 Escanxaques charged in, accusing the people of the Great Settlement of murder and claiming that "it was here they had killed the Spaniards, surrounding them with fire and burning them." They also declared that one of the Spanish victims had survived the fire and, although "badly crippled" from his burns, was alive and held captive in this very town. The Great Settlement's representatives replied "that they knew nothing about what was said and not to believe what those

Indians said because they were mortal enemies who killed and ate each other." They explained that the war was not their fault—the Great Settlement had "tried to make friends," but the "warlike" and cannibalistic Escanxaques had "refused."

Like de Soto and Coronado before him, Oñate found himself trapped between two opposing versions of the Arkansas Valley. Confused and unable to find any information on the alleged survivor, Oñate decided to turn around. But he would have to pass by the Escanxaques to get home. Meeting on their way out, the Spaniards desperately thrust their hands into the air, which they believed was the customary sign of peace, and had the interpreter remind the Escanxaques that "we were all friends." According to some accounts, the Escanxaques replied that they "did not wish to be friends of the Spaniards but to kill them." The only reply that another Spanish participant remembered was a volley of arrows. After several hours of battle, the Spanish fled back across the Plains, grumbling that the Escanxaques had not played fair because they had only "pretended to be friendly."

On their frantic return, Oñate's forces carried off several boys and girls to train in Christianity and Spanish translation skills. One of these young people, whom the Spaniards christened Miguel, would spark the next round of Spanish hopes of Quivira. On the journey back to Mexico, Miguel drew a map with circles of different sizes to represent the eastern Plains. These included his birthplace, Tancoa, a town with agriculture, many people, and a great chief, perhaps the town that de Soto called Tanico, part of the Caya chiefdom. As a youth, Miguel had been taken prisoner by the people of Aguacane and transported to that town, perhaps the Aguacay that Moscoso stumbled through during his disastrous attempt to find New Spain. Miguel had lived in Aguacane for several years, until its people joined its ally the Escanxaques against the Spanish and the people of the Great Settlement. Most importantly to his Spanish audience, Miguel described "much gold" in the region. He recalled seeing gold pieces and vessels at Tancoa, bought with meat and hides. Like El Turco and Jusepe Gutiérrez before him, Miguel spoke in words and symbols for which Spaniards had to make interpretive leaps. But by now, stories of Quivira were wearing thin. Some believed Miguel and wanted to return, but others agreed with a soldier named Baltasar Martínez Coxedor, who suspected that "this Indian is telling what the soldiers and those who questioned him wanted to hear."[68]

No Spaniards followed Miguel onto the Plains, and he probably lived his life in Mexico or New Mexico, unless he found a way home without a Spanish escort. Throughout the seventeenth century, the Spanish, and the

French once they heard the tales, dreamed of Quivira's precious metals and souls. Its rumored "numerous gold mines" were one of the reasons for Louis Jolliet's and Jacques Marquette's voyage seventy years later. And Europeans bought Quiviran slaves from Plains traders. But after Oñate's disaster, the Spanish finally decided that the lands to the north offered more dangers than benefits. Most Indians of the Arkansas Valley had formed the same conclusion about the Spanish much sooner.[69]

Natives of the mid-continent possessed some of the faults they found in Spaniards—violence, dissimulation, bullying, bluster—but they generally knew when to use each. In future centuries, Europeans would learn how to work within North American diplomatic systems, but sixteenth-century Spaniards overstepped their bounds and became liabilities. The successes of Pizarro and Cortés were so dazzling that, even though their successors saw *encomiendas* as a theoretical way in which they could profit from their explorations, in practice it proved difficult for them to conceive of any material goals besides gold or strategies besides dividing and conquering. To make matters worse, they brought nothing to trade. If Arkansas Valley residents considered some people "the quartz people" and others "the flint people," they may have called the Spanish "people who demand but give nothing in return." The Spaniards' uselessness and obnoxiousness united even enemies against them.

If they had learned more compatible methods, given up on gold, and brought goods to distribute, the Spanish might have established a sphere of interest across North America in the sixteenth century and stalled French and British expansion. If so, the later British footholds in Virginia and Massachusetts might not have grown so steadily into an Anglo-dominated United States across the continent. But conquistadors had visions of gold and power, and the Indians of the Arkansas Valley came to believe that Spanish contact was not worth the cost. Many of them apparently decided that the best they could hope for was to be rid of the Spanish and make sure none ever returned. Killing them all would probably have been the most effective means of bringing about that result, but Indians settled for demonstrating their ability to kill them if they did return.

*   *   *

One result of these Indians' success is that subsequent decades are even more difficult to divine. Arkansas Valley people responded to change borne by the transitory Spaniards and to the continuing dynamics of their native land. We know little of these years, especially near the Mississippi, where no Europeans visited for more than a century after 1543. What we do know is that, by the mid-1600s, the great chiefdoms—Casqui, Pacaha, Anilco, Guachoya—were gone, and for another century no population centers north of Mexico would approach them in size or centralization. The causes probably included climate change, depleted fields, drought, floods, warfare, and new European diseases. Before 1492, smallpox, measles, mumps, rubella, diphtheria, whooping cough, chicken pox, influenza, malaria, typhoid fever, cholera, pneumonia, yellow fever, and scarlet fever were unknown in the Americas, and American Indians had not developed resistance to them. Because only the healthiest Spaniards survived to reach the mid-continent, probably neither de Soto's nor Coronado's men brought these diseases there directly, with the possible exception of typhoid. The places where de Soto wintered, including Utiangue and Aminoya, would have provided ideal conditions for passing typhoid if a Spanish carrier's waste contaminated food or entered the water system. Reproducing rapidly, the expedition's pigs probably brought tuberculosis, trichinosis, and other diseases, which they could easily have spread to the region's deer and to humans who ate the pork or venison or came into contact with their waste.[70]

Archaeological finds suggest that most of the destruction from disease came to the mid-continent in waves of epidemics spread through native trading networks in the late sixteenth and seventeenth centuries. Thus the trade and diplomatic ties essential to survival became carriers of disease and disruption. If any of Coronado's or de Soto's men had smallpox or whooping cough, they may have carried it to Tampa Bay or New Mexico, from whence the diseases could have spread slowly across North America. Historical evidence reveals that neighboring regions with sustained European contact in the seventeenth century suffered from European diseases. New Mexico reported fevers and smallpox in the 1630s. Smallpox and other diseases hit the Great Lakes and New France in the 1630s and 1640s. By the end of the century, various diseases had spread through the Caddoan peoples in Texas. Trade and raids could have brought disease from any of these sites to the Arkansas Valley.[71]

Varying types of settlements probably experienced diverse effects. Those living close together in nucleated towns in the lower Arkansas Valley likely proved more susceptible than those dispersed on farms higher upriver. Still, less centralized places like Quivira also suffered population decline and disruption of their old ways of life, many of them becoming more Plains-oriented as their Mississippian trading partners disappeared. Surprisingly, no Europeans who arrived in the seventeenth century heard tales of mass death. It is possible that disease hit incrementally so that it became "normal" to have periodic waves of death or that scholars have overestimated the destruction. On the other hand, perhaps the disruption was too great for traditional rituals of commemoration, too personal to tell Europeans, or, as anthropologist Raymond D. Fogelson has surmised, so traumatic that it could not be remembered.[72]

It is difficult to estimate sixteenth- and seventeenth-century population loss. De Soto's chroniclers called the lower Arkansas Valley "the most densely populated" of all the lands they visited.[73] They may have exaggerated its cities to account for their defeat there, but archaeological findings indicate a dense population and a large number of communities, as does the Spaniards' ability to survive on food from Indians. A reasonable range of estimates for the 1541 Arkansas Valley east of the Plains (from Quivira to the Mississippi and from the White River to the Red) seems somewhere between 300,000 and 1,000,000. One hundred fifty years later, the French estimated fewer than 20,000 people. These French observers certainly missed people, perhaps tens of thousands of people. On the other hand, some people whom the French visited were recent immigrants to the Arkansas Valley. Whatever the magnitude, it seems clear that the population was dramatically and tragically lower in 1700 than it had been when the Chief of Casqui first heard that roving bandits had entered his territory.[74]

But disease did not stop North American history. Indians adapted as they had in the past. While many historians have portrayed disease as a force driving out Indian agency, Paul Kelton has recently shown that some southeastern Indians responded to disease in ways that reduced psychological damage and even saved lives. While in some places, loss of life may have led people to repudiate their leaders for their inability to combat the epidemics, in others, they may have relied on their old leaders and beliefs more than ever.[75]

It appears that disease played a significant role in the decline of Mississippian communities but was not the only force of change. In the lower valley, war may have continued to accelerate, perhaps even destroying some societies after the Spaniards left (although anti-Spanish coalitions could instead have decreased tension). Perhaps a newcomer took advantage of divisions, playing societies against one another and succeeding where de Soto and Coronado had failed. Some towns such as Pacaha and Casqui broke up, but Natchez and others remained, adapting to new changes without falling. Other chiefdoms moved to safer places. Not only disease and political change but also new plants and animals available because of the Columbian

exchange probably changed people's relations with the natural world, altering their cultures in ways we can never pin down. Whatever happened, the
people of the Arkansas Valley continued to use and modify older ways to
negotiate the unprecedented changes of the seventeenth century.[76]

It is even harder to know how the Arkansas Valley remembered the
Spanish visitors. In 1695, a group of Apaches reported to Spaniards in New
Mexico that some Quivirans whom they had enslaved told them a story of
white men who came to their towns, made war on everyone, then went away,
only to come again at long intervals to repeat the same process. To the
Apaches and Quivirans, this was a cyclical story of comings and goings, dis-
ruptions and times in between. The nervous Spanish interpreted it as evidence that the French had visited Quivira from the East. But as historian
Elizabeth John has observed, these visitors sound more like the Spanish
themselves. It is easy to believe that Quivirans and their neighbors retold stories of Coronado, de Soto, Oñate, and others "on winter nights" for a century, possibly adding morals about the responsibilities of guests and the
foolishness of greedy strangers.[77]

*   *   *

As strange as Spaniards were, the people of the Arkansas Valley did not view
them as wholly different from themselves. Rather, they dealt with the
Spaniards in the long-established ways of their native ground, attempting to
fit the newcomers into older understandings and practices of trade and
diplomacy. When the Spaniards refused to be incorporated, the valley's people drove them out, through violence in the lower valley and by discouraging
them farther upstream. Cortés and Pizarro had forged Indian alliances that
enabled their successes. De Soto and Coronado wandered isolated across the
continent and failed miserably. Spanish colonization of the Arkansas Valley
ended before it began.

The Valley changed so dramatically in the following decades that its earlier history is wrapped in haze, for the descendants of those who lived there
earlier, for late seventeenth-century European explorers who tried to use the
de Soto and Coronado accounts as travel guides, and for those of us today
who try to imagine that world. Still, as historian Daniel K. Richter has
pointed out, "1492 did not rend the fabric of the continent's time." The descendants of El Turco's and Casqui's kin and neighbors remained. They
traded and hunted along similar routes and in similar ways. Their history
and beliefs affected how they dealt with the new challenges.[78]

Despite changes, declensions, and disappearances, for the foreseeable future the mid-continent would remain an Indian place. It had changed in the past and would continue to change as new peoples—Indian and European— arrived. Unlike sixteenth-century Spaniards, these later newcomers would bring more reasonable demands, more experience in Indian diplomacy, and more desire to adapt to local ways of cross-cultural relations.

Chapter 3

Negotiators of a New Land, 1650–1740

In 1998, near the mouth of the Arkansas River, archaeologists found the remains of a multicultural society, probably the late seventeenth- and eighteenth-century Quapaw town of Osotouy. They found evidence of the town's ties to other peoples regionally and beyond the Atlantic. Pottery shards remain from vessels made locally by Quapaws, across the Mississippi in Natchez country, and in New Spain, France, Italy, and England. Mixed with silt from the river lie glass beads fired in Europe and thick green pieces of bottles that once held French brandy. The lead musket balls and shot found here came from Europe, but using guns had become standard enough during the life of this town that local artisans made gunflints when the ones that came with their guns wore down or fell off in battle. Arrowheads reveal the continuing importance of bows and arrows. Large numbers of scrapers testify to the work that Quapaw women did preparing deer and bison hides for the European market, from the animals that Quapaw and French men hunted.

This thriving town's incorporation of European material culture re- flects the changed nature of Indian-European relations since the days of Guachoya, Anilco, Casqui, Pacaha, and Quivira. While those sixteenth- century residents of the valley rejected Spaniards as dangerous and useless, the late seventeenth-century Quapaws purposefully intertwined their lives with those of Europeans. Indeed, wrought iron nails found at the site suggest the presence of French-style wooden buildings in the town, as well as the Quapaws' own daub houses. Probably occupied by a handful of early traders or soldiers, these buildings could not have been built in Osotouy if the Qua- paws had not wanted them there.[1]

Part of the appeal of the French stemmed from their willingness to co- operate. Unlike their sixteenth-century Spanish counterparts, the French came to stay. In the intervening century, Spain's interest in the region north of New Mexico and Florida had declined, and the French and English had rushed in to establish their own colonies. The French had established a

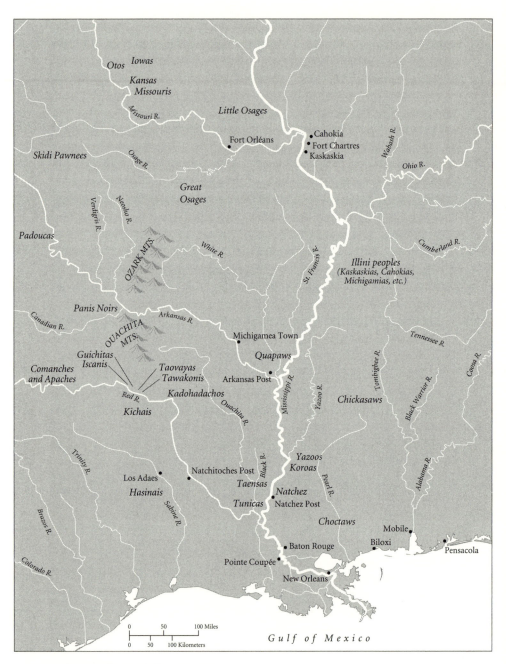

Map 3. Arkansas Valley, 1670s–1750s.

fur-trading colony in Canada and now sought to expand those operations south along the potentially useful Mississippi River, hoping both to make profits and to fend off English designs. Certainly, individual traders, missionaries, and bureaucrats hoped to leave after making their fortunes, redeeming some souls, or performing service for the monarchy that would get them promoted to more appealing offices. But French Louisiana as a colony was to be permanent. The sixteenth-century Spaniards' lack of goods and their desire to acquire quick gold by dividing and conquering Indians had made these intruders useless or worse for the region's native peoples. In contrast, the French brought not demands and destruction but valued trade goods. They came with valuable ties to European manufacturing, and they intended to form lasting Indian connections, indispensable to their own economic, religious, and imperial goals. Therefore, the French had considerably more incentive to learn and comply with native methods of cross-cultural relations and land use. And by the late seventeenth century, they had already learned much about North American Indian ways, particularly the importance of ceremonial exchange. The French would fit themselves more successfully to the Arkansas Valley than had the sixteenth-century Spanish.[2]

European alliances also became more appealing because of local circumstances. Casquis and other sixteenth-century native peoples had only temporary use for Europeans—winning a battle, frightening an enemy, learning new sources of spiritual power. But a great deal had changed since 1543. Most of the Mississippian chiefdoms had fallen, their diminished descendants dispersing across the land. In this less stable world, people found themselves surrounded by unfamiliar peoples. De Soto and Coronado had been aberrant—people of unclear allegiance, history, and motives. Now newcomers were more common, including Indian refugees dispersed from far-off fallen Mississippian towns as well as local Mississippian peoples with social and political structures so altered that their motives and allegiances had changed.[3]

Smaller in population, occasionally victimized by Indians bearing European arms, and less certain of their own importance, most seventeenth-century people of the mid-continent were prepared to court these new Europeans with more patience than had previous residents. The French were lucky that times had changed. Trade, religious conversion, and supremacy over European rivals all required the help of native peoples. Some of the French would fulfill their dreams and some would fail, but none would control the Indians. Rather, the native peoples of the Arkansas Valley in particular

TABLE 1. Indian Peoples of the Mid-Continent, 1670s–1750s

Name	Language group	Prior history
Apaches	Athabaskan	descended from Querechos, southern Plains
Chickasaws	Muskogean	descended from Mississippian Chicaça
Choctaws	Muskogean	descended from Mississippians
Comanches	Uto-Aztecan/Shoshoean	moving south from the northwestern Plains
Guichitas	Caddoan	descended from Quivira, Tula, Naguatex, Aguacane, and/or Escanxaque; become Wichitas
Hasinais	Caddoan	become Caddos
Iowas	Chiwere Siouan	probably moved west from the Great Lakes
Iscanis	Caddoan	descended from Quivira, Tula, Naguatex, Aguacane, and/or Escanxaque; become Wichitas
Kadohadachos	Caddoan	become Caddos
Kansas	Dhegiha Siouan	probably moved west from the Ohio Valley
Kaskaskias	Algonquian	part of the Illinois culture group
Kichais	Caddoan	descended from Quivira, Tula, Naguatex, Aguacane, and/or Escanxaque
Koroas	Tunican	descended from Mississippians, possibly Coligua
Michigameas	Algonquian	part of the Illinois culture group
Missouris	Chiwere Siouan	probably moved west from the Great Lakes
Natchez	Tunican	descended from Mississippians, possibly Quigaltam
Osages	Dhegiha Siouan	probably from the Ohio Valley, possibly descended from Mississippians or Hopewell, but also possibly Escanxaque
Otos	Chiwere Siouan	probably moved west from the Great Lakes
Padoucas	Athabaskan (prob.)	probably Plains Apaches, possibly descended from Escanxaque
Panimahas	Caddoan	also known as Skidi Pawnees
Panis Noirs	Caddoan	descended from Quivira, Tula, Naguatex, Aguacane, and/or Escanxaque; become Pawnees
Peorias	Algonquian	part of the Illinois culture group

TABLE 1. (*continued*)

Name	Language group	Prior history
Quapaws	Dhegiha Siouan	probably from the Ohio Valley, possibly descended from Mississippians or Hopewell, but also possibly Pacaha
Taensas	Muskogean (prob.)	descended from Mississippians
Taovayas	Caddoan	descended from Quivira, Tula, Naguatex, Aguacane, and/or Escanxaque; become Wichitas
Tawakonis	Caddoan	descended from Quivira, Tula, Naguatex, Aguacane, and/or Escanxaque; become Wichitas
Tunicas	Tunican	descended from Mississippians, probably Pacaha and/or others of the lower Arkansas Valley
Yazoos	Tunican	descended from Mississippians

and the mid-continent in general would fit the French into their world, into their established rituals of trade and alliance, of friendship and rivalry.

The Quapaws, not the Spanish, French, or English, would have the greatest effect on the seventeenth-century Arkansas Valley. The Quapaws achieved what they wanted from their alliances with the French and with select native peoples—reciprocal exchange relations, weapons, and assistance against their enemies. To support their French alliance, the Quapaws created an image of themselves as steadfast French allies. Probably newcomers themselves, they used the French to establish the lower Arkansas Valley as their own native ground.

*   *   *

The first French emissaries assumed that the people they met at the mouth of the Arkansas River had long-time and uncontested possession of their homeland, but the Quapaws' history was more complicated than that. The lack of information on the lower Arkansas Valley between 1543 and 1673 makes their origins difficult to determine. Quapaw oral histories and early European accounts suggest that the turmoil caused by Iroquoian-speakers' use of Dutch weapons to expand their territory had compelled the Quapaws to leave the Ohio River Valley in the early seventeenth century. In the West, the Quapaws in turn drove away the Mississippian peoples who lived there. Because the Quapaws are Dhegiha Siouan speakers, an Ohio Valley origin makes sense. Oral, documentary, and linguistic evidence support this explanation best, but there are other possibilities. Quapaws today speak of an Ohio Valley migration but possibly one that took place in time to meet de Soto, possibly at Pacaha, 100 miles north of their location by the 1670s. The word *Quapaw*, or *Kappa* as it was spelled in the seventeenth century, sounds a great deal like *Pacaha* and even more like the spelling of one of de Soto's chroniclers, *Capaha*. Although linguistic evidence suggests that Pacaha was Tunican, it could have been Siouan. Kappa and the other Quapaw towns may have moved the 100 miles south from Pacaha and settled on the ruins of Anilco. Or perhaps both explanations are valid—refugees from Pacaha and even Cahokia could have combined with newcomers from the Ohio Valley.[4]

In any case, the Quapaws were new to their location in 1673, when merchant Louis Jolliet and Jesuit priest Jacques Marquette descended the Mississippi from Canada. By then, they lived in four allied towns near the juncture of the Arkansas and Mississippi rivers—Osotouy, Kappa, Tourima, and Tonginga, which probably sat just east of the Mississippi. In the seventeenth century, they usually told outsiders to call them *Akamsea*, or *Arkansas*. They also called their river by that name, probably to associate their identity with their new home. The Quapaw people took advantage of French alliance and trade goods and the power vacuum left by disease. While French traders, priests, and government officials came to Louisiana with diverse agendas, the Quapaws were able to present a relatively united front, working to draw all French into serving Quapaw interests.[5]

Despite change and population decline, the Arkansas River Valley remained as diverse a place as in the 1540s. In the late seventeenth century, people speaking variants of at least four unrelated language groups lived in scores of towns. The Quapaws occupied the mouth of the river. In the central valley lived Caddoan-speaking peoples including the Taovayas, Iscanis, Guichitas, Tawakonis, and Panis Noirs. Probably the descendants of Quivira, Tula, Naguatex, Aguacane, and perhaps the Escanxaques, these peoples would join the Wichita and Pawnee confederacies in the next century. Some 15,000 of these people had moved southeast down the Arkansas River after Oñate's visit in 1600 to settle near the Canadian River's juncture with the Arkansas. Dozens of other Caddoan-speaking peoples lived along the Red River and would confederate into the Caddo nation in the late eighteenth and nineteenth centuries. More than 400 miles farther west lived Apache bands, who were beginning to use Spanish horses to become buffalo hunters on the vast Plains.[6]

South of the Arkansas were the Mississippian Tunicas, who probably had moved south from one or several of the chiefdoms that de Soto encountered near the Arkansas River. In a seasonal town north of the Arkansas lived the Michigameas, an Algonquian-speaking Illinois group. Farther north, on the White, Osage, and Missouri rivers, lived the Osage and Missouri peoples, who spoke Siouan languages. Across the Mississippi from the mouth of the Arkansas lived Mississippian descendants—the powerful Chickasaws to the north and the Yazoos, Koroas (perhaps the descendants of Coligua), Taensas, and Natchez (perhaps Quigaltam) to the south. These peoples were far from homogeneous or united. The Chickasaws were matrilineal, while the Quapaws and Osages were patrilineal. The Natchez were fairly centralized, while the individual Quapaw towns ruled themselves and, within towns, shared decision-making broadly. The Guichitas were short and stocky, while the Osages often stood over six feet tall.[7]

Whatever brought the Quapaws to the Arkansas Valley, by 1673 they found themselves dangerously isolated. Older residents disputed the relative newcomers' right to settle there. Perhaps the Quapaw towns were aggregations of separate peoples, and their unstable chiefs sought the economic and spiritual power of foreign alliances to bolster their political authority. Clearly, they faced challenges. The Tunicas, Yazoos, and Koroas to the south regularly attacked the Quapaws, probably seeking to expel them from their own former territory. Farther west in the Arkansas Valley, Taovayas, Iscanis, Guichitas, Tawakonis, and Panis Noirs clashed with Quapaw hunters. Iroquoian-speakers occasionally expanded their raids in Illinois country across the Mississippi to attack the Quapaws. To make matters worse, Chickasaw bands were beginning to take Quapaw slaves, hundreds of whom they traded to the English at Charles Town for guns, ammunition, and horses. The people that de Soto and Coronado had met in the Arkansas Valley could afford to reject the Spaniards. Blocked from Dutch and English trade in the East by Iroquoian peoples and the Chickasaws and from Spanish trade by Apaches, the Quapaws needed to establish allies, particularly those who could provide weapons.[8]

Still, the Quapaws maintained control over their relations with the French. The Quapaws welcomed the French when they offered something useful—such as guns—but rejected their attempts to disturb native religious practices, land use, or relations with other peoples. The Quapaws, like most of the mid-continent's native peoples, chose what they wanted from Europeans. When French interests coincided with Indian interests and when French newcomers conformed to Indian practices of peace-making and trade, the

French were successful. When the French clashed with Indian ways and desires, they failed, at best going bankrupt or going home, at worst dying by Indian hands.

To the Quapaws, the French were not a dominant intruder but simply another of the region's diverse peoples, one connected to sources of powerful goods. In 1673, the Quapaws introduced Jolliet and Marquette to their methods of establishing good relations. As for most peoples of the eastern woodlands and the Mississippi basin, reciprocal goods exchange reflected and sustained friendly relations. European cloth, kettles, needles, and knives were useful for hunting, fighting, tattooing, doing beadwork, and making clothes. Guns were a powerful force for frightening an enemy. Although not as accurate as bows and arrows, they had improved since the 1540s. Their noise and smoke and the grisly carnage that resulted when they did hit their targets made people whose enemies had them want that power themselves. Like the shells, copper, and quartz crystals of older trade networks, glass and porcelain beads were pleasing for adorning clothing, musical instruments, arms, necks, ears, and noses and important for conveying messages and conducting various rituals. Goods also had political uses. Hospitality and generosity were the bedrock of mutual trust. When a visiting delegation arrived, the Quapaws always performed the calumet ceremony with them and served an elaborate meal, the reciprocal responsibility of the host. As in previous centuries, trade goods, food, and politics were bound together, with hospitality and gifts symbolizing ties between peoples.[9]

Reciprocity in diplomatic relationships mirrored reciprocity within Quapaw society. Leaders distributed goods widely among their people. Rather than a hierarchic chain of command, the Quapaw political structure was decentralized and depended on mutual obligations. The chiefs did not rule their people but instead were important participants in shared decision-making who created and maintained influence and respect by fulfilling their obligations within the community. The Quapaws expected their chiefs, like their visitors, to be generous with presents. Similarly, women gave men and children their agricultural produce, while men provided the products of the hunt.[10]

By the seventeenth century, it appears that Mississippian decline led some people to distrust concentrated power. Authority both within societies and over foreign relations spread more broadly across most populations. Many North American Indians had come to disapprove of accumulating wealth and valued giving more than receiving. Some peoples probably returned to their own cultures' earlier nomadic taboos against storing wealth.

Figure 4. Mississippi Valley welcoming ceremony. This is Jean-Bernard Bossu's probably exaggerated depiction of Mississippi Valley Indians' welcoming ceremonies. From Bossu's *Nouveaux voyages dans l'Amérique septentrionale* (Amsterdam, 1777). Courtesy Dechert Collection, University of Pennsylvania.

In addition, if those who never lived in large cities suffered less from disease, they and former urbanites alike may have inferred that centralized chiefdoms and accumulation of goods tempted disaster.[11]

The Quapaws' gift-based economy required the incorporation of would-be traders into Quapaw systems of reciprocity. They welcomed outsiders with elaborate ceremonies, which lasted well into the night, and sometimes several days. Some historians have interpreted the elaborate welcoming ceremonies that Europeans received as evidence that Indians believed that Europeans were gods or kings, but there is no reason to believe that Indians did not welcome first-time Indian visitors with similar ceremonies. Once incorporated, newcomers became fictive kin and members of the community instead of outsiders. Like blood kin, they now had a role in Quapaw networks of reciprocity. The Quapaws expected their adopted French kin to appreciate their hospitality and to reciprocate with trade goods, both to important leaders and to individuals who established specific fictive kin relationships.[12]

For their part, the French arrived in the mid-continent with their own traditions of reciprocal and obligatory gift-giving. Not only did they share European beliefs regarding diplomatic generosity and the obligation of rulers to the ruled, but they had come to value gift exchange even more highly in North America because it was already the primary way of doing business there. Decades before Jolliet and Marquette canoed down the Mississippi, traders in New France learned the necessity of presents to establish and maintain trade relations, missionaries discovered that gifts made Indians more attentive listeners, and governors began to give presents to recruit and acknowledge allies.[13]

Serendipitous similarities between French and Indian diplomacy helped the two peoples to become friends. In both societies, men were responsible for greeting outsiders, and a particular man usually had the primary authority to speak during ceremonies of contact. When Jolliet, the leader of his party, met the Quapaws, they led him to the diplomatic chief. Both leaders were accustomed to one-on-one negotiation. Meeting with an analogous counterpart was easier than negotiating some more alien system. In reality, these superficial similarities masked major differences in the French and Quapaw political systems. The French assumed that they were negotiating with a supreme leader, but Quapaw chiefs did not have coercive power over other Quapaws. The men and women in a circle around the leaders were political participants witnessing and approving a ceremony invalid without their presence. The diplomatic chief was one of many chiefs with varying roles. Every Quapaw belonged to a clan, which had specific rights and responsibilities for

rituals and practices. Representatives of the clans came together to make political decisions for the whole. In contrast, Jolliet and Marquette lived in a
monarchy and a rigid social hierarchy. Royally appointed, Jolliet had power
over the men he commanded. For the French, a male leader of an all-male
party mirrored gender inequality within their broader society. In contrast,
while the Quapaw diplomatic chief was male, women wielded considerable
economic and political power. They farmed the fields that provided for the
community, distributed the harvest, participated in councils, and occasionally served as chiefs. Their role in welcoming newcomers by presenting the
food that they had grown and prepared was an essential part of diplomatic
ritual.[14]

Luckily for the Frenchmen and the Quapaws, the differences between
their societies were easy to ignore. It was in both Quapaw and French interest to build a friendship based on what they had in common. The most important similarity was their desire to agree upon rituals that would establish
their rights to the Arkansas Valley—the Quapaws to live and hunt and the
French to hunt, trade, and travel. The most important aspect of French rituals of alliance was gaining native consent, which the Quapaws were happy
to grant, as long as the French served their interests and complied with
Quapaw rituals. By legitimating each other's rights, each hoped to deny
the claims of others: the Caddoan, Tunica, Yazoo, and Koroa rivals of the
Quapaws and the English and Spanish rivals of the French.[15]

The French had ambitious plans for a place where hundreds of different
communities with various goals and priorities vastly outnumbered them.
Like most colonizers, the French in Louisiana demonstrated a disdain for
demographics as well as tremendous self-confidence. French cartographers
wrote "La Louisiane" across the vast middle of North America, from the headwaters of the Mississippi to the Gulf and from just east of Santa Fe to the
Appalachians, borders the Spanish and English disputed indignantly, and
which were irrelevant to the Native American majority. Trader Jolliet and
Father Marquette represented twin French goals—the fur trade and conversion to Catholicism. With Spain established in Mexico, New Mexico, and
Florida and the English on the Atlantic, the Mississippi Valley seemed to be
France's last chance for a mainland colony south of Canada.[16]

From the Quapaws and other native peoples, Jolliet and Marquette
found the friendship they desired, but, like its symbols, that friendship was
more on Indian terms than European. The Quapaws did not invent reciprocal friendship, but they were particularly good at it. They were masters of
diplomacy because they had to be. As people who had probably fled one

homeland and who faced challenges from their current neighbors, the Quapaws were eager to attract new friends to help them maintain their tenuous hold on the lower Arkansas River. Their history instilled in the Quapaws a degree of flexibility that groups with longer tenures on the land seldom possessed. Indeed, Quapaws today regard themselves as a flexible people, who value harmony and kindness and who survived their tumultuous history in part by purposefully working with their neighbors, adopting newcomers, and adapting to change. In the colonial period, they consistently portrayed themselves as whatever newcomers wanted them to be, in order to recruit new friends who would advance Quapaw interests. From initial welcoming ceremonies through decades of interactions, they incorporated Europeans into the reciprocal obligations of friendship.[17]

* * *

The Quapaws actively courted potentially useful neighbors. After seven years passed with no follow-up to Jolliet's and Marquette's visit, Quapaws heard from other Indians about the new French mission at Kaskaskia, Illinois. Quapaw representatives traveled to Kaskaskia with some Osages and Chickasaws to present deerskins and other hides to the Frenchmen. Beyond their deerskins, the delegates offered to broker trade in the region. They told the French that the Mississippi was navigable to the Gulf of Mexico and that "all the nations of the lower Mississippi would come to dance the Calumet of peace." Above all, the delegates declared, they wanted to "establish a good relationship, & commerce with the French Nation."[18]

The Indian delegations offered the French exactly what would draw them to the lower Mississippi Valley: an environment of peace, abundant hides, and a river that would easily carry those hides to sea. The delegations sought to recruit French trade and alliance to increase their own power at home. The Quapaws and Chickasaws probably also hoped to make peace with each other by substituting French trade for English goods that the Chickasaws acquired by capturing Quapaws to sell as slaves. In any case, the delegation exaggerated harmony in their homeland. Two years later, the Sieur de La Salle's small expedition and its Indian escorts took the Quapaws up on their offer to introduce the French to the other peoples of the lower Mississippi Valley. Accordingly, when they arrived at Kappa, its inhabitants escorted them to the three other Quapaw towns and to their allies the Taensas, fifty leagues down the Mississippi. Each place welcomed the newcomers with elaborate rituals, surely directed at the Indian visitors from the East as well as the French. These rituals included speeches (translated by an Illinois interpreter), the calumet ceremony, feasting, and gift-giving. La Salle provided axes, knives, and glass beads, while the Quapaws gave buffalo skins, domestic fowl, corn, dried fruit, guides, a Chickasaw woman, and a young Mosopelea slave, whose people the Taensas were conquering.[19]

Despite the Quapaws' recruitment campaign, they were not an ideal trading partner for the French. The Quapaws simply did not have much to give traders. They were a primarily agricultural people. Quapaw women were productive farmers who raised corn, beans, squashes, pumpkins, sunflowers, melons, lamb's-quarter, mulberries, persimmons, plums, and muscadines, much as their sixteenth-century predecessors had. They had already incorporated crops spread from European sources, including peaches and watermelons. Quapaw women were renowned for their cooking. They stewed corn in earthen jars, seasoning it with fruit or with squash. Travelers noted their various cornbreads, including a persimmon bread that always drew compliments. The Quapaws also raised turkeys and geese. They smoked meats and made earthen pots, oval wooden platters, elaborately-painted deerskins, and dugout canoes, all of which they traded widely. Quapaw men hunted duck and other game birds, rabbit, deer, bear, buffalo, and fish. However, ample agricultural production and fear of neighboring enemies limited their range to nearby streams, forests, and meadows.[20]

Despite their plentiful subsistence, the Quapaws had little that Europeans wanted and little desire to change. Instead, they attempted to change French ideas of desirable trade. After conducting the calumet ceremony with La Salle's lieutenant Henri Joutel in 1687, the Quapaws gave him the pipe that they had shared, a few bison, otter, and deer skins, and a collar made of seashells. In return, the Frenchmen presented the Quapaws with a gun, two hatchets, six knives, 100 charges of powder and musket balls, and some glass-bead bracelets. When the French provided additional presents, the Quapaws agreed to send guides to lead the Frenchmen to Illinois.[21]

These exchanges provided each group with goods or services that it could not easily provide for itself. The Quapaws could not make guns, although they had probably tried. The French did not know the way to Illinois. The trade, performed in the context of the calumet ceremony, confirmed the Quapaw-French friendship. To the Quapaws, alliance with the French provided mutually beneficial support in a dangerous world. They shared with most Indian peoples in North America a belief that alliances were reciprocal links among groups and among individuals within those groups. Allies were not necessarily equal partners, but each partner had responsibilities that it could not take lightly. A significant portion of goods' value lay in the relationships that they represented.[22]

This small-scale exchange was ideal for the Quapaws, who only needed guns to protect themselves and their lands against enemies mostly armed with bows and arrows, but it was not the large volume of hides that major French traders had in mind. They particularly wanted beaver pelts, which commanded the highest prices because of European demand for fashionable, warm, and waterproof hats and coats. But the Quapaws wore otter robes, not beaver, and showed little interest in changing their practices of hunting and preparing pelts. Besides, the beavers of this temperate clime never grew the thick furs that Canadian beavers did. Traders could sell deer and buffalo skins for leather in France, but the Quapaws did not produce many of these either.[23]

Henri de Tonti, a French officer born to Italian parents, hoped to build a large-scale fur trade on the Arkansas River. He received a land grant and a trading concession near the Quapaws from La Salle on his way through in 1682. In the spring of 1686, Tonti installed six men beside the town of Osotouy to protect his claim, provide a way station for La Salle's explorations of the western shore of the Mississippi, and acquire furs from the Quapaws. The men built a house and a fence, the first French establishment west of the Mississippi. They gave it the grandiose name of "The Fort and Mission of St. Étienne." More realistically for six men and a hut, they referred to it as "aux Arcs," meaning at the home of the Arkansas, or Quapaws.[24]

The Quapaws allowed this post because it served their interests. Their earlier efforts to attract European traders indicate that they must have welcomed Tonti's offer of a permanent post. Allowing the post in no way compromised Quapaw sovereignty. They were not selling the land but rather granting Tonti and his men space for their trading post and residence. Had the men proved troublesome, the Quapaws had the right to dispossess them. But they were useful, and the presence of armed allies probably assisted the Quapaws' land claims. However, these traders failed to persuade the Quapaws to increase their hunting significantly. They provided for themselves well already and simply wanted a few extra goods for self-protection. The Quapaws wanted European alliance and trade, but on their own terms. To make matters worse for Tonti, Iroquoian attacks imperiled the trade route between this post and New France. By the early 1700s, he abandoned his dream of a trading empire on the Arkansas.[25]

The Quapaws refused to change their economy radically, but some

French *voyageurs* (independent traders) did build a successful small-scale enterprise by adapting to Quapaw ways. When *voyageurs*, and their guns, began to accompany Quapaw hunting expeditions, Quapaw men felt more comfortable venturing farther afield. As a result, Quapaws killed a few more bison, bear, and deer and thus could exchange more hides and bear oil for useful goods—guns, powder, shot, knives, needles, razors, vermilion (red dye), cloth, wool blankets, shirts, and sometimes brandy. The *voyageurs* collected the products of Quapaw hunting as well as from their own efforts and those of their *engagés* (indentured servants). And hunting together reinforced their friendship, conforming to the Quapaw ideal of fruitful relations. Established in the Quapaw towns, *voyageurs* could also trade with the peoples whom the Quapaws invited—other Indian groups and occasionally the Spanish and the British—and they sent dried buffalo meat and bear oil downriver to New Orleans to feed its settlers and soldiers. Thus, the *voyageurs* and their Quapaw hosts became a new source of trade on an old trading path. Still, the Quapaws never became intensive hunters. Visiting in the 1760s, Philip Pittman remarked, "they hunt litle more than for their common subsistence."[26] In a typical year, they provided only 1,000 of the 50,000 deerskins that Louisiana sent to France. For the officer and soldiers sometimes stationed on the Quapaws' land, they provided a limited amount of food and served as guides and mediators. In return, the Quapaws got what they wanted. As early as 1714, French travelers described them as "almost all armed with guns," which they used "very skilfully."[27]

Because the Quapaws were able to draw the French into their customs of commerce, the European-style market did not make major changes to the Arkansas Valley. Eric Hinderaker has written of the Ohio Valley that, whereas Indians used to "hunt only for what they needed," the market "caused Indians to overhunt." He divides exchanges into Indian-defined reciprocity for the purpose of alliance-building versus the European-defined marketplace where "it was traders and merchants who set the terms of exchange." In the Arkansas Valley, however, it was *Indian* traders and policymakers who set the terms. When the Quapaws began feeding goods into the European market, they still controlled the volume and associated ritual, and there is no evidence that the meaning of exchange changed for them. As in the past, Quapaws used the new goods for spiritual, political, military, diplomatic, and material needs and desires. While European goods and traders did spread rapidly across the continent, historians tend to exaggerate the "pre-market" nature of pre-colonial North America. Indians in the Arkansas Valley had never restricted hunting to basic needs. Similarly, it is easy to overestimate the effects of the European way of exchange. In reality, older reasons and methods remained alongside changes, and change itself was hardly new.[28]

While the French did not direct change, change happened. For example, when the Quapaws acquired direct French trade, they altered their relations with the Michigameas. In the late seventeenth century, some Michigameas lived part of the year west of the Mississippi. They hunted with the Quapaws in summer. In winter, they carried the products of their own and Quapaw hunting to the French at Fort Chartes, east of the Mississippi, near the rest of the Michigameas. The following summer, these Michigamea intermediaries would return west with hatchets, knives, and beads for themselves and the Quapaws. Michigameas interpreted between the Quapaws and people who spoke Algonquian languages, including early French explorers. But when the Quapaws began trading directly with the French, the Michigameas lost their role as intermediaries and abandoned their western settlement. At least one woman stayed behind, moving into a Quapaw town, serving as an interpreter, and probably marrying or being adopted into the Quapaws. But the growing Quapaw-French relationship squeezed out her compatriots.[29]

More damaging changes resulted from disease. Ironically, French-borne diseases made French friendship more important to the Quapaws. Having lost population to European diseases before the French arrived, the Quapaws suffered another round of epidemics at the end of the seventeenth century. Visiting in December 1698 after a wave of smallpox, Father Jean François Buisson de St. Cosme found the Kappa town, "once so numerous[,] entirely destroyed by war and sickness." According to him, smallpox had "carried off the greatest part of them. There was nothing to be seen in the village but graves."[30] In reality, Kappa was not "entirely destroyed," but the Quapaws did suffer terrible devastation. While there were at least 5,000 Quapaws in the 1680s, the population dropped below 2,000 by 1700. Although they still greatly outnumbered the French in their region, the losses increased their desire for neighbors and friends to help them defend their lands.[31]

*   *   *

The Quapaws recruited various settlers to enhance their security. John Law's financial debacle provided an early group of recruits. In 1717, the French crown leased Louisiana and Illinois (the entire Mississippi basin) to Law's Company of the West. Echoing Spanish hopes nearly 200 years earlier, Law launched a major campaign throughout western Europe to attract investors. One promoter claimed that, because gold had been found in the mountains of New Mexico, it was "impossible" that rivers, such as the Arkansas, that flowed east from those mountains "should not be equally fruitful." Law displayed gold ingots supposedly (but surely not) mined in Louisiana.[32]

Law also hoped to reap profits by supplying the new French posts in the Illinois country. With Quapaw permission, Law's Company of the West established a military post near Kappa to guard the convoys of flatboats and canoes that would ascend the Mississippi from New Orleans with supplies and trade goods. Law planned an agricultural colony nearby, which would sell agricultural products to his "Arkansas Post" as well as to Illinois and New Orleans. In the summer of 1721, nearly 100 black slaves and white indentured *engagés* (usually committed to three years of service) arrived at the mouth of the Arkansas to prepare the way for the vast settlement of mostly German *habitants* (agrarian settlers) to whom Law had granted land. But by then rumors had spread in France that Louisiana offered more disease and starvation than gold or gems. Investors unloaded shares in a panic, and Law fled France.[33]

When the *habitants* did not arrive, the Company of the West—now renamed the Company of the Indies—moved the slaves to work farms nearer New Orleans and freed most of the *engagés* from their indentures. Most left, but some stayed to take the place of the *habitants*. Because these settlers found Law's unbroken land difficult to break, the Quapaws in 1722 invited them to farm fields previously worked by Quapaw women on the banks of the Arkansas near Osotouy, farmland available because of disease. Sixteen Frenchmen, six Frenchwomen, four French servants, and a number of children moved to Osotouy to farm and live beside the Quapaws. Soon they were farming successfully, but the Company of the Indies frustrated their hopes in 1724 when it cut costs to its unprofitable colony by ceasing Mississippi River convoys and withdrawing the garrison from the Arkansas Post.[34]

With no market for their goods and no soldiers to protect them, more of these settlers left, probably to try farming closer to New Orleans or Illinois. Those who stayed increasingly depended on Quapaw friendship and adopted Quapaw ways. Many gave up farming and became full-time hunters. They lived and hunted near the Quapaws, who protected them and in bad times fed them. When the convoys began again and the garrison returned at the beginning of the 1730s, the French settlers did not resume their agrarian pursuits but continued to hunt deer, buffalo, and bear for the market. With Quapaw help, they salted meat and sold it and bear oil, which the French used as a butter substitute and mosquito repellent. They grew a little tobacco to consume and to sell to Indians and traders.[35]

While delta lands to the south would later prove the ideal climate for profitable sugar, rice, and cotton plantations, clearing and planting that land would require expelling its original inhabitants and importing workers, usually enslaved. In contrast, the banks of the Arkansas, as Quapaw women knew, were ideal for small-scale agriculture and trade. One French official lamented the laziness of most settlers, who preferred trading to growing tobacco on plantations. British Captain Harry Gordon, who floated down the Mississippi from the mouth of the Ohio in 1766, called them neither farmers nor traders but simply "the few Banditti at Arkansas." But the French who lived on the Arkansas River had learned the safest and easiest way to make their way in this new world.[36]

The Quapaws also controlled smaller-scale population movement across their lands. They developed a policy that soldiers, indentured servants, slaves, or accused criminals who ran away from the French could seek refuge in the house of a Quapaw spiritual leader. If the Quapaws gave them sanctuary, the runaways could live in the *voyageur* settlement, which was nestled among the Quapaw towns and under their protection. When French officials tried to capture these runaways, the Quapaws insisted that the terms of their alliance allowed them to establish a sanctuary from French justice. Their success in enforcing their decisions vividly reveals their continuing sovereignty over their lands.

Desertion was a constant problem for the French as opportunities in the fur trade lured scores of soldiers away from their duty. Sometimes soldiers deserted en masse. In 1751, while the Arkansas Post commandant was on a trip to New Orleans, the corporal in charge and all of the garrison deserted together, taking the commandant's trade goods and the fort's supplies with them. Others were deserters from private service, *engagés* who illegally left their employers to hunt for their own profit in western Louisiana. Many of these deserters hunted and traded with the Quapaws. Like the *voyageurs*, deserters made valuable hunting partners, and the Quapaws quietly adopted many of them as fictive kin.[37]

The Quapaws chose whom they protected and whom they handed back to the French. Probably only a portion of these cases appears in the records. In 1744, the commandant of the Arkansas Post pardoned a deserter at the Quapaws' request. Eight years later, the post's commandant tried to arrest a *voyageur*, Martin Hurtubise, for treason because he had told the Quapaws that the French were going to kill their men and take their women as slaves. The Quapaws hid Hurtubise and refused to give him up for trial.[38]

In 1756, Jean Baptiste Bernard, a soldier at the post, killed a corporal in his company and, with three other soldiers, took refuge in the same house, asking Ouyayonsas, the chief in charge of the sacred cabin, for asylum. The chief accepted the request because, the Quapaws explained, anyone who took refuge there was "washed clean of his crime." This time, French officials said the Quapaws were going too far. They could protect deserters, unruly *voyageurs*, and runaway laborers, but a murderer was a different matter. Ouyayonsas must have seen some justice in the French claim. He allowed French officials to send the soldiers to New Orleans for trial, but he and another chief, Guedelonguay, insisted on accompanying the party. In New Orleans, Chief Guedelonguay told Governor Louis Billouart, Chevalier de Kerlérec, that the Quapaws regarded soldiers at the Arkansas Post as their "own children." The chief reminded the governor that the Quapaws were loyal allies and had sometimes surrendered prisoners at French request, including six slaves, five Choctaws, and two Britons. The chief warned Kerlérec that Ouyayonsas "would sooner lose his life than allow the refugee to suffer the penalty for his crime" and might react violently if the French executed Bernard and the others. Taking all this into consideration, the governor decided to pardon the Frenchmen. The Quapaws were vital French friends who performed important favors. When they asked for a favor in return, the French listened.[39]

The Quapaws protected men like Bernard and Hurtubise because they were members of their community. They had probably lived nearby for years and were closer friends of the Quapaws than the more transitory French commandants. Guedelonguay and the other chiefs considered these men their dependents and felt responsible for them. They probably also believed that they were the best judge of "crime" on their lands and that these men did not deserve the punishments of imprisonment and death that might await them.

By the 1760s, the Quapaws were occasionally welcoming runaway slaves as well. On one occasion five African slaves found their way to the Quapaws. When French officials tried to re-capture them, the Quapaws refused (in part, the commandant suspected, because he could not pay a high price for them). As the runaways had hoped, Quapaw jurisdiction prevailed. Runaways from French authority recognized the Quapaws' jurisdiction over the lower Arkansas Valley, and French officials and masters who failed to reclaim their soldiers, servants, or slaves had to acknowledge Indian power as well.[40]

By end of the eighteenth century, the French settlement near the Quapaw towns was full of deserters of one kind or another. The 1785 census showed that one-sixth of the non-Indians living on the lower Arkansas were "free people of color," by far the largest percentage in Louisiana or West Florida. Like slaves and free blacks across rural Louisiana, they probably farmed on a small scale, hunted for game, and participated in what historian Daniel H. Usner, Jr., has labeled the frontier exchange economy—regional trade in a variety of goods and services among diverse people in the lower Mississippi Valley.[41]

The Quapaws also recruited friendly Indian refugees to settle near them. In the Illinois country to the east, as French settlers began to farm and raise livestock, conflicts with Illinois Indians increased. In the 1750s, a band of Michigameas and another Illinois group moved to the lower Arkansas, lured by abundant and compliant French trade, the lack of French agriculture, and a history of trading relations with the Quapaws. But this time the Quapaws would be the intermediaries. The newcomers settled near the Quapaw town of Tourima and placed themselves under the protection of that town's chief. The immigrants in turn added to the security of the entire community on the Arkansas River. Once a land of large chiefdoms, the lower Arkansas Valley was now home to French, African, and Illinois hunters and small producers living in a cluster of permanent settlements and supervised by the Quapaws.[42]

Gradually, Indian and European residents of the lower Arkansas Valley grew more interdependent. The Quapaws needed European guns, but as the archaeology shows, they began making their own gunflints and still used bows and arrows. Perhaps because of declining population and Chickasaw raids, the Quapaw town of Tonginga moved west from its previous location, probably east of the Mississippi. Kappa moved farther up the Arkansas River from the Mississippi to be nearer the other Quapaw towns and the *voyageur* settlement. Kappa's move left Lieutenant La Boulaye and his dozen soldiers at the Arkansas Post, near the Mississippi, dangerously exposed to Chickasaw attacks. In late 1721 or early 1722, he moved the garrison near Osotuoy and the *voyageurs* in order to "live more comfortably." La Boulaye knew what many historians of colonialism have missed—European forts did not necessarily dominate Indians. The fort could not have survived without the Quapaws' approval and support. After Kappa and the French garrison moved, Tourima and Tonginga, near the mouth of the Arkansas, were the most exposed Quapaw towns. They gradually moved closer together for protection. By 1727, they had physically consolidated into one town, at first called "Tourima and Tonginga" and later simply Tourima.[43]

Quapaws, Europeans, Africans, and Illinois hunted together, lived and farmed in adjacent towns and fields, and traded furs, food, and other material goods. Osotuoy, Kappa, Tourima, and Tonginga became cosmopolitan

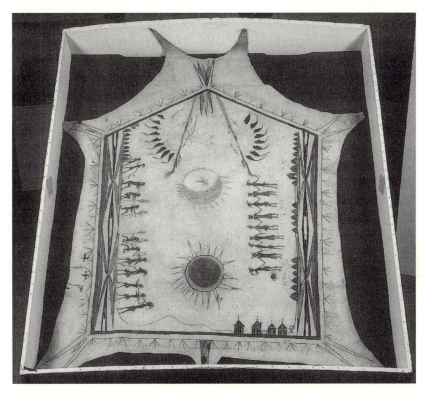

Figure 5. Quapaw painted deerskin. This deerskin shows the Quapaw towns, the neighboring French community, and a battle, perhaps against the Chickasaws. Courtesy the University of Arkansas Museum.

towns. Not only did French and Indian goods circulate, but also Italian beads and Chinese porcelain. The allies' desires coincided, and the Quapaws practiced rituals that incorporated the newcomers smoothly. They all settled into a mutually beneficial network of economic and occasionally familial relationships that lasted for more than a century. By 1758, a French observer could note that the Quapaws and the French were "more like brothers than like neighbors."[44] A deerskin, probably painted by a Quapaw in the 1730s or 1740s, depicts their own towns and the French settlement. In the scene, Quapaw warriors stop at the French settlement on their way to a battle, probably against the Chickasaws. Clearly, the artist saw the French as a friendly neighbor with whom to consult and collect supplies before a battle against a common enemy. A French friend even helped to complete the painting by writing the names of the Quapaw towns over the picture of each one.[45]

Despite the closeness of French-Quapaw relations, it appears that few Quapaw women married or bore children with their French neighbors, in contrast to other parts of New France, where traders intermarried into Indian tribes and fathered *métis* (mixed) children. As intimate as they were on many levels, there is little evidence of any sexual contact between the French and the Quapaws in the seventeenth and eighteenth centuries. The parish records for the Arkansas Post, which only begin in the 1760s, identify only one Quapaw woman who married or bore children with a French man. Another young Quapaw woman and the son and grandson of a Quapaw chief were baptized in 1789, and in 1797 a Quapaw child was baptized and a Quapaw woman received a Christian burial. In contrast to these few examples, the parish records show the Christian baptisms, marriages, and burials of scores of Indians from distant tribes, probably captives. All of this made for a complex community, which included diverse Indians, Europeans, and Africans being baptized, marrying, and serving as godparents. But it seems that few Quapaws lived within the French community—they lived nearby, in their own communities, and formed their own families.[46]

Some clue to the lack of Quapaw-French sexual liaisons may lie in the fact that the Quapaws are patrilineal, reckoning descent through the male line. Matrilineal societies often encouraged pairing between their women and French men because the children of such unions would belong to their mothers' people, and the traders would become linked to their wives' families. The Quapaws incorporated Indian women, who either willingly became part of a town, as the Michigamea interpreter did, or were captured. Quapaw women were likely aware that they too could be captured and incorporated into an alien society. Thus, the patrilineal Quapaws might have been willing to incorporate French women into their families, but the few of them who came to the Arkansas Valley usually came with French husbands. In contrast, a foreign man who married a Quapaw woman would have no lineage, no place in Quapaw society, and neither would their children. Adoption by an older Quapaw man made more sense than marriage. Also, because they linked the French with the new diseases, Quapaw women may have feared sexual contact with French men. According to *voyageurs* in the early 1720s, the Quapaws believed that any woman who had sex with a French man would die. Over time, as such taboos lost strength and the Quapaws adopted French (and occasionally British) men, intermarrying would have been easier, but it does not appear in the records. More likely, the few women who wanted to marry French men moved into their patrilineal, patrilocal households and became fully part of the French community.[47]

Canadian traders accustomed to using marriage to establish trading relationships may have tried to change Quapaw lineage customs, but they did not succeed. In contrast to the Quapaws, the French had only mild taboos about sex with Indians. In the early eighteenth century, French missionaries at times encouraged French men to marry Indian women in the hope of serving French colonial aims through the Christianization and "cultural colonization," as historian Jennifer Spear puts it, of these women and their children. In addition, missionaries hoped that encouraging Catholic marriage would dissuade French men from entering non-marriage relationships with Indian women and becoming culturally colonized by their Indian partners. In the lower Arkansas Valley, the lack of a large *métis* population suggests that the French wisely chose to respect Quapaw gender relations and guidelines for interactions.[48]

* * *

As with other potential friends and allies, the Quapaws welcomed Catholic priests into their towns. According to Father Marquette, the Quapaws "manifested a great desire to retain me among them, that I might instruct them." Marquette interpreted the Quapaws' effusive welcome and invitation to remain as evidence that they cherished religious teachings. In reality, the Quapaws sought to draw priests into their gift-based economy. The Quapaws sought the same kind of friendship with Marquette that they did with other Frenchmen. To Quapaw eyes, Frenchmen—whether traders, soldiers, or priests—were potential valuable allies and bearers of European wares, some of which might be spiritual. To their frustration, Catholic priests found befriending the Quapaws effortless but converting them impossible.[49]

Quapaw exchanges with Father Paul Du Poisson, their missionary in the 1720s, reveal the centrality of reciprocal generosity and hospitality to the Quapaw definition of friendship. Two young men asked Du Poisson to adopt them as his sons, explaining that the adoption would mean that when they returned from the hunt, each adopted son "would cast, *without design*, his game at my feet." According to them, *without design* meant that they were not trading with Du Poisson, but giving him the game. Still, the men would expect the priest to invite his "sons" to sit down and join his meal. Perhaps also, the next time a "son" visited, his "father" might give him some vermilion dye and gunpowder. To Du Poisson, understandably, this arrangement seemed a lot like trading. But to the Quapaws, giving and receiving were meaningful acts that proved friendship and respect. On another occasion, Du Poisson shared a pipe with a chief visiting his home. The chief in return gave him a deer skin painted in different colors with designs of calumets and animals, for which the Quapaws were famous. When Du Poisson asked what the chief wanted in return, the chief replied, insulted, "I have given without design . . . am I trading with my father?" But a few minutes further into the conversation, the chief happened to mention that his wife could use a little salt and that his son was out of gunpowder.[50]

To the Quapaws, all Frenchmen had desirable goods, and exchange with any of them should take place within a close relationship and should strengthen that relationship. Thus, priests who became individual Quapaws' adoptive fathers accepted even more responsibility for reciprocal generosity toward their "sons." As men in a patrilineal society, priests transformed their "sons" into Frenchmen, albeit men who did not surrender their Quapaw identity. Because priests seemed to possess particular access to spiritual power, Indians likely valued priests' gifts even more than those of French traders or government officials.

Still, priests felt that the Quapaws were treating them like traders. They interpreted the Quapaws' insistence on gift exchange as greed, not the basis of friendship. To Du Poisson, "gratitude is a virtue of which they have not the slightest idea."[51] To the Quapaws, gratitude was not what they owed the French—each group should give of what it had, and priests brought lots, knowing that gifts inspired attention. When La Salle's expedition stopped at the Quapaw towns in 1682, they discovered the goods that Father Louis Hennepin had brought for other peoples and "only reluctantly let us take our merchandise away." Hennepin believed that only the duty imposed by having exchanged calumets with him prevented them from taking the goods by force. While Hennepin thought that the Quapaws were trying to extract everything they could from him, they saw his refusal as a betrayal of their newly-formed friendship. His explanation that he had withheld the goods to give them to other Indians, possibly the Quapaws' enemies, certainly did not assuage their anger.[52]

Although priests' involvement in gift exchange helped them to establish themselves among the Quapaws and other native peoples, it could also be deadly. In 1702, Koroa Indians killed Father Foucault, the first priest stationed at the Arkansas Post, while on a trip from there to Mobile. Catholics saw these priests as martyrs, but the Indians who killed them apparently saw them simply as Frenchmen, and Frenchmen were bearers of French merchandise. To the Koroas, Father Foucault provided munitions to their enemies the Quapaws. They may even have suspected that he was going to Mobile in order to get weapons for the Quapaws to use against them. Priests were not supposed to be involved in the arms trade, but they did carry supplies of powder and shot. Consequently, their worldly goods made them more dangerous than Catholicism did.[53]

Priests did not survive long on the Arkansas River. The priest sent to accompany the aborted Law settlement in 1721 quickly died. The Natchez killed Du Poisson less than two years after his arrival in 1727. In 1728, the Jesuits promised the French government to build six churches and six rectories across Louisiana within the year, including on the Arkansas River, but the priests had trouble simply getting to their destinations, and they soon abandoned most of their ambitions. Priests came and went in the 1740s, but none stayed. Jesuit priest Louis Carette established himself near the Quapaws in 1750 but abandoned the mission eight years later, unable to convert the Quapaws or even to command respect from his French congregation. Because the commandant refused to build a chapel in the fort, Father Carette had to say mass in the dining room, which was crowded with swearing soldiers and noisy food preparations. At the end of one mass, a chicken flew over the altar and overturned the chalice. Carette was appalled that the Frenchmen jeered at this spilling of the transubstantiated blood of Christ. Surrounded by French heathens, Carette despaired of converting Indians. In the 1640s, the Jesuit order had decided that adapting to Indian ways attracted more conversions than demanding that Indians change, but adapting brought them no success in the Arkansas Valley. After Father Carette gave up, the Arkansas Valley had no resident priest for the next forty years.[54]

The lack of priests and the Quapaws' indifference kept Christian influence low. Spiritual practices and especially beliefs are among the most difficult aspects of eighteenth-century Quapaw life to know. They may have incorporated selected aspects of Catholicism into their spirituality, perhaps adding the trinity and saints, the cross, sacraments, and prayers to their rituals and beliefs. However they regarded the elements of Christianity, it is clear that the Quapaws did not discard their pre-existing spirituality, as French priests advised. The Quapaws continued to celebrate their planting and Green Corn ceremonies and to abide by their own structures of more than twenty clans and two moieties—the Earth People, responsible for the rituals to bring physical and material well-being, and the Sky People, with jurisdiction over spiritual well-being.[55]

* * *

As they did with traders and priests, the Quapaws also incorporated Louisiana's French officials into their customs and obligations. By adopting the diplomatic forms of their new friends and neighbors, French administrators installed themselves in Louisiana. But establishing Louisiana as French in the minds of other Europeans was a perpetual project. French officials feared the Spanish, who loomed menacingly both on the southeastern border with Florida and, particularly, the western border, where Spain founded Texas in the 1690s in response to La Salle's expedition. In 1721, the Spanish established the capital of Texas at Los Adaes, just twelve miles from French Natchitoches. On the other hand, some French believed that the Spanish were so cruel that Indians living in Spanish colonies would surely rise up against them and help the French win all of New Spain. Antagonism toward the Spanish ebbed over time, just as British power in the East escalated. French officials feared that the British were "pursuing their ambitions further," with their sights on Louisiana. The French presence in Louisiana successfully prevented British settlement, but British traders and government agents regularly traveled west to court France's allies, including the Quapaws.[56]

France could not control its "colony" by force. Although officials regularly requested more soldiers and arms to "intimidate the Indians," desertions locally and war in Europe made troop numbers in Louisiana fluctuate wildly.[57] At times, fewer than 200 soldiers were stationed on both sides of the Mississippi, and the numbers may never have reached 1,000. The Arkansas garrison ranged from none to fifty, usually hovering at about twelve. The *voyageurs* who crossed the land were more loyal to their own interests and often to their Indian trading partners than to French officials, as the French hierarchy was well aware. Etienne de Périer, Louisiana governor in 1729, petitioned his superior to strengthen the Louisiana government in order to "subdue the inhabitants of this area who are just *voyageurs* and *coureurs de bois* who work that trade only because they want to be their own masters and who would easily withhold their obedience from the King if we were not prepared to repress them." Even had all French men of military age been ready to fight for France, they would have been grossly outnumbered. Policymakers in France occasionally proposed forcing the region's native peoples into missions, where they could be supervised and converted, but local commandants knew that demographics required them to win over Indians, not to dominate them. With so few soldiers and settlers, the French had to depend on their Indian allies.[58]

Imperial rivalries across most of North America took the form of competition for Indian allies. As Louisiana Governor Pierre François de Rigaud, Marquis de Vaudreuil, put it in 1750, until the crown saw fit "to send to this colony sufficient forces for acting with firmness," "we can do nothing by ourselves."[59] There were simply too many Indians and not enough French for any other means of colonization. Unable to enforce their will, garrisons at places like the Arkansas Post worked simply to "maintain our alliance with the Indians."[60] In addition, local commandants' economic interest often lay in Indian friendship. As in most French western posts, the Arkansas Post commandant was in charge of the fur trade. He issued trading permits, oversaw the conveyance of goods, and traded for personal gain, both with Indians and French settlers. For both political and personal reasons, commandants preferred keeping their Indian neighbors happy over trying to command them.[61]

Not following Indian protocol could be disastrous, as La Salle's attempt to found a French colony in the lower Mississippi Valley proved. In 1685, La Salle landed some 200 men and women on the Texas shore. When he led a small expedition north, searching in vain for the Mississippi River and the French settlements at Illinois, some of his men mutinied and killed their leader. The colonists were stranded, and the colony disappeared. Henri Joutel, an officer who survived, bitterly reflected that if La Salle had *befriended* Indians instead of fearfully *shooting* any he saw, Indians could have told them how to find the Mississippi, and there would have been no mutiny.[62]

Wiser French abided by Indian protocols for establishing and maintaining diplomatic relations, as any Frenchman who sat with a smile pasted on his face for hours through interminable speeches, songs, and dances long remembered. After La Salle's murder, his brother Cavelier, Joutel, and a few other stragglers made their way north, looking for French Illinois. They were delighted to stumble across Osotouy and find two of the Frenchmen that Tonti had recently stationed there. After the opening ceremonies, the Quapaw elders asked Cavelier to perform the calumet ceremony. Despite his fatigue, Cavelier recognized that these were people "whom we need" and agreed. After some time, Cavelier sought an excuse to leave, telling the Chief that he was unwell and asking if he could put his nephew in his place. The singing continued through the night, and in the morning they performed more ceremonies, which the weary chronicler Joutel found "not worth describing."[63]

A French official might occasionally bow out of a long night, but someone had to participate, or the alliance would not stand. The ceremonial speeches, dances, and songs were as vital a part of diplomacy as gifts and sharing a smoke. Like most seventeenth- and eighteenth-century Native Americans, the Quapaws were an oral culture and a society whose leaders' power depended on the will of the people. Thus, public participation in and witnessing of political and diplomatic rituals was vital, clamorous, and protracted. Each time a French expedition encountered the Quapaws, they conducted rituals to renew the alliance, and when new governors and other Louisiana officials took their offices, Quapaw delegations traveled to their headquarters to conduct the calumet ceremony with them personally.[64]

At some point in the early eighteenth century, the French became participants in the rituals of choosing and ratifying new Quapaw chiefs. Such occasions traditionally involved participation and witnessing by Quapaw men and women. Now their French neighbors joined them. Unsurprisingly, part of French officials' role became providing presents to celebrate the installation. In addition, French officials began to recognize authority with medals, which symbolized the importance of the chief and his people to the French empire. Long before the French arrived, influence within Quapaw society had depended on prestige, which was always provisional and depended upon possessions rich in the symbolism of power. European medals, flags, and other symbols of recognition enabled chiefs and warriors to signify their status to other Indian peoples and white traders as well as to their own people.[65]

Over time, the Quapaws became more politically centralized, probably because of population losses, the consolidation of the towns of Tonginga and Tourima, and French symbols of power. Decisions were still made communally, but more often as a single people than as separate towns. By the 1750s, the Quapaw office of "great chief" emerged. This was a new position but one that remained bound by the system of mutual obligations and shared power. In fact, the great chief's power may have been limited to conducting foreign relations. Quapaw chieftanships in general may have become more permanent with European recognition, but neither French symbols nor heredity guaranteed succession, and chiefs had to work to maintain their positions.[66]

Individual Quapaws used the changes to increase their influence within Quapaw society. In 1752, Commandant Paul Augustin Le Pelletier de La Houssaye recognized Guedelonguay as great chief over the four Quapaw towns. Guedelonguay may have used La Houssaye to validate the existence of this office and Guedelonguay's own candidacy for it. Apparently another Quapaw man was in consideration because his mother was a chief and his deceased father had been one as well. Guedelonguay may have used the French medal and other goods, which he could distribute, to consolidate his position. Thus, the French played an important role in Quapaw politics, recognizing leaders and perhaps altering leadership roles. Still, Quapaws individually and generally retained more control over their politics, and the French could implement no changes without at least some Quapaw participation.[67]

Presents and other signs of respect from external figures of authority helped a chief to maintain influence over the Quapaw community, but always within strong limits enforced by communal norms. And other sources of goods balanced the chiefs' sources, including women's agricultural products, war party chiefs' booty, and goods that individual Indians earned as guides or hunters. While European diseases had decreased chiefly power after the Mississippian era, now European goods and alliance began to build up that power again, but restrictions within Indian communities would prevent radical centralization. Perhaps the Quapaws had negative memories of the powerful chiefdoms of the Mississippian era. In any case, they would never support a chief completely beholden to outsiders.[68]

Official French-Indian relations worked best when each side could assist the other. To the Quapaws, the French were desired allies and traders, not conquerors. It did not bother them that the French crown called Louisiana its "colony." The region's native peoples knew that the French did not rule the mid-continent. In 1683, on a hill near Kappa, La Salle raised a cross and King Louis XIV's coat of arms, declaring that he was taking "possession in the name of His Majesty, and of his heirs and successors to his crown, of the country of Louisiana and of all its lands, provinces, countries, peoples, nations, mines, minerals, ports, harbors, seas, its straits and roads." These symbols meant a great deal to the French and their European rivals but did not diminish the Quapaws' sovereignty one bit. Similarly, French forts and French names on French maps signified possession to European rivals but did not trouble the people who ruled on the ground.[69]

Having common enemies brought the Quapaws closer to French officials. When a Koroa party killed Father Foucault and three other Frenchmen in 1702, the Quapaws took the opportunity to attack and win a victory over their old enemy. In praising the Quapaws, Governor Jean Baptiste Le Moyne, Sieur de Bienville, gave them a gift. Thereafter, French administrators regularly recognized Quapaw victories against common enemies through a ceremony with gifts for the victors. This arrangement helped the understaffed French (who could not fight their enemies alone), complied with Quapaw notions of generosity, and reinforced the Quapaw-French alliance.[70]

The Quapaws sought to influence their friends' choices of other friends and enemies and the ways in which their friends interacted with each.

Usually friendly hosts, the Quapaws' hospitality ended when their guests threatened to trade with their rivals. When Jolliet and Marquette mentioned that they intended to continue following the Mississippi to the sea, the Quapaws warned their guests that the trip would be extremely dangerous because the Indians to the south were armed and dangerous. The last thing that the Quapaws wanted was for their new-found suppliers to trade with their enemies. When La Salle accepted the Quapaws' invitation to facilitate alliance with the other peoples of the lower Mississippi, the guides chose whom he would meet. They explained that they were at war with the Chickasaws, on the east bank of the Mississippi. Farther downriver, the guides pointed out Tunica and Yazoo lands, warning La Salle that they were "enemies of the Arkansas [Quapaws] and Taenseas." When they passed a Tunica town on the east bank, the Quapaws told La Salle that "it was necessary to disembark there and that we would conquer them easily with our arms." At his insistence, the Quapaws abandoned this plan and did introduce the French to the Natchez and Koroas, but they clearly advocated French alliance with their allies the Taensas. Rather than making peace with all, as they had promised, the Quapaws introduced La Salle to their friends and asked for "assistance against their enemies."[71]

The Quapaws also regulated French relations with peoples to the west. In 1719, Kadohadacho and Kichai guides led Jean-Baptiste Bénard de La Harpe from their towns on the Red River northwest through the Ouachita Mountains to a Tawakoni town on the Arkansas, probably El Turco's Quivira. Narrowly escaping a conflict with an Osage party, La Harpe found several thousand Tawakonis, Taovayas, Guichitas, Iscanis, and probably Panis Noirs gathered to celebrate the arrival of their Indian allies and the French and African men that they brought, the first large expedition to reach the central Arkansas Valley since Juan de Oñate more than a century earlier. The chiefs told La Harpe that all the peoples of the central Arkansas wished to ally with the French, who "would bring weapons for them to defend themselves against their enemies." In return, they promised horses, bison robes, salt, tobacco, and slaves. They described their river as navigable as far as Spanish settlements and boasted "that their country was beautiful, full of domesticated bison, of horses and of deer." One chief whispered to La Harpe that they also had "some yellow metal," which "the Spanish value very highly." Like the Quapaws, these people knew about Europeans—their desire for Indian alliances, the goods they brought, and the products they wanted—and they knew what to say to persuade them to return.[72]

But when La Harpe tried to reach those towns again in 1722, this time by ascending the Arkansas River, the Quapaws did everything they could to dissuade him from his purpose. They refused to describe the route to La Harpe, stating that they were "unhappy with his expedition," fearing that he "might make alliances with rival nations." They warned him that Osage Indians had attacked another French party that had tried to buy horses from the towns upstream. That party had left seven months earlier and had not been seen since. Looking around the gathering crowd, La Harpe noticed that the women and old men were weeping. Falling into their trap, he asked them why, to which they replied that they were mourning for the certain death of La Harpe and his men if they persisted in this folly. The Quapaws would only give the Frenchmen a small amount of corn and beans for their journey and refused to sell them a canoe at any price, despite the fact that La Harpe could see more than thirty in their towns. Angry and even more determined, the Frenchmen stole a canoe. As they were struggling to paddle upstream, Quapaw warriors caught up with them, declaring that they were "hungry for killing Frenchmen." La Harpe's men surrendered the canoe and sat down on the bank to make one themselves. Clearly, the Quapaws opposed La Harpe's mission. When a priest traveling down the Mississippi had upset his canoe near Kappa a few years earlier, the Quapaws had readily given him a new canoe as well as provisions for his journey. Circumstances were different for traders heading *up* the Arkansas. Eventually, Quapaw opposition, short supplies, dysentery, and mutinous troops persuaded La Harpe to give up on the mission.[73]

At the same time, other Indians were attempting to muddy the Quapaw-French alliance. Clearly, the Quapaws' upstream neighbors and the Red River Caddoans hoped to break the Quapaws' barricade by attracting traders from the south. And some Indians contradicted the Quapaws' image of being dedicated to the French. In 1730, a Choctaw chief casually asked a French officer from Mobile if any French lived at the Arkansas. When the officer replied that some did, the chief told him that he expected "they were dead" because he had "heard it said that [the Quapaw] nation was going to attack." Although not held hostage to Indian tales as the sixteenth-century Spaniards had been, the French still depended on information from Indians, and tales of attacks and massacres became a particularly sensitive topic for the French after the Natchez killed their French neighbors in 1729.[74]

*   *   *

The eighteenth-century history of the Natchez provides a contrast to the Quapaws' willingness to teach newcomers how to conform to native expectations

Figure 6. *Marche du Calumet de Paix.* In this scene, the Natchez conduct a calumet ceremony with four bored but obligated Frenchmen. From Antoine Simon Le Page du Pratz, *Histoire de la Louisiane* (Paris, 1758). Courtesy Dechert Collection, University of Pennsylvania.

of inter-cultural relations. Located on the east bank of the Mississippi near present-day Natchez, Mississippi, the Natchez likely descended from Quigaltam, the powerful chiefdom that expelled de Soto. Beginning in 1682, when some 15,000 armed Natchez warriors scared off La Salle's party, relations with the French were shaky. The Natchez had incorporated some former

Mississippians as subordinates and, in the early 1700s, did the same with the French settlements that they allowed on their lands. But the French insisted on having prime farmland and numerous settlers and slaves to work it. When French traders and officials proved less pliable than the Natchez expected, they raided French settlements and sent representatives to meet with potential allies, including the Tunicas, Yazoos, Koroas, Illinois, Chickasaws, Choctaws, and African slaves.[75]

At eight in the morning of November 28, 1729, Natchez warriors knocked at the doors of their French neighbors and asked to borrow guns for a hunting expedition. Then they turned the guns on their owners, killing nearly all the Frenchmen, including the commandant and Father Du Poisson, who happened to be visiting. The Natchez captured the slaves and most of the French women and children and burned the houses and sheds, destroying thousands of pounds of tobacco. Some historians have labeled this attack an uprising or rebellion, but the Natchez did not see it this way. They were the dominant people casting out the disrespectful newcomers who would not play by Natchez rules. Encouraged by the Natchez, the Yazoos and Koroas killed their Jesuit missionary, the French who were in their post, and several ill-fated traders who happened to pass along the Mississippi. Koroa women, who apparently had the authority to determine the fate of captives, decreed that five French women and four children be taken to the Chickasaws and sold rather than killed.[76]

The war that followed gave the Quapaws an opportunity to defeat their old enemies and bolster their alliances, including that with the French. The Quapaws swore to the French that "while one Akensas [Quapaw] should be remaining, the Natchez and the Yazous should never be without an enemy." French officials believed that Quapaw fighting proved their devotion to the French, but the Quapaws had long fought these peoples to their south. Rather than fighting for the French, they were delighted to have an agitated ally who would provide troops, supplies, and encouragement against their long-time enemies. As in their other policies, the Quapaws fought for their own objectives and on their own terms. Historians have often divided North American Indians into pro-British, pro-French, and pro-Spanish factions, making the same mistake that European commanders occasionally did. In contrast, historians never label the British "pro-Mohawk" and the French "pro-Huron." Like European groups, Native American groups were primarily pro-themselves. Individuals might disagree over the most advantageous alliance policy, but the choice was in the service of native goals, whether personal or communal.[77]

The war destroyed both Natchez and French plans for the Natchez homeland. After three years of attacks and counterattacks, by the summer of 1732, most Natchez, Yazoos, and Koroas were dead, enslaved and shipped to the Caribbean, or refugees among the Chickasaws, Creeks, and Cherokees. Hundreds of French had also died during the war, and their plan to build plantations on Indian land had ended. The Natchez had resented and resisted imperious men and women who disrespected Natchez leaders and demanded exclusive rights to farm on lands belonging to the Indians. It is possible that Law's settlers might have suffered the same fate at the hands of the Quapaws had Law pursued his plans for plantations in the Arkansas Valley, but the Quapaws were more accustomed to accommodating others, and they might have worked within those circumstances with a bit more finesse than the Natchez did. Fortunately for the Quapaws, they did not have to make such decisions. Instead, they welcomed isolated French refugees and wholeheartedly joined the fight against their old enemies.[78]

The Natchez War forced Natchez neighbors to choose sides. Previously, the Chickasaws had used their strategic position between the British and the French to gain concessions from both. When war broke out, the French tried to recruit the Chickasaws, who readily accepted their gifts and trade, but when Natchez, Yazoo, and Koroa refugees hid out in Chickasaw country, the Chickasaws could not remain neutral. The Chickasaws sent emissaries to the Quapaws, as well as to the Choctaws, Cherokees, and several Illinois peoples, declaring that the French were nearly defeated and proposing that they all join with the Natchez, Yazoos, and Koroas against the French. But the Quapaws had fought the Natchez, Yazoos, Koroas, and Chickasaws in the past. The Chickasaws' decision to side with the others accentuated the Quapaw-Chickasaw rivalry. Rejecting the Chickasaws and finding common cause with the French, the Quapaws repeatedly raided the Chickasaws throughout the 1730s. A Chickasaw map from 1737 shows the Quapaws as a clear enemy of the Chickasaws, although the Chickasaw war chief who drew the map remarked that he hoped to "make peace."[79]

Despite their common interest in the war, the Quapaws and the French disagreed on tactics. Quapaw parties preferred to raid the Chickasaws, take the spoils, and receive rewards from their French friends. But the French wanted to destroy the offending tribes once and for all. At first the Quapaws cooperated when Bienville proposed striking from the west with a large war party, composed of 1,000 French soldiers, more than 300 African slaves, Choctaws, Quapaws, Indians and French civilians from the Illinois country, and an Iroquois contingent, which the Quapaws proposed to recruit. In

December 1737, Quapaws led a French party to explore the route from the Mississippi to the Chickasaw towns.[80]

As the French repeatedly postponed the attack because of delayed supplies and lack of communication among New Orleans, Arkansas, Illinois, and the promised Iroquois, the Quapaws became frustrated. In addition, French officials vacillated between including the Choctaws and keeping them out of the battle for fear they would demand high prices for their services. In 1739, the Quapaws helped to build forts on both sides of the Mississippi to house the troops and supplies arriving in preparation for the attack. Then they waited. For months, Quapaw, French, Illinois, and Iroquois warriors urged Bienville to commence the fight. But Bienville wanted everything to be ready first, including roads built to the Chickasaw towns for his heavy artillery. His war strategy must have seemed absurd to the Quapaws, for whom the best military tactic was surprise attack. Building a road to the enemy's town certainly spoiled the surprise. French soldiers were no happier with the delay and exposure to potential Chickasaw assaults, and they grew more mutinous as provisions ran out and illness decreased their ranks. In January 1740, a contingent of French soldiers, acting without orders, sent a message to the Chickasaws saying that if they surrendered the Natchez refugees and cast out the English, the French would make peace. The Quapaws and the rest of the Indian allies gave up and went home, and Bienville had to accept a Chickasaw peace plan.[81]

When the peace proved short-lived and Chickasaws began to inflict heavy damage on French convoys, the Quapaws persuaded the French to accept an alternative war plan. The Quapaws fought the Chickasaws whenever they wished, in parties of thirty to fifty warriors who could strike quickly and escape without major casualties. In describing the raids to his superior, Governor Vaudreuil claimed to have "engaged" them. However, it is clear that the Quapaws were now in charge of their effort. The French contributed by paying for Chickasaw scalps. As in many cases, Indian allies molded French customs to their own practices and benefit. Historian Brett Rushforth has shown that Indian slavery in New France stemmed at least in part from Indians' insistence on the appropriateness of captives as alliance-sealing gifts. As in New France, the Quapaws' expectations and definitions generally prevailed. Enemies' scalps had likely been a longstanding customary alliance gift to symbolize the death of a common enemy. Nor did the French interfere when Quapaw attacks occasionally hit the Choctaws.[82]

Despite the fact that French officials in no way controlled their Indian alliances, they had to pay for them. Over the colonial period, the Quapaws and other native peoples successfully institutionalized gift-giving. Present distribution, at first only for special occasions such as a first meeting, became a regular expectation. By the 1750s, commandants gave the Quapaws and other allies annual presents to reaffirm their alliance and to compete with British and Spanish inducements. These presents included flags to symbolize the alliance and muskets and coats for important chiefs, as well as abundant trade goods. In addition, presents accompanied rituals for new chiefs, requests for military or other assistance, or simply to bolster a sagging friendship. At each of these meetings, in addition to presents, the French had to fulfill the obligations of hosts with several nights of elaborate feasts. With food shortages common, the meals for the delegations at times came from the mouths of French soldiers.[83]

The Quapaws' friendship with the French government required regular cultivation. Unlike the *voyageurs* and *habitants* who lived with the Quapaws, local commandants and colonial governors came and went, and their highest priority was generally the well-being of the colony. Friendship with the Quapaws was important because it forwarded this goal. Officials knew that gifts would confirm the alliance, but frequent shortages of goods threatened the relationship. In 1701, the crown spent 24,773 livres on presents for Louisiana's Indians, but expenses for the War of Spanish Succession, combined with graft in the first Louisiana administration, decreased the annual budget for presents to 4,000 livres by 1712. By the 1740s, the government was spending 14,000 livres per year, still significantly below former levels. To make matters worse, Louisiana's high inflation rate meant that a livre bought fewer presents than it had in 1701, and the goods supply thinned again during the Seven Years' War.[84]

When the Quapaws felt that they were not receiving adequate material recognition, they threatened French officials. In 1745, Quapaw leaders warned the commandant whom the French had stationed near Kappa that they no longer were receiving their "needs" from the French "on the previous terms" and that if supplies did not improve, they would see the British again, who, they claimed, "every day offer to establish themselves" at the Quapaw towns. In fact, the Quapaws had negotiated and traded sporadically with other European traders since at least 1700. In 1706, they made an official peace with Carolina, brokered by trader Thomas Welch. As the French and British colonies expanded in the eighteenth century, they increasingly threatened each other. Each side with good reason suspected the other of trying to take over the continent.[85]

While French officials expected their alliance to be exclusive, the Quapaws did not see any problem with being friends of the British as well. They did not consider themselves under French command, and they placed their own needs above those of the French government. On May 10, 1749, Chickasaw chief Paya Mataha led 150 warriors against the Arkansas Post. The young commandant, First Ensign Louis Xavier Martin Delino de Chalmette, and his twelve soldiers were no match for the Chickasaws, who killed six Frenchmen and captured eight French women and children. The Quapaws did not defend the fort, in part because Tourima and Tonginga had moved farther up the Arkansas River to escape recent flooding.[86]

To encourage timelier help the next time, Governor Vaudreuil followed the Quapaws' advice to increase the troop strength at the post to fifty men and to move the fort several leagues up the Arkansas to be nearer the Quapaws, despite the fact that it was more difficult to protect the convoy from that position. When he appointed a new commandant, Vaudreuil picked Lieutenant La Houssaye, an experienced officer with "familiarity with the Indian nations of that place," particularly the Quapaws, who, Vaudreuil remarked, "merit commendation for the attachment which they have always had for the French." The governor knew that the fort needed the Quapaws more than the Quapaws needed the fort. After the 1749 Chickasaw attack, 300 warriors, nearly the Quapaws' entire force, patrolled the area to ensure that the Chickasaws had left. Smaller parties raided the Chickasaws throughout the next year.[87]

Still, the Quapaws were not at France's beck and call. In December 1752, after a Chickasaw attack on the convoy, the Quapaws refused to send war parties out or to escort the convoy downriver. According to Commandant La Houssaye, "they are busy with their corn harvest." A more likely reason was the rumor circulating among the Quapaws that the convoy had brought "considerable presents" for them from the governor but that La Houssaye was keeping them for himself.[88]

Although the Quapaws never completely trusted French officials, they did build a friendship that served well enough. Unable to eliminate all friction, French and Quapaw leaders nonetheless developed ways of preventing their misunderstandings and peccadillos from jeopardizing their alliance. When the next Louisiana governor, Kerlérec, heard that the Quapaws believed that La Houssaye was withholding presents, he did what those who started the rumor may have intended. The governor invited eighteen Quapaw chiefs and other leaders to be his guests in New Orleans for two weeks, where he paid them every attention.[89]

Similarly, Quapaw chiefs and the French commandant averted a potential rift in the fall of 1754. An Indian war party clashed with a French detachment near the Natchez Post, killing a lieutenant and a sergeant. After the battle, on top of each corpse, French soldiers discovered a tomahawk, which they recognized as Quapaw. Natchez Post Commandant Henri d'Orgon immediately reported to Kerlérec that the Quapaws had violated their alliance and recommended that he send troops to protect the Arkansas Post against an imminent Quapaw attack. Governor Kerlérec doubted the report, given what he knew of Quapaw-French history. But ignoring it might mean the loss of an important post, which the French had rebuilt only five years earlier after the Chickasaw attack. Kerlérec dispatched sixty additional soldiers to Arkansas.

In response, the Quapaws accused the Chickasaws of slander. The chiefs explained to Arkansas Commandant Charles Marie de Reggio that the Chickasaws could easily have retrieved the tomahawks from the corpses of Chickasaws whom Quapaw warriors had killed the previous winter. The Chickasaws would then have placed the tomahawks on the bodies of the French whom they killed near Natchez in order to create trouble for the Quapaw-French alliance. De Reggio immediately wrote Governor Kerlérec, adopting the chiefs' explanation of the misunderstanding and assuring him of the Quapaws' undiminished friendship. Of course, it is possible that a renegade Quapaw party killed the French soldiers, but even if Quapaws were responsible, it was in the interest of the Quapaw chiefs, Commandant de Reggio, and Governor Kerlérec to blame the Chickasaws. The chiefs did not want the incident to transform French officials and their army into enemies. As for the French, they felt that the Chickasaws, the British, the remaining Natchez, and occasionally the Choctaws were quite enough enemies without adding the Quapaws.[90]

French and Quapaw officials had to work out their differences because their friendship had become mutually indispensable. Both felt increasingly vulnerable by the mid-eighteenth century. The Quapaws had lost military capacity because of their population decline. As the Chickasaws accelerated their raids, the Quapaws' need for French munitions increased. Alliance with France provided troops and arms, which boosted Quapaw security. The French felt less secure in Louisiana after the shocking events at Natchez, Yazoo, and Koroa and under the growing threat of the British. In 1743, Governor Vaudreuil acknowledged that British traders' superior goods and lower prices complicated alliances with Indians east of the Mississippi, such as the Choctaws. Living near the French, the British, and the Spanish, they could forge multiple European alliances. Thus, tensions in the East increased the value of dependable allies west of the Mississippi.[91]

Over time, the Quapaws created an image of themselves as steadfast French allies. By the 1750s, French observers invariably referred to the

Quapaws as "a nation celebrated for the attachment that it has always had for the French."[92] In a 1758 memoir, Governor Kerlérec devoted several pages to praise of the Quapaws, calling them the only nation "that has never wet its hands in French blood." According to Kerlérec, the Quapaws, "although proud and haughty with their enemies, are kind, affable, and on easy terms with the French." Indeed, their attachment to the French was so great that "in vain did the *English* have solicitations made." But Kerlérec's source was a bit suspect—the Quapaws themselves. As his memoir noted, their reputation for loyalty came from the fact that "they boast of it in all their speeches."[93] Not only did they highlight their own friendship with the French by calling themselves the only nation with no history of violence against the French, but they also downgraded their Indian neighbors into second-class French friends. In July 1764, a Quapaw delegation told Acting Governor Jean-Jacques-Blaise D'Abbadie: "You are surrounded by tribes who do not observe the word of the French. It is not the same with us. We have always listened, and have never reddened our hands with the blood of the French." The Quapaws had given the French their valuable friendship and could also withdraw it. French officials would do all that they could to keep it.[94]

*   *   *

The Quapaws neither surrendered to nor resisted colonialism. Neither would have made sense to them, given the weakness of the French. Rather, accustomed to operating in a cross-cultural world, the Quapaws enlisted Europeans into their service, persuading them to adopt Quapaw practices of reciprocity. By building connections with Europeans and selected Indians, often with the lure of facilitating good relations among them, the Quapaws staved off isolation and increased their security. They received the goods and respect that they wanted, even when what they offered in return was not what their French friends wanted. Of the French, only the *voyageurs* and successful runaways found the relationship satisfyingly reciprocal and were able to make the Arkansas Valley their own and their descendants' native ground. All of the companies that attempted to make money running Louisiana folded. Tonti gave up entirely on the Arkansas River. Most of Law's settlers never even arrived, and many of those who did left the Arkansas Valley to pursue agricultural ambitions elsewhere. Priests gained few if any souls. Officials found themselves paying tribute to the Quapaws without receiving in return a monopoly on their friendship. Governor Bienville complained in May 1733 that "ever since they observed how weakly the French made war on the

Natchez, they have held our nation in supreme contempt." Not only did the Quapaws demand presents but "they have insolently claimed to require as tribute the presents that the King would gladly give of his own free will." Indians insisted that the goods they received from their weak French friends were tribute, not charity.[95]

French and Indians alike knew that the French did not control the mid-continent. To succeed at all, they had to adapt to local customs, goods demands, and rivalries and base their colonial claims on Indian sovereignty. While the Quapaws thwarted direct French interference in their internal religious, social, gender, and economic arrangements, they involved themselves in some matters that French officials considered internal to French governance, including dealing with deserters and other renegade French. Still, the presence of the French brought change to the Arkansas Valley. Disease weakened the Quapaws, while French trade changed the balance of power throughout the mid-continent. The French did not determine what changes would occur, but Indians could not always either. Some people prospered while others faltered. The Quapaws used their diplomatic and incorporative skills to channel change in ways that enhanced their sovereignty and status on the lower Arkansas River, leaving them in a stronger position by the 1730s than they had been in 1673. At the same time, another group was finding similar success with a very different style of consolidating and maintaining power, the Osage Indians.

Chapter 4

An Empire in the West, 1700–1777

The Quapaws were not the only people living near the Mississippi River who maximized their own French trade at the expense of their
enemies to the west. In 1719, the year of La Harpe's only successful visit to the
central Arkansas Valley, the Osage Indians enthusiastically welcomed trader
Claude Charles Du Tisné and his interpreter into their towns on the Osage
River, north of the Arkansas. As with the Quapaws, the Osages' welcoming
tone changed when their visitors voiced their intention to continue their
mission by journeying south to the Taovaya towns of the central Arkansas
Valley. After much discussion, the Osages consented to a compromise. They
allowed the two men to make the trip but with only three guns, so that the
Osages could be fairly confident that Du Tisné was not trading guns to their
rivals. The Osages did not stop there. They secretly sent a courier ahead to
the Taovayas with an alarming message—two Frenchmen were coming to
entrap and enslave them.[1]

Over the course of the eighteenth century, the Osage people used their
relatively large numbers and location between French traders on the Mississippi and the resources of the near western prairies and plains to develop one
of the largest trading systems in North America and to wield enormous
power over both their Indian and European neighbors. Like the Quapaws,
the Osages controlled their relations with Europeans and used them for their
own ends. But the Osages chose a different path. The Quapaws enhanced
their security in a limited space, employing diplomatic more often than military means and avoiding armed conflict except under the least risky conditions. In contrast, the Osages used their connections with the French trading
empire to forcibly expand, taking military risks to gain advantages over their
neighbors. When the Spanish took over the administration of Louisiana
from the French in the 1760s, the Osages compelled them to continue facilitating Osage dominance and thwarted Spain's attempts to establish its own
rule. The Osages proved far more successful than either France or Spain at
building a mid-continental empire. Throughout the eighteenth century, they

expanded their native ground and became the region's primary economic and military power.

*   *   *

The earlier history of the Osages has some similarities with that of the Quapaws. Both are Dhegiha Siouan speakers who probably moved west from the Ohio Valley around the same time. As with the Quapaws, some versions of Osage pre-colonial history contend that they were a Hopewellian or Mississippian society east of the Mississippi, perhaps Cahokia. Others believe the Osages had lived in their homes south of the Missouri River for centuries before 1700. Some have suggested that Osage ancestors included the Escanxaques, the people who tried to enlist Juan de Oñate against the Great Settlement in 1601. In any case, in the eighteenth century, the Osages lived along the Missouri and Osage rivers in what is now the state of Missouri. They called themselves Niukonska, the Little Ones of the Middle Waters. Their population totaled about 10,000, much larger than any of their neighbors.[2]

Osage expansion would dramatically change living patterns of Caddoan peoples in the central Arkansas and Red river valleys. By the late 1700s, the Osages would expel the Taovayas, Tawakonis, Iscanis, Guichitas, and Panis Noirs (most of whom eventually became the Wichitas) from the central Arkansas Valley and the Kadohadacho alliance (a part of the future Caddo Confederacy) and the Kichais from the Great Bend of Red River. Throughout the eighteenth century, the Osages intimidated their neighbors. They must have been terrifying, with their faces painted red, their heads shaved except for one lock pulled straight skyward, most over six feet tall, swooping in on their horses.[3]

Osage expansion would prove the greatest force of the eighteenth-century mid-continent, but, as historian David La Vere has pointed out, the Osages began the century with nothing to trade. Osage women farmed, but so did their Wichita neighbors to the southwest. Therefore, they had no interest in giving the Osages the products that they hunted on the Plains, which the Osages could have sold east. Instead of forging alliances with the Osages, these peoples of the central Arkansas Valley blocked Osage access to wild horses and opportunities to trade with or raid the Spanish by attacking the Osages when they hunted along the Arkansas, much as they did the Quapaws. If the Osages did descend from the Escanxaques, the battle at the Great Settlement may have been part of this struggle, one that the Osages were losing by 1700. However, in the coming years, the peoples of the central Arkansas Valley would regret not befriending the Osages. Once connected to the French trading empire, the Osages lengthened and intensified their hunts, becoming major commercial hunters in the lands previously controlled by Caddoans. Although the market rose and fell over time, French traders generally wanted the bison, deer, and bear products that the Osages could now provide.[4]

Despite initially having little to sell, the Osages were a bit more prepared for large-scale trade than the Quapaws. The Osages seem to have escaped the worst effects of European epidemics by spreading out into smaller bands for much of the year instead of concentrating in towns. Despite opposition on the Plains, once armed with French weapons, the Osages' large numbers allowed them to hunt more extensively than the Quapaws. Also, Osage cultural beliefs and practices easily accommodated European trade. In Osage society, valued men were successful warriors and Plains hunters. Expanding their hunting range and violently excluding Caddoan hunters from French trade increased Osage men's opportunities to prove their manhood. In contrast, diplomacy seems to have been Quapaw men's most valued sphere, perhaps because encouraging belligerence in their young men would have been too dangerous.[5]

Warfare served many purposes for the Osages. In battles and raids, young men proved themselves and gained influence and prestige within their society. For Osage men, hunting, trading, and warfare were all part of the same process of establishing their individual prestige and collective dominance over their lands and their neighbors. Indeed, Osage historian John Joseph Mathews blamed his ancestors' violence on individual men's "urge to attain glory as a warrior and to be noticed and honored, the intense urge to be wise and pontifical and make statements of wisdom, and the desire to be able to give generously."[6] It is impossible to determine exactly what parts of Osage cosmology developed before 1700 and what changed as a result of eighteenth-century expansion. Over time at least, the Osages came to value courage and valor enough that their most glorified symbols included the lynx, wolf, puma, and black bear. According to a ritual recorded in the early twentieth century, upon killing their own prey, these brave animals "uttered a cry of triumph, and spake, saying: Thus shall the little ones [the Osages] utter a cry of triumph over the fallen foe."[7] Osage oral history records that, at first, the Osage great chief was a military leader. Only later did the council of elder spiritual leaders, known as the "Little Old Men," decide to balance that chief's authority with another hereditary chief, responsible for keeping peace.[8]

As well as brave, the Osages today consider themselves outward-looking. While the Quapaws sought to accommodate and channel change, the Osages went looking for it. Osages describe the key elements of their cosmology as making sense of the world and looking toward the future. Osage history certainly reflects this drive for change and expanding involvement in the world. Some of these beliefs may have been results rather than sources of eighteenth-century Osage history. Whenever they began, warfare and trade became more important to the Osages over the course of the eighteenth century.[9]

Like the Quapaws, the Osages recruited trade from the East. Although they had periodically fought bands of Illinois Indians, they began to trade with them in the late seventeenth century, traveling to Kaskaskia and other towns that had access to French trade. In their 1680 trip there with the Quapaws and Chickasaws, they surely traded with the Kaskaskia Indians, an Illinois group, as well as with the French. When French Catholics founded missions at Kaskaskia in 1699 and Cahokia in 1700 across from the mouth of the Missouri, Osage bands probably took the products of their hunting and slave-raiding expeditions there. They and some Missouri Indians, who lived nearby and also spoke a Siouan language, joined Ottawas, Potawatomis, Sauks, Menominees, and some Illinois in a battle against the Fox and Mascoutins at Fort Detroit in 1712, returning with captives and French powder and ball. Perhaps they also traveled farther south, where the Quapaws may have facilitated trade between the Osages and the French as they did for other native peoples. Before long, trade came west, mostly in the hands of *voyageurs*. But many early explorers and traders who ascended the Missouri missed the Osage River tributary. Probably to waylay westward-bound traders, both for trade and to dissuade them from continuing to the west, several bands of Osages moved north to the Missouri River in the early eighteenth century and settled near their allies the Missouris. This division became known as the Little Osages, while those who remained on the Osage River called themselves the Great Osages.[10]

Besides attracting European trade for themselves, the other key to the Osage rise to power was preventing European goods from reaching Osage enemies to the west. The Osages welcomed French traders into their own towns but attacked and sometimes killed those who tried to reach potential customers farther west, as well as Indian and white hunters poaching on Osage lands (according to Osage definitions). In the winter of 1721–1722, several *voyageurs* from Illinois made it across the Mississippi and up the Missouri to trade with the Kansa Indians, a people who had probably migrated across the Mississippi with the Osages and the Quapaws. In response, the Osages attacked the next *voyageurs* who passed through Osage towns, plundering their goods and, according to one report, killing three of them. The Osages only shared trade with their close allies, the Missouris. Richard White has shown that the refugees and displaced peoples of the eighteenth-century Great Lakes region did not resist sharing French trade among themselves. Indeed, their common French alliance served as a unifying part of their identity. In contrast, Osage identity and success became increasingly dependent on reserving French alliance for themselves.[11]

The Osages acquired their own French trading post in 1722 as a result of French-Spanish rivalry. Alarmed by news of Du Tisné's 1719 expedition, the Spanish commandant at Santa Fe determined to protect New Mexico's eastern border. In July 1720, he sent a caravan of over 100 Spaniards and Indians under the command of Pedro de Villasur and led by Frenchman Jean de l'Archévèque, one of La Salle's assassins who had taken refuge in New Mexico. Pawnees attacked and killed most of this party and took their goods. Despite Villasur's failure, French Governor Bienville feared that the next Spanish effort to recruit Indians between Louisiana and New Mexico would be more successful. In his worst nightmares, the Spanish conspired to overthrow French Louisiana with the powerful Padoucas. To counter Spanish ambitions, Bienville established a post, Fort Orléans, on the Missouri River near the Missouri and Little Osage towns. The post's orders were to keep the peace with France's Indian allies, provide them with munitions, trade with the Spanish if peace reigned, and protect Louisiana in case of Spanish attack. To secure local Indians' allegiance, the Company of the Indies invited Osage and Missouri chiefs to Paris, "to inspire in the barbarians a favorable impression of the French, and thus to attach them to this nation," as they believed the British and Spanish had done with their Indian allies.[12]

In September 1725, an Osage man called Boganienhin, a Missouri man and woman, and representatives of neighboring peoples accompanied the commandant of the new Fort Orléans, Etienne de Bourgmont, to Paris. There, they attended an opera, visited Versailles and other sights, and exchanged speeches and gifts with French notables, including King Louis XV. Boganienhin returned to his home with a royal medallion on a gold chain, a painting of his audience with the King, and goods to distribute among the Osages. We do not know if he returned with "a favorable impression," but there is no reason to think that his opinion of his own people declined.[13]

The Osages now had their own trading post, but it came at a price, sharing it with other Indians. The French intended the post as a center not only for the Osages and Missouris but also for peoples farther west—Kansas, Otos, Iowas, Pawnees, and especially Padoucas. The Osages were unenthusiastic about the trip that Bourgmont took after Paris, a journey from Fort Orléans to the Padoucas, with the purpose of making peace with others that they met along the way. Unable to dissuade Bourgmont from going and unwilling to disrupt their useful French relationship by violence, 100 Missouris and 64 Osages set out with him in July 1724. Upriver, they all performed the calumet ceremony with the Kansas. With a Kansa delegation in tow, the party now included some 300 warriors and chiefs, 300 women, 500 children, hundreds of dogs dragging the baggage, and 200 Padouca slaves to return to their people. However, soon the Osages and most of the Missouris turned back. The remainder performed peace ceremonies with the Otos, Iowas, Panimahas (Skidi Pawnees), and finally the Padoucas. The Padouca chiefs promised the French and Indians to mediate peace and trade between all of them and the Spanish, in return for which the chief asked Bourgmont to "send some Frenchmen to trade with us." Although the Osages were not present to hear these words, Bourgmont's journey surely inspired in them a renewed desire to isolate the Padoucas and undermine their plan of becoming the center of Plains trade.[14]

To Osage relief, the French and Padouca plan failed. Part of the reason was that the French could not afford it. In 1728, the new governor, Etienne de Périer, complained of the Company of the Indies' meager appropriations for Fort Orléans. As the governor pointed out, "you advise . . . the officer in charge of this post to have presents sent, but you only budget 800 [livres] for those of the Indians and the expenses that he will have to undertake in order to win them over," despite the fact that the Osage "nation is huge" and full of demands. Périer suggested that 3,000 livres per year for the first two years "would not have been too much." Because the Company assigned only eight soldiers to the post, the French did not have the force to protect the fort without giving presents. Governor Périer concluded that, with a troop strength that low, the fort was "absolutely useless." To make matters worse, most soldiers sent to Fort Orléans deserted along the way there, and the Company withdrew the garrison entirely in 1729 to save expenses.[15]

The failure to support the fort stymied French ambitions in the West but served Osage and Missouri objectives nicely. Traders' interest in the Missouri and Osage rivers increased, and trade there grew throughout the eighteenth century. Spreading goods as far as the Padoucas proved too expensive, but the French did pour funds into their remaining allies, including the Osages. The French bought far more furs than their markets could absorb,

Figure 7. Eighteenth-century musket. This .77-caliber 1717 French flintlock musket is similar to those that the French army used and probably like those that the Osages imported. Courtesy National Museum of American History, Smithsonian Institution, Washington, D.C.

knowing that commerce was the key to Indian alliances, which in turn enabled them to retain their "colony." For their part, the Osages became powerful and domineering but by no means isolated. While they alienated many of their Indian neighbors, the Osages cultivated European connections, acquiring cloth, axes, knives, beads, rum, needles for tattooing, and the guns and ammunition that fueled their expansion. When French traders, explorers, or officials arrived without guns, even if they brought powder and ball, the Osages showed their discontent. By the 1750s, Osage-French trade was so active that Indians in Illinois complained that "the French traders carry their best goods to the Missouri tribes." Osage women became skilled at preparing buffalo and deer hides for market. Each season, they cleaned, dried, and dressed thousands of furs and shaved and tanned most of them to make leather. As historian J. Frederick Fausz has pointed out, women's expanded fur trade work is evident in the fact that retired warriors began to cook the meals for their towns. Women simply no longer had the time.[16]

With a new market and new arms, the Osages made life difficult for Caddoan peoples in the central Arkansas Valley. The Osages traded not only the products of their own hunt but also hides, horses, mules, and slaves that they raided from the Kichais, Taovayas, Iscanis, Guichitas, Tawakonis, and Panis Noirs. These Caddoan peoples whom La Harpe and Du Tisné had visited in 1719 found themselves squeezed in the middle. As their enemies acquired guns, their own need for them increased. But they found French connections difficult to develop. There were many reasons for traders to choose not to visit them. Their towns were nearly 300 miles farther upriver than the Quapaws or Osages, and long periods of low water in the late summer and fall made traveling there difficult. More decisive was opposition from the Quapaws and the Osages. The central valley was also cut off from the West, where Apache bands used their access to Spanish horses to dominate the southern Plains, blockade Spanish trade, and capture central

Arkansas Valley Caddoans to sell to New Mexico. Beginning in the 1690s, Spanish Franciscans established missions in Texas among the Caddoan Hasinais but spread not firearms, as the Hasinais hoped, but disease to the peoples of the central Red and Arkansas river valleys. In the early eighteenth century, Chickasaw traders occasionally brought English goods west, but these trips were rare.[17]

Although only sporadically occupied, the Arkansas Post and Fort Orléans further isolated the central Valley peoples by concentrating French trade near the Quapaw, Osage, and Missouri towns. Centralized trade provided both convenience and power, because those with trade could guard access, inviting their friends and excluding their enemies. By the time of La Harpe's and Du Tisné's visits, the Kichais had already abandoned the Arkansas River for a safer location on the Red River. In the 1730s, Osage raids prompted the Tawakonis to move south from the Arkansas to the Red River, where they hoped to acquire French trade at the towns of their Kadohadacho allies. Still on the Arkansas River, the Taovayas, Guichitas, and Iscanis moved closer together to defend against the Osages.

The Osages continued blockading and raiding the central Arkansas Valley. In 1733, an Osage party reportedly killed eleven French hunters on the Arkansas, although it later turned out that all but two had gotten away. In January 1742, a party of thirty-five Osage warriors captured seven horses, a mule, and two scalps from the Caddoan towns on the central Arkansas. Prior to their raid, they had encountered Sieur Fabry de la Bruyère and offered him any horses and slaves they might capture, but on their return they realized that he did not want horses to take east to sell but rather to carry his merchandise farther west. They accused him of seeking out the Caddoans and Padoucas "to make an alliance with them and to trade guns with them." Not reassured by his claim that his intention was to visit the Spanish, they refused to sell him any horses and cautioned him not to try going by canoe, the party's leader attesting that he "had always found [the river] without water." Ultimately, Fabry had to turn around without reaching the Arkansas River. The Osages controlled French and Indian access to the central Arkansas Valley and established their own sovereignty over the region.[18]

*   *   *

Although the Osages were relatively populous, if other groups in the region had united, they would have outnumbered the Osages. The fact that their rivals did not get along facilitated the Osage rise to dominance. Just west of the

Osages, the Kansa Indians bore the brunt of fighting the northern Pawnee bands, whom they and the Osages had pushed west in earlier times. By the 1750s, the war and smallpox had devastated the Kansas, and some fled west to the Kansas Valley, decreasing their population on the Missouri River to fewer than 2,000.[19]

The Osages worked to dissuade their neighbors from joining against them. Relations with the less numerous Missouris generally remained good. Occasional clashes suggest some tensions as Osage power grew, but the Missouris seem to have found Osage alliance preferable to Osage enmity. Observing what happened to those whom the Osages opposed, the Missouris decided to tie their fortunes to them. In return, the Osages did not attack traders visiting the Missouris. Although Quapaw and Osage parties occasionally clashed when the Osages hunted too far down the Arkansas River for the Quapaws' comfort, their hunting patterns generally did not conflict, and they occasionally fought together against the Caddoan peoples. Having fought these upstream peoples for their right to the lower Arkansas Valley, the Quapaws generally sided with their fellow newcomers. In 1730, after the Quapaws suffered a major attack by a Caddoan party, most of the nation traveled north to the Osages, their allies, to propose a joint attack. In response, the Osages further increased their attacks on the central Arkansas.[20]

Despite the Osages' growing power, they could not afford a break with the French. When Osages killed whites, it was almost always because the latter were attempting to get past the Osages in order to trade with Osage enemies. The Osages felt justified in raiding or even killing them but could not allow these attacks to alienate the French entirely and thus threaten the flow of goods. In order to smooth over differences, the Osages developed a ritualized means of explaining, apologizing for, and using European goods to cover deaths. Osage leaders repeatedly asked to restore "good friendship" and declared that they did not want "to cause any more trouble" after their young men attacked French *voyageurs* or France's Indian allies.[21]

Within their own society, the Osages had developed methods for dealing with murder while minimizing social discord. When an Osage murdered another Osage, the victim's clan theoretically had to kill the culprit and bring the culprit's scalp to the grave of the victim. This practice could easily get out of hand, as one mourning clan interpreted its own violence as retribution, but the clan that it aggrieved saw the retributive killing as a new murder, requiring new retribution. To prevent this cycle of violence, the Osages had developed ritual substitutes for capital punishment. One way was for the clan to substitute the scalp of an alien enemy for the murderer's scalp, a choice that could redirect the violence outside the society and, especially in wartime, make the violence productive rather than destructive, at least from the Osage perspective. Thus, while European justice punished the responsible individual, Osage justice could be satisfied without individual punishment. Justice could even be served without physical punishment at all, if the aggrieved clan agreed. The murderer, the murderer's representatives, or a third party could ceremonially present the clan with elaborate apologies, explanations, and gifts or a captive to compensate for, or "cover," the death. If the clan accepted the overtures, it would not seek vengeance. Ritualized procedures of public gift presentation and formal announcement of the clan's decision, all witnessed by the community as a whole, made the process dependable and binding.[22]

The Osages handled murder between two Indian peoples much as they did intra-Osage killings. When an Osage was involved in a murder with an Indian of a different nation, the aggrieved nation might raid and kill representatives of the murderer's nation. If that nation played fairly, it would interpret the battle as an act of justice rather than a declaration of war and would not retaliate. But this practice was as dangerous as compensatory violence between Osages, because it could easily escalate into war. As in intra-Osage murder, the murderer's nation could substitute ritual gifts and explanations to cover the crime. In their dealings with the French, the Osages would expect the newcomers to abide by native forms of cross-cultural justice.[23]

Dealing with *voyageurs*' deaths was essential to preventing a French-Osage war. A cross-cultural killing could be either a murder or the first casualty of war. Neither the Osages nor the French wanted war. The Osages needed French trade to acquire guns and ammunition. For their part, the French could not defeat the Osages, who numbered nearly 10,000. There were only a few hundred French soldiers to defend all of Louisiana, which included the entire Mississippi basin from the Great Plains to the Appalachians— about one soldier for every 1,000 square miles. Wars in Europe and the fact that Louisiana was France's farthest and least valuable colony meant that few of the empire's resources reached it. Over the course of the colony's history, the French government granted it to various companies, but each ended up returning it to the crown when profits proved elusive.[24]

Relative power often determines whose idea of justice prevails in cross-cultural crime and punishment. In the eighteenth century, the Osages became the most powerful people in the western Mississippi Valley. When the French established the colony of Louisiana, its administrators instituted European-style justice systems for French colonists, vesting local executives, as representatives of the king, with the authority to judge and punish crime. But the Osages held more power over crimes involving Osages.[25]

In 1749, a Great Osage party killed two *voyageurs*. The Osages and Iowas, who were also suspected, sent several chiefs to the Illinois country's Fort Chartes to accept blame and ask the fort's commander, Jean Baptiste Benoist, Sieur de St. Claire, to petition Governor Vaudreuil for "mercy." Vaudreuil decided that "to add to the number of our Enemies for trifling reasons" would be suicidal. Rather, the governor instructed the Illinois commandant to assure the Osages "that we will forget the past and that I would very much like to renew our friendship."[26] Vaudreuil's superiors approved of the pardon because they too recognized the importance of the Osages as a large group on the border with Spanish America. Threatened by the British on one side and by the Spanish on the other, and surrounded by Indians whose loyalty they doubted, the French could not raise serious or sustained objections to Osage violence and expansion. The Osages felt justified in killing these *voyageurs*, but the chiefs recognized the need for some sort of amends to prevent a rupture in their relations with the French generally. By apologizing and receiving the governor's pardon, they incorporated the French officials into customary intertribal justice. For their part, the French considered the Osages more important than the unruly *voyageur* victims. As unlicensed traders operating far from French officials' control, *voyageurs* brought officials plenty of trouble and few, if any, profits. Vaudreuil called the victims "very ill fellows."[27]

Later that year, a Little Osage band killed a *voyageur* named Giguiere and his slave. When French officials protested, several Little Osage leaders crossed the Mississippi to inform Commandant St. Claire that they had executed the murderer, whose scalp they brought as confirmation. As a murderer's representatives would do within Osage society, the chiefs conducted a formalized ritual of accepting blame and asking for pardon. French officials accepted the Osages' word as sufficient justice because they could not afford a break with the powerful Osages. As La Harpe put it, "however friendly they may be with the French, this nation is perfidious, and it is wise to be on one's guard."[28]

Unfortunately for the Osage chiefs, Missouri Indians began to spread the word that the scalp in fact belonged to the brother of the culprit, who had initially fled but had since returned to the Osage towns. The Osages may have been attempting to protect an important man and perhaps get rid of a troublesome one. Caught, the Little Osage chiefs bound "the real murderer," as they now said, and delivered him to Fort Chartes. When French officials asked some Missouris present at this second surrender whether the Osages had it right this time, they claimed to be uncertain who was the guilty man. French officials had two choices—accept the Osages' claim (again) that this was the culprit or risk more conflict than they could handle. They chose the former.

Rather than rebuffing their form of justice, French officials accepted, both times, the Osages' claim of the surrendered man's guilt. In fact, in his official report, Governor of New France Pierre Jacques de Taffanel, Marquis de La Jonquière, praised their "submission" and "honesty."[29] French officials had learned that it was best not to quibble over the determination of guilt. At the same time, the Osages made concessions to French conceptions of justice by accepting blame and at least pretending to punish individuals, even if they were not necessarily the guilty parties. This ability to construct a common fiction in order to smooth over conflict mirrors the creative misunderstandings that Richard White finds in the Great Lakes. In the case of the Osages and the French, the "misunderstandings" seem intentional on both sides.[30]

The flexibility of Osage war parties and the decentralized nature of Osage society helped the chiefs to define the violence as isolated events, not general Osage policy. A full-scale Osage war would have required elaborate discussions and debate, then more than a week of ceremonies to prepare the tribal war party. In addition, there is evidence from nineteenth-century ethnography that large-scale war parties could only assemble in the summer. In contrast, individual clans could raise small, temporary parties for war or raiding without all the fuss, and hunting parties could become raiding parties if the need arose. Thus, these had a more flexible response time, and Osage chiefs could more easily describe them as renegade parties, not representing Osage policy.[31]

Besides preventing an Osage war, the French wanted to keep peace among their many allies, making Louisiana more stable and easier to defend against British incursions, which increasingly threatened in the 1740s and 1750s as French-British rivalry escalated toward the Seven Years' War. Exploiting the French desire for peace, Indians incorporated French mediators and goods into older practices of ritual compensation. For example, in December 1751, Missouri Indians killed an Osage man and took his herd of horses. When French traders who were with the Missouris learned of the raid, they feared Osage reprisal. To preempt an Osage attack, the French traders gave the Missouris goods to present to the Osages. By expending their own resources, the traders prevented further violence, which could have been bad for business and for their own health.[32]

Before the eighteenth century, compensation and rhetoric appear to have been equally vital components of preventing retributive killing among the native peoples of the mid-continent. With European involvement in both European-Indian justice and inter-tribal justice, the tradition developed for representatives of the accused to provide the ritual explanations, pleas for pardon, and promises not to commit future violence. Europeans, no matter who had killed whom, provided most of the goods required to cover the crime. With their access to valued goods and their desire to keep peace among their allies, the French assumed a role within older practices of peacekeeping. The French developed a similar role in other places as well. Richard White calls mediation "the heart of the alliance" between the French (and later the British) and their Native American allies in the Great Lakes region.[33]

As with the Quapaws, Osage society changed as a result of its contact with Europeans, but the French did not direct change. Over the course of the eighteenth century, the Osages apparently shifted from a patrilocal to matrilocal residence system, with husbands now moving to live in their wives' households rather than the reverse. Anthropologist Garrick Alan Bailey has traced the reason to the new clan war parties, which left all of the men of a family gone at once and for longer periods than in the past as they ranged farther for slaves and horses. The men would be away for months and might even all die in a disastrous battle, leaving the household with no hunters. In contrast, a matrilocal household would include men of many different clans. The Osages also created a position of Protector of the Land. This chief was charged with "protecting the Osage domain against uninvited intruders" and frightening off or killing any who stole animals that belonged to the Osages. This office assisted Osage trade and expansion.[34]

Archaeological findings indicate that the Osages replaced older goods with European ones when the new ones suited them better. Town sites from the late eighteenth century reveal that Osages increasingly used guns and copper and iron kettles but still made bows and arrows and pottery. Iron knives were so superior to stone knives that they apparently converted almost completely, while older stone hide scrapers and stone pipes remained preferable to imported iron scrapers and clay pipes. Even by the 1830s, most Osages continued to use hides and furs as well as cloth in their clothing. In material culture as well as other practices, Osages adopted what they found useful and rejected what they did not.[35]

*　*　*

In 1745, the French again attempted to establish a broader trade in the mid-continent. Canadian merchant Sieur Deruïsseau built a new post on the

Missouri River. Directly confronting the Osage blockade, he threatened to ban Osages from the post unless the Osages permitted the post's traders to deal with the Iscanis, Taovayas, Guichitas, and Panis Noirs for Spanish horses. The Osages reluctantly assented. To the Frenchmen's delight, the Comanches increased their sales of horses and buffalo hides to the Iscanis, Taovayas, Guichitas, and Panis Noirs, who in turn sold these goods, along with products of their hunt, to the French for munitions. The Iscanis, Taovayas, Guichitas, and Panis Noirs reserved some French arms for themselves and sold the rest, plus their own agricultural products, to the Comanches, who used the arms to protect themselves against the Osages and Apaches.[36]

At the same time, Alexis Grappe, a member of the 1741 Fabry expedition that the Osages had turned back, came north from New Orleans to found a trading post at a Kadohadacho town on the Red River. By the next decade, traders were traveling north from there to the Tawakonis on the Red River and the Iscanis and other towns on the central Arkansas. By coming from the south, they bypassed Osage scouts. Through this channel, French officials sent presents and offers of a permanent alliance. Using the Comanches as intermediaries, these towns also increased their trade with the Spanish, who promised in 1760 to build a mission and presidio nearby. To the Osages, these were disastrous developments. Armed with French guns and new alliances, Taovayas, Guichitas, Iscanis, and Panis Noirs joined with Comanche warriors in an attack on a Great Osage town in which they killed twenty-two Great Osage elders. Flushed with their success, they tried, but apparently failed, to recruit Chickasaws to join their alliance.[37]

Not only did the Osages face greater military resistance because their economic monopoly ended, but their diplomatic monopoly also eroded. When an Osage party raided Kadohadachos on the Red River in 1751, the Kadohadachos had a direct line of complaint to the French. At their urging, French Governor Vaudreuil began to think that it might be time to stop Osage expansion. That August, he ordered Illinois commandant Jean Jacques de Macarty Mactique to feel out French allies in Illinois for the possibility of going after "this worrisome and turbulent nation" to "punish a nation that knows neither friends nor allies." When Macarty charged the Osages with attacking the Kadohadachos, the Osage chiefs explained that a group of Kadohadachos had invited several Osages to share a meal only to kill them as they ate. Not an act of aggression, the raids justly avenged this gross violation of the dictates of hospitality. The Osage chiefs promised to perform the calumet ceremony with the Kadohadachos.[38]

Despite their wishes to control the Osages, Macarty and Vaudreuil had little choice but to accept their excuses and promises. Another British war was imminent. Rumors circulated of a British-inspired Indian conspiracy to massacre the French, who shuddered at the memory of Natchez. According to reports, the British and their Indian allies in Illinois had sent messengers to all the nations of the mid-continent, including the Osages and Quapaws, to encourage them to turn against the French. Some said that the Osages had accepted their offer and were making plans to attack the Arkansas Post or the French posts on the east side of the Mississippi. Rather than make trouble over Kadohadacho-Osage relations, Macarty concentrated on what was best for the impending French-British conflict. He accepted the Osages' explanations, while using the occasion to urge them to reject British overtures and to fight for the French if open warfare came.[39]

War did come. Clashes in the Ohio Valley ignited the imperial tensions that had been smoldering since the 1740s. The Seven Years' War was a war for North America, in which Europeans sought to expand their empires and Indians east of the Mississippi seized the opportunity to work for their own objectives, whether destroying intrusive colonial settlements or expanding their own power. West of the Mississippi, the Osages did not fight with the British or the French. Instead, they took advantage of wartime exigencies to reinstate their trade restrictions and establish control over most of the Arkansas Valley. As Macarty and Vaudreuil had realized in 1751, the French could not afford to alienate the Osages. In a 1758 report, Governor Kerlérec stressed the "great importance to show consideration to this nation." The Osages still received French goods from Canada and New Orleans, but attenuated supply lines decreased the available goods and left nothing for the Indian towns farther from the Mississippi. Illicit British traders, who had occasionally smuggled goods past French and Osage regulators, now did not dare to venture beyond the Osages. And the Spanish never built their promised mission and presidio on the central Arkansas. During the war, outgunned by the Osages and suffering more outbreaks of disease, most of the Iscanis, Taovayas, and Guichitas abandoned the Arkansas and joined the Tawakonis on the Red River. The Taovayas built an impressive fortification there, but it too would soon fall to the Osages. The Panis Noirs moved north into present-day Kansas and Nebraska to join the Panimahas. By 1758, the Osages controlled 500 miles of the Arkansas River Valley, between the Quapaws in the east and the Comanches in the far west.[40]

The Osages made efforts to keep the peace with the Quapaws on their southeastern border. Inevitably, clashes sometimes occurred, but diplomacy could smooth over problems, as it did with the French. In February 1764, an

Osage delegation visited the lower Arkansas Valley to perform the calumet ceremony with the Quapaws and French there. According to now-established custom, the French commandant gave out presents to confirm the reconciliation.[41]

French officials' jobs would have been easier if they could have controlled their Indian allies. Still, they could comfort themselves with the fact that other colonial administrators faced the same difficulties. According to Kerlérec, Indians believed that the French were better friends than the British, and the most the British could buy with all of their low-priced goods and treacherous recruitment of French allies was neutrality, not friendship. Indeed, across most of the continent in the eighteenth century, Europeans could only "rule" by persuasion, and friendship could be more powerful than material goods.[42]

Still, the British won the Seven Years' War. Because most of the fighting took place far from the mid-continent, the news of 1763 came as a shock to the region's Indians and French alike. France had ceded Canada and Louisiana east of the Mississippi to the British. In the complicated post-war negotiations, France's ally Spain gave Florida to the British, and France transferred the western half of Louisiana, including the Arkansas Valley, to Spain. The people of the Arkansas Valley would now have to teach the Spanish the responsibilities that they were inheriting from France.

*   *   *

Much had changed since de Soto and Coronado had tramped through the heart of the continent. Guachoya, Anilco, Pacaha, and Casqui had fallen; Osage, Quapaw, French, and African newcomers had arrived; the descendants of Quivira were fleeing Osage expansion. While their sixteenth-century predecessors could make little use or sense of Europeans, eighteenth-century Indians had become intricately involved with them. Indians knew what they wanted from Europeans and how to get it, although some were succeeding more than others. While sixteenth-century residents had expelled the troublesome interlopers, eighteenth-century Indians had incorporated them into their diplomatic, economic, judicial, and familial ways, making them a vital piece of a cross-cultural world.

The Spanish had changed too. Nearly 300 years in the Americas had made them more permanent settlers. No longer seeking gold, they hoped to establish what the French government had wanted from Louisiana, a colony to stand against the British. Spanish administrators knew that they would need Indian allies if Louisiana were to serve as a barrier between British expansion and New Spain. Spanish officials dreamed of populating Louisiana with Spanish settlers, but it was difficult to lure them to this place, far from Spanish population centers and lacking in sources of wealth. If the Spanish wanted to protect Louisiana from French enemies within and British enemies without, they would need Indian friends.[43]

While de Soto and Coronado had outfitted and financed their expeditions personally and through investors, the State ran eighteenth-century Spanish colonialism. The changes began in the conquistadors' time. In 1500, King Ferdinand and Queen Isabella had declared that natives were the subjects of Castile, not the playthings of fortune-seekers. Felipe II expanded the crown's power at the end of the sixteenth century, a centralizing trend that continued over the following centuries, particularly under the Enlightenment-influenced Bourbons. Spain's Bourbon monarchs sought reforms that would rationalize governance and decrease the power of the church. Contrary to the stereotype of backwards Spanish colonialism, they strove to construct a "modern" empire, with freer trade and rational bureaucrats. In the 1700s, Felipe V and Carlos III strengthened and reformed the colonial bureaucracy, centralized language customs, and increased their control over the church by banishing the Jesuits from the colonies and cracking down on the Inquisition.[44]

The Spanish empire prided itself on its power and organization. Therefore, while Spanish officials' goals for Louisiana resembled French goals, they wanted to correct what they saw as French laxity. The first Spanish governor of Louisiana, Antonio de Ulloa, decreased the power of the local Superior Council and imposed price controls on trade goods coming from the West Indies. He intended these price controls to assist Louisiana consumers, but they angered leading merchants, who made great profits from importing these goods. In November 1768, these merchants led the French residents of New Orleans in rebellion against Spanish authority, expelling Governor Ulloa from the colony. King Carlos III promptly sent General Alejandro O'Reilly to put down the uprising. Irish by birth, O'Reilly had joined the Spanish army at the age of ten to fight British imperialism. Like many other Irish "Wild Geese," O'Reilly became an effective agent of Spanish imperialism. By the time that Carlos III sent him to Louisiana, O'Reilly had fought in several wars and most recently quelled the 1766 Esquilache riots outside the king's palace. The general landed at New Orleans on July 24, 1769, at the head of more than 2,000 troops. He easily vanquished the rebels with an impressive demonstration of Spanish power, without resort to violence, and set about instituting Spanish rule throughout Louisiana.[45]

Governor O'Reilly's policies in Louisiana reflect the ideals of the Bourbon Reforms. To decrease the power of the church, he instituted a policy whereby the government appointed priests and paid their salaries and expenses. The governor established public schools to teach Spanish and a Cabildo to restore some local governance to Louisianans. He regulated local institutions from billiard parlors to pharmacies. O'Reilly would also try to follow the Bourbon crown's new Indian policy. In previous centuries, the Spanish had sought to conquer native peoples by "civilizing" them. Civil and religious leaders agreed that Indians should adopt Spanish law, dress, marriage practices, and other signs of "civilization." But this "Culture of the Conquest" had declined by 1763. To protect its vast North American empire, which spread from California to Louisiana and from the headwaters of the Mississippi south to Tierra del Fuego, Spain sought Indian allies and effective ways to control them through secularized and centralized Indian policy.[46]

In reality, Spain lacked the resources to implement the Bourbon Reforms on all of the Indians within its empire. Louisiana was a distant and relatively insignificant edge of the Spanish empire and thus received few of the empire's resources. What resulted was a hodgepodge of methods. In New Mexico and Texas, Spanish officials attempted an expensive and unsuccessful military conquest of Plains Indians. In California, the Spanish disregarded the Bourbon Reforms and re-instituted an old means of Indian relations, the mission system. Franciscan friars worked to make native Californians into industrious, Christian subjects of the Spanish empire.[47]

Louisiana was the most appropriate place to institute Bourbon Indian policy, by adopting the French policy of negotiating with Louisiana's native peoples but with a tighter hand on the reins. To discourage warfare, O'Reilly outlawed Indian slavery and the trade in horses and mules. Trade in Louisiana was to be more free than in much of New Spain, but all traders had to be licensed, unlike in French Louisiana. But O'Reilly's vision of controlling Louisiana's Indian and French residents proved a fantasy. The balance of power weighed against Spain. On this far northern edge, the permanent army for Louisiana never exceeded 1,000 troops, and the force at the Arkansas Post fluctuated between fifteen and fifty soldiers. Nearly 1,000 Quapaws lived near the fort, thousands of Osages ruled the river farther up, and bands from other tribes periodically hunted along the river. Several hundred French *habitants* and *voyageurs* lived along the region's rivers, who were no more Spain's to command than were the Indians. In fact, most avoided the posts because they were trading without Spanish licenses or because they owed money to merchants there who had financed their hunting expeditions.[48]

Indians controlled the mid-continent, and individual chiefs, traders, and interpreters had more influence over daily workings than did the Spanish bureaucracy. Spanish officials believed that the French role in Indian diplomacy was to provide moderate presents, issue orders, and discipline transgressions. They assumed that the French had been in control. They did not understand that French officials had not ruled Louisiana but instead had obtained allies by adopting native practices and extending trade and gifts to native peoples. The Quapaws and the Osages would spend the next decade teaching the Spanish to be a generous friend and developing another new friend—the British. Thus both groups of Indians would maintain and even increase their connections to European sources of power and goods.

*   *   *

According to Spanish officials, the new town and post of St. Louis was to be the center for fur trade and diplomacy with the Osages and their neighbors. Just across the Mississippi from the remains of Cahokia, St. Louis would serve Spanish policy by controlling the dangerous Osages, who could have trade and presents in abundance there, under the eye of the commandant, but nowhere else. Other avenues of trade and presents, including on the Arkansas River, were forbidden because, Spanish officials believed, centralizing all dealings with the Osages would make them easier to control. If they misbehaved, the Spanish could cut off trade and presents from that one source. The Spanish hoped to draw the Osages back northeastward, away from the Arkansas and Red rivers, because Osage expansion had upset potential allies like the Wichitas, Kadohadachos, and Pawnees and encouraged unlicensed French *voyageurs* who operated outside of the Spanish trading system.[49]

The Osages and other Indians in the area quickly seized on St. Louis as a useful regional center. Indeed, French families, lingering in the lower Missouri Valley after their government left, established an agricultural economy in part to feed the Indian delegations that visited St. Louis almost constantly. It also became a center for diverse Indian groups to negotiate with one another, with or without Spanish facilitators, all at the expense of their Spanish hosts. Because the creation of St. Louis fostered more permanent and larger French-run trading operations, ties increased between Osage and French families.

The Osages adopted French traders and interpreters, who then sometimes married Osage women. The Osages wholeheartedly used St. Louis for diplomacy and trade; however, they refused to confine these activities to one Spanish-defined location. The Osages were growing in power, not declining.[50]

At the very time that the Spanish were designing their system of control, the Osages were expanding farther south. When the French government left Louisiana in 1763, the situation of the Taovayas, Iscanis, Guichitas, and Tawakonis, who had all fled the Arkansas River, became even more dire. While some *voyageurs* still traded with them, they lost their official traders and presents and gradually moved southwest deeper into Texas from the 1760s through 1780s. On the Red River, disease and warfare drastically decreased the population of Kadohadachos by 1770. They abandoned their old towns north of the Red River and merged into a smaller number of towns south of the river.[51]

When Osages raided the Taovayas, Iscanis, Guichitas, Tawakonis, Kadohadachos, or *voyageurs* attempting to trade with them, the Spanish government forbade trade with the Osages. If their plan of limiting Osage trade to St. Louis had worked, these punitive trade sanctions might have had some effect. But Spanish officials could not enforce their trade sanctions because *voyageurs* did not agree with the policy. Most *voyageurs* believed that the whole St. Louis plan was created by prominent St. Louis merchants to monopolize Osage trade. They particularly suspected Auguste Chouteau, whose family had founded St. Louis.

As long as the Osages could acquire weapons and other goods through illegal trade and pillaging, Spain had no power to compel them to move. In 1774, despite a trade embargo, some Indians from Illinois saw "seven canoes loaded with every type of merchandise and ammunition" in one Osage town.[52] The St. Louis trade report of May 19, 1775, listed both the Little Osages and the Great Osages as "forbidden," according to Spanish regulations. Yet it reported a combined total of nine traders and 22,200 pounds of furs received from them that year, more than from any other group.[53]

Many people would have liked to stop that trade, including a chief of one of the Wichita towns, who begged the Spanish to prohibit hunters and traders from supplying the Osages with ammunition to fight his people. But the Spanish could not stop the *voyageurs*. In vain, governors urged commandants of the Arkansas Post to stop trade on the Arkansas River, but *voyageurs* and Osage hunters had long traded there, and the founding of St. Louis did not change their practice. Shorthanded and busy with the Quapaws, commandants did not dare to challenge the Osages and made no serious efforts to stop illegal trade. In 1770, at least one trading camp on the Arkansas was known as "having been founded for the purpose of supplying the Osages." The Spanish had little control over this vast borderland whose populations had no reason to be loyal Spanish subjects.[54]

The major flaw in Spain's policy regarding the Osages was assuming that both the Spanish and the Osages were centralized powers. The Spanish could not stop the Osage trade because it was not centralized. The governor could not simply turn off the spout in St. Louis and expect all Osage trade to dry up. Hundreds of individual *voyageurs* worked along the rivers and streams of Louisiana. They exchanged guns, ammunition, and other goods for furs and skins, which they sold illegally to legitimate French and Spanish merchants in New Orleans or smuggled into British territory in West Florida or Canada. The British government's 1774 Quebec Act, which declared that Canada extended as far south as the Ohio River, encouraged British and French Canadian traders to extend from Michilimackinac and Detroit on the Great Lakes and Prairie du Chien on the upper Mississippi into Spanish Louisiana and to ship the furs to Montreal. In 1772, Jean Marie Ducharmé, a French resident of now-British Cahokia, Illinois, transported 1,500 pounds of British goods from Canada up the Missouri River to trade with the Osages and Missouris. Canadian firms even employed French Louisiana traders, leaving the Spanish little ability to distinguish "Spanish" Louisiana trade from "British" Canadian.[55]

Similarly, Spanish policymakers assumed that Osage chiefs had the power to prevent violence. The Osage chiefs at times encouraged this belief in order to gain more recognition and goods from Spanish officials, but it was far from true. Individual Osage bands spearheaded Osage expansion by hunting and raiding farther afield each year. There is no evidence that the Osage chiefs opposed the expansion, but if they had wanted to stop it, they could not have. Like Quapaw chiefs and Spanish governors, Osage chiefs did not command their people. Chiefs would promise that there would be no more raids on the Arkansas or that the Osages were all moving back to the Missouri Valley, but they had no power to put those promises into effect.

Not only did the Osages continue trading on the Arkansas, they also kept trade open at St. Louis most of the time, despite continuing their raids on their enemies. The Osage leadership on the Missouri and Osage rivers protected their gifts and trade at St. Louis by denouncing the raids and claiming that they were committed by unruly Osage factions. With the exception of a few troublemakers, the chiefs alleged, the Osage people generally were good friends of the Spanish. In July 1772, the Great Osage chiefs blamed the Little Osages for recent raids on the Arkansas River. As the chiefs explained, "there is but one part of the nation which makes an effort to withdraw from the rest. This part commits all the depredations." They called the Little Osages "one of the most restless, most inclined to thievery, and most evil-intentioned of all the nations." St. Louis Commandant Pedro Piernas was eager to believe the Great Osages' accusations. As he put it, the Little Osages were one of "the least numerous of all and the easiest to reduce by means of extermination." In contrast, the Great Osages constituted the majority of the largest and most powerful nation in the region, and the most profitable to Spanish trade. The commandant believed that destroying the "evil" band would stop the violence on the Arkansas without endangering the profits of the Great Osage trade at St. Louis. Tension between the Little Osages and St. Louis grew.[56]

Later that month, a party of Little Osages and Missouris broke into a Spanish fort outside St. Louis and stole its supplies. Emboldened by their success, the young men charged into St. Louis itself and erected a British flag. Co-opting a European symbol, the Little Osages struck back with a powerful symbol of independence from the Spanish and French. They showed their access to British goods and, most of all, demonstrated their own daring and power. Everyone knew the dreadful retribution that would face any European or Indian who dared to steal *Osage* supplies or storm uninvited into an *Osage* town.[57]

As French settlers' calls to avenge the Osage effrontery mounted, the Spanish government considered war. While St. Louis Commandant Piernas had advocated war on only the Little Osages, Governor O'Reilly's successor, Luis de Unzaga y Amezaga, wanted to kill them all. Like his European counterparts in other times and places, he was so frustrated with Indian power that he brooded in 1772, "there is no other remedy than their extermination since the tolerance which we have had with them, instead of attracting them, has made them insolent." But Unzaga knew that he lacked the forces to adopt this policy. As important as the colony was to its local officials, higher-ups did not see it as equal to Mexico or other colonies. Therefore, the Spanish could not defeat, much less "exterminate," thousands of Osages. Governor Unzaga hoped to persuade other Indian nations to destroy them but knew that Indian recruits were hard to come by and expensive to outfit. He suspected he would have to "find easier means."[58]

Piernas and the Osages did find easier means, a peace agreement. In St. Louis on April 4, 1773, 130 Great and Little Osages surrendered three men allegedly responsible for all of the attacks on the Arkansas River and St. Louis in the preceding decade. The Osages promised to keep the new peace, saying that, if they failed, the Quapaws should attack and destroy them because they would "no longer deserve indulgence." The band that harassed St. Louis had gone too far, and the Great and Little Osage leadership moved quickly to prevent a major break in their friendship with Spain. They made peace in St. Louis, but only there.[59]

If anything, Osage expansion accelerated against the Caddoan peoples on the Red River. Just a month after the St. Louis peace, Osage warriors began a series of assaults. They stole horses from some *voyageurs* near Natchitoches and raided a Kichai town, killing five men and capturing three women. The Kadohadachos moved closer together to improve their security and, by the late 1770s, referred to part of their former homeland in the Great Bend flood plain as "the Prairie of the Enemy." The Spanish were powerless to stop this violence. As long as *voyageurs* resisted their trade policies and the crown refused to send more troops, neither Spaniards nor Indians could challenge Osage dominance.[60]

Still, the St. Louis peace created a system of negotiations that allowed the Spanish to pretend that they had influence over the Osages. In a formalized version of how the Osages smoothed over raids with the French, chiefs regularly traveled to St. Louis to explain and apologize for Osage violence and to confirm their friendship with Spain. These meetings calmed relations with the Spanish but did nothing to prevent future violence. The next time that an Osage band attacked a Frenchman or Indian, the chiefs would travel to St. Louis again. Despite their desire to control Louisiana's native peoples, most Spanish officials tacitly accepted this system.

One exception was Natchitoches commandant Athanase de Mézières, who witnessed Osage violence on the Red River and repeatedly heard Kadohadachos' and others' pleas for Spanish assistance. Disgusted with his comrades' inability to stop Osage violence, de Mézières charged that the St. Louis peace had actually increased raiding on the Red River. Surely echoing Kadohadacho opinion, he said that every time the Osages feared military or economic punishment, "they will exert themselves to excite the pity of the commandant of [St. Louis] with humble messages, with pretended weeping, with presents, and even with offers of the heads of those whom they will claim to be the instigators of the last uprising. The dangerous conclusion that they have repented having resulted from this, they will be pardoned for their atrocities, or, to put it better, invited to perpetrate new ones." Indeed, the Osages continued to get presents and trade at St. Louis and to deflect Spanish retribution.[61]

In 1781, on hearing that the Spanish had again banned Osage trade, an Osage party traveled to the Spanish Arkansas Post, where they surrendered the Spanish symbols of recognition—a medal, flag, and commission—belonging to Brucaiguais, the man they said was guilty of the attacks. They explained that they would have surrendered him but that he was dying and could not travel. But they offered several "chiefs," they said, as hostages in his place. The Arkansas commandant approved this peace measure and provided the representatives with abundant provisions to escort the hostages to New Orleans. The next morning he awoke to find that the Osage representatives had gone home, taking with them the provisions, as well as all of the "hostages." Brucaiguais, the supposed culprit, was involved in a leadership dispute with another young Osage, Cashesegra. This party may have been willing to finger Brucaiguais because it was on Cashesegra's side. In any case, the supposedly "dying" Brucaiguais lived many more years. On other occasions, Osages brought hostages to answer for past offenses or as insurance against new ones, but these hostages were not the "chiefs" Osage representatives claimed them to be. At times they were not even Osage.[62]

After 1773, formal diplomacy and pardoning took place regularly at St. Louis and occasionally at the Arkansas Post, while quieter illegal trade continued along the Arkansas River. In the past, Osage bands had attacked native peoples on the Arkansas and Red rivers and *voyageurs* trespassing on Osage lands or attempting to ascend the Arkansas to trade with other peoples. Peace in St. Louis allowed the Osages to continue this policy throughout the Spanish period. Even when Spanish governors grew frustrated with the system and forbade trade, illegal trade continued. When sanctions failed and Osage delegations arrived to make amends, Spanish administrators always relented.[63]

*   *   *

Like the Quapaws, the Osages used their geographic and logistic advantages to recruit European trade and employ it in their relations with other Indians. But the Osages chose a far more ambitious path. As the eighteenth century progressed, they increasingly shaped European-Indian relations in the mid-continent. They isolated some peoples while integrating others, such as the Missouris and Quapaws, on Osage terms. Spanish colonialism was too ineffective even to prevent Osages from planting a British flag in the heart of Spanish St. Louis. In the eighteenth-century mid-continent, Osage, not European, sovereignty was dominant. The French and Spanish only maintained their colonial claims by appeasing the Osages.

The Osages became more deeply involved in the world market than the Quapaws. Foreign goods changed the extent of Osage hunting and provided new routes to power for young Osage men, although the council retained its influence for the time being. As hunting and warfare increased and the Osages became more dominant over and estranged from most of their neighbors, their ideas about themselves and the world must have transformed. While war and the hunt had informed Osage masculinity in earlier times, now the unprecedented success of both increased their importance. Men's valor had changed Osage history. While women's economic importance remained strong through preparing hides, working in hunting camps, and continuing to farm, their place probably became less central than in the past. Not all Osage descendants would take pride in their people's violent past. In his 1961 book, John Joseph Mathews lamented the "haughty insolence" that characterized his people "for a century and a half."[64]

Still, as Mathews recognized, the changes resulted from Osage choices. In a world rapidly being colonized by European powers, who would have liked nothing better than to subordinate Indians to their colonial states, the Osages conducted a successful policy of violence, both against their European would-be colonizers and their Indian neighbors. In the process, the Osages became the most powerful people in the region and established it as their native ground. To the south, the success of Osage policies of violence would soon pose serious challenges to Quapaw diplomacy.

Chapter 5
New Alliances, 1765–1800

In 1773, Quapaw leaders told the Spanish commandant of the Arkansas Post that they remained "very irritated at the Osages, because they are not good nor will they ever be." They pointed out that in the seven months since the Osage-Spanish peace agreement in St. Louis, the Osages had already robbed three hunting parties on the Arkansas River. The Quapaws had two problems. First, the Osages threatened to undermine Quapaw power. Previously, the Quapaws had maintained relatively friendly terms with the Osages. An Osage party had struck some Quapaws in 1751, but the two groups apparently healed their differences diplomatically, without the assistance of Europeans. The Quapaws and Osages occasionally even fought together. But by the mid-1760s, the Osages had become dangerously powerful, while the Quapaws' numbers had probably fallen under 1,000. The second problem involved the Spanish more directly. Although many French traders and settlers remained in the region after the Seven Years' War, the Quapaws' carefully cultivated and lucrative diplomatic relationship with France had ended. The Quapaws worried that Osage expansion and the loss of French officials might endanger their hold on the lower Arkansas. If the Osages became the sole recipients of Spanish presents and frightened off French traders, the Quapaws might lose access to the weapons that they needed to protect themselves.[1]

In danger of becoming isolated, the Quapaws adapted to changing times. In order to retain their native ground, they cultivated three new allies—the Spanish, Spain's British rivals, and their own erstwhile enemies the Chickasaws. The Chickasaws could be a powerful ally, and they could help the Quapaws to acquire British trade and alliance. In turn, alliance with the Chickasaws and British could help the Quapaws to persuade the Spanish to behave like good allies. From the moment of Spanish arrival, the Quapaws worked to persuade the Spanish not to favor the Osages but instead to conduct Quapaw diplomacy as the French government had. Thus, in case the Osages targeted the Quapaws, they would have strong allies. To appreciate

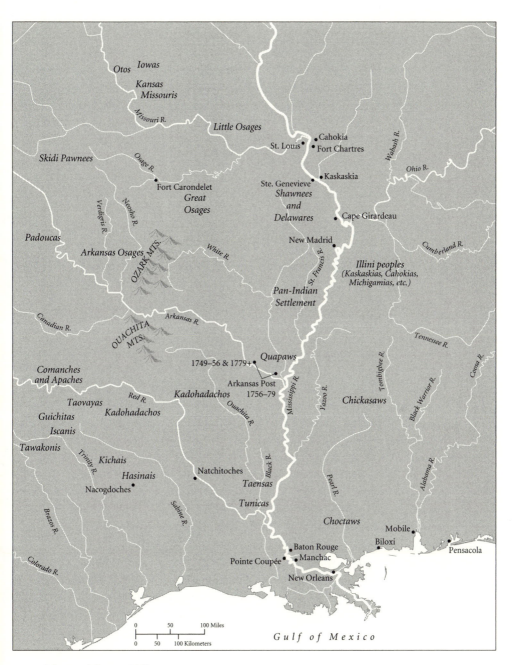

Map 4. Arkansas Valley, 1770s–1790s.

the Quapaw position, we must backtrack to the end of the Seven Years' War, the results of which spurred them to seek change.

*   *   *

Beginning in 1763, rumors circulated among the Quapaws that the French were leaving Louisiana. That July and the following year, delegations traveled to New Orleans to meet with Acting Governor Jean-Jacques-Blaise D'Abbadie, reconfirm the Quapaw-French alliance, and collect presents. He admitted that France had lost the war, but little else changed in the first few years. The Spanish took some time establishing themselves, so the French continued to staff Louisiana's forts.[2]

In 1766, Quapaw Great Chief Cazenonpoint learned from the French commandant of the Arkansas Post, Le Gros de la Grandcour, that the new Spanish Governor, Antonio de Ulloa, had finally arrived to take possession of Louisiana. Therefore, the commandant explained, he was now a Spanish employee, and Cazenonpoint's people should transfer their French alliance to Spain. Unsurprised, the chief promised to carry the Spanish "in his heart as he did all the French." The Quapaws expected to incorporate the Spanish into their kinship and trading patterns as they had French officials. They wanted the Spanish to take on French alliance responsibilities—ceremonial diplomacy and the requisite accompanying guns, gunpowder, ball, blankets, knives, and needles. For their part, the Quapaws offered knowledge of the land and its peoples and steady friendship in a contested place. As allies of the French for nearly a century, the Quapaws had clear expectations of what each alliance partner should provide.[3]

The Spanish quickly disappointed. To the Quapaws, forging an alliance with a new people required them to join in speeches, dances, and reciprocal gift-giving. Yet their new ally did not appear. Grandcour continued to command the Arkansas Post with his handful of French soldiers. The only change was negative. Gifts, which had increased during the war, stopped coming. Frustrated that no invitation arrived to seal the new alliance with the Spanish governor in New Orleans, Cazenonpoint took a delegation south anyway, as did many other native Louisianans. Despite the lack of invitation, the chief insisted that the governor pay the bills for the New Orleans visit, as his French predecessors had done. In New Orleans, Governor Ulloa paid for the unsolicited visit and promised the Quapaws annual presents.[4]

Unfortunately, unpaid French debts had greatly devalued paper currency. After paying for Indian visits to New Orleans, the governor lacked the funds to begin annual presents or even to pay his soldiers. These budget problems meant no gifts could be sent to the Arkansas Post. Spanish poverty seemed like disrespect to the Quapaws, who wanted goods both for their material value and as signs of friendship from their new ally. Local commandants found themselves trapped between, on the one hand, their superiors' orders to maintain peaceful and cheap relations with native peoples and, on the other, the reality of Indian expectations and power.[5]

Because qualified Spaniards were rare in 1760s Louisiana, the first three commandants were Frenchmen—Grandcour, Alexandre de Clouet, and François Desmazellières. On the surface, a frontier command was a profitable acquisition. A commandant could both trade with Indians and speculate by outfitting white and Indian hunters in exchange for liens on their goods. But because Spanish budgets were tight, a commandant had to draw on his own resources for Indian presents and hospitality to build the Spanish-Quapaw alliance on which his own safety and success depended. The more successful a commandant was at Indian relations, the less money he made from his position. While commandants found this reality frustrating, to Indians it made perfect sense. Skilled diplomats and leaders gave their wealth away.

The Quapaws immediately began instructing Spain's representatives regarding Quapaw requirements. At his first meeting with Clouet in February 1768, the Quapaw chief asked him to "remind" the governor that they had not yet received their annual present. If Clouet could not deliver, the chief offered to travel to New Orleans again to remind the governor himself. Clouet was a ten-year veteran of Louisiana politics and understood Indian power. Knowing that the supply ship had not even reached New Orleans, he gave the Quapaws goods from his own stores to appease them. In fact, he had to be so generous that he feared he would not have enough corn left to feed his soldiers.[6]

When the Quapaws complained that Spain was a stingy ally and threatened to desert to the British, Clouet gave presents and reassurances that Spain would prove as faithful and beneficial a friend as France. The commandant knew he needed the native peoples of the Arkansas River Valley if he wanted to protect New Spain from the British conquest that had overrun New France. He declined to enforce Spanish trade restrictions and repeatedly violated official policy limiting Indian presents. Keeping the Quapaws satisfied required irritating the governor, who reprimanded Clouet for using soldiers' supplies as Indian presents. Exasperated with the governor's lack of comprehension of local circumstances, the commandant carefully explained that in order to "continue to fulfill your intentions for the peace and tranquillity that I am to make reign among the red men . . . it is absolutely necessary to keep some goods in addition to the annual present for the operation of the post." Clouet knew that Louisiana depended on Indians and that Indian alliances required constant attention. He explained that "the Indians would indeed go to the British if I didn't give them presents from time to time."[7]

When the Quapaw town of Tourima's second chief died in 1769, the Quapaws sought the opportunity to teach the Spanish one of their responsibilities. With the French, the choosing of a new chief had been a time of ceremony and presents. Because Clouet was not a truly Spanish leader, the Quapaws proposed traveling to New Orleans so that the governor could ratify their chosen replacement, a man called Angaska. But the New Orleans rebellion was raging, and Clouet knew that the governor had fled, news that the Quapaws may also have heard. Clouet ratified the choice in the governor's name and promised that the governor would send a medal to Angaska and the other chiefs, who did not yet have Spanish replacements for their French medals. The commandant gave a gift to the dead chief's family and treated the mourners to some liquor. His violations of official policy were numerous—making promises without official approval, giving from the army's storehouse, and distributing liquor to Indians—but his letter to the new governor insisted that his methods were "of little expense to the King," compared with the cost of losing Quapaw friendship. Thus, Clouet sought a compromise to strengthen the Spanish-Quapaw alliance.[8]

In 1769, after quelling the rebellion, General Alejandro O'Reilly appointed a new commandant in the hope that he would rule with a stronger hand than Clouet. Governor O'Reilly expected the new Arkansas commandant, François Desmazellières, to impress and command the Indians of his jurisdiction, much as O'Reilly had cowed the French rebels in New Orleans. The governor ordered the commandant to make the Indians of the Arkansas River Valley "understand that they owe submission only to the King." The Spanish would continue the French practice of annual presents, but the Indians would "not receive another thing from the King's account."[9]

Moving quickly to instruct this latest commandant, the Quapaws told him that they had heard a rumor that "the Spanish would no longer give presents." This accusation particularly irritated Desmazellières because he had just hauled their annual present up the Mississippi. Regardless, he mitigated O'Reilly's imperious orders by reassuring the Quapaws that the friendship would continue as it had in the past and accepting their invitation to visit each of their towns. Prior experience in Indian diplomacy had taught Desmazellières the importance of flexibility and generosity. As a captain in the French Louisiana army since 1750, he had led supply missions between Canada and the Illinois country and frequently negotiated with Indians. At the Arkansas Post, he ignored the mandate to give no additional presents. He regularly distributed flour and rum to the Quapaws and to visiting Indian bands. "A couple of barrels [of rum] per year would satisfy the Indians," he assured O'Reilly pragmatically, "and would not cost a great sum." In the heart of Quapaw country, armed only with speeches, imposing Spanish rule was impossible.[10]

Nevertheless, the Quapaws were not pleased with the Spanish. They suspected, correctly, that Clouet's and Desmazellières's efforts were only stop-gap measures, not Spanish policy. The governors seemed disrespectful and imperious. The Quapaws complained and pointedly informed the Spanish that they were not following the French precedent. In October 1770, all the Quapaw leaders came to the post to tell Desmazellières that "when the country belonged to France," they had plenty of goods and good prices for their furs. In contrast, Spanish stinginess "made their young people do foolish things" because they did not even have "anything to cover themselves with." The French were wisely generous and fair; the Spanish risked trouble by providing bad prices and inferior merchandise.[11]

In pressing the Spanish to be the kind of ally the French had been, the Quapaws idealized the history of their relations with the French. It is not clear that the French government had been more generous. Like their Spanish successors, French administrators had repeatedly tried to curtail their Indian expenses. Once the budgetary crisis of the transition ebbed, the Spanish crown budgeted some 3,000 pesos annually in presents for Louisiana, 500 pesos of which went to the Quapaws, plus the commandant's un-reimbursed supplements. The Spanish gift was not a reduction from most years in French Louisiana. Before the war, French budgets for both sides of the Mississippi (double the number of Indians) had ranged from about 800 to 5,000 pesos. War against the British had increased the French budget for Indian presents, but even at the zenith, the budget equaled about 10,000 pesos, most of which supplied Indians fighting east of the Mississippi. The French regime, like the Spanish, was troubled by frequent shortages due to storms, administrative blunders, Chickasaw attacks, and low rivers. As with the Spanish, the Quapaws had frequently needed to remind the French to fulfill their alliance responsibilities.[12]

But when reminded, French officials usually compensated for lapses.

When the Quapaws seemed disgruntled, officials would pay them special attentions, as Governor Kerlérec had in 1753. In response to Quapaw dissatisfaction with their commandant, that governor had splendidly hosted Quapaw dignitaries in New Orleans. Because the French government did not institute rigid trade restrictions, trade flowed freely from individual *voyageurs.* Most French officials also knew when to be flexible to avoid endangering Indian alliances. For example, French officials seldom enforced the official ban on liquor sales to Indians. Lax enforcement pleased their allies and helped French traders compete with the British. Finally, officials throughout the French hierarchy verbally demonstrated respect for their allies. They accepted the Quapaws' self-created image as loyal partners worthy of special attention and respectful diplomacy. Indians had taught the French to be flexible in the service of perpetually reaffirmed relations.[13]

Grandcour, Clouet, and Desmazellières practiced these techniques, but it is not clear whether the Quapaws saw these men as French, Spanish, or something in between. It was clear to the Quapaws that the commandants' Spanish superiors viewed the relationship as little more than a bother. They did not send Spanish medals, which would have signified the chiefs' personal and the Quapaws' general importance to the Spanish. The governors' resistance to any meeting that might require presents further marred relations.

*   *   *

Viewing the Spanish as less reliable than their French predecessors, the Quapaws simultaneously forged new connections to the East with the Chickasaws and the British. After the Seven Years' War split Louisiana between Britain and Spain, the Mississippi River made a stark dividing line on European maps, a line that meant much less on the ground. Indians and Europeans continued to trade, hunt, forge alliances, and fight wars on both sides of the Mississippi. Because records do not exist from most Quapaw-Chickasaw diplomacy, it is hard to know exactly what sparked their alliance. The Osage threat certainly gave both a common worry. The French government's withdrawal enhanced the Quapaws' interest. France had supported them in their conflicts with the Chickasaws, but the Spanish and British usually discouraged Indian warfare on the Mississippi.

Whatever the impetus, in the 1760s and 1770s, Quapaw-Chickasaw relations steadily improved. They held peace talks and diplomatic ceremonies to establish and maintain their new relationship. The Quapaws offered the Chickasaws access to their hunting lands, which the Chickasaws valued as game declined east of the Mississippi. For the Quapaws, hunting with Chickasaws increased their strength in case of an Osage attack. The Quapaws brought promises of ties with the Spanish, while the Chickasaws could provide British links. Thus, both the Quapaws and Chickasaws could diversify their sources of goods, preventing either from becoming isolated should its main source of trade decline. In 1770, five or six Quapaw families settled east of the Mississippi, on Chickasaw lands, to strengthen ties between their peoples.[14]

The Chickasaw-Quapaw rapprochement led each side to share its friends with the other. The Chickasaws mediated between the Quapaws and the British. In 1765, as British troops prepared to occupy the formerly French posts in Illinois, Chickasaws and Choctaws promised their British allies that they would send delegations to the Quapaws asking that they not oppose British occupation. Better practitioners of Indian diplomacy than the Spanish, the Chickasaws and Choctaws surely brought presents to the Quapaws. Quapaw delegations carried calumets to British Natchez in 1766 through 1768, describing, with some exaggeration, the "many Presents" that the Spanish had given them. Under Chickasaw influence, the British began imagining the usefulness of the Quapaws as an ally. Southern District Superintendent for Indian Affairs John Stuart described the Quapaws as an important component of a British plan to protect their side of the Mississippi with a barrier of Indian allies against Spanish aggression. To encourage the alliance, Indian presents given out at Natchez included gorgets (large necklaces with engraved symbols of British alliance) for Quapaw leaders.[15]

The Quapaws understood both their value to the British and how much British recruitment frightened Spanish officials. Quapaw chiefs used their growing association with the Chickasaws and the British to compel the Spanish to be more compliant friends. Rather than hiding their new alliance, the chiefs regularly told Commandant Clouet that they would surrender their British gorgets if the Spanish would finally deliver their medals. If you "give us milk of Spain," the chiefs promised, "we will always listen to you" and not to the British. But they threatened that continued failure to provide goods and recognition would drive them into the arms of Spain's enemy.[16]

When Clouet's superiors failed to respond, the Quapaws asked a British merchant to build a trading post on the eastern bank of the Mississippi River, to provide easy access from the towns on the other side. Quapaws publicly rejoiced when construction began in the summer of 1768. They crowed to Commandant Clouet that "among the three fathers"—Spanish, French, and British—"there will be at least one who is not hardhearted toward his children, who must have milk." Mixing their parental metaphors, the Quapaws made it clear that the European role in their alliance was providing sustenance in the form of gifts.[17]

The Quapaws channeled their disgust with Spain's shortcomings into a greater willingness to ally and trade openly with Spain's enemy. To the Quapaws, the Spanish were doubly pathetic: too poor and stingy to provide worthy goods and too weak to keep out British traders. The French rebellion in New Orleans only increased these incursions. Ten British traders traveled to the Quapaw towns in February 1769, including a woman who established a tavern in one of the towns. Free from Spain's mercantilist restrictions and supply problems, they provided lower prices and plentiful trade goods, such as brass kettles, looking glasses, ribbons, hoes, thread, manufactured fabric and shirts, and rum. When the commandant protested this British establishment right under his nose, the Quapaws answered that if the Spanish should "continue to be poor," the Quapaws would find themselves "a more affluent friend."[18]

The British honeymoon soon ended for the Quapaws. To recruit new customers, British traders had lavishly dispensed goods on credit to Quapaw hunters, but by the late summer of 1769, the Quapaws had not notably increased their hunting, and they traded most of what they did hunt to their *voyageurs*, as they long had. The Quapaws' "affluent" friends became disappointed creditors. Neither Quapaw nor Spanish authorities had any incentive to help them collect. Also, O'Reilly's victory at New Orleans that July and his determination to rule Louisiana with a stronger hand made illegal trading less appealing. By September, the only Britons remaining in the Quapaw towns were the tavern owner and her husband, who, Commandant Clouet noted, "has reason to regret having listened to his wife and issued credit, for which he will never be paid."[19]

The sudden alteration in British generosity shocked the Quapaws. Offended by British traders, they turned to a British post commander. In August 1769, one of the Quapaw chiefs traveled to Fort Chartres on the British side of the Mississippi River. According to Clouet, the chief, "in the style of all the men of his color asked the commander for some evidence of his good will," in the form of presents. In the previous two years, this fort had spent far beyond its budget for Indian presents, incurring irritation from superiors in the British Empire, pressed themselves by Seven Years' War debt and colonial tax resistance. Having nothing to give, the commandant prevented the chief from entering the fort. The British officer may also have feared that hosting Indians from the Spanish side of the Mississippi would disturb the

peace with Spain. Throughout the late 1760s and 1770s, British officials debated whether it was more advantageous to respect Spain's right to Louisiana
or to undermine Spain by recruiting its allies.[20]

But the Quapaw chief expected respect from both British and Spanish
friends. Not only were British trade and presents in the Quapaws' interest,
but rejecting a potential friend was not the Quapaw way. Thus, the British
commander's refusal to welcome them seemed inexplicable and offensive.
Unable to get into the fort, these Quapaws forced other Britons to give them
goods. The chief and his men boarded two British barges on the Mississippi
and took some flour, a coat, and several hats. When Clouet learned of the
raid, he warned the chief that a British war would be in neither of their interests. The chief replied "very curtly" that the British had strained his patience.
According to the chief, British officials were inciting Chickasaw attacks on
French hunters north of the Arkansas River, perhaps threatening the nascent
Quapaw-Chickasaw alliance. The chief had plenty of bile for the Spanish as
well, accusing both European nations of being stingy with presents. Clouet
calmed the chief's agitation with several bottles of liquor.[21] In subsequent
meetings, the Quapaws assured Clouet that they preferred their "natural
father," the Spanish, to their "adopted one," the British, whose "milk could
dry up."[22]

In the meantime, the Quapaws were brokering an alliance between the
Spanish and Chickasaws. In 1770, Chickasaw Chief Paya Mataha, who had led
war parties against the Quapaws in the past, accepted a Spanish flag and
medal. Like the Quapaws with the British, the Chickasaws hinted to the
Spanish that they might be willing to move west of the Mississippi. Some
may have, but mainly for the purpose of keeping relations good with the
Quapaws.[23]

The Chickasaws and Quapaws also used their new alliance to share
Indian allies and to encourage common enmities. In 1770, the Chickasaws
brokered peace between the Quapaws and Choctaws, who then occasionally
joined hunts on the Arkansas River. The Quapaws discussed fighting the
Kickapoos with Paya Mataha in 1770. The *Pennsylvania Gazette* reported in
1772 that "the warlike Nation of the Arkansas [Quapaws] have determined to
join the Chickesaws, Shawanese and Cherokees, in a War against the Kickapoos, for killing some English Settlers on the Ohio and Mississippi," although clearly the Chickasaws had been recruiting allies because of attacks
on *Chickasaws*.[24] But that same year, some Quapaws told the Deputy Superintendent of Indian Affairs for Mississippi, John Thomas, that the French
had been recruiting them to join the Kickapoo side, and that the Spanish

were complicit because, as Thomas put it, "the outposts are commanded by French officers." After some presents, the Quapaws agreed again to join the Chickasaws, Shawnees, and Cherokees against the Kickapoos.[25]

In reality, the Quapaws fought none of these people. With another intra-European war appearing likely, it is possible that the Quapaws were looking to forge a much larger peace than simply with the Chickasaws and a few of their allies. According to a 1772 report, the Quapaws were encouraging the Creeks, Cherokees, and Illinois that if war broke out among Britain, Spain, and France, "all the red people is to be at peace," refusing to be drawn in.[26] The Cherokees apparently had other ideas. That same year, they apparently invited the Quapaws and Chickasaws to fight with them, but John Stuart was not sure against whom—maybe the Choctaws, maybe the Kickapoos, maybe the British.[27]

Whatever other coalitions they were forming, the Quapaws continued to work on their British alliance. In the early 1770s, they received medals and trade goods from Deputy Superintendent Thomas. The man leading this Quapaw effort was Chief Gran Migre, a name he may have earned for his migrations east of the Mississippi. Although he promised Commandant Desmazellières in October 1770 that he would make no more visits to Mobile, the next summer he traveled with a Chickasaw delegation to British Pensacola, where he received gifts including pictures of the British king and queen, the kind of alliance token than the Spanish had failed to provide. When Gran Migre returned to Quapaw lands, he spread the friendly messages of British and Chickasaw negotiators.[28]

Gran Migre was probably functioning as a *fanemingo*, or "squirrel king," a diplomatic office among the Chickasaws. When the Chickasaws forged peace with another people, each would adopt a fanemingo from the other side. As a fanemingo, Gran Migre would still live with his fellow Quapaws, but he would safeguard the calumet used to make the peace and would work to keep relations good between the new allies. If his fellow chiefs and warriors contemplated war against the Chickasaws, the fanemingo would work to dissuade them. If he failed, his office obligated him to warn Chickasaws of an impending attack. If Gran Migre was the Quapaw fanemingo for the Chickasaws, and perhaps for the British, Paya Mataha and perhaps John Thomas may have served parallel roles, each working for Quapaw interests among his own people. British officials certainly felt tempted by the idea of an ally within the Spanish empire. Thomas claimed that he could protect the British coast and maybe even capture New Orleans with Chickasaw and Quapaw forces. Charles Stuart, the Deputy Superintendent of Indian Affairs stationed at Mobile, interpreted the Quapaws' requests for a British flag and traders as evidence that the Spanish had not successfully supplanted the French.[29]

Chickasaw Chief Paya Mataha worked to seal the Quapaw-British alliance. At Mobile in 1771, he negotiated "a treaty of Friendship" between Quapaw and British officials. But apparently some resentment lingered. One Chickasaw reportedly called one of the Quapaw delegates a woman and spat rum in his face. Nonetheless, some thirty-five Quapaws came with Chickasaws to the second Mobile Congress the following January, even though British officials, who could not afford to host a large delegation, discouraged the Quapaws' attendance. At the second Congress, Paya Mataha symbolically presented the Quapaws' eagle feather calumet for the British to smoke, declaring, "this Calumet was given me by the Querpha Chief . . . in Token of Friendship." He asked the British to smoke and to keep the Calumet "as a memorial of the Faith mutually Pledged by my nation and the Querphas." John Stuart encouraged the delegates to beware of rebellious colonists and stand with the British. The Quapaws heard both Stuart's requests and southeastern Indians' complaints about unruly traders and settlers, but they also noticed the lack of presents, although the British officials promised to deliver some when their supplies increased.[30]

In the aftermath of the bloody and costly conflicts of the 1750s and 1760s and with the rising threat of rebellion in the East, Britain wanted to avoid war with Spain, which equally dreaded an expensive war. Local officials on the border between the empires sought to avoid conflict by agreeing which Indian allies belonged to which empire. In New Orleans in the early spring of 1772, Thomas met with Spanish Governor Unzaga. Apparently attempting to back out of his role as fanemingo, Thomas promised Unzaga not to give British medals to the Quapaws. In return, the governor agreed to take back the medals he had given the Tunicas, who lived on the "British" side of the Mississippi.[31]

In reality, an agreement between two European officials regarding Indian alignments carried no weight if Indians did not agree. Indian strategies rested on allying with multiple sources of European goods, and their diplomacy immediately rendered meaningless Thomas's and Unzaga's pact. After meeting with the governor in New Orleans, the Quapaw Great Chief and ninety-one other Quapaws dropped in on Thomas at Manchac, a British post south of Natchez. They described to him the "valuable quantity of presents" they had just received from Unzaga as well as from New Orleans merchants and planters, who had promised to send them a barge "loaded with presents," to encourage them to fight the British. This threat persuaded Thomas to abandon his agreement with Unzaga only a few days after they had made it and to resume his fanemingo responsibilities. He explained to John Stuart that only "strong arguments and good presents" managed to dissuade the Quapaws from declaring war on the British. More expenditures went to hosting their visit and provisioning them for the remainder of their trip (for which Governor Unzaga had surely also provisioned them). The Quapaw chiefs were "very loud" in their complaints that the British had reneged on their promise to send traders and presents, and they made Thomas pledge that in six months he would meet them at Manchac or Natchez, where they would bring all the principal chiefs and warriors and Thomas would present British medals.[32] Fearing that Thomas's diplomatic efforts with the Quapaws would spark war with Spain, his superiors suspended him from his position as Deputy Superintendent in June 1772. Being the Quapaws' fanemingo created a conflict of interest with his main job. Thomas's suspension disappointed the Quapaws. When the British interpreter gave them the news, they told him that they had planned to massacre the Spanish at the Arkansas Post that very night, but now would have to cancel their plans. They continued to try to meet with British officials to express their disappointment with both them and the Spanish. As Thomas explained, the Quapaws "are their own Masters, and not Subjects of or depending on *the King of Spain*," or anybody else.[33]

While the Quapaws and Chickasaws helped each other to build new friendships with other peoples, they reinforced the impression that the Osages were a threat. In 1772, rumors circulated among the British that the Quapaws and the Spanish were recruiting the Chickasaws to fight the Osages. Joint Quapaw-Chickasaw war parties went out. In 1775, thirty Chickasaws arrived to confer with the Quapaws about a joint attack on the Osages. A large war party of four chiefs and seventy Quapaw and Chickasaw warriors set out, after circulating a rumor that the Caddos (including the Kadohadachos and Hasinais) and some Wichita groups were going to join their party. They returned nine days later without having engaged the Osages, apparently having convinced the Osages to disperse. When Chickasaws and Quapaws did kill Osages, they sold the scalps to the Arkansas Post. But they certainly did not attack the Osages to please the Spanish. In April 1778, a Quapaw-Chickasaw party apparently thwarted a Spanish peace effort by attacking an Osage peace delegation.[34]

For the Quapaws, these new relationships served as a useful threat against the Spanish. When Desmazellières arrived in 1770, the chiefs urged him to be generous, explaining that his predecessor Clouet had forced them into the arms of the British by stifling trade and denying presents and that Desmazellières might do the same unless he gave them a drink every time they came to the post. The Quapaws regularly grumbled about the short-comings of the Spanish nation and occasionally threatened to desert the post entirely and move east of the Mississippi. In August 1770, some Quapaws told Desmazellières that they wanted to "strike down the first Spaniard that they could find." Fortunately for Spaniards, there were none to be found.[35]

* * *

Spanish governors did not blame their tight budgets or lack of hospitality for the Quapaws' dissatisfaction. Rather, they believed that if Indians were out of control, it was because their commandant needed to employ a firmer hand. Governor O'Reilly and his successor Unzaga repeatedly chided local com-mandants for giving in to the demand for presents when "sweet words re-garding the gentleness of our Government and its justice and fairness" were enough to persuade Indians that the Spanish knew their best interest. If commandants would patiently explain that chiefs were not allowed to visit New Orleans and that the presents would arrive eventually, Indians, like sen-sible children, would recognize and defer to Spanish wisdom and benevo-lence. In 1770, Governor Unzaga finally found a real Spanish officer surely up to the task.[36]

Fernando de Leyba had no experience running a frontier outpost or dealing with Indians. Born in Spain, he had come to Louisiana in August 1769 as a soldier in General O'Reilly's regiment, composed of outsiders brought to put down the French rebellion. Therefore, Leyba's first experiences in Louisiana were O'Reilly's demonstration of overwhelming might and his im-perial ceremony reinstating Spanish control over New Orleans. As an officer, Leyba knew how to lead soldiers and impress weak enemies but not how to juggle the lofty expectations of his superiors with the conflicting demands of the powerful players of the mid-continent. Having been in Louisiana for a mere year and a half, the new commandant had little or no experience with native peoples. While his experienced predecessors had ignored their superi-ors' ill-advised orders, Leyba believed in his mission to control the Indians and reduce expenditures. He soon found himself caught between the de-mands of a hierarchy that trained and rewarded him and the realities of local conditions, in which Indians held the upper hand.[37]

In Leyba, the Quapaws at last had a Spaniard with whom to confirm

Figure 8. Spanish peace medal. Spanish officials distributed these medals in the name of Carlos III. This side proclaims the king as "an excellent father." The other side commemorates the 1765 marriage between his son and Maria Louisa of Parma. Courtesy Jefferson National Expansion Memorial, St. Louis.

their alliance, but he instead confirmed their worst fears about Spanish intentions. Leyba finally brought a medal for Quapaw Great Chief Cazenonpoint to exchange for his old French one. But to the chief's shock, the Spanish medal was smaller than the French one. Cazenonpoint expected his new medal to symbolize both the Quapaw-Spanish alliance and Cazenonpoint's status as great chief. To the chief, the smaller medal indicated that Quapaw alliance meant less to the Spanish than it had to the French. And it was a personal insult as well. For Cazenonpoint to surrender a large for a small medal could be seen as a ritual of diminution, which would expose him to a ridicule fatal to his standing among his people. It was clear that the Spaniard did not understand the contingent nature of his own or Great Chief Cazenonpoint's authority.[38]

If Leyba had known that Cazenonpoint's displeasure could make his job as commandant nearly impossible, he might have ensured that the medal be a grandiose one. Grandcour, Clouet, and Desmazellières would have bestowed extra gifts on the chief to compensate for the deficiency or have apologized and promised to write the governor to request a more appropriate medal. Instead, Leyba made feeble attempts to persuade the chief that the size did not reflect Spain's estimation of him or his tribe. Rebuffing Leyba's flattery, Cazenonpoint demanded his French medal, which Leyba grudgingly returned.

Worse still, the guns that Leyba had brought to the post for the Quapaws were of poor quality, as he admitted in his report to the governor. Perhaps they had gotten wet and rusty on the trip across the Atlantic, or they may simply have been less well-made than French muskets. Cazenonpoint and the other chiefs accused Leyba of "disarming" them by giving them "useless" weapons. They predicted "that being defenseless the Spaniards or some other Nation of Indians could destroy them, and if this did not happen, they would kill one another off, because they would not have other ways of feeding their families." Leyba had thus made them vulnerable to attack or competition over scarce food, perhaps intentionally, they charged. Shoddy weaponry implied a weak alliance and "bad faith." Cazenonpoint and the other chiefs saw that Leyba, and Spain itself, had a lot to learn about making and keeping friends.[39]

Leyba viewed his attempts at hospitality differently from the chief. Leyba had entertained the Quapaws for several days following his arrival at the post. He hosted Cazenonpoint and other chiefs for several meals at his own table. On the 350 other visiting Quapaws, Leyba lavished a cow, a 280-pound barrel of flour (which he had to borrow from a *habitant*), and fifty-seven bottles of brandy. He believed that his expenditures were more than generous, given that his superiors had ordered him to economize, but Cazenonpoint kept taking offense. At one dinner, Leyba neglected to provide presents to the dozen men in the chief's retinue, so Cazenonpoint distributed food to them from Leyba's own table. After several days of these expensive dinners, Leyba tried to free himself from the obligation. He informed the chief that he was not invited to dinner that night because Leyba himself would not be eating. Incredulous and offended, the chief left without saying a word or giving Leyba his hand. He later declared to the interpreter that "it was impossible that [Leyba] was not planning to dine."

When Leyba protested to the Quapaws that the king's budget only provided for the annual presents, not for additional expenses, they replied simply that the king was "rich." In their first meetings with the Quapaws, Spanish officials had probably boasted of the wealth and size of their empire. The Quapaws turned these assertions back on the Spanish, asking why, then, did they insist on economizing. When Leyba tried to enforce his superiors' orders regarding economy in an overextended empire, the Quapaws saw stinginess and disrespect. When the Quapaws insisted on the obligatory symbols of their alliance, Leyba saw excessive and ungrateful demands.[40]

Following their disappointing first meeting with Leyba in the spring of 1771, Cazenonpoint and the other Quapaw chiefs spent a year showing the commandant that their people were essential to the maintenance of Spain's claims on Louisiana and Leyba's authority and safety at the post. Barely a month after Leyba's arrival, the Quapaws were seething. According to Leyba, they "breathed nothing but fury and disgust at Spain." Cazenonpoint was full of "various insults and even insolence." The Quapaws threatened to travel to New Orleans to demand that the governor replace Leyba with a French-born commandant.[41] They occasionally displayed their displeasure with violence. In November, a Quapaw man discovered that his horse was missing and blamed the Spanish. Brandishing his knife, the man declared, "I'm going to kill a Spaniard," then found and wounded one. Leyba's report to the governor acknowledged his own inability to arrest and punish the culprit "because of the lack of forces."[42]

In early 1772, Cazenonpoint traveled to New Orleans to ask the governor to appoint a new commandant. The chief charged that Leyba treated his people with "scorn," endangering the Quapaw-Spanish alliance. He reminded the governor that the British had been courting his people. Just as Leyba had earlier offended Cazenonpoint's sensibilities, the chief now violated Leyba's sense of propriety. By ignoring the Spanish chain of command and complaining to Leyba's superior, Cazenonpoint was undermining the commandant's authority just as the small medal had undermined Cazenonpoint's. The governor did not replace Leyba but promised the chief that in the future Leyba would be "all affability." His next letter to Leyba pointedly instructed him to be so, without, however, providing additional presents. Again, Leyba was trapped between Quapaw expectations and the constraints of his own superiors.[43]

Rather than acknowledging the Quapaw argument that Spain was not honoring its alliance, Leyba blamed French interpreters for turning the Quapaws against Spain. Indeed, the interpreters that Leyba relied on were the very men who had long lived with the Quapaws. They tended to put Quapaw interests, as well as their own, above those of the Spanish. In 1771, Leyba fired one interpreter and appointed a new one, Nicholas Labucière. Born in Marseilles, Labucière had been a French soldier assigned to the Arkansas Post in the last years of French Louisiana. When Spain acquired Louisiana, Frenchmen like Labucière lost their government positions and thus their livelihoods.

In 1763, the Quapaws invited Labucière to live in one of their towns, in part to work on his language skills. Quapaw training enabled Labucière to make himself valuable to the Spanish. In 1771, Leyba appointed him Quapaw interpreter, a position that paid a substantial ten pesos per month.[44]

The importance of the interpreter reveals the limits of Spanish power. Not only did Leyba depend on the Quapaws for peace on the frontier, he had to rely on a local Frenchman to communicate at all with Cazenonpoint. Within two months of appointing Labucière, Leyba fired him too. The commandant accused Labucière of speaking badly about the Spanish and consorting with the British. In the spring of 1772, the commandant heard rumors that British traders at Manchac were trying to recruit the deposed Labucière as their interpreter to attract more Quapaw business.[45]

Leyba felt that he needed to act quickly to prevent the British from gaining this advantage, but he knew that prosecuting Labucière for treason would infuriate the Quapaws, so he quietly arrested the interpreter one night and tried to sneak him out to New Orleans for trial. But Labucière called out to a passing Quapaw, "tell my father (the Great chief) what is happening to me, make him come help me." In response, Cazenonpoint came to the post with several warriors to declare that he had assembled his men in the forest, and that at his call, they would attack the post. After much negotiation, many presents, and more than sixty pesos for the chief, Cazenonpoint agreed that the interpreter could go to trial but that if he had not returned in three months, "the Post would be put to the knife." On his way home, Cazenonpoint sent one of his men back to the post, instructing him to bring him a barrel of brandy or Leyba's scalp. Leyba sent the brandy. These actions pointedly reminded Leyba that he was nearly alone, surrounded by Indians, and that angering the Quapaws could cost him his life. But Cazenonpoint did not resort to actual violence; he wanted to make the Spanish alliance more to his liking, not destroy it. Still, Leyba judged the threats so credible that he considered evacuating his wife and daughters from the post. To calm the Quapaws, Leyba distributed even more brandy, bread, and powder to them from his own stores.[46]

Leyba yielded to Quapaw power. He began to provide even more presents and be more patient and responsive to Quapaw demands. He recognized that "there is no other remedy" to his paradoxical situation than a paradoxical solution—to "give them more than what I am able to" and more than "any of my predecessors have given, since this colony was ours."[47] Leyba abandoned the policy of limiting gifts to the annual present. He succeeded in getting the 1773 annual presents delivered early, and the quality and quantity of the guns and other goods pleased the Quapaws. When Cazenonpoint received his part of the present, he apologized to Leyba for the "bad treatment" shown him. Chief Cazenonpoint admitted that he was, as Leyba recorded, "becoming ashamed . . . of the evil with which he had repaid me for the favors which I was continually giving him." Guatanika, the chief of the Quapaw town of Kappa, told Leyba that he was "improving every day." Others joined in the somewhat backhanded compliments. Cazenonpoint apparently decided that pressing for the return of the dishonored Labucière was not in the Quapaws' interest and let the matter rest.[48]

The Quapaws stopped talking to Leyba about British alliance, but their interactions east of the Mississippi continued. In early 1772, Gran Migre accepted a Spanish medal, but by May he was again making regular trips east in his role as fanemingo. In November 1773, Gran Migre apparently installed a British trader next door to him as his son-in-law, adopted son, and personal trader. The other chiefs denounced him to Leyba, but this may have been a ploy. In 1774, thirty-four Quapaws, possibly led by Gran Migre, proposed alliance to British West Florida Governor Peter Chester at Natchez, who hoped to get them to fight with the British and Chickasaws against the Creeks. Chester referred them to the reinstated Deputy Superintendent of Indian Affairs John Thomas, who this time declined because Superintendent John Stuart had warned him to refuse. Although the other Quapaw chiefs probably exaggerated their disapproval of Gran Migre, his work may have been controversial. According to Spanish reports, another Quapaw man killed Gran Migre in December 1775 when they were both drinking with a British party.[49]

When Great Chief Cazenonpoint died in the spring of 1773, the Quapaws chose his nine- or ten-year-old son as the new chief and asked Leyba to choose an interim chief. By extending this honor to Leyba, the Quapaws showed that they would meet their alliance obligations when the Spanish fulfilled theirs. Leyba's careful response demonstrated his awareness of the importance of showing respect to the Quapaws. He first graciously declined the offer. When the Quapaws continued to press him for assistance, Leyba convened the Quapaws. He cautiously offered the nomination of Guatanika and then polled each of those present to gain their approval. To celebrate and show his respect for the chiefs, Leyba threw a party for the people, distributed presents, and lowered the prices in his store. The commandant was now acting as a helpful and generous ally. He wielded some influence, but it was influence granted to him by the Quapaws, and he showed no signs of his previous imperious behavior.[50]

By demonstrating their power to go behind Leyba's back to his superior in New Orleans and to desert to the British, the Quapaw chiefs had persuaded Leyba of his limited power. He learned the importance of keeping them supplied with timely and substantial presents and treating them as indispensable friends rather than as subordinates or unreasonable supplicants. He recognized that, rather than carrying out his superiors' commands, he had to lobby them to meet Quapaw needs, in effect serving as the Quapaws' Spanish fanemingo.

In 1776, Governor Unzaga backed down from O'Reilly's policy and appointed a Frenchman as the next Arkansas commandant, Balthazár de Villiers. An experienced officer, Villiers knew the importance of Indian presents and rituals. He had come to Louisiana from France in 1749, a full twenty years before Leyba. During the French regime, Villiers had been an officer at Balize, at the mouth of the Mississippi. For nine years under the Spanish, he had commanded two posts in southern Louisiana, Natchitoches and Pointe Coupée. These posts were similar to the Arkansas Post in their small size and large number of Indian neighbors. In addition, Quapaws often hunted in these lands south of the Arkansas River, so they had met Villiers on several occasions.[51]

The new commandant arrived more aware of his limitations than Leyba had been. He knew that he would have to negotiate exaggerated official expectations, few local resources, and superior Indian numbers. Because he was French, his superiors would more closely scrutinize his performance. To cultivate Quapaw support, Villiers consistently and forcefully lobbied the Spanish governor to send goods to the Quapaws, and he regularly drew on his own stores as well to provide powder, ball, hatchets, blankets, salt, brandy, and other goods to Quapaw chiefs.[52]

Not confident in their new commandant's pliability, the Quapaws persistently pressured Villiers for the first couple of years. He privately called them "drunkards and rascals" who were "more trouble than they are worth." He despaired that the British might conquer Louisiana and then Mexico because of their ability to court the Quapaws and other Indians. He was certain that "these savages belong to whoever gives them presents" and that "receiving nothing or almost nothing from Spain they would go over to the English in a minute." He grumbled that such a small nation could compel burdensome gift-giving and continual "acquiescing to their importance." But the Quapaws were in charge, and Villiers did not complain to them.[53]

* * *

Between 1763 and 1780, the Quapaws and the Osages instructed Spanish officials in Indian expectations and power. The Spanish crown had intended to adopt French policy in Louisiana, but Spanish officials misunderstood how that policy had worked. They thought that the French had instructed Indians on how to behave and rewarded obedience with reasonable annual presents. The Spanish believed that negotiating with native peoples was simply a less costly way of conquering them. The Quapaws and Osages demonstrated that Spain was the weaker partner. Both drew the Spanish into an even more useful role than French officials had played. At the same time, both native peoples maintained their relations with French traders and settlers, often using them for purposes contrary to Spanish policies.

As the Quapaws and Osages pursued similar strategies with the Spanish, their relations with each other broke down. The Quapaws watched with alarm as Osage dominance grew in the lower valley. In the early 1770s, Quapaw parties patrolled their hunting lands to warn the Osages not to expand farther in their direction. When the Osages attacked Quapaws or their allies or ventured too close to Quapaw territory, the Quapaws sent out large war parties to threaten and sometimes engage the Osages, at an asking price from the Spanish of "powder, bullets, and six pesos for each Osage scalp." This sword-rattling only occasionally resulted in actual armed conflict. The Quapaws did not send war parties to attack the Osages high up the Arkansas or in the Osage towns, and they did not challenge Osage expansion outside of Quapaw hunting lands.[54]

There might have been no Quapaw-Osage tension had it not been for Quapaw friendships with *voyageurs* on the Arkansas. Many of the victims of Osage raids were these *voyageurs*, for whose safety the Quapaws felt some responsibility, as well as sorrow for their losses. Their French neighbors continually pressured the Quapaws to avenge Osage attacks. When Quapaw war parties did go out, French families hailed their return with embraces and thanks, calling them their "protectors and avengers."[55]

As their French fictive kin pressured the Quapaws to fight, the Quapaws persuaded Spanish commandants to support their forays. The Quapaws wanted the Spanish to supply and reward these raids, as the French had done in the Chickasaw War. But while the French had advocated war against the Chickasaws, the Spanish feared starting trouble with the Osages. In 1771, Cazenonpoint and Leyba made a deal. Leyba would host Osage-Quapaw peace negotiations. If the Quapaws and Osages accepted the peace terms, the Spanish would hold on to Osage hostages for as long as it took for the Quapaws to trust Osage sincerity. If the Osages would not agree to the terms, Leyba would not protest if the Quapaws and Caddos "destroy them."[56] However, before any Osages arrived at the negotiations, a French man returned

from upriver with the untimely news that Osages had killed his five companions and, by his estimate, "more than forty men who hid in different places
along the river are probably dead by now" because the Osages "have spread
blood and fire to all the river" and left "no place for them to hide."[57]

Quapaws struck back hard at Osage intrusions. In the spring of 1772,
Quapaws successfully attacked an Osage party, killing one and running the
rest off. Cazenonpoint and forty warriors presented the one scalp to Leyba,
who had to pay the increased price of 25 pesos in goods and brandy. Over the
following several years, the Quapaws sent out more war parties and hung
Osage scalps on the Spanish fort as a grisly warning to the Osages that the
Quapaws and Spanish were allied against them. In the spring of 1775, five Osages attempted to steal horses from the settlement that Michigameas and
other Illinois had established near the Quapaws in the 1750s. Indians in this
settlement killed three of the raiders, scared off the others, and brought the
scalps to the chief of the Quapaw town of Tourima, Angaska. Several Quapaw parties set out to seek the two Osages who had escaped. Encouraged by
Quapaw victories, Spanish officials began to push for all-out war, but the
Quapaws demurred. They followed their own interests, attacking the Osages
when they got too close, not when Spanish officials told them to. Indeed,
they often received Spanish arms by promising to engage the Osages, then
failed to fight. In 1775, joint Quapaw-Chickasaw parties went out against the
Osages but returned "because (according to those Nations) some of the warriors of the parties fell sick."[58]

Weary of funding Quapaw protection that did little to rein in Osage attacks farther west and south, the Spanish again proposed a Quapaw-Osage
peace. Historian Wendy St. Jean persuasively argues that Commandant
Villiers's fears of a Quapaw-Chickasaw-British alliance led him to urge a
Quapaw-Osage-Spanish one instead. If the Osages posed no threat, the Quapaws' need for allies east of the Mississippi would decline. But it was also
probably an Osage proposal—they certainly would not have come to negotiate simply to please the Spanish. After refusing several peace offers, the Quapaws finally agreed to hold a peace conference in 1777.[59]

That April, the Osages sent a delegation of five men and one woman
(there in part to show the group's peaceful intentions). Meeting with the
Spanish and Quapaws at the Arkansas Post, the chief of the delegation "cried
a great deal and deplored the actions that had been committed." In turn,
Quapaw Chief Guatanika "reproached him severely for their bad conduct."
With some rewriting of history, he declared that, "having taken up arms in
order to avenge the blood of their Spanish brothers, . . . they would have

never laid them down on their own," except that he knew that the Spanish governor "desired that all nations on his lands be tranquil and live in Peace." Guatanika warned the Osage chief that he had known the Osages to violate peace treaties and that this would be their last chance. In front of the Osage party, Villiers embraced the Quapaw chiefs as "our best friends and allies." Then all settled in for three hours of speeches, hand-shaking all around, and plenty of Villiers's food, drink, and presents. The commandant concluded that the Quapaws had emerged victorious: "Thus a handful of Indians have by their valor subjected a nation beyond comparison more numerous than they."[60] Villiers was impressed with the Quapaws, whom the Osages were asking for peace. The Quapaws had scolded them and dictated the terms.[61]

However, the Spanish desire to control trade undermined the truce before the year was out. In the peace negotiations, Villiers had promised the Osages an official trader on the Arkansas River. Governor Bernardo de Gálvez, who was appointed to succeed Unzaga in 1776, overturned Villiers's agreement. In a disastrous decision for the residents of the Arkansas Valley, he ordered Villiers not to send the trader. When the Osages arrived at the appointed place on the Arkansas River but did not find the promised trader, they sent a party of seven men to remind Villiers of his obligation. As this party traveled to the Arkansas Post, a large party of Taovayas, Guichitas, and Iscanis from the Red River attacked and killed five of them. The two survivors rushed back to report the treachery to the larger group of Osages, who subsequently robbed and killed the first people they encountered, three Frenchmen. Quapaw scouts reported to Villiers that the Osages displayed the French scalps prominently in their towns and that, nonetheless, St. Louis traders were continuing to trade with the Osages. Throughout 1777, Osage raiders repeatedly attacked French hunters and traders on the Arkansas. Both they and the Quapaws blamed the Spanish.[62]

After the failed Arkansas peace, Villiers got tough. In 1778, a party of twenty-five Osages pillaged on the river. When they came to the post to make excuses and get trade, Villiers "assembled as many men as I could," surrounded the Osages with "armed soldiers with every means to make them fear for their lives," and seized their arms. He asked the Quapaw chief who was present "why he was bringing me these dogs whose hands were still dripping with the blood of the King's subjects, and why he had not killed them." The chief replied that he had not wanted to attack the Osages without Spanish consent. Then Villiers put two of the Osages in irons. After three days, he returned only one to his comrades, instructing him, "I set you free to return to your village and tell your nation that I am holding your friend hostage, in shackles, and that I will not let him loose until you have brought me the principal leaders of the gang." Knowing Osage skills at diplomacy, Villiers demanded "unequivocal proof of their repentance."[63]

The Quapaws may have been impressed with Villiers's commanding exhibition, but they were weary of peace talks. When the Osages sent the leaders that Villiers had requested to the Arkansas Post, a party of Quapaws and Chickasaws attacked them, killing one. These were Quapaw lands, and Quapaws determined how to deal with intruders. In 1780, an Osage party visited the post in peace, then pillaged their way back up the Arkansas River, leaving two Frenchmen dead. By then, some *voyageurs* had been robbed ten times each and were deeply in debt for their losses. In response, the Quapaws sent out larger, more frequent, and more deadly war parties. In April, they killed at least twelve Osages, captured ten more, and took twenty-four horses. Quapaw raids were successful. By 1780, the Osages seem to have deferred to Quapaw sovereignty in the lower Arkansas River, while continuing their domination higher upriver and their expansion farther southwest. As involved as Europeans had become in the politics of the region, the disputes and decisions of the Osages, Quapaws, and Chickasaws were having the greatest effects.[64]

*   *   *

The revolt of Britain's American colonies in 1775 created problems for their neighbors on the continent, and the Arkansas Valley's Indians and Europeans felt its reverberations. Spanish King Carlos III was not inclined to support the overthrow of another colonial power, yet this could prove his best opportunity to challenge Britain. In 1778, he decided to join his ally France against the British. After the declaration of war, Louisiana Governor Bernardo de Gálvez ordered all British traders to leave Louisiana and seized their boats on the Mississippi. Spanish troops under the governor's command defeated the British at Manchac, Baton Rouge, and Natchez in 1779, Mobile in 1780, and finally Pensacola in May 1781, regaining the formerly French and Spanish posts.[65]

As the British retreated, the Quapaws moved to solidify Spanish relations. Angaska, the chief of the Quapaw town of Tourima, made a particularly public transformation. Chief Angaska had sporadically negotiated with the British and in the mid-1770s had accepted a British medal and flag, perhaps taking over Gran Migre's fanemingo duties. Soon after arriving at the Arkansas Post in 1776, Commandant Villiers had withheld Angaska's annual present, demanding that he surrender his British medal. The chief acquiesced, but soon was again meeting with the British. However, when war began, the chief renounced his British ties. Villiers and Angaska found themselves in similar situations. Although Commandant Villiers and Chief Angaska had important titles, they lacked coercive power. Over time, each man used the other to boost his legitimacy among his own people and with the other group. Having the ear of a powerful chief not only gave Villiers some influence among the Quapaws but also enhanced his reputation among his Spanish superiors as an expert at the tricky job of dealing with Louisiana Indians.[66]

In turn, Angaska used his relationship with Villiers to ensure that Spanish presents flowed steadily, to keep Spanish demands modest, and to gain legitimacy and rank among the Quapaws. When Villiers arrived, Guatanika was serving as interim great chief. But in the late 1770s, Cazenonpoint's son came of age. Believing that the young chief had too little influence among his people to serve Spain's interests, Villiers helped Angaska to rise to the position of great chief. It is not clear exactly how Villiers and Angaska succeeded. The chief of Kappa, not Tourima, usually served as the great chief. In an assembly, the commandant told the Quapaws that the deceased chief's young son was not capable of leading his people and that Angaska should be declared great chief instead. Villiers chose an opportune time to make the request. The Quapaws had come to the post to collect their presents, including needed arms. It is probable that many Quapaws were unhappy with the young chief as well and that Angaska had been maneuvering within the tribe for the position as great chief.[67]

While Angaska's and Villiers's action was unprecedented, it was not entirely beyond the bounds of Quapaw customs. Power within Quapaw society had to be earned and maintained, and seeking outside assistance toward those goals was not unusual. In 1752, French Commandant Paul Augustin Le Pelletier de La Houssaye had assisted in Guedelonguay's appointment. After Cazenonpoint's death, several Quapaw leaders had lobbied Leyba for his endorsement of them for interim chief. It also seems likely that the Quapaws let Villiers choose Angaska as "great chief" in part because of the shared nature of authority within their society. Angaska could be their liaison to Villiers and in charge of diplomatic relations without commanding power over the other village chiefs. Guatanika, for instance, remained chief of Kappa. In 1783, he and another chief refused to accompany Angaska on a scouting mission, indicating that Angaska's power within Quapaw society remained limited.[68]

Like the Quapaws, the Chickasaws found their multiple alliance strategy complicated by the American Revolution. While the British wanted the Chickasaws to scout and raid along the Mississippi, Ohio, and Tennessee rivers, most Chickasaws hoped to stay out of this Anglo civil war. Some Chickasaws regularly aggravated British fears by accepting Spanish medals in return for their British ones, then turning the Spanish medals over to the British in return for new British ones. In 1780, Chickasaws showed British Superintendent of Indian Affairs for the Mississippi District Alexander Cameron a letter from Governor Gálvez recruiting them. They assured Cameron that they were "still firm and loyal," but they clearly were also demonstrating that they had options. However, after Gálvez took British Natchez in 1779, Loyalists from there sought refuge among the Chickasaws, just as Natchez Indian refugees had fled from French, Quapaw, and Choctaw attacks to Chickasaw protection in the 1730s. At the same time that Britain's retreat increased Spain's importance for the Chickasaws, the presence of these Loyalists threatened to disrupt the fledgling alliance.[69]

The main irritant was James Colbert, a Scottish trader who lived in the Chickasaw nation and had fathered at least six children with three Chickasaw women. By the late 1770s, he and his sons and other relatives were raiding Spanish shipments on the Mississippi between St. Louis and the Arkansas Post, assisted by Chickasaw warriors and white and black refugees from Natchez. These raids disrupted commerce and endangered Spaniards, including the St. Louis commandant's wife, Anicanora Ramos, taken prisoner in 1782. Because some Chickasaws joined Colbert's forces and others fenced his stolen goods, some historians have portrayed him as the leader of the Chickasaws, an assumption that would have pleased him very much. But few if any Chickasaws regarded him as their leader. In 1770, one group had complained to British officials that white hunting parties, including James Colbert's, were intruders on their lands. These Chickasaws, at least, did not see Colbert as one of their own, much less their leader.[70]

As Gálvez's forces pushed the British east, the Chickasaws, Quapaws, and Spanish attempted to strengthen their alliance. As usual, the Quapaws mediated. Angaska carried Spanish flags to the Chickasaws in the early 1780s. But Colbert's raids threatened the alliance. Because of his Chickasaw connections and some Chickasaw participation, the Spanish associated his raids with the Chickasaws generally and expected Chickasaw alliance obligations to include cracking down on Colbert's party. When it became clear that Chickasaw leadership had no such power (and perhaps no such desire), each of the three groups found it in its interest to distinguish Colbert's raids from general Chickasaw policy. Natchez refugees in the 1730s had drawn the Chickasaws into war against peoples west of the Mississippi. All determined not to let Colbert do the same in the 1780s.[71]

The Spanish had two choices: accept the Chickasaw chiefs' explanation that Colbert's raids had nothing to do with them or fight the Chickasaw nation. In 1782, Esteban Miró, the man whom Governor Gálvez left in charge of Louisiana while he fought the British in West Florida, considered the latter choice: for a decisive attack on the Chickasaws, he would need 1,000 Spanish soldiers, 400 French *habitants*, 400 Indian allies, "many boats, . . . all the instruments of war, ammunition and provisions." With Louisiana's troops occupying West Florida, he had no hope of raising these forces or supplies.

Instead of war, the Spanish would accept the Chickasaws' disassociation from Colbert and attempt to use the Quapaws for a two-pronged strategy: strengthening the Chickasaw alliance and fighting Colbert's "Pirates." In Miró's plan, Quapaw chiefs should "invite the grand Chief of the [Chickasaws] to come and give me his hand in order to attract him to our side, and if I am not wholly successful in that, at least to induce him to keep his nation neutral." At the same time, Miró had an agent surreptitiously encourage Kickapoos and Mascoutins in the Illinois country to attack the Chickasaws in order to make Spanish alliance more necessary. The Spanish had learned to lower their ambitions in Louisiana. When O'Reilly was governor, he might have ordered local commandants to make the Chickasaws to stop raiding, or to get the Quapaws to fight them. In contrast, Miró's plan would require expenditures on hospitality and presents but would cost far less than war. Not only were Miró's means more modest, so too were his goals. He would not object if the Chickasaws accepted friendship and presents from the Spanish and the British, if only they would stay neutral in the war.[72]

The Quapaws and Chickasaws readily agreed to the diplomatic half of the plan. In the summer of 1782, Chickasaw delegates again traveled west of the Mississippi to confer with the Spanish in St. Louis, and they continued their Quapaw diplomacy. The Quapaws mustered less enthusiasm for the other part of Miró's plan, fighting Colbert's forces. Even though Chickasaw chiefs claimed Colbert acted on his own, his forces included Chickasaws. Even his sons, as members of Chickasaw matrilineages, were Chickasaw. Too strong a retaliation against Colbert could spark a Chickasaw war. The Quapaws refused to let Europeans and renegades destroy a decade of their own peace-building. Rather than follow Miró's plan, they avoided armed conflict, choosing instead less risky means of assisting the Spanish. Angaska led spy missions of Quapaws and *habitants* to see what Colbert was doing. In 1783,

Figure 9. Quapaw warriors. Armed with guns, bows, and arrows, these young men track an enemy and paint a symbol on a tree. From A. Antoine De Saint Gervais, *Nouvel album des peuples ou collection de tableaux* (Paris, 1835). Courtesy Library of Congress, Washington, D.C.

one of these parties captured an Anglo-American family whom they found on the Mississippi River without a passport. To show their affability, they offered to kill the children if the Spanish wished. The Quapaws would send out spies and capture non-threatening intruders but were not interested in angering the Chickasaws and risking their lives to protect Spanish convoys.[73]

Most Quapaws did not even fight when Colbert's forces attacked the Arkansas Post itself on April 17, 1783. The attacking force included Colbert's sons, at least sixty whites, a dozen Chickasaws, and a few blacks. To defend the post, Villiers's successor, Jacobo Du Breuil, could muster only thirty Spanish soldiers, the four Quapaws who happened to be in the fort that night, and a handful of neighboring *habitants*. To defend his post against its more numerous assailants, Du Breuil hatched a daring plan, rooted in his knowledge of white men's conceptions of Indians. The commandant sent out a detachment of fifteen soldiers and ordered them to "yell like attacking Indians." Scared that the Quapaws were coming, Colbert's men fled, yelling, *"run run they have Indians!"* Having regrouped east of the post, the attackers sent one of the prisoners whom they had taken, Maria Luisa Valé, with a message that warned the commandant that if he sent the Quapaws against them, they would kill the remaining prisoners. Despite the warning, one of the four Quapaws in the fort ran into their midst to "plant a hatchet in the ground in the middle of them." Imagining hundreds of hatchet-bearing Quapaw warriors, Colbert's forces took the prisoners they had captured and "embarked on their boats and kept going all night notwithstanding a heavy rain" until they reached the east bank of the Mississippi.[74]

Despite this one Quapaw's act of heroism, most Quapaws did not feel that defending the Spanish from other Europeans was their responsibility. During the attack, Du Breuil sent a messenger to the nearest Quapaw town, Kappa, asking for help. Kappa's Chief Guatanika answered that it was "not his job to help the Whites make War on one another."[75] Furious, Du Breuil confronted Angaska the next day. The great chief explained that once he learned of the attack, he tried to assemble his warriors but could not because "they were scattered in the mountains, some hunting[,] others seeking rations to sustain their families" because that year's harvest "had failed entirely." It had indeed been a bad year, and food was short for everyone in the region. But Guatanika, at least, had been less than a mile away and knew that the battle was raging. At the heart of the Quapaws' inaction lay the refusal to define their friendship with the Spanish as a military alliance. Even if Angaska wanted to assemble warriors, the majority of Quapaws agreed with Guatanika. They did not feel obligated to defend their Spanish friends against British and Chickasaw fighters, who were Spanish enemies, not Quapaw ones.[76]

Chief Angaska, as usual, found a less dangerous way to defuse Spanish anger. The day after the attack, Angaska crossed the Mississippi with 100 Quapaws and twenty Spanish soldiers. According to Du Breuil, Angaska took the large force "so that after rescuing all of our people they could fall upon the enemy." But the chief did not intend to start a fight. Rather, he used his diplomatic skills to full effect. He left his men behind and confronted the opposition alone. Angaska informed Colbert that he had brought 250 men with him (twice his true force) to "come looking for all of the prisoners." According to Angaska, Colbert instantly surrendered Lieutenant Villars (Maria Luisa Valé's husband) and most of the other prisoners. Villars and Angaska tried to persuade Colbert to release the remaining prisoners: four soldiers, the son of a *habitant,* and three slaves. When Colbert refused, the chief and the lieutenant took the released prisoners home and gave up on the others. Without a potentially destructive engagement, Angaska rescued most of the prisoners. When a war party of eighty French *habitants* and Spanish soldiers engaged Colbert's forces a month later, only four Quapaws joined them.[77]

Although Du Breuil grumbled at the Quapaws' failure to defend the post or Spanish convoys on the Mississippi, he was powerless to coerce them. The commandant felt certain that the Quapaw shortcomings were not a result of his failure to nurture their friendship with goods. He alleged that "never have they seen themselves so entertained, showered with Gifts[;] they themselves admit it." But the commandant knew that the Quapaws had the power to define the nature of their relationship. He concluded that "if I had more Forces I might be able to conduct myself otherwise." As conditions stood, he had to acknowledge the return of most of the prisoners with gifts and words of thanks, surely through clenched teeth.[78]

The Quapaws profited from these affairs with little risk. Between January and April 1783, the Quapaws received 157 pounds of powder and 314 pounds of musket balls for military expeditions, yet there is no evidence that they fired a single shot in battle. For Angaska's sortie to rescue the prisoners, Du Breuil gave each of the 100 Quapaw soldiers a pound of powder and two pounds of balls. In contrast, each of the Spanish soldiers received a half pound of powder and a pound of balls. For the soldiers, it was a supply for battle; for the Quapaws, it was a supply plus a payment for helping the Spanish to rescue *their* prisoners. Angaska's diplomacy left the Quapaws supplied with 100 pounds of powder and 200 pounds of balls, to use entirely for their own purposes.[79]

Chickasaws and Quapaws worked together to distance the Chickasaws from Colbert in the minds of the Spanish. In August, his forces attacked a group of French hunters on the White River, killing at least two and taking all of their pelts from eight months of hunting. In response, Chickasaw chiefs sent a Quapaw emissary to tell Du Breuil that "those who committed those hostilities were the followers of Colbert" and that the Chickasaws refused to receive his forces in their towns "because of the crimes they had committed." Later that August, a Chickasaw delegation came to the Arkansas Post to, as Du Breuil recorded, "ratify the peace that their Great Chief had resolved to establish forever with the Spanish." The ambassadors assured Du Breuil that "except for Colbert's family, all were very satisfied with the new friendship which they had contracted, and that they saw clearly that all the promises of Colbert had never been anything but lies." According to them, Colbert depicted the Spanish as abusive and deceitful and assured them that the British would return to resume the war, but the Chickasaws saw through his deceptions. The Spanish accepted the Chickasaws' explanations. Du Breuil gave them presents "to destroy the bad impressions that Colbert wants to give of Our Government." It remained in the Spanish interest to view Colbert as an isolated enemy and the Chickasaws and Quapaws as reliable friends.[80]

On June 23, 1784, a Chickasaw delegation made a formal peace with Spain, specifically naming the Quapaws as one of the nations they would in future live with "in the most perfect union" of "Peace and friendship." Although they certainly did not take responsibility for Colbert's raids, they promised to use "all possible means" of "preventing the Piracies that the white and Indian vagabonds regularly commit up the Mississippi River." In return for their promise to trade with no other white men, the Spanish guaranteed the Chickasaws "permanent and unalterable Commerce at the fairest prices."[81]

In the heart of North America, Indian-European alliances were unequal partnerships in which the Spanish gave presents and respect and participated in necessary ceremonies. In return, they could maintain enough of a presence in Louisiana to threaten other Europeans. The compromise worked. Through the 1790s, Anglo-Americans viewed the Spanish alliance system as formidable. Each non-Indian nation believed that Indians were such a potential menace if allowed to fall into a rival European alliance, that simply securing them, even if passively, in one's own alliance was worth the trouble and cost. Europeans designed this trap for themselves. Indians were numerous and militarily powerful, but they were seldom, if ever, under the command of European military strategists. Each non-Indian power knew that it could not mobilize the Indians living in its jurisdictions, but each suspected that the others did hold such power over their own Indian allies.

* * *

The Spanish had come a long way in the short time since Leyba's command and were finally learning the rules of the native ground, much to the benefit of their empire. Indeed, at the end of the Revolution, Spain held the formerly British posts on the eastern bank of the Mississippi and claimed lands from the Ohio River to the Gulf, as far east as the Flint River in Georgia. The man who implemented Spain's policy for these eastern lands was Louisiana

Governor and hero of the battles of the Gulf Coast, Bernardo de Gálvez. To secure West Florida, Gálvez recruited Indian allies, applying the principles of friendship that he had learned in Louisiana to native peoples across the Southeast, including the Creeks, Choctaws, and Cherokees.[82]

In 1785, Gálvez succeeded his father as Viceroy of New Spain, inheriting a jurisdiction that stretched from southern Mexico to the Canadian border and from the Californias to Cuba. Gálvez drew on the education that the Quapaws, Osages, and others in Louisiana had given him and his subordinates over the past decade to devise a more consistent and realistic Indian policy for northern New Spain. As governor of Louisiana, he had written to his uncle, the secretary of state: "The knowledge which I have acquired since I have been in this colony . . . impels me to desire that in our other establishments they should be treated in the same way." He concluded that keeping Indians "friendly by means of presents" was the way for the King to "keep them very contented for ten years with what he spends in one year in making war upon them." To Gálvez, Indians raided because they could not get what they wanted otherwise. The solution was to provide them with those things so that they would not make war—horses, mules, guns, powder, and other manufactured goods such as cloth, paint, and ornaments. Gálvez's short-term goal was friendship; his long-term goal was the same as the king's, dominance. If native peoples grew dependent on Spanish trade, they would "forget how to make war upon us" and would eventually be "unable to do without us." "Accustomed to guns and powder," they would forget how to make and use bows and arrows and become dependent on European goods.[83]

But the Quapaws had no intention of becoming dependent on one ally; in fact, the prospects of many Indians from the East depended on them. The outcome of the American Revolution had created more willing immigrants. Like the Spanish, Indians who had fought against the American colonists' rebellion did not accept domination and invasion based on the Treaty of Paris, to which they had not been party. After the Revolution ended, Shawnees, Delawares (a group forced out of the mid-Atlantic colonies), Miamis, Abenakis, and other Indians in the Ohio Valley continued the fight after Britain and its colonies made peace, winning major victories over the United States Army until demoralized at the Battle of Fallen Timbers in 1794. In the Treaty of Greenville the following year, the nations of the Ohio Valley made peace, ceding vast lands that would become the state of Ohio and parts of Michigan, Indiana, and Illinois.

The traumas of war and the aftermath of land cessions drove many people in the Ohio Valley and throughout the East to seek a safer life west of the Mississippi. In the 1770s and 1780s, Chickasaws, Choctaws, and Cherokees increasingly hunted along the Arkansas, and some Delawares and Shawnees moved to Cape Girardeau, Missouri, south of St. Louis. In the 1790s, this settlement increased, and Cherokees, Shawnees, Miamis, Abenakis, and some Illinois, including Kaskaskias and Peorias, settled on the St. Francis River, not far from the remains of Pacaha. After the turn of the century, some of these Cherokees moved south to the Arkansas River, at the invitation of the Quapaws.[84]

These immigrants discovered that they would have to comply with Quapaw and Spanish desires and practices if they wanted opportunities in the mid-continent. An early contingent of Kaskaskias requested permission to move to the White River, but the Quapaws and Spaniards insisted that they settle closer by, on the Arkansas River, presumably where they could be better observed and controlled. In 1787, a small party of Abenakis arrived at the Arkansas Post to trade pelts for brandy and other goods. According to later reports, they tarried to drink with some Quapaws. At some point in the evening, a fight broke out, and some of the Abenakis beat two Quapaws "so severely that one of them died that night, and the other was a long time sick and near death." By giving out presents and commiserating over the deleterious effects of alcohol on judgment, Commandant Du Breuil managed to dissuade the Quapaws from vengeance, at least long enough for the Abenakis to escape, and he declared that no alcohol should be sold to the Abenakis or Quapaws until they patched up their differences. Not wanting to lose their newfound trading opportunities on the Arkansas, an Abenaki delegation arrived that May to make peace with the Quapaws.[85]

What happened next illuminates the role that African slaves played in cross-cultural relations, a role that rarely made it into commandants' reports. The Spanish trader who had earlier provided the brandy heard of the Abenakis' coming and illegally sent Luis and Cesar, the slaves who helped him run his business, to trade with the delegation before it arrived. Luis was a Catholic native of New Orleans who, in his twenty years, had learned Indian languages, including one that allowed him to speak with the Abenakis. He and thirty-year-old Cesar sold them two flasks of brandy and a keg of rum. As a result, the party that intended to come in peace "became drunk and arrived at this post," threatening several Quapaws who were there. After the Quapaws killed one Abenaki, the others retreated. Under subsequent questioning from the new commandant, Josef Bernard Valliere d'Hauterive, Luis and Cesar both admitted that they knew of the order not to trade liquor but reminded Valliere that, as Cesar testified, "he is a slave, and is compelled to do what his master tells him to do." This glimpse of the lives of Luis and Cesar—negotiating with Indians, trading illegally, and using their enslaved status to avoid punishment—gives us a hint of the complications of the Arkansas Valley that the sources rarely provide.[86]

After sobering up, the Abenakis tried to heal relations with the Quapaws. After negotiating their own peace, the Quapaws escorted them to the Arkansas Post, where the Abenaki chief exchanged his British medal for a Spanish one. Presumably with Quapaw approval, the Abenakis discussed going to meet with the Osages as well, because they wanted to settle on lands northwest of the Quapaw towns. Certainly getting Osage approval for their settlement would make it more viable. However, something soon went wrong again. Two years later, Valliere and Chief Guatanika denied groups of Abenakis and Miamis use of the Arkansas River. Guatanika told their messengers, "I do not want you to come on our land; there is plenty of it elsewhere." Fearing that these rivals might ally with the Caddos and subvert Quapaw control of the lower Arkansas, he proposed to the Caddos that neither ally with "foreign" Indians, or there might be a Caddo-Quapaw war.[87]

As circumstances for Indians in the East worsened, the requests continued. In January 1790, a Miami chief called Pacane and his Miami and Illinois followers fled west after a Kentucky militia raid killed some of their kinsmen. Their plight became more complicated because a large party of Chickasaws who had recently killed three Illinois and captured four others simultaneously arrived at the Quapaw towns. The Quapaws were such skilled diplomats that it is difficult to discern their motives or even their actions from Spanish documents. Clearly, they sought to balance their Chickasaw allies' wishes, Spanish desires that everyone be at peace, and their own need to preserve control over their lands and game. On hearing of the Chickasaws' arrival, Pacane's band sought Spanish protection at the Arkansas Post. Apparently trying to keep the peace, Quapaw chiefs led three Chickasaw chiefs—Tanapea, Coolabe, and Pani Mata—to the post to meet with Valliere. Tanapea explained that they had attacked the Illinois because "the Illinois had killed two of his brothers." He gave Valliere the four Illinois captives but then pointedly remarked that Quapaws had offered ten horses for them. Desperately trying to keep the peace, Valliere gave the chiefs an astonishingly large gift: "fifteen white blankets, eight of [a fine wool], fifteen shirts, two pounds of vermilion dye, four small barrels of rum, thirty pounds of powder, sixty of ball, twenty-four knives, twelve mirrors, three rolls of tobacco" and "five days' rations" for the sixty-seven visiting Chickasaws. In addition to getting the captives, Pacane's band also received gifts, as did the freed captives themselves. Everyone satisfied, and Valliere considerably poorer, Pacane surrendered his British medal in return for a Spanish one, and the Quapaw and Chickasaw chiefs "gave him the usual honors, with which he was well-pleased."[88]

Nevertheless, the Quapaws did not want these prospective settlers. Later that month, a Chickasaw and Quapaw war party chased some Illinois into Caddo territory and killed several. Pacane himself settled near Ste. Geneviève but kept seeking to move to the lower Arkansas. The Quapaws continued to block him from settling on Quapaw lands or farther upstream. That summer, when the latest commandant, Captain Juan Ignace Delino de Chalmette, asked the Quapaws why they were preventing Miamis and Illinois from passing through to settle on Caddo lands, the Quapaws replied that, on the contrary, they had "received them into their villages, giving them everything they needed" and had "never had the slightest difficulty with them." In fact, they insisted, they "never did anything without its having been dictated by the commandant of this post." Whether the Quapaws intended their remark sarcastically or not, they were clearly following their own agendas. Their Chickasaw and Spanish alliances worked to maintain their own dominance in the region. The Chickasaws offered powerful assistance in warfare and diplomacy, and the Quapaws were glad to hunt with them for the abundant game of the lower Arkansas River. The Spanish provided important goods and asked little in return. In contrast, permanent settlers allied with the Caddos were too dangerous.[89]

*   *   *

With these new arrivals, the lower Arkansas Valley might have become more like the "middle ground" of the Great Lakes, where a mélange of refugees forged common practices, interests, and even identity from their mutual positions of weakness. Like the refugees who fled to that region in the seventeenth century, these newcomers were escaping enemy attacks and declining resources in their homelands. The difference between the Great Lakes middle ground and the Arkansas Valley's successive and contested native grounds was that the resident peoples had already established precedents for integrating (or rejecting) new arrivals. The Quapaws shaped new Indians' and Europeans' impressions of the region and persuaded them that Quapaw approval and methods were essential to peace. Their evolving methods do show the influence of their decades of relations with Europeans. The Quapaws, the

Chickasaws, and the newcomers acknowledged a legitimacy that Spanish medals and ceremonies conveyed for establishing a group's right to live and hunt in Arkansas. Chief Pacane came to the Arkansas Post because he wanted protection and the return of his captives. The Chickasaws came to sell their Illinois prisoners for the highest possible price. Still, Spanish approval was not enough. These were Quapaw lands. The French, Spanish, Chickasaws, Choctaws, and Cherokees served Quapaw needs and played by Quapaw rules. The Miamis and Abenakis, too cozy with the Caddos, were not welcome. For the Quapaws, their home remained their native ground.

The Quapaws adapted to changing times in order to maintain this native ground. By the 1790s, they had forged strong connections with the Spanish and Chickasaws. Through diplomacy and a few uncharacteristic but impressive military confrontations on their own territory, they had held back Osage incursions. The Spanish found that Indian borders held more force than European-defined ones. Like the Osages, the Quapaws not only persuaded the Spanish to conduct diplomacy as the French had but constructed an idealized version of French generosity and persuaded the Spanish to emulate that fiction. Spaniards' aims of colonial control failed, yet following Indian dictates provided them with a fairly stable hold on the heart of the continent. Although sometimes rocky, new relationships helped the Quapaws to maintain their position on the Arkansas River. As new Indian and European allies strengthened their friendships and mutual security, their thoughts began to turn to a joint war against the region's greatest power, the Osages.

Chapter 6
Better at Making Peace Than War, *1790–1808*

In 1790, a group of Delaware Indians arrived on foot at the French settlement of Ste. Geneviève, on the Mississippi River between St. Louis and the Arkansas Post. They carried their saddles, vividly demonstrating that an Osage band had stolen their horses. Many Indians and Europeans were suffering from Osage violence. The Delawares, Shawnees, Miamis, Illinois, Abenakis, Chickasaws, and Choctaws—beginning to hunt and settle in Louisiana as game diminished and settlers increased in the East—found that Osage attacks endangered their plans. The Osages occasionally raided French settlements, including Ste. Geneviève, whose people well understood the Delawares' frustration. French traders feared for their lives every time they went upriver. The Caddo and the Wichita peoples had lost their homelands and were continuing to suffer Osage attacks even after moving south to the Red River. On the lower Arkansas, the Quapaw Indians sometimes clashed with the Osages. Finally, the Spanish soldiers and officials who had to hear all of their neighbors' complaints about Osage violence would very much have liked to establish control over that troublesome people.[1]

Despite this common goal, the connections established in the region provided no precedent or structure for forming such a coalition. Most people who had moved to the Arkansas Valley since the mid-1600s legitimated their rights there based on alliance with the Quapaws, who in turn used their alliances to bolster their own legitimacy and security. They forged and maintained friendships, which fostered exchange. Exchange enhanced security by providing weapons, either directly from Europeans or through Indians with European trading connections. The customs that the Quapaws had imposed on their native ground worked well for making peace but faltered when the object was war.

Unlike their Mississippian predecessors, the Quapaws placed a greater value on peace than war, and their system did not provide a means of compelling allies to fight a common enemy. The various peoples had methods of inducing their own people to fight. With varying degrees of success, European officials could command their soldiers, and native societies could incite their warriors to an agreed-upon battle. But attempts at sustained war had generally failed. This lack of military unity would prevent a common war in the 1790s against the Osages, even though the other peoples of the region defined them as a common enemy. It would prove even less feasible to mount a military challenge to the next expansionist power, the United States, which at the dawn of the nineteenth century seemed much less threatening than the Osages.

*   *   *

Most neighbors of the Osages wanted to make war on them. In 1790, a group of Peorias, Shawnees, and others living between the Quapaws and St. Louis complained to Spanish officials of Osage attacks. The Shawnees threatened that if conditions did not improve, they would move back across the Mississippi and forge an alliance with the United States against the Spanish. Victims of Osage attacks as well, Ste. Geneviève's French residents added their voices to the call for action.[2]

Governor Miró's successor, François Luis Hector, Barón de Carondelet, was willing. He instructed his commandants in 1792 to arm Indian nations, including the Quapaws, Caddos, Chickasaws, Choctaws, and French hunters to fight the Osages in order to "finish with them once and for all."[3] Carondelet proclaimed that "any subject of His Majesty, or individual of the other nations, white or red, may overrun the Great and Little Osages, kill them and destroy their families, as they are disturbers of the prosperity of all the nations." He believed it necessary "to humiliate or destroy those barbarians," who were the enemy of all Spain's friends.[4] He ordered "a general expedition against the Osages" from Arkansas, St. Louis, New Madrid, and Natchitoches, led by the Quapaws. Heady from his victories serving under Gálvez's command in West Florida and light on colonial experience, the new governor had not yet absorbed the lessons of the native ground. Of Flemish ancestry, Carondelet had been the governor of San Salvador, Guatamala, where Indians had significantly smaller numbers and less power than in Louisiana. For his grand plans to destroy the Osages, Carondelet budgeted no expenses but powder and ball.[5]

Orders alone would do little to commence war. Indians expected Spanish troops to fight alongside them and Spanish officials to supply guns, ammunition, and food not only for the expeditions but also for defending their homes against inevitable Osage reprisals. But the Spanish did not have troops to spare and could not afford the necessary supplies. Indians insisted that, at the very least, traders had to stop providing the Osages with weapons. Otherwise, they said, war against the heavily-armed Osages would be suicide. The Spanish government agreed to ban trade with the Osages. If goods had stopped reaching the Osages, they might have become isolated and vulnerable; however, those who profited from the Osage trade protected it. Every time the governor banned trade, influential St. Louis merchants lobbied hard to reinstate it. Local Spanish officials generally agreed, because they made money from licensing traders. When trade with the Osages was forbidden, their traders did not buy licenses.[6]

The Spanish government did sporadically crack down on official trade, but illicit trade continued unabated on the Missouri and especially the Arkansas rivers. An Osage woman testified that ten barges of goods had arrived at the Osage towns in the summer of 1792, during an Osage trade ban. Trade with the Osages was simply too valuable. During the 1790s the Arkansas Post trade with the Osages alone was worth four times the local settlers' entire agricultural output. Osage trade was similarly important to St. Louis, where the lieutenant governor called their trade the best at the post. A colony dependent on the fur trade was not likely to stop trading with its most profitable partner.[7]

Even if the Spanish could have stopped all trading with the Osages, the embargo could not be as effective as their native allies wished. The Osages could simply take what they needed. When official trade slowed, the Osages increased their raids on *voyageurs* supplying other Indian nations. If these traders were abiding by trade sanctions and not delivering to the Osage towns, an Osage party was likely to stop them and strip them of all their goods. And the Osages had another source of European goods, British traders from Canada, who eagerly traded behind the back of their Spanish enemy. With fewer than 1,000 troops spread over all of Louisiana—about one soldier for every 200 square miles—Spanish officials could do little to enforce trade policy.[8]

Spain's Indian allies were disgusted at the ineffective embargo. A Chickasaw man named Thomas conveyed the frustration of many when he reminded the Spanish that they "had closed all the roads and had forbidden the white men to carry goods into their villages" so that they could strike the Osages without fear. Yet, Thomas charged, the Osages were "well clad in new blankets" and well-supplied with new guns because goods were pouring into their villages. Thomas explained that St. Louis traders "take guns, powder, and ball to the Osages and buy from them all this booty which they steal from the Spaniards and red men on the rivers and . . . they kill all the whites of Natchitoches and Arkansas and all the red men of this region who cannot hunt without being killed or plundered by the Osages." "Ah! my father," Thomas continued, "if the great chief of New Orleans had all those who carry goods to the Osages killed, there would be no one to carry [them] and . . . we could plan to attack their village."[9]

When the Spanish reprimanded their allies for not fighting the Osages, Thomas and others in turn blamed the Spanish for allowing traders to give an enemy the trade goods that only friends deserved. Indians would fight the Osages, Thomas said, if Europeans would stop giving them weapons. At Cape Girardeau, Miami Chief Pacane accused Europeans of only following their own interests and love of money. A Caddo chief charged the Spanish with failure to "treat the Osages as enemies."[10] One can imagine the growing reluctance among warriors when Lieutenant Governor Zenon Trudeau informed them: "war having been declared at [your] solicitation," they could "expect nothing of us" except munitions "indispensably necessary . . . for each expedition."[11]

Unsurprisingly, war did not ensue. When Lieutenant Governor Trudeau attempted to organize an attack on the Osages returning from their summer hunt in 1793, only 100 warriors gathered in St. Louis. Most nations sent their regrets. Some from the East explained that the Americans would march against them if they left home. Others claimed that they could not leave their wives and children alone because other tribes with which they were at war "might easily attack and destroy [our] families" in the warriors' absence.[12]

The Quapaws, too, repeatedly frustrated the Spanish with their "inability" to confront the Osages. In 1786, Commandant Jacobo Du Breuil reported that Quapaw warriors had "abandoned the whites" with whom they were pursuing Osage raiders.[13] In response to Du Breuil's report, Governor Miró agreed that the Quapaws "have not conducted themselves on this occasion with the activity and zeal that I expected of them after the fine words and promises they made here to be ready whenever we might need them. It is necessary for you to reprimand them severely, and bring them to see that they do not know their own true interest, and that in protecting the Osage they are protecting a viper which will gnaw their entrails."[14] How the Quapaws responded to this advice is not recorded, but they did not change their policy regarding the Osages. They knew their "own true interest" better than Miró. The Quapaws continued promising to fight the Osages, in order to get supplies and prevent a rupture with the Spanish. Two months later, Spanish officials in Natchitoches stated that the Quapaw great chief was leading a multi-tribal anti-Osage offensive, which never materialized. In 1789, three parties of Quapaws set out against the Osages but returned "without having found any."[15]

In the 1730s, the Quapaws had willingly fought the Natchez, long belligerent and by then outnumbered. Regarding the more powerful Chickasaws, the Quapaws had pursued a policy of more selective raiding and eventually forged a peace with them. The Osage case proved even more delicate. With their numerous and well-armed war parties, they were a dangerous enemy. Despite the Quapaws' frustration with Spanish appeasement of the Osages in the 1770s, the Quapaws hesitated now. With the Osages' proven ability to banish enemies from the Arkansas River, war could endanger Quapaw security. And the Quapaws could draw on an affinity with the Osages that they did not have with the Natchez, Chickasaws, or Spanish. The Quapaws and Osages negotiated, possibly emphasizing their common ancestry, customs, language, and history of fighting the Caddoan peoples of the central Arkansas Valley. Both the Quapaws and Osages found it in their interest to keep peace.

The Quapaws may have frustrated their Chickasaw allies with their reluctance to engage the Osages. Coordinated Quapaw and Chickasaw war parties set out in the late summer of 1789, but only the Chickasaws found an Osage battle. This pattern continued in the 1790s, when Chickasaws occasionally clashed with the Osages and escaped with scalps and slaves. Probably more a rhetorical threat than a real one to the Quapaws, the Osages provided a perfect opportunity for the Quapaws to aggrandize their own importance to their allies, European and Indian. As against the Chickasaws during the American Revolution, the Quapaws pursued a consistent strategy of railing against enemies, collecting the arms to fight them, and avoiding real battles. They were such skilled diplomats that their charade never endangered good relations with their European or Chickasaw allies.[16]

Under any circumstances it would have been difficult to organize such a large and diverse population to fight a war to destroy another people, but the fact that the organizing was a complete failure reveals that Spain's allies were not eager to fight the Osages if the Spanish did not back them up completely. In 1793, a Spanish envoy instructed the Shawnees to "prepare themselves for an expedition against the Osages," and to "set a time and a meeting place with all the nations of the lower part of the river and of Mexico." The Shawnee leaders replied that they were eager to fight, but "that it was not up to them to fix a time, but to their father to set it for his children."[17] Spain's

Native American allies believed the Spanish role in their alliance was to organize and supply their multi-party Osage war. If the Spanish did not fulfill their role, their friends would not do it for them. While sustaining a rhetoric of belligerence, they quietly refused to make war on the Osages. In 1793, Trudeau explained to Carondelet that all the tribes were technically "at war" with the Osages but that "one does not see any of them killing more than two Osages in a year; and they will never succeed in destroying them."[18] Without full support from the Spanish, Louisiana's native peoples would not engage the dangerous Osages in an all-out war. They might occasionally skirmish, to defend themselves or to support their own interests, but no more.

If local French settlers had fought with them, the Indians might have been more willing to endanger their own lives, but French Louisianans were reluctant to plunge into an Osage war, even though they regularly suffered from Osage attacks. The residents of Ste. Geneviève reflected this reluctance in the face of a powerful enemy. Osage parties had continually pillaged the town and its hunters. In a joint letter to the governor in 1790, residents had complained that the Osages "take our Horses, kill our Cattle, plunder the French and Indian Hunters," and generally made life in Ste. Geneviève dangerous and unprofitable. The residents demanded that the governor punish these "Bandits."[19] But once war seemed a real possibility in 1793, they were not so sure. As Trudeau explained, "the inhabitants of Ste. Geneviève, who have talked the loudest about punishing this nation, are today the first ones ready to sacrifice even the rest of their horses in order to have peace." They were afraid even to work in their fields for fear of Osage reprisals, and they did not volunteer to fight the Osages. Spanish officials did not want to pressure them. Following the French Revolution, war broke out between Spain and France in 1793, and some officials feared that French radicals in Louisiana would rise up against them.[20]

*   *   *

Most Osages did not want all-out war either. As had been the case in the region throughout its history, even its strongest people were not completely independent. The Osages needed European weapons, and they were beginning to worry about united enemies. They knew of the Chickasaw-Quapaw peace, and they faced both tension with newcomers from the East and continuing battles with the Caddos. To make matters worse, Pawnees were beginning to come south from their towns on the Loup and Platte rivers into Osage country.[21]

The Osages further decreased the viability of a coalition war by coming to the negotiating table. In 1786, Governor Gálvez had ordered officials to give even the most belligerent adversaries peace "whenever they ask for it."[22] Osage leaders took full advantage of this loophole, deflecting war by continually asking for peace. They portrayed themselves and their people as friends of the Spanish. As in the past, they blamed the raids on a few restless young men, who did not understand the importance of friendly relations. The Arkansas River became key to this explanation. Beginning in the mid-eighteenth century, as they displaced the Caddo and Wichita peoples, some Osage hunting bands had begun living on the central Arkansas River for most of the year in order to protect their hunting grounds and to trade along the river. Naturally, most Osage attacks on rival hunters and traders occurred in these lands. For decades, Osage leaders had seen little reason to make excuses for these attacks, but now they hoped to deflect the blame.

Beginning in the 1790s, Osage negotiators developed a rhetorical dissociation between the "legitimate" Osage "nation" and a so-called "outlaw band" on the Arkansas. Osage leaders responded to Spanish accusations of violence by bemoaning their lack of control over the renegade band. For example, in 1792 an Osage chief blamed "young men" in the Arkansas hunting grounds for recent raids, explaining that he would have more control over these "bad" warriors if trade resumed. The Spanish accepted his explanation and rescinded a recently-declared trade ban.[23] After several horse thefts and murders on the Arkansas River in 1793, Osage ambassadors accused "bad men" over whom chiefs had no power. They described the Arkansas band as mixed-bloods and "allied to women of their enemies" who clearly "cannot be their brothers." Spanish acceptance of these explanations helped the Osages to deflect Spanish ire and to obviate the sort of coalition against them that might have driven the Osages from the Arkansas River entirely.[24]

Regardless of the chiefs' hand-wringing, the "Arkansas band" was still connected to Osage society and policies. In 1785, St. Louis Commandant Francisco Cruzat officially recognized two Osage men as the "medal chiefs" of the Arkansas band. Yet trader Benito Vasquez met up with them in one of the Osage River towns that March, where they appeared to be at home. Vasquez "reprimanded them for having deceived the governor by telling him that they had settled on the [Arkansas] river, and for stealing from the French hunters who were in that place." The two men replied that they "had not promised their father to settle on that river" and claimed that it must have been the interpreter who misled the Spaniards into thinking they had promised to settle there.[25] Despite the Spanish attempt to pin them down,

Osages went back and forth from the Arkansas to Missouri valleys. In Osage society, bands were not necessarily permanent groupings. They could form and dissolve from one season to the next. By the 1760s, Osage Peace Chief Clermont held primary responsibility for keeping order within the nation. But he did not have the power to control bands, especially when they were far away from him. It was to the benefit of Clermont and the other chiefs to deny affiliation with the men committing robberies and murders on the Arkansas. There was a cooperative relationship between the Osage leadership and bands on the Arkansas but not a relationship that the chiefs controlled.[26]

The Arkansas bands were led by younger warriors, who used the Arkansas Valley's relative independence and plentiful opportunities for hunting, trade, and raiding to increase their prestige within the nation. In previous decades, young men's access to European trade enhanced their prestige and power within the Osage people and their own families, but being a permanent chief apparently still required the correct clan membership and heredity. Opportunities on the Arkansas and relations with Spanish authorities could open new routes to leadership, as they did for the young warrior Cashesegra in the 1780s. Cashesegra often served as a war party chief, a temporary office, but was apparently not of the proper clan to be a permanent chief. Nonetheless, Cashesegra persuaded Commandant Du Breuil to give him a medal, signifying chiefly status. The surrender of Brucaigais's medal, discussed in Chapter 4, likely resulted from the rivalry between these two men living on the Arkansas. Brucaigais was of the correct clan to be a peace chief, and his father was a chief. Outraged that Du Breuil had given Cashesegra a medal, Brucaigais went to New Orleans to complain. In 1780, a rumor circulated that Brucaigais was leading a war party because he feared other Osage chiefs' power. Soon thereafter, other Osages accused him of the attacks on the Arkansas. While the Arkansas bands had not separated from the rest of the Osages, expansion did provide new opportunities for young men. Some of those who might benefit from a relaxing of the rules pushed for change, while others defended the old ways of assigning authority. Unfortunately, we know little of these conflicts because they took place far from the knowledge (and influence) of European record-keepers.[27]

Clermont and the other main Osage chiefs needed to maintain their European connections in order to ward off war and to control Osage warriors. Their chance came in a plan developed with St. Louis traders Auguste and Pierre Chouteau in 1794. The brothers would build a fort and trading post near the Great and Little Osage towns in the Missouri Valley. When the Chouteaus described the plan to Governor Carondelet, they proposed "subjecting" the Osages by building and maintaining this shrewdly named Fort Carondelet. In return, the Spanish granted the Chouteaus a monopoly on official Osage trade.[28] The Osages knew the fort would not subject them. Rather, traders on their doorstep would provide a more convenient, safer, and steadier source of European goods. By 1795, the Chouteaus reported that the Osages were "proud" of the fort, which they regarded "as their own property." To them, having their own fort signified their people's preeminence in the region. They asserted that their friendship with the Spanish made them strong. Without the Spanish, they said, "we have no nerves in our arms and we can scarcely move our bows." But "now that they will not abandon us any more," their arms had become "so large and so strong that we can break trees."[29] When raids occurred, as they still did, the Chouteaus mediated to preserve the general Spanish-Osage friendship. When Osages pillaged a hunter on the Arkansas River that summer, Auguste Chouteau persuaded them to return his horses and weapons and to put "a price upon the head of the first [war party chief] whose band would do evil." In Osage style, the Chouteaus blamed "some evil subjects" for committing all the raids. The Osages continued to take horses from Ste. Geneviève, but less frequently and only when they could nab them without violence. The Chouteaus, the Osages, and the Spanish all found it in their interest to agree that isolated raiders did not undermine their friendship.[30]

Historians have generally claimed that the Chouteaus established "control" over the Osages in order to build their trading empire, which lasted from the 1760s well into the nineteenth century. The Chouteaus certainly benefited, but Osage leaders' friendship with the Chouteaus was a mutually profitable one. From sources in New Orleans, Illinois, Detroit, Michilimackinac, Montreal, and London, the Chouteaus distributed an astonishing amount of goods, much ordered by the Osages. From 1790 through 1803, the Chouteaus imported hundreds of guns, blankets, needles, mirrors, tomahawks, and hatchets, thousands of pins, knives, and silver earrings, hundreds of pounds of vermilion war paint, literally tons of lead, hundreds of thousands of beads, scores of hats, over 2,000 scarlet ribbons, and 10,000 gun flints, as well as bracelets, steel spurs, shoes, ivory combs, rum, rope, bridles, kettles, barrels of gunpowder, and yards and yards of silk, calico, canvas, wool, chintz, linen, muslin, and thread. European goods flowed to the Osages in unprecedented quantity, diversity, and reliability.[31]

Despite the fort, the Osages fought when they wanted, as did their Indian enemies. Europeans could not prevent Indian-Indian battles any more than they could generate them. After the Osages sealed the peace with the

Spanish in New Orleans, a Chickasaw chief who had lost a son to the Osages led a retaliation party that killed a Great Osage Chief named La Fou and Little Osage chiefs La Vente and Le Soldat du Chene, as they were returning from New Orleans. Carondelet prayed that the Osages would get the story straight and blame the Chickasaws, not the Spanish. In 1795, a Caddo killed an Osage chief's father-in-law, and a 100-man vengeance party set out despite the Chouteaus' efforts. Neither were the Chouteaus able to stop illegal trading and occasional raids on the Arkansas River. In 1797, Osages traded with the commandant at the Arkansas Post, then killed a hunter from the post and took several horses from a neighboring settlement. In response to the governor's reprimand, the Chouteaus protested that they could not possibly be expected to control this dangerous tribe completely and that the Spanish should be happy that the raids were less frequent than they had been before the fort was built.[32]

The compromise was good enough for the Spanish. Troublesome friends were better than resolute enemies. In response to the continuing raids on the Arkansas, Lieutenant Governor Trudeau concluded in 1798 that "without doubt the Osages have been harmful in the river of Arkansas, but I do not know whether it would be prudent to break with them in a point in which they leave the important district of [St. Louis] at peace." The Osages were powerful and profitable friends, while the *voyageur* victims were, as Trudeau put it, "the scum of the posts."[33]

Sometimes Spanish officials tried to use division between the Missouri and Arkansas bands to their advantage. By 1800, there was a new Osage Great Chief, Pawhuska. His nickname, White Hair, reportedly came from his taking the wig of an American at Arthur St. Clair's 1791 defeat at the hands of the Ohio Valley Indian confederacy, although that story is almost certainly apocryphal given the Osage animosity to those Indians. In 1800, a new governor of Louisiana, the Marqués de Casa Calvo, told Pawhuska that, if the Arkansas Osages were truly responsible for all the stealing and murdering, he should destroy the Arkansas band. But the Arkansas Osages were still connected through familial and political bonds with the rest of the tribe, and Pawhuska was not going to fight them. Instead, he brought to St. Louis Arkansas Osage chief La Cheniere, many members of the Arkansas band, and a man whom Pawhuska called the "commander" of the murderers. Referring to La Cheniere and his band, Chief Pawhuska asked the Spanish commandant of St. Louis, Carlos de Hault de Lassus, to "unstop" their ears and "tell them for thyself that they should reunite to my village and cease their raids against the whites." Chief La Cheniere, in Osage tradition, said that he wanted to reunite but that his young men would not listen. De Lassus put the alleged "commander" in irons and, wanting to show the chiefs his desire for harmony, invited the large group to dinner. There he gave them presents in a quantity that Governor Casa Calvo later deemed "excessive."[34]

As the Osage leaders had hoped, de Lassus declared that because they had brought the one who was to blame, he was satisfied. In a rhetorical exaggeration of Spanish power, de Lassus declared that he would quell his desire for vengeance, not end trade (which, he claimed, he was just about to do), and not send the Great Osages to destroy the Arkansas Osages. Pawhuska assured de Lassus, "I bewail daily the sorrow that our young men cause." La Cheniere promised that he would try to get his band to reunite with the Great Osages and then asked de Lassus to return the prisoner. De Lassus said he would petition for his release if the bands reunited and for his execution if they did not. Although Pawhuska claimed the next year that the Arkansas Osages had, according to their promise, joined him in the north, the Osages did not stop living and raiding on the Arkansas. The fate of the prisoner is unclear, but so is his legitimacy. It was not unusual for the Osages to surrender a bogus "culprit." Although slight, these concessions helped Spanish officials to save face by providing justification for not fighting the Osages.[35]

*   *   *

While war against the Osages failed to materialize, a new expansionist power, the United States, was gaining strength in the East. Western native peoples had difficulty imagining that this new power could threaten them, but Indians from the East and Europeans saw troubling warning signs. Many Anglo-Americans felt that, by defeating the British, they had won the right to settle on any lands that the British had claimed before the Revolution. They spread rapidly across the Appalachians, scorning Indian and Spanish claims. With good reason, Governor Carondelet worried about the "unmeasured ambition of a new and vigorous people, hostile to all subjection, advancing and multiplying in the silence of peace and almost unknown, with a prodigious rapidity."[36]

These tenacious invaders were indeed "hostile to all subjection," including (and perhaps especially) by their own leaders. With no power to tax, the United States Congress needed the revenue that would result from selling public lands in the West. But under the Articles of Confederation, the United States government had no real powers over the states, who also claimed jurisdiction over western lands. In fact, some states' claims stretched all the way to the Pacific. In turn, the states could not control frontier elites, who rushed in to survey and profit from selling off vast "unclaimed" areas, most of which were in fact claimed by various Indians, the Spanish, the United States Congress, *and* a couple of states. Even these elites had little power to prove their claims over those of other speculators or to exclude squatters. These propertyless men and women hoped to take advantage of the opportunities of a new country to become elite themselves. For many Anglo-Americans, these were not simply property disputes. They were conflicts over *liberty*, a concept that citizens of the new United States had fought for but defined in radically different ways. Even more decentralized than the Osages, Anglo-Americans posed a threat difficult for Indians and Spaniards to comprehend, predict, and counteract.[37]

Given the new American nation's land hunger, it was in Spanish and Indian interest to band together. Carondelet's defense plan for the East relied on the Choctaws, Chickasaws, Creeks, and Cherokees. He hoped that, "fearful of the usurpations of the Americans," they would "be disposed to make the most destructive war on them whenever incited by presents and arms." In the governor's plan, the Osages, Quapaws, Shawnees, and Delawares west of the Mississippi would form a second line of defense. With the Osages an essential part of this defense, Carondelet had to give up fighting them. Periodic rumors that the Osages might join France in an attempt to take Louisiana from Spain made courting them even more important. If the Osages were happy with the Spanish, a powerful friend would join the Spanish sphere.[38]

But a European-Indian coalition that included the Osages was hardly feasible after years of trying to make war on them. The Osages had long traded with the British, and they correctly believed that they could profit from United States traders. The Osages in the late 1790s had little reason to suspect that the United States would prove less malleable than the Spanish. The Osages had dominated Louisiana by protecting their lands with violence, providing irresistible trade opportunities, and negotiating to win the Spanish over. Even though they heard rumors of large numbers of settlers devouring eastern lands, their domination in Louisiana seemed too secure to give them much worry. With little affinity for the Europeans and Indians who had aspired to make war on them and little fear of the United States, the Osages were not going to join the Spanish coalition.

Other Louisiana Indians were not much more excited about the prospect of war against the United States. The failure to organize against the Osages had left a bitter taste in the mouths of everyone involved. Because of skillful negotiating, the Osages continued to receive trade and presents, including munitions. In the eyes of neighboring Indians, not only did the Osages still get the tools to fight Spain's friends, the Osages also received more respect, a respect that they did not deserve. Osage boasts that they had a fort of their own were particularly galling. When the Spanish began to look for allies against the United States in the mid-1790s, the nations they tried to recruit used the Spanish inability to organize retribution on the Osages in their explanations of why they felt no obligation to risk their lives for the Spanish.

In 1794, the Shawnees living on the St. Francis River sent a messenger named Ne-tom-si-ca to chastise the Spanish for their hypocrisy. He reminded the Spanish that the Osage war "has been avoided by delays, or by other pretexts." Yet now the Spanish summoned them "in their necessity." Ne-tom-si-ca pointedly asked how his people could leave their homes to fight for the Spanish, not knowing "where to place their families in order that they may be sheltered from . . . the Osages and . . . the American enemy." Now the Shawnees had two powerful enemies, and they needed to take care of their own defense.[39]

In their response to the same call for assistance, the Miamis charged that the Spanish had lied when they promised to ban Osage trade. They were doubly appalled when they discovered that the Spanish were at that very moment sending a new shipment of artillery to the Osage towns. Having failed to fight the Osages together, other Indians and Europeans could neither organize themselves to defend Louisiana nor recruit the powerful Osages to that effort.[40]

Indians did not accept Spain's delineation of pro-Spanish and pro-American sides. British traders from the Great Lakes continued to trade with Louisiana's native peoples, and British agents may have recruited them. Any observer could see that alliances were not black and white. In the 1790s, hoping to re-open the Mississippi to American trade, Revolutionary War hero George Rogers Clark plotted with "Citizen" Edmond Genêt, the French ambassador to the United States, to seize Louisiana for France and possibly go after Mexico as well. In 1787, American Revolutionary War General James Wilkinson swore allegiance to Spain and became a Spanish agent. In return, Spain paid him a yearly stipend and granted him the exclusive right to sell Kentucky produce in New Orleans. He promised Governor Miró to recruit other Kentuckians to secede from Virginia and the United States and to form their own nation, which would ally with Spain. Wilkinson repeatedly assured the Spanish that Kentuckians were leaning toward secession and finagled funds for encouraging them, until Kentucky statehood in 1792. After that, he continued to spy for Spain. In return for his pay, all that Wilkinson ever managed to deliver was news of Westerners' fantasies of invading Florida or Louisiana, which only served to put the Spanish more on edge.[41]

While resenting Anglo-Americans, Spanish officials envied their large population, which, at least in the Spanish view, enabled them to transcend Indian politics. St. Louis Commandant Trudeau looked forward to the day when "these settlements, having been assured by a numerous population, may themselves lend to the Government aid and a strong hand to punish this tribe [the Osages] and any other which transgresses order."[42] More immediately, the Spanish needed population to counter the Anglo-American onslaught. Carondelet recommended recruiting various Europeans for such vital places as the Arkansas River Valley. In his plan, European immigrants would serve as soldiers in the Louisiana Regiment for five years and then "marry and devote themselves to the cultivation of the soil for another five years during which they would be compelled to serve as militiamen."[43] Kaskaskia Commandant Barthélemi Tardiveau agreed, writing, "it has now become urgent to place an obstacle to the rapid westward progress of the Americans and to raise a barrier between these enterprizing people and the Spanish possessions." Officials tried to lure Germans from Philadelphia, Flemish and Swiss settlers, and French people dispossessed by their country's revolution.[44]

Settlement efforts were somewhat successful in the fertile lands near New Orleans, but the Spanish were not able to persuade many settlers to move into the mid-continent. A few deserters from Canadian trading boats accepted the invitation to linger in St. Louis, but Commandant Trudeau reported despondently that they all preferred to trade and were "definitely not cultivators."[45] By 1785, the lower Mississippi Valley, on both sides of the river, had an estimated total white and black population of 30,471, with nine settlements of over 1,000 people. In contrast, the Arkansas Post had only 196 non-Indian residents, primarily traders, hunters, and soldiers. St. Louis and Natchitoches were not much larger. Anglo-American settlers were an obvious choice, although the Spanish feared that they would facilitate Louisiana's acquisition by the United States. In the *Kentucky Gazette*, Miró offered potential settlers plots of 320 acres, but only a few Anglo-Americans took up the offer. In 1797, there was one small Anglo-American settlement on the Missouri River, none on the Arkansas, and a few scattered settlers in between. For now, there was plenty of land to settle east of the Mississippi, and most Anglo-Americans preferred to live under neither the Spanish monarchy nor the Catholic church.[46]

Unable to attract many white settlers, Spanish officials tried to persuade resident French hunters and traders to settle down and farm. They believed that agricultural settlers would be better Spanish subjects than the roving, unruly *voyageurs*. In 1792, the retired Miró argued to colonial administrators in Madrid that if Arkansas Valley traders would abandon their trade, they would be forced to cultivate the land and would get into less trouble with the Osages. But even many of the new settlers preferred the adventure and profits of the fur trade to agriculture.[47]

Indians comprised the largest source of potential immigrants. In 1784, a party of Iroquois, Cherokee, Shawnee, Chickasaw, Choctaw, and Delaware representatives came to St. Louis complaining of the Anglo-American "plague of locusts" east of the Mississippi. The lieutenant governor promised them that all the Spanish inhabitants of the region "will receive you in their homes as if you all belonged to our nation." To Spaniards and eastern Indians, everyone else was a friend when the enemy was this growing plague of locusts.[48] Indians who depended mostly on agriculture, as did the Cherokees, fit Spanish desires better than did white hunters. They would farm, hate the Americans, and have a good influence on the Osages, making "the habits of those savages more gentle."[49] As an inducement to settlement, the Spanish assured Indians that they recognized Indian land possession. The governor referred to eastern land that "belongs to the Chickasaw nation, although the Anglo-Americans consider it as belonging to them" and to the Ohio Valley "under the domination of the United States of America" but "disputed by several Indian nations, who are in reality the rightful owners of it." Having learned the importance of sharing the land, Spanish officials used that understanding to woo Indians who found their sovereignty eroded by the expanding Anglo-Americans. Osage, Quapaw, Chickasaw, Cherokee, French, African, Illinois, Miami, Shawnee, German, Flemish, and Swiss friends living side-by-side across the mid-continent just might be able to keep it "Spanish."[50]

*   *   *

The Osages and Quapaws did not agree that the United States threat superseded all others or that retaining the Spanish should be their highest goal. Rather, they continued the policies they long had. The Quapaws relied on hospitality, negotiation, and reciprocity to maintain their place and draw newcomers in on Quapaw terms. The Osages continued to balance violent expansion with careful diplomacy. Both assumed that they could fit the United States into these older strategies. At first, they were right.

On October 1, 1800, Napoleon strong-armed Spanish King Carlos IV into returning Louisiana to France. Had French administrators moved back into Louisiana, the result might have been similar to what occurred in 1763. As happened then, various groups would have shifted their strategies and alliances, but the system of shared European and Indian native ground might well have continued long into the nineteenth century. But by 1803, Napoleon was facing renewed war with Britain and rebellion in St. Domingue and had not yet even taken possession of Louisiana. He decided to sell it to the United States and concentrate on his European empire. The frustrated last commandant of St. Louis scrawled "The Devil may take all!" as his trade book entry for 1804. The Spanish turned their backs on the friendships they had established in the Mississippi Valley and retreated to New Spain. They left only a tiny number of settlers, some crumbling forts, and place names that would soon be spoken with a different accent.[51]

After 1803, Indians west of the Mississippi would have to deal with a radically new vision of Indian-white relations. United States expectations of Indian relations bore some similarities to Spain's initial hopes for the region. Like Alejandro O'Reilly forty years earlier, United States officials believed they had the upper hand in Indian affairs. But cross-cultural friendship in the mid-continent had never conferred the right to interfere with another group's internal political, social, or economic arrangements or to seize its land. Now, United States officials demanded radical change.

United States officials and reformers proposed a "civilization policy," in which Indians would stop hunting and would instead support themselves entirely with agriculture and household production. Reducing each sex's range (moving women from farmlands into the household and men from hunting lands onto farms) would free up land for eastern native peoples. Louisiana, particularly the Arkansas Valley, would be a training ground for "civilization," where Christian missionaries and federal agents would teach both long-resident Indians and newcomers from the East how to live like whites. Indian men would become industrious, Christian, law-abiding farmers and small producers. Indian women would stop farming and learn, as one missionary put it, "the use of the needle, the spinning-wheel, the loom, and all kinds of domestic manufactures . . . common in civilized families." Meanwhile, the children and grandchildren of Anglo-American farmers would gradually move west toward the Mississippi. By the time white farmers needed Louisiana, the Indians there would be autonomous farmers who could spare land that they no longer needed for hunting. French and Spanish colonizers had held similarly gendered views of work and would have liked to influence Indian politics, economics, and religion, but most had known better than to try changing Arkansas Valley Indians' internal societies.[52]

Thomas Jefferson and like-minded United States officials and reformers believed that "all humankind had passed through savagery and barbarism before gaining civilization," and that Native Americans simply lived in an earlier stage of development. They urged Indians to dissolve their own political and social structures and assimilate into white society. Otherwise, as anachronisms in an agrarian and commercial society, they were doomed to extinction. The facts that many Anglo-Americans made their living from the hunt and were illiterate, that the United States had won its independence through warfare, and that most native peoples farmed already did not distract Jefferson and his elite contemporaries from their false dichotomy of civilized whites and backward Indians.[53]

As they had with the French and Spanish, Arkansas Valley Indians denied United States efforts to change and control them and instead pulled the newcomers into native ways of diplomacy and land distribution. After a century of weaving Europeans into their networks, they neither illustrated Jefferson's diagnosis nor needed his cure. As many Native Americans would point out in the coming years, Jefferson's plan was more advantageous to land-hungry Anglo-Americans than to Indians expected to surrender their lands and their cultures. Officials would face an impossible task in persuading the region's native peoples that radically changing their lives and allowing their lands to become a dumping ground for Indian refugees from the East was in their interest.

The native peoples of the mid-continent did not need to learn a new way of life. They did not waste land. They supported themselves from multiple sources—farming, hunting, horse-breeding, trading. They were not static, facing a stark choice between ancient ways and Anglo-borne re-education. The Osages had established a fur-trading empire, using European trade networks to expand their dominions and gain the upper hand over their Indian neighbors. They received $63,000 in goods for their furs in 1806 alone. The Quapaws, Chickasaws, French, and Spanish had developed networks of friendship that facilitated all of their access to land. They had already disproved Jefferson's theory that Indians and whites could have a future together only if Indians surrendered their lifeways and their independence.[54]

The Osages and their neighbors had participated in a global economy for a century. No starving hunter-gatherers, they had built a market-based economy that provided a higher material standard of living than many a scrabbling white farm family. Most Indians did not agree that their only choices were losing their lands or extinction. The Quapaws welcomed settlers, but on Quapaw terms. The Osages were unwilling to make way for settlers, Indian or white. Until Indians could be persuaded that Jefferson's plan was in their best interest, implementing it would require coercion. But in 1803, the United States stationed even fewer soldiers in Louisiana than the Spanish had. At the time of the Louisiana Purchase, fewer than 2,000 troops were scattered over all the lands west of the Appalachians. After the Purchase, these troops had to cover Louisiana as well, leaving both the old forts and the new undermanned. Only sixteen men held the post on the Arkansas River, and not many more staffed the region's other posts. The garrisons suffered from debilitating illnesses and a lack of supplies, further weakening their forces. In any case, the federal government was hesitant to use regular troops against the Indians after confederated Indians in the 1790s Ohio Valley inflicted over 1,000 casualties on the small American army. Without more troops, the United States stood in the same position as the Spanish and French in earlier times.[55]

Instead, the region's native peoples did what they were good at, making allies. They drew federal officials into their long-established patterns of diplomacy. They compelled the federal government to become the kind of friend that the French and the Spanish had been, providing ceremonial and material signs of respect and alliance. In response, Jefferson and his agents pledged that the United States would become Indians' "fathers and friends" and "friends & protectors."[56] When Jefferson used the word *father*, he meant a wise instructor and disciplinarian, but the Quapaws and Osages turned these metaphors into signifiers of responsibility to provide goods, as they had with the French and Spanish.

Louisiana's native peoples were able to push federal Indian policy toward older patterns of friendship in part because of the continuing presence in the region of the British, who continued their long-standing trade from Canada, and the Spanish, who contested the legality of the Louisiana Purchase. One stipulation of Carlos IV's cession had been that, if Napoleon decided to abandon the territory, Spain would have the option of regaining it. Because of this clause, the Spanish considered the Louisiana Purchase invalid. Within the Purchase, rumors abounded that the Spanish planned to give the Floridas to the United States in order to regain Louisiana. Disputes over Louisiana's borders added to the tension. Because Texas and Florida were Spanish territories, the French had not bothered to delineate the boundaries of Louisiana when it became Spanish in 1763. Predictably, the United States asserted that the Purchase included Texas and West Florida, and the Spanish refused to evacuate the contested posts, including Nacogdoches, Baton Rouge, Mobile, and Pensacola. Making relations more complicated, Jefferson appointed Spanish spy James Wilkinson as the first governor of the Louisiana Territory. For a decade after 1803, all sides attempted to recruit native peoples to their cause.[57]

With war threatening, the loyalty of Louisiana's French-speaking citizens by no means clear, and rumors flying that Aaron Burr was leading 30,000 men against the Spanish or the United States, or possibly both, and possibly with British help, the native peoples of the region retained a great deal of influence. In 1805, the governor of New Mexico sent Spanish troops throughout contested western Louisiana, strengthening Indian friendships by distributing medals and spreading rumors of an imminent war against the United States. In 1807, the Spanish government sent a message to its Indian friends on the east side of the Mississippi saying that "in case any circumstances should arise, which may render an appeal to the bloody hatchet necessary, they may always rely on their old Friends for such advice as will contribute to their welfare & happiness."[58]

As in the past, Indian relations remained the key to colonial possession. Spanish officials warned Indians that this new republic was a duplicitous friend that would provide Indian nations with "nothing but ejection from their lands."[59] Wilkinson suspected that British agents were saying to Indians, "Beware of the Americans, they mean to take your country from you, as they have done that of your Red bretheren East of the Mississippi."[60] When Indians told federal officials that Europeans claimed that the United States pretended to befriend Indians in order to steal their lands, United States officials responded with an alternative vision, Indian and Anglo-American *natives* as the rightful co-possessors of America. Indian Agent John Sibley told the Caddos and other Red River peoples assembled at Natchitoches in the summer of 1807, "it is now so long since our Ancestors Came from beyond the great Water that we have no remembrance of it, we ourselves are Natives of the Same land that you are, in Other words White Indians."[61] In the same tone, Jefferson assured the Osages that now that "the strangers" (Europeans) had left Louisiana, the red and white people there were "all now one family," Americans.[62]

But Indians knew that the Europeans were not strangers and that they had not gone far. Like Wilkinson, Indians exploited these rivalries for their own interests. By consistently informing federal officials of what their Spanish and British counterparts were saying about them, the mid-continent's native peoples demonstrated that there was demand for their friendship.

When the United States failed to meet their expectations, they threatened to join the Spanish or the British to throw the United States out of Louisiana.[63]

*   *   *

As Jefferson determined to teach them how to live differently, the Osages and Quapaws set out to teach the United States that Indians held the power and would determine how their new friend would act. Historians have called this kind of action "playing-off" one European power against another, but that term would overemphasize the role of non-Indians in this set of relationships. The mid-continent's native peoples used connections with Europeans and the United States much as they always had—to gain an advantage in their more pressing foreign relations, those with other powerful native peoples.

By no means fearing the United States, the Osages worked to draw the new nation into their sphere. For their part, United States officials recognized the importance of courting the Osages, the strongest military power and largest landholder in Louisiana. Jefferson's administration feared that if the Osages were "not made our friends" they would "become our enemies" and make gaining control over Louisiana much more difficult. For the moment, the United States had to avoid armed conflict with the Osages. For the long run, Jefferson had his eye on their land.[64]

In 1804, the Osages eagerly accepted Jefferson's invitation to become the first Indian delegation from the Louisiana Purchase to visit Washington. In the spring of 1804, Chief Pawhuska and eleven other Osage leaders left their towns on the Osage River. The trip began badly. A Sauk war party killed one of the chiefs, Bel Oiseau, before the delegation even got to St. Louis. When the delegation arrived in Washington in July, Jefferson expressed his sorrow at the death of Chief Bel Oiseau and promised that the United States would help its friends the Osages and punish their enemies. Jefferson conformed to the Osage ideal of a good ally, giving them medals, showering them with gifts, promising them trade, and appointing their longtime trader Pierre Chouteau as their agent. Equating their nations, Jefferson said, "the great spirit has given you strength & has given us strength, not that we might hurt one another, but to do each other all the good in our power," through trade and friendship. Pawhuska used the opening to complain of the Arkansas Osages, who were beginning to pose a greater challenge to his leadership than Jefferson's people possibly could. He requested Jefferson's help in reuniting his people. The Osages continued on to Baltimore, Philadelphia, and New York, visits that Jefferson likened to Lewis and Clark's explorations of Osage country.[65]

The Osages were pleased with their respectful and generous new ally. As the Spanish receded, the Osages needed a new source of goods to help them dominate the region. Jefferson's attentions suggested that the United States might even prove a more reliable friend than the ever-complaining and economizing Spanish. According to James Bruff, the military commander of Upper Louisiana, the Osage chiefs returned from Washington "loaded with valuable presents & puffed up with ideas of their great superiority to other nations." The Osages had every reason to believe that their new friends would assist their dominance, not impede it. Fearing no retribution, some of the Osages on their return trip reportedly plundered a group of white hunters.[66]

As the Osages hoped, the United States facilitated Osage dominance. War against the Osages would have disrupted Jefferson's plans for Louisiana by discouraging Indian immigration from the East. And once immigrants did start coming in large numbers, mediation would be more necessary than ever. In contrast to the Spanish, Secretary of War Henry Dearborn directed Indians not to make war against the Osages. The Osages were friends of the United States, and other Indians would have to acknowledge "the impropriety of their prosecuting war against any nation or tribes of Indians who are in amity with us."[67] The United States took on the responsibility of encouraging its allies to make peace with one another. When the War Department made treaties with Sauks and Foxes of the upper Mississippi River, for example, part of the agreement was that they stop fighting the Osages.[68]

The Osages saw that mediation by Jefferson's administration could work to their advantage as immigration from the East increased. Between 1803 and 1805, Illinois, Sauk, Delaware, Miami, Potawatomi, and Shawnee chiefs ceded tens of thousands of square miles to the United States. Thousands of these Indians began to hunt west of the Mississippi, and hundreds settled permanently on the Missouri, White, and St. Francis rivers. Supplied by Canadian traders and desperately in need of new territory, these immigrants attempted to take it from their old Osage enemies, who struck back. In March 1805, Kaskaskia chief Jean Baptiste Ducoigne threatened that 3,000 warriors were marching from the Ohio Valley to punish the Osages for their raids and either destroy them or push them off their lands so that "we will be able to Support our Wives and Childrens and give them meat." As in the past, no united effort resulted, but small scale raids increased dramatically.[69]

Figure 10. *Pawhuska*, by Charles Evret de Saint-Memin. Pawhuska was Great Chief of the Osages by 1800. Saint-Memin probably painted this portrait during the Osage visit to Washington in 1806. Courtesy New-York Historical Society.

By 1805, the Osages were clashing with these Indians from the East and Arikaras, Kansas, Pawnees, Otos, and possibly even Missouris to the west. While native Caddos and immigrant Cherokees, Chickasaws, Creeks, and Choctaws occasionally struck Osages on the Arkansas River, the brunt of war fell on the Osages who lived in the north, near the Missouri and Osage rivers. The United States and the Osages had a common interest in restoring peace. In September 1805, twenty Great and Little Osage chiefs from the towns near the Missouri River made a peace treaty with the Delawares, Miamis,

Potawatomis, Kickapoos, Sauks, Foxes, Kaskaskias, Iowas, and the Des Moines River Sioux in which they agreed to settle their disputes through mediation by the United States rather than through violence. The United States adopted European precedents by promising presents, protection from anyone who violated the treaty, and steady trade.[70]

The Osages held the United States responsible for its promises of protection and friendship. In late 1805, a Potawatomi party attacked a Little Osage hunting camp south of the Missouri River, while the hunters were away. They killed more than thirty women and children and captured about sixty others. Soon thereafter, two Little Osage chiefs appeared before Governor Wilkinson with their heads bowed, their eyes filled with tears, their faces smeared with mud, their clothing rent, and their American medals in their hands. They told the governor that they had not expected to need to guard their families closely because the president had promised that they would be safe, "yet have Red Men spilt our Blood, destroyed our flesh, & carried our Wives, & Children into Captivity there to treat them like Beasts."[71] Surely this was the time for the United States to prove its friendship by redeeming the captives. The Potawatomis had passed most of them on to Kickapoos, Sauks, and Foxes, and the Osages would have had great difficulty in recovering them. While Osage warriors had more power in the mid-continent than did the United States Army, they recognized the wide reach of the federal government's influence. As one Osage man, whose family was among the captives, flattered Secretary Dearborn: "your voice is a well known sound, which reaches thro' every forest, and is obeyed by the Red People however hostile to each other, and where ever dispersed over this extended country."[72]

Fulfilling the treaty obligation did not come cheap. United States officials ransomed 46 Osage captives, paying as much as $150 each. In addition, the government gave the Osages $500 in goods to discourage revenge and spent over $10,000 on expenses for another Osage trip to Washington. In the summer of 1806, Zebulon Pike ascended the Missouri River to the Osage villages with the ransomed prisoners and the returning delegation from Washington. In the formal ceremony celebrating the captives' return, Sans Oreilles, a Little Osage chief whose wife and children had been captured, told his people: "Osage, you now see your wives, your brothers, your daughters, your sons, redeemed from captivity. Who did this? was it the Spaniards? No. The French? No. Had either of those people been governors of the country, your relatives might have rotted in captivity, and you never would have seen them; but the Americans stretched forth their hands, and they are returned to you!!" The Osages were pleased and grateful. In the interpreter's English translation at least, Sans Oreilles catered to the European-American vocabulary of governance. Still, they considered Wilkinson's and Pike's actions as a reflection, not of Osage weakness, but of their importance to the United States.[73]

Although the Osages wanted assistance with their eastern enemies, they rejected interference in their other foreign relations, even when Pike asked at the most opportune moment. Amidst the speeches, dances, and feasts of boiled pumpkins and buffalo meat, sweet corn cooked with bear fat, watermelons, and—courtesy of Sans Oreilles—tea and pastries, Pike arose to explain that he was bound to explore the western reaches of Louisiana. He requested guides and horses and offered to mediate peace between the Osages and the Kansa Indians along the way if some of the Osage chiefs came too. Pike assumed that, grateful for the returned captives and eager for peace with a longtime enemy, the Osages would readily agree.[74]

But the Osage chiefs did not relish the prospect of venturing unprotected across the open Plains to make peace with a people they had controlled through violence for decades. In fact, Osage parties were marching on the Kansas at that very moment. And they were offended at the impropriety of Pike's requesting a mission, then asking *them* to supply it. The Spanish and French had learned to accompany requests with presents, not more requests. The Osages would only lend a handful of horses (and charged him $40 to $50 apiece), despite the fact that Pike could see at least 700 horses in the towns. Four chiefs, including Sans Oreilles and Jean Lafond, reluctantly agreed to go, as did several warriors and one woman. But within a week, the chiefs had turned back. They were not interested in facilitating United States ties with their western enemies or serving as Pike's attendants. Still, Pike's attempts may have sparked subsequent peace efforts. Osage-Kansa violence soon ended, and they traded and raided other Indians together in the future.[75]

The Osages living on the Arkansas River benefited from United States friendship as well. At first, when Chief Pawhuska blamed them for raids on hunters, Governor Wilkinson outlawed trade with them. In response, the Arkansas Osages sent a delegation in 1805 to the Arkansas Post, where the Office of Indian Trade had established a factory (trading post). They asked to exchange their Spanish medals and flag for "similar tokens of friendship" from the new occupants of the post. They wanted to conduct the rituals and receive the symbols "recognizing them as Friends." Their efforts worked. By the next summer, Osages were trading regularly at the Arkansas Post. Jacob Bright established the first legal trading post at one of the Osage towns on the Arkansas River. Auguste Chouteau, who had previously conducted some illegal trade there, increased his efforts to compete with Bright.[76]

With steady trade on the Missouri and unprecedented legal trade on the Arkansas, the Osages used competition to their advantage and thereby improved their access to goods. To court the Arkansas Osage chiefs, Bright hosted them for coffee every morning, wine or whiskey at noon, and tea in the evening. But hospitality could not take the place of good prices. When Bright disputed the amount of goods he should pay for Osage products and services, Arkansas Osage Chief Clermont II, the son of the former great chief, rose to his feet, towering over the trader, and asked if he understood that he was talking to "the greatest Chief of all his Nation." Wisely, Bright answered "yes" and paid the Osages the prices they demanded. The trader had nothing to complain about. In only two years, his firm would make $15,000 in profits, mostly with the Osages.[77]

As with the Spanish, the Osages retained their access to trade and presents by blaming various factions for their continuing raids. Pawhuska blamed the Arkansas Osages. In turn, Arkansas Chief Clermont II claimed that he had cast off the epaulets that the Spanish had given him and was "now an American," but he warned that another Arkansas Osage chief, Cashesegra, "liked the spaniards." When Jacob Bright asked him about recent Osage raids on the Arkansas, Chief Clermont II turned the tables on Pawhuska, claiming that "it is not my People who steal Horses and rob the People on this River, it is the white hairs [Pawhuska's] people who do."[78] The old Great Chief Clermont's death around the turn of the century had heightened leadership tensions into real trouble. With some help from the Chouteaus and the fact that he was of the right lineage, Pawhuska had become the Osage great chief, despite the fact that the rightful hereditary chief was apparently Clermont's son, then a small boy. By 1806, the boy had taken on his father's name and established a rival power base on the Arkansas. The young chief told anyone who would listen that Pawhuska had usurped his chieftanship. He denounced Pawhuska and Chouteau as his "mortal enemies."[79]

Like the Spanish, the United States tolerated excuses from the Osages. Their location was too strategically important. To their southwest lay the disputed border with New Spain. Knowing that the Caddos and other Indians on the Red River remained involved with the Spanish, federal officials found it particularly important to "conciliate the friendship of the Ozages living on the arcansa river," because they could be a powerful buffer for the mouth of the Mississippi. After all, securing the port of New Orleans was the main reason Jefferson had sent Robert Livingston and James Monroe to negotiate with Napoleon in 1803.[80]

The Osages and the United States government were equally pleased with their new friendship, but their reasoning was ultimately incompatible. The Osages believed that they would be able to use the United States to maintain their dominance in Louisiana. In the Osage vision, American arms would enable them to continue their violent protection of their land. United States influence would dissuade the Ohio Valley peoples from organized retribution. The Osages assumed that their greater importance would prevent Anglo-American objections to their methods. In contrast, Jefferson and his agents hoped to use this friendship to convert the Osages to their vision of Louisiana. In their view, gifts of plows, mills, and other tools of husbandry would lessen Osage reliance on hunting. A reduced need for land, gratitude toward the United States, and harmony with their neighbors would then ease them into land cessions. Holding vastly different opinions of their long-term relationship (and of who was dominant now), both partners were pleased with how it was faring so far.

Other peoples were less pleased. They had watched the Osages manipulate the Spanish into assisting their own expansion at the expense of their Indian neighbors and feared an American sequel. The Choctaws raided shipments of goods to the Osages, but they could not inflict enough damage to make supplying the Osages unprofitable. The Osages encouraged the perception of favoritism, bragging about Jefferson's attentions and their new trading posts. Osage enemies developed what Major Bruff termed a "universal jealousy."[81] They charged that, if Anglo-Americans had been in the midcontinent for the past century, they would know that the Osages were the "enemies of the whites and of all other Indian nations." Rather than capitulating to the Osages, the United States should consider them the enemy of all. But the over-extended United States—like France and Spain before it—was not going to alienate its powerful new friends.[82]

* * *

Like their neighbors, the Quapaws were grossly insulted when they heard that Jefferson had invited the Osage chiefs to Washington but had not even sent them a representative. This new nation was showing a shocking ignorance of history. In the past, when Europeans or Indians arrived at the Arkansas Valley, they had quickly recognized the importance of the Quapaws, with their friendly welcome, knowledge, and good relations with most locals. The Quapaws hoped that the Anglo-Americans would come to regard them as "our best friends and allies," as the French and Spanish had termed them. But while federal administrators recognized the importance of giving annual presents to the Osages, the Quapaws did not seem large or important enough to warrant such recognition.[83]

Over the previous century, the Quapaws' need for assistance had grown, and their lives had become intertwined with those of Europeans. Disease had continued to diminish the Quapaw population, which was down to only 600 by 1805. Like the Osages, the Quapaws needed to protect their lands and game from increasing numbers of Indian and white settlers from the East. By 1806, newcomers outnumbered the Quapaws. Friendly neighbors could help the Quapaws maintain their position, but undependable ones could make their situation more precarious. Establishing and maintaining good relations remained essential.[84]

The Quapaws wanted to make sure that their new friends at the post publicly acknowledged the Quapaw right to their villages and their hunting grounds nearby. Although small in number locally, Europeans and Euro-Americans could recognize legitimacy in a way that others respected. Because they extended across thousands of miles and scores of native peoples, these colonizing nations carried an outside authority. In the past, Quapaws and Europeans had supported each other's place on the lower Arkansas. The thought that Spain's replacement was not aware of the Quapaws' role must have been alarming. They determined to teach the United States some history. When United States Factor John Treat arrived to establish a trading post near their towns in 1805, the Quapaws saw their chance. Although Treat explained that he merely ran the trading post and had no authority to negotiate with them on behalf of his government, the chiefs pushed him into the role that Spanish commandants had played.

The Quapaw chiefs carefully explained to Treat the responsibilities that the United States had inherited, much as they had to Commandant Leyba three decades earlier. The United States should formally recognize their people, "not forgetting the presents." Officials should provide annual ceremonies and deliver the Quapaws' accustomed annual present: $600 worth of powder, lead, blankets, and fabrics, plus rifles for all the chiefs. And they should prevent outsiders from driving the Quapaws off their lands.[85] The Quapaws were specific about goods. They refused to accept goods that they did not want or found of low quality. Some kinds of cloth were too heavy, and the blankets Treat brought at first had red stripes rather than what they wanted, "a very Broad and deep Blue Stripe." They did not want the shoes, axes, and hoes that he brought. They did judge the guns, saddles, and brass kettles of "excellent" quality and reasonable price but had to inform him that the kettles were "too large." Quapaw women needed "at least eight or ten" smaller ones for each large one.[86]

Spain was both the model that the United States should follow and the alternative to whom the Quapaws could resort if their new friend failed to meet their expectations. The chiefs wore their Spanish medals when visiting the trading factory and reminded Treat that they had not received "any such token of Friendship from their present Father."[87] Like the Osages, the Quapaws used their former relationships with European governments to demonstrate how the United States should view them—not as a subject people but as an essential ally. If Treat's government delivered the customary medals and presents, the Quapaws promised to be valuable and steadfast friends. If the United States refused, the Quapaws would remain allied to the Spanish, who lingered, after all, not far to the west. To make this point, mounted Quapaw scouts periodically rode into the post, declaring that they had come to see if the Spanish had returned yet. They pointedly informed Treat that "they were long our Friends, who presented the Chiefs with medals and annually bestowed presents to all in our villages," neither of which the United States had provided.[88]

United States officials hoped that the Quapaws would provide early proof that the civilization policy was beneficial to Indians. Treat wrote Secretary Dearborn in 1806 that the friendly and peaceful Quapaws "present to us the fairest prospect of Civilization than any of the Indian Tribes I have beheld in all my intercourse among the Aborigines of our Country."[89] To Treat, the Quapaws were on the right track to civilization. With his help, he believed, they might soon get there. In response, Dearborn encouraged Treat to promote "the Introduction of some of the arts of Civilization, the improvement of Agriculture and domestic manufactures" among the Quapaws.[90]

The Quapaws declared that they did not need to change—they were already a settled, agricultural people. Their chiefs told Treat that they found the wish that they "become more accustom'd to cultivating the soil" a bit odd. If the Americans paid any attention, they would know that the Quapaws already farmed corn and bred horses to such an extent "as enables a supply to many of the Inhabitants." Not only were they already an agricultural people, but they were farming more successfully than the white settlers, many of whom depended on Quapaw provisions. When Treat instructed the Indians to change their methods of production, the Quapaws told him to take a closer look.[91]

Quapaws could not understand why the United States did not recognize their long-settled life of mixed agriculture and hunting. They lived in permanent villages and fed themselves largely by farming. Over the previous century, they had increased their production of food and livestock for the local market. They hunted only to supplement their diet. Whereas most Indians on the edge of the Plains made yearly hunting expeditions lasting several months, in which the entire population participated, Quapaw hunts lasted only a matter of weeks, and Quapaw women remained in their towns to tend the fields.[92]

Still, officials like Treat and Dearborn insisted that the Quapaws fell somewhere between civilized and savage. Quapaw men were industrious in raising horses to sell, but they got their meat mostly from the hunt and not from domesticated livestock. In growing corn for the market, the Quapaws seemed to fit the agrarian ideal—except that Quapaw men did not perform the farmwork. Agriculture was women's work in Quapaw society. Anglo-Americans believed that Indian men forced their women into the "drudgery" of farming while the men enjoyed the hunt. Agrarian sexism blinded Anglo-Americans to the fact that Quapaw women were farmers producing for the market. To Anglo-Americans, agricultural production for the market was only part of being a civilized people. Quapaw gender roles would have to change as well. To be truly civilized, Quapaw men would have to become the farmers.[93]

None of this made sense to the Quapaws or any of the mid-continent's Indian nations. Whether a friend or an enemy, everyone had always treated them as independent peoples. Bernardo de Gálvez had sought to create dependency, but he had not told them of his plan, and his subordinates had negotiated with them on the level of one independent people to another. A basic element of colonialism had always been missing: the ability to transform other societies to the colonizers' ends. In the mid-continent, the "colonizers" had conformed to the customs and dictates of the "colonized." Despite larger ambitions, in practice, the United States initially conformed to older models.

The Quapaws achieved some of their goals for their United States relationship. Their pressure persuaded the secretary of war in 1808 to send medals and military uniforms for the Quapaw chiefs and budget $800 annually for their presents. They also forced Treat into a commandant-like role of facilitating and witnessing the resolution of intertribal disputes. One evening in the spring of 1807, a party of Chickasaw men settled into one of the Quapaw longhouses to drink and celebrate their successful winter hunt. The night grew late, the Chickasaws got drunker and livelier, and the Quapaw women in town judiciously decided to remove to the nearby town where the Quapaw men had settled for the night. As the women and children were departing, a gun went off. According to the women, an eight-year-old Quapaw child had been carrying the gun and had accidentally fired it. The bullet, after passing through the side of the longhouse, wounded two of the Chickasaws, one of whom died a few days later. When the dead man's friends insisted that the child be "sacrificed" to atone for the death, the Quapaws looked to the United States to both protect the child and prevent a rupture in the Quapaw-Chickasaw friendship. At their request, Treat wrote Thomas Dwight, the Chickasaw agent east of the Mississippi, to explain the Quapaws' side of the story. With Treat's and Dwight's intervention, the Chickasaws agreed to view the incident "as accident" and retract their demand for revenge.[94]

Quapaws needed United States recognition, mediation, trade, and presents to maintain their land and hunting rights on this increasingly crowded borderland. This new ally had a tendency to preach inadvisable change and underestimate the Quapaws' importance. But teaching the Spanish had required time. After five years of interactions, it appeared that the United States was learning too. These officials would report, as their French and Spanish predecessors had, that each Quapaw speech began with the "usual assurance, that his nation had always been friendly to the white people."[95]

*   *   *

In the 1790s, Spanish officials, French hunters and traders, Quapaws, Caddos, Shawnees, and Chickasaws attempted a joint military action against the bothersome Osages. This alliance failed because each group refused to subordinate its own interests to the war effort. The Osages were able to stave off isolation by maintaining ties with Europeans and probably Quapaws. When the United States expanded west, the region's contentious history made uniting against this new threat even less feasible than the failed anti-Osage coalition had been.

The Arkansas Valley's native residents had failed at war, but they were experts at peace. They wanted to establish connections with the United States, not fight it. In the first decade after the Louisiana Purchase, the federal government met native Louisianans' expectations of a valuable and malleable friend. Officials lavished presents, operated trading posts at cost, acknowledged important leaders, mediated among crowded neighbors, and made no mention of land cessions. After some prodding, they complied with the Quapaws' demand to be included in the largesse. They accepted Pawhuska's explanation that the Arkansas bands were responsible for Osage violence, but when negotiating with the Arkansas bands, federal officials showed nothing but respect, and Jefferson hosted their chiefs in Washington on a later visit.[96]

Trade goods and presents flowed to the mid-continent. Indians demanded and received a steady flow of beads, rifles, tomahawks, flags, blankets, ear bobs, and vermilion dye, as well as goods new to them—blue coats with silver lace, green petticoats, black silk handkerchiefs, and paintbrushes. They were quite specific in their requests. The Osages insisted on smooth-bored guns, which could fire rocks or any small objects when bullets were in short supply, while most Indians preferred the accuracy of rifles. A white calico with a brilliant red design caused quite a stir at the Arkansas Post in 1806, and Treat had to order more. The secretary of war acknowledged the importance of gifts, in "a moderate amount," but native Louisianans pushed expenses far beyond moderate.[97] Expenditures far exceeded budgets. In the years before the War of 1812, Louisiana Indian relations cost four times as much as the territory's civil government. In a typical year, the Osages alone received $4,300 worth of presents. Like the French and Spanish, United States administrators found trying to colonize the Arkansas Valley a costly business.[98]

Likewise, Jefferson's attempts to change Indians' consumption patterns in order to facilitate societal change were showing no signs of success. The president had banned the sale of alcohol, hoping Indians would become more peaceful and civilized if freed from its influence. Indeed, alcohol was controversial in native societies. Some Indians believed, with justification, that alcohol weakened their communities and caused unnecessary violence. But the policy was unenforceable, as local traders avoided ineffectual trade officials, and even the government supplied liquor to attract and appease Indian allies. Alcohol had long been a part of European trade and presents and an important symbol of hospitality when whites received Indians, as Commandant Leyba had learned. To pacify and profit from Indians, both local officials and traders provided Kentucky whiskey by the barrel.[99]

Even more unworkable was an attempt to slow the flow of arms to Indians. When a rumor spread that the governor might prohibit firearms trade up the Missouri River, St. Louis merchants carefully explained that there would be no fur trade without an arms trade. The Indians sold furs for firearms, which they used to hunt more furs, as well as the meat for their sustenance. Depriving the Indians of arms would not only endanger profits but drive these friendly nations into the hands of Spanish or British suppliers. In reality, most Indians seemed to prefer the rapid fire and small entry wounds of bows and arrows for the hunt, but it would not have been politic for the merchants to mention the role of guns in shooting (or at least threatening) human targets. By the 1800s, Indians in the mid-continent needed the goods that Europe and the United States manufactured, but they retained power over the type, price, and quantity of those goods. As in the past, would-be colonizers paid the regions' real owners to gain any rights to claim this native ground.[100]

To the Osages, the United States had made a natural alliance with the strongest power in the region. They had no doubt that diplomacy, as with other negotiating partners in the past, would be on their own terms. Even though they heard rumors of large numbers of settlers devouring eastern lands, their historical domination of the mid-continent was too great to give them much worry. And the federal government promised to remove any white settlers who did encroach on Indian land there. The Quapaws were less satisfied with their new ally's level of engagement with them. They still had some work to do in teaching the United States the requirements and limits of their alliance, but they had laid the foundation for good relations. Both used the United States to gain advantages in their more pressing relations with other Indians. Supplied with trade, presents, and official recognition and able to deflect unreasonable demands, the Quapaws and especially the Osages were still in control. But in this ever-changing land, the status quo would not last.[101]

Chapter 7
A New Order, 1808–1822

Between the 1790s and 1820, some 5,000 settlers crossed the Mississippi to build farms and ranches along the Arkansas River between the Quapaw and Arkansas Osage towns and to hunt deer, bear, and buffalo for profit on Osage lands upriver. Beginning in the 1810s, these settlers engaged the Arkansas Osages in a bloody decade-long war, simultaneously waging a political battle to convince the United States government to view the Osages as an enemy of progress and to compel land cessions from them. The settlers eventually defeated the Osages militarily and politically, ending those Indians' century-long domination and forcing them off their prime hunting and farming lands. This is a familiar story in nineteenth-century America; however, these early trans-Mississippi expansionists were not Anglo-Americans, but Cherokees.

Cherokee settlers from the East crossed the Mississippi to build farms and ranches along the lower Arkansas River and to hunt farther west. These Cherokees were taking advantage of United States officials' and reformers' desire to use the region as an "Indian Territory" to which their country could move southeastern Indians. Cherokee immigrants' familiarity with both Indian and United States ways would allow them to make the Arkansas Valley their own native ground. As the Cherokees fought the Osages for these lands, they adopted the Anglo-American myth of western lands as an uninhabited wilderness, drawing a metaphorical border between themselves as "civilized" and the Osages as "savage." Having already established good relations with the United States, the Cherokees built connections with the Quapaws and other Indians in the mid-continent, organizing an anti-Osage coalition and isolating the Osages. Whereas Spanish attempts to subdue the Osages had failed miserably, the Cherokee alliance would be more successful. And the Cherokees would prove a more useful ally to the Quapaws and their friends than the United States had been.

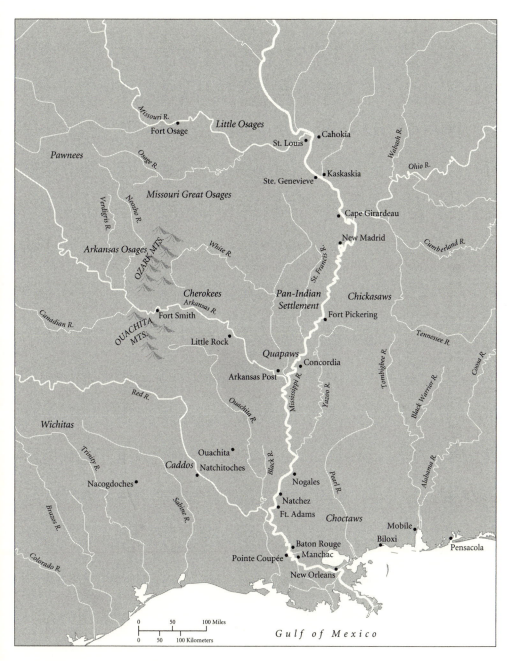

Map 5. Arkansas Valley, early 1800s.

*   *   *

The Cherokee Trail of Tears of 1838 has a deserved reputation as one of the cruelest injustices of American history. The United States army forced over 10,000 Cherokees away from their homes in Georgia to travel more than 1,000 miles to lands west of the Mississippi. At least 4,000 died as a result. But why did some Cherokees move west in earlier decades? For these Cherokees, the Arkansas Valley provided opportunities that European settlement had eroded in the East. Cherokees had crossed the Mississippi on hunting expeditions since at least the 1780s, and some stayed there year round. With only a tiny white population, the lands west of the Mississippi were better for hunting. The game was more plentiful, fewer farms impeded their hunting parties, the Quapaws were welcoming, and most of the whites who did live there were, conveniently, traders.[1]

Whether a Cherokee hunter came seasonally or permanently, the Arkansas Valley provided a place to continue practices that, by the late eighteenth century, were threatened in the East. Hunting and making war defined Cherokee manhood. The rise of the fur trade only heightened this definition of masculinity, as hunting became more profitable. But hunting for meat and furs could no longer provide subsistence in most of Cherokee country at the end of the eighteenth century. The number of animals had declined as competition from Indian and white hunters increased. After 1794, warfare also became less viable. Some Cherokees had continued their war against the American revolutionaries after Britain made peace in 1783, but white frontiersmen defeated the Cherokees a decade later, and the chiefs strongly discouraged further fighting.[2]

The decline of hunting and warfare diminished not only Cherokee men's ability to provide for their communities but also their gender-specific ceremonies, which centered on war and the hunt. And young men had difficulty proving themselves, as traditional routes to individual prestige declined. A young man who had not earned a war title was still a child. Federal officials urged Cherokee men to farm, but farming was women's work. A man who farmed was no longer a man. Across the Mississippi, Cherokee men could fulfill their masculine roles—hunting the abundant game along the St. Francis, White, and Arkansas rivers, trading hides for European goods, and fighting the Osages. The Osages made a formidable enemy, but one that seemed less dangerous than the United States. To many Cherokees, including Sequoyah, the inventor of the Cherokee syllabary, moving west was the best way to resist acculturation.[3]

To some Cherokees, the Arkansas Valley provided a place to escape the rapidly changing East. Quapaws, Caddos, Shawnees, and Delawares made abundant and eager allies and trading partners, in contrast to the East, where Anglo-Americans increasingly encircled the Cherokees and limited their engagement with other peoples. In addition, as historian Dixie Ray Haggard has pointed out, the Ozark Mountains looked like the southern Appalachians. The region's natural environment—its appearance and resources—made it a place where Cherokees could transfer fairly place-specific ways of interacting with all that made up the life essence of the world, not only its human component.[4]

The Cherokees who moved west in the late eighteenth century settled on the St. Francis River, in the old region of Pacaha and Casqui. By the fall of 1805, they were pushing the limits of the St. Francis Valley for territory and game. Hunting farther west, they suffered Osage raids, as did all interlopers. Some Cherokees began moving to the north bank of the Arkansas, just up-river from the Quapaws and hunting there and along the nearby White River. They figured that if they accepted the Quapaws' invitation, they could hunt nearer home and better protect themselves against the Osages. As for the Quapaws, a strong and indebted ally to the west would provide an ideal Osage buffer and partner to "carry their warfare against their Common Enemy the Osages."[5]

Westward migration became controversial in Cherokee society in the nineteenth century. Chief Doublehead and other chiefs from the Chicka-mauga towns on the Tennessee River had led the Cherokee Council since the 1770s, but in 1807, the Cherokee opposition executed Doublehead and deposed his fellow chiefs for signing land cession agreements. Many Cherokees vehemently, and some violently, objected to any further land sales or exchanges. While protecting their remaining lands decreased the appeal of westward migration for most Cherokees, it made emigration more appealing and even obligatory for others. As one set of chiefs toppled the Council that had approved the treaties and created a new governing structure, violence and social upheaval resulted. In May 1808, Jefferson told a Cherokee delegation in Washington that, should some of them "chuse to continue the hunter life," the United States "will give to them leave to go, if they chuse it, & settle on our lands beyond the Mississippi where some Cherokees are already settled, and where game is plenty."[6] He meant the Arkansas Valley. With tensions flaring, some Cherokees decided to accept his offer to help them move west. Most emigrants sought a place where they could hunt, fight new enemies, forge new alliances, re-create older ways of interacting with the land,

and escape the civil unrest. Others, such as deposed chiefs Tolluntuskee and Duwali, probably feared for their lives. In January and February 1810, some 1,000 Cherokees left their homes throughout Cherokee country and headed west.[7]

These immigrants joined the Cherokee settlement on the Arkansas River. The remaining St. Francis Cherokee communities also moved to the Arkasnas after the New Madrid earthquakes of 1811 and 1812 rocked the St. Francis basin, creating a swampy and unstable backwater. The St. Francis Valley had been a commons, where Cherokees, Chickasaws, Shawnees, Delawares, Miamis, French, and Anglo-Americans hunted and lived on land they recognized as shared. The Arkansas and White rivers were different. There, the Osages saw the Cherokee immigrants as squatters and poachers.[8]

*   *   *

Arkansas Valley Indians had forced United States officials to negotiate along older lines, but the United States retained Jefferson's goal of land cessions, to acquire land first for southeastern Indians and later for Anglo-Americans. United States officials hoped that current concessions to native Louisianans' demands would help to encourage acceptance of eastern Indians. Vacant land and peace, supervised by federal officials, would in turn make Louisiana appealing to more Indians from the East. This was mostly wishful thinking. The Quapaws and the Osages challenged Anglo-American definitions of civilization and savagery and scorned the attempts of an alien people to change their successful ways of life. They made decisions based on their own defined needs. The Quapaws welcomed Cherokees and other friendly newcomers to bolster Quapaw security. The Osages rejected the idea of sharing land with challengers.[9]

In September 1808, Osage Chief Pawhuska signed a treaty with William Clark, ceding some 50,000 square miles of land between the Arkansas and Missouri rivers to the United States. The Osage fur trade was more profitable than ever before. Their lands had never extended farther. New encroachments from the East were balanced by the acquisition of a new mediator clearly on their side. How, then, did Clark persuade them to give up so much land? Indeed, Clark and his superiors asked themselves the same question. But to Pawhuska, the treaty was no defeat, but rather a traditional strategy of negotiation with outsiders to deal with internal problems in the Osage nation.

Recent deaths from disease had accentuated internal Osage tensions. In the fall of 1806, several Osages apparently caught a strain of influenza in St. Louis and carried it back to their northern towns when they returned with Pike in September 1806. Over the following four months, some 200 Osages died. Some Osages came to the conclusion that this unknown and unprecedentedly deadly strain "was visited upon them by Captain Pike."[10] In 1807 and early 1808, Osage warriors attacked Anglo-Americans who had recently settled west of St. Louis. The Osages had tolerated these settlements in the interest of friendship with the United States, but warriors angry over Osage deaths found them a logical target. The warriors stole horses and goods they could use but also destroyed symbols of Anglo-American culture. The raiding parties hacked up furniture, ripped open feather beds, and killed cattle. In response, Upper Louisiana Territorial Governor Meriwether Lewis forbade trade with the Osages and ordered all traders on the Missouri River to return to St. Louis, first destroying any gunpowder or ammunition that the Osages might be able to steal.[11]

Fearful that these angry warriors would destroy his people's alliance with the United States and leave them vulnerable to their many enemies, Chief Pawhuska had to respond. He did so in the standard way of Osage chiefs. In June 1808, Pawhuska and the Little Osage great chief, Nichu Malli, visited Governor Lewis to apologize for the attacks and to explain that the warriors had acted without the chiefs' approval. As in the past, the chiefs' claim that warriors were not under their control was both true and convenient. Understanding his awkward position, Pawhuska laid it on thick. He claimed that he could no longer govern his people and that "the United States will have to do it." Lewis took him literally. He interpreted the chiefs' age-old strategy as Osage civil war, telling the secretary of war that most Great Osages had "cast off all allegiance to the United States" and to Pawhuska. Lewis instructed the chiefs to assemble all Osages friendly to the United States three months later at Fire Prairie on the Missouri River, some sixty miles north of the northern Osage towns. He called neighboring Shawnee, Delaware, Kickapoo, Iowa, and Sioux chiefs to St. Louis and announced to them that any Osages who did not go to Fire Prairie were no longer under his government's protection.[12]

The two parties came to Fire Prairie in September 1808 with vastly different ideas on how to acquire and defend land. The Osages had conquered extensive land, maintaining their control over it through violence against intruders and manipulation of their European friends. Through ritual avowals of friendship and promises to change, the Osages had deflected retribution, maintained their access to arms, and protected their lands. Pawhuska came to Fire Prairie to perform the ritual once again. But to William Clark, the ne-gotiator for the United States, land was exchanged on paper. Even a military conquest generally required a treaty, and a signed treaty alone was sufficient for land transfer. Not coincidentally, Clark brought a treaty with him.

Pawhuska's and Clark's divergent assumptions led them to vastly differ-ent interpretations of what happened at Fire Prairie on September 14. First, Pawhuska followed Osage custom, asking Clark not to hold his whole nation responsible "for the bad Conduct of a Fiew."[13] Pawhuska expected Clark to accept the chiefs' explanations, vacuously warn them against future trans-gressions, and send them home laden with presents. Big Red Head, as the Osages called Clark, did agree that the United States would compensate Os-age victims, but he also gave the chiefs a piece of paper to sign. Through the interpreter, Clark explained that, in signing this treaty, the Osages would agree to give up their lands east of Fire Prairie. In return, the United States would build Fort Osage at Fire Prairie to house a garrison for their protec-tion, goods for their benefit, and a blacksmith to mend their weapons and tools. In addition, they would immediately receive guns, powder, ball, paint, and blankets. They would get another $1,200 in goods the following fall. Eager to mend the rift and acquire the proffered benefits, the chiefs agreed to the treaty, which seemed consistent with past Osage policy. Indeed, accord-ing to Clark, they said he "was doing them a great Service." Clark's journal recorded that the Osage delegates found particularly appealing his sugges-tion "that it was better that they should be on the lands of the U.S. where they Could Hunt without the fear of other Indians attacking them for their Country, than being in continual dread of all the eastern Tribes whom they knew wished to distroy them & possess their Country." Like the Chouteaus' Fort Carondelet in 1794, the post at Fire Prairie would signify Osage impor-tance and provide needed goods. And it might be a place of refuge for Osage non-combatants from attacks while the hunters were away. The Osages spent the night dancing and singing while Clark hunkered down in his tent with, as he recorded in his atrocious spelling, a "very Serios" case of "Desentary."[14]

Clark's stomach troubles did not prevent his rushing back to St. Louis in triumph. In his view of events, he had stared down the most powerful tribe in Louisiana and won. He had greatly advanced his country's goals for Louisiana, not only without provoking a war, but "fer a verry Small Sum."[15] The land cession, which Lewis described to Jefferson as "nearly equal to the State of Virginia," would tempt more Indian immigrants, including the Cherokees to whom Jefferson had already promised Arkansas Valley lands. The treaty also encouraged the Osages to move to Fire Prairie and develop their farming skills, with the help of the mill and plows promised by the treaty. It encouraged the Arkansas Osages to reunite with their northern counterparts, a goal that Pawhuska had advocated at his meeting with Jefferson in the summer of 1804 and thereafter. If all the Osages could be settled, peaceful, and free from any continuing Spanish or British influence, more land cessions would surely follow.[16]

While Lewis and Clark saw the land cession as a major victory, it did not have the same significance for the Osage signatories. Much of this land actually belonged to the Quapaws anyway, and other parts had been settled by Cherokees, Chickasaws, Shawnees, Delawares, and whites. The Osages only controlled the western edge of this "cession." And apparently, the Osage chiefs believed that what they were selling was the right to share the hunting lands between Fire Prairie and the westernmost Anglo-American settlements. When a rumor circulated that Clark believed the treaty gave whites and other Indians the right to *settle* on those lands, a group of Osages objected. They charged that Pawhuska and the other chiefs did not have the right to approve of the treaty without a full council. In response, those who had signed the treaty defended themselves, explaining that they had intended to grant "no more than the privilege of hunting in that tract of country." If the treaty stated otherwise, they said, the interpreter must have translated it incorrectly.[17]

Haggling over the words contained in a written document must have seemed particularly alien after centuries in which Europeans had adapted to Indian-developed public rituals that orally sealed agreements. While the heart of any agreement between European powers lay in a written and signed treaty, when Indians were involved, colonial Europeans had adopted the native practice of viewing the entire official proceedings, including speeches, as the agreement itself. With the English, a written treaty was one of several vital components. French and Spanish negotiators usually did not insist on a signed document at all.[18]

The Osages were accustomed to setting the terms of diplomacy and land use. While Anglo-Americans believed that people who bought land also bought the right to do with it what they wanted, the Osages defined land rights according to multiple uses. Different people could have various rights of usufruct, the right to use the land in a specific way. The Osages owned the right to farm and live in permanent towns on the Osage and Missouri rivers, and by conquest they had extended that right farther south. But their hunting rights spanned a far greater territory. The Osages considered some parts of this land theirs alone to hunt, while other places, such as the lower

Arkansas, they generally shared with Quapaw hunters. The French and Spanish had been too weak to insist on anything but carving out land possession within Osage usufruct definitions. Certainly French farmers owned plots near the mouth of the Missouri, but the Osage had not sold these lands, only accepted the newcomers as generally useful neighbors, easily controlled by an occasional raid to curb unwanted behavior.[19]

To the Osages, sharing their hunting lands east of Fire Prairie seemed a fair exchange for peaceful United States relations and a new trading fort. When a larger group of Osages signed the treaty the following November, the exact meaning of the land cession remained vague. Lewis said that he intended the land for white and friendly Indian hunters, not settlers, and the treaty itself stated that the Osages could hunt anywhere in the ceded territory, outside of white settlements, at least until the United States assigned it to other Indians. Pierre Chouteau, interpreting between English and Osage, seems to have encouraged the confusion for his own benefit. After Clark's meeting with Pawhuska in September, the treaty was amended to include a large land grant for Chouteau, although the amendment was excised in the final version. At the least, Chouteau stressed the (temporarily) continuing Osage right to hunt in those lands and downplayed the (permanent) right of the United States to settle Indians or whites there later, and he could easily have lied outright about the treaty's terms. For years afterward, the Osages maintained that they had understood that the ceded lands would be a shared hunting territory.[20]

Another reason that Pawhuska and Little Osage Chief Nichu Malli agreed to the 1808 treaty was the growing division between their towns and those on the Arkansas. What had begun in the 1770s as a largely rhetorical division was becoming an actual political schism that challenged Osage leadership structures. "Party chiefs" had traditionally led hunting or war parties but relinquished their authority when the party disbanded at the end of the hunt or the battle. Parties that settled on the Arkansas did not disband. Their leaders assumed an unprecedented role—the permanent party chief. One of these, Cashesegra, had received a medal from Commandant Jacobo Du Breuil in 1783 for rescuing two white hunters. The medal had angered Chiefs Clermont and Jean LaFond because Cashesegra was apparently not of the proper clan to be a chief. In the early 1800s, Great and Little Osages moved to the Arkansas for game, relief from warfare in the north, access to the trading house that Auguste Chouteau set up after losing his Osage monopoly to rival trader Manuel Lisa in 1802, and distance from Anglo-Americans after the influenza outbreak of 1806 and its violent aftermath.[21]

The 1808 treaty only increased allegations that Chief Pawhuska was a usurper. In December 1808, the young Clermont II traveled down the river with 200 Arkansas Osages to declare that they had been "betrayed cheated and belied."[22] More disgruntled Osages joined the Arkansas bands. While about one-third of all Osages lived on the Arkansas in 1803, more than half, close to 3,000, lived there by the 1810s. Zebulon Pike described the Osage towns as fast becoming separate nations. Both Pike and Treat suspected that, if the towns ever did reunite, it was more likely on the Arkansas, where Clermont II's band was "daily becoming more powerful."[23]

By 1808, the Osages had made some major concessions and suffered some serious internal divisions, both of which would endanger their dominance in the future. Nevertheless, they believed that they retained the upper hand. Needing their United States alliance to stave off their Ohio Valley enemies, the northern Osages believed that the 1808 treaty, at least as they interpreted it, was in their interest. The Arkansas chiefs eventually signed the treaty too, after being promised more presents and diplomatic attention than they had received in the past, thereby bolstering their position in relation to the northern leaders. In general, the Osages, like the Quapaws, were optimistic about their prospects. Immigrants were crowding them a bit, and internal Osage politics could be smoother, but they seemed to have persuaded the United States to help them protect their leading place in the region.[24]

* * *

In 1805, Tenskwatawa, the Shawnee prophet, began to spread the word that all Indians should join together. With his brother Tecumseh and other leaders, he founded a pan-Indian movement to oppose Anglo-American expansion into the Ohio Valley. From 1807 through 1814, Tecumseh, Tenskwatawa, and other leaders of the movement attempted to heal old wounds with the Osages and recruit them to fight the United States. Around 1812, the Arkansas Osages gathered in great numbers to hear Tecumseh's proposal. The 1808 treaty must have lent some credence to his warning that the white men at first only asked for a little land to live on, but soon "nothing will satisfy them but the whole of our hunting grounds." Still, they could not quite agree to Tecumseh's idea that "we all belong to one family." Nor did it ring true for them that "the blood of many of our fathers and brothers has run like water on the ground, to satisfy the avarice of the white men."[25]

After some debate, the Osages rejected the offer. They also declined one in 1813 from Red Stick Creeks, a related nativist movement that also sought to unite Indians against the United States. The Osages had fought eastern

Indians for decades, and the clashes continued even as these nations fought the United States. Tenskwatawa and Tecumseh asked others to see themselves as "Indians," but the Osages still saw Tenskwatawa and Tecumseh as Shawnees. Breaking off contact with whites was an alien idea that went against more than a century of Osage experience. The Osages did not believe that the United States could pose as great a threat as the Indians of the Ohio Valley. Besides some easily frightened settlers on the outskirts of St. Louis, the United States seemed only to want trade and land for its forts. Sharing the land with this kind of friend was mutually beneficial, while the Shawnees and other eastern peoples had always come as poachers and warriors.[26]

The Osages probably became even more wary when the confederation mentioned needing a place of refuge in case of defeat. In the East, Choctaw chief Pushmataha declined joining the confederacy because of the strength of the United States, saying it would be "a war against a people whose territories are now far greater than our own, and who are far better provided with all necessary implements of war, with men, guns, horses, wealth, far beyond that of all our race combined."[27] The Osages declined the confederacy's offer for the opposite reason—they did not believe that the United States posed a threat. In the East, Choctaws, Shawnees, Cherokees, and Anglo-Americans lived in a world drawn increasingly along racial lines. But for Osages, other Indians posed the greatest challenges, and people of European descent were tractable trading partners. It would not have served Osage interests to identify all whites as adversaries or all Indians as allies. Perhaps for similar reasons, fearing the Osages more than the United States, Shawnees and Delawares living west of the Mississippi also showed little interest in the war.[28]

Indeed, the United States made extra efforts during the war to preserve their friendship. Fighting against the Indian confederacy and against Great Britain in the War of 1812 increased the federal government's need to appease its Indian friends in the mid-continent. If the conflict spread across the Mississippi, tens of thousands of Indians might join in open war. The Osages used this fear to their advantage, warning the United States that they were tempted to heed Tenskwatawa's call to fight for "the common interests of the red people."[29] The War Department increased agents' budgets for presents to persuade local chiefs that the United States valued their friendship. The Osages particularly benefited. In 1813, Acting Missouri Territorial Governor Frederick Bates gave the Osages the annuities intended for the Sauks and Foxes, hoping that the Osages would at least stay neutral. In the spring of 1813, Bates went one step further. He asked them to join the fight against Tecumseh's forces.[30]

The Osages took this opportunity to show themselves a "resolute and constant friend to the united States" as well as "Sworn ennemies" to these enemies of the United States.[31] After all, the Osages were already at war with these Indian nations. When Bates asked the Osages for 200 warriors, 500 volunteered, eager to fight a joint war with their powerful new friends against their longtime enemies. But before they got to St. Louis, an order arrived from General Benjamin Howard directing them not to come. Inciting the Osages proved too controversial for the Anglo-American settlers west of St. Louis, who had been the targets of Osage violence in 1807 and 1808. Upon hearing that Osage warriors might join the war, they had immediately written their Congressional delegate in Washington to protest the plan. To these whites, "savage allies" would only add to the danger posed by "savage foes." Rather than distinguishing between friendly and unfriendly peoples, these Anglo-American settlers saw the Osages as equally dangerous savages. The French and Spanish had fought in Louisiana with Indians by their sides, and Anglo-Americans in the Ohio country recruited Indian allies there. But Anglo-American settlers near St. Louis felt outnumbered by Indians and less directly threatened by the confederacy fighting east of the Mississippi. They feared armed and organized Osage warriors, whatever side they were on. The Osages were disappointed, and offended as well.[32]

As the war progressed, the War Department more seriously considered accepting Osage assistance. On July 19, 1814, United States troops surrendered Prairie du Chien, high up on the Mississippi, opening the river to British Canada. Rumors flew that the British were building a fort on the Mississippi from which to recruit the native peoples of the mid-continent. If the British army and navy captured New Orleans, they would gain control of the Mississippi. That August, British forces temporarily seized Washington. William Clark, now Missouri's territorial governor, asked the secretary of war for permission to engage Osage warriors against enemy Indians, reasoning that "those Missouri Tribes must either be engaged for us; or they will be opposed to us."[33]

The war ended before the Osages could become involved. In December 1814 the United States and Great Britain made peace. The following month, before receiving news of the treaty, Jackson defeated the British at New Orleans. Meanwhile, Spain's attention to border disputes with the United States had declined, after Napoleon appointed his brother king of Spain and civil turmoil ensued. Gradually Spain lost West and East Florida. With Britain gone, there would be only one European-American power in the Mississippi Valley. The United States ended the War of 1812 feeling dominant in the East and the West and free to crush, civilize, or expel the Indians that remained.[34]

Both federal policymakers and the native peoples of the mid-continent had reason to believe that their newly-established friendships were going well. Laden with Anglo-American supplies and support, the Osages assumed that they would continue their military dominance. The Quapaws had persuaded the United States to acknowledge their land rights and diplomatic importance, while Indian immigrants from the East appreciated the government's mediation efforts and diplomatic recognition. For their part, federal policymakers believed that they were steadily, if furtively, gaining control over western Indians through peace, trade, and presents. Tecumseh's and Tenskwatawa's confederacy demonstrated that eastern Indians would not all go quietly west, but there were signs of success too. Many Shawnees and Delawares had agreed to move to Louisiana to escape the war, and thousands of Cherokees and other southeastern Indians had moved west. Federal officials believed that if they could keep the peace and gradually urge land cessions in the West, more would surely follow.

* * *

Cherokees had a mission for the lands west of the Mississippi. They knew that the "vacant lands" that Jefferson promised them were occupied by the Osages, who for a century had used their large numbers and access to European weapons to expand their territory, not contract it. In Jefferson's plan, the land cessions and the incoming Indians would encourage Louisiana's native peoples to cease living from the hunt, a change that in turn would prompt additional land cessions. In reality, the arrival of Cherokee immigrants prompted not spontaneous Osage life changes, but an Osage-Cherokee war. When Cherokees moved to the Arkansas River in the 1810s, began hunting even beyond the boundaries of the disputed 1808 cession, and ventured farther west to buy horses from the Pawnees, Osage warriors attacked and killed them, as they had always dealt with competitors.[35]

The Cherokees would achieve greater military and diplomatic success than had any previous Osage enemies. More populous and better armed than past rivals, the Cherokees also had more experience fighting full-scale wars. They inflicted unprecedented damage on Osage raiding parties. In the fall of 1817, in response to recurrent raids, Tolluntuskee, Tekatoka, and other Arkansas Cherokee leaders assembled their warriors and recruited some eastern Cherokees, Delawares, Shawnees, Quapaws, Chickasaws, Caddos,

Choctaws, and Anglo-Americans. Some 600 men advanced on Clermont II's town while he and the warriors were away hunting. As a witness later recalled, "a scene of outrage and bloodshed ensued." The invaders burned down the town, destroyed the corn and sweet potato crops, killed over thirty people, and took 100 prisoners as well as horses and other spoils. The Cherokee-led multi-tribal strike far surpassed any raids the Spanish had been able to inspire. More raids followed, while Pawnees and Comanches also occasionally attacked from the west.[36]

When the Osages commenced their customary negotiations to stop the violence, the Cherokees and the United States demanded land. With the Spanish and British gone, the Osages had to maintain good relations with the United States, now their only source of guns. In 1816, they negotiated a peace with the Arkansas Cherokees through the Cherokee agent, William Lovely. The Osages agreed to give the United States much of their remaining lands along the Arkansas River in what became known as Lovely's Purchase. In the final treaty, signed in 1818, they ceded almost 100 miles of riverfront, from below Fort Smith (near the current Oklahoma border) up to the Verdigris falls. United States officials paid them a small amount of money and goods and agreed to pay American "citizens the full value of such property as they can legally prove to have been stolen or destroyed by the said Osage."[37]

United States officials, who wrote the treaties, interpreted them as Osage capitulation to the plan of filling Louisiana with Indian refugees. True, the Osages had learned their lesson in the wrong way. They were supposed to discover that they had too much land by developing ways of using their land more efficiently. But if Cherokee violence pushed the Osages down this path a little faster, federal officials were not going to complain. The need for a place to put eastern native peoples was too urgent. Officials including Territorial Governor William Clark and Secretary of War John C. Calhoun also feared that any failure to provide the western Cherokees with land would discourage emigration by other southeastern Indians.[38]

For their part, the Osages hoped to protect their valuable friendship with the United States by sharing some land with Anglo-Americans. The Osages did not mind a few white settlers. In general, Osages valued white neighbors. European traders and merchants had brought manufactured goods to trade for furs, skins, salt, and horses. Because these whites usually settled in very small numbers, the Osages could plunder or kill them if they overstepped their bounds, with little repercussion from overextended colonial governments. In contrast, thousands of Cherokee hunters were dangerous rivals for the game the Osages needed to trade for arms and other goods.

When the Cherokees settled on the ceded lands, the Arkansas Osages objected. They had agreed to share some of their lands but bitterly denied that the United States had the power to transfer the lands to their enemy. In 1820, Arkansas Osage representatives told Arkansas's first territorial governor, James Miller, that they "never would have sold these lands to the United States to be given to other Indians, particularly the Cherokees."[39] Arkansas Osage parties attacked Cherokee hunting parties and, when federal officials protested, defended their right to raid or kill Cherokees "encroaching on the Osage hunting grounds." They had not intended to invite a rival people to take their game and make war on their towns. To the Osages, Clark and other officials had deceived them as to the meaning of the treaties. They accused Clark personally and the United States generally of pretending to be their friend only to get their lands, a goal the Spanish, the British, and Tecumseh had all predicted in the past.[40]

Central to Osage understanding of the treaties was a distinction between land rights and game rights. In 1821, Arkansas Osage Chief Clermont II conceded that land cessions gave whites and maybe other Indians the right to settle on the lands in question, but he did not relinquish his people's right to hunt there. Clermont protested the Cherokees' assumption that the ceded lands were theirs for settling and hunting. In his mind, when Jefferson "sent the Cherokees on this side of the great River and gave them Land we had sold him he Certainly did not give to the Cherokees all the Beaver, Bear, Buffaloe and Deer on our Lands." Others could settle on formerly Osage lands without gaining the right to all of the game, or the right to exclude the Osages. "We Sold him Land but not the game on our Land," the chief declared.[41]

In contrast, the Cherokees believed that they had won the right to Osage lands by treaty, conquest, and settlement. To Cherokees who moved west, Jefferson had promised lands of their choosing, and federal representatives had negotiated land cessions from the Osages. Thus, the Cherokees concluded, the lands were legally theirs for settlement and hunting. Furthermore, they had earned those lands by conquest. They persuaded Secretary Calhoun to conclude (prematurely) in 1818 that "it seems fair that the Osages, who . . . have been beaten in the contest," should either give the Cherokees the land they requested or at least "grant them an undisturbed passage to and from their hunting grounds."[42] Finally, the Cherokees pointed to their farms and ranches as evidence that they were developing land that the Osages had wasted. The Cherokee improvements impressed Governor Clark so much that he decided "it would be Just" to give the Osage lands to the Cherokees.

The visual signs of Cherokee "civilization" outweighed the fact that they were squatting on Osage land.[43]

The Arkansas Osages fought back. They fought a brutal war against their Cherokee neighbors. Osage parties raided and killed Cherokee hunters on the contested lands. In return, Cherokees sacked Osage hunting camps and agricultural towns. On one occasion, Cherokees stole forty Osage horses, killing four and wounding three and leaving them behind as a signal of disrespect to their Osage owners. For four years, "deadly hate" reigned, as one observer put it.[44]

Osages had been involved in captive-taking for at least a century, but this war left an unprecedented written record in which we can discover more about some captives' experiences. Cherokees traded one young Osage girl to a white man, who, when confronted with illegally owning an Indian slave, claimed that she was mulatto. After Governor Miller offered a reward for her return, some Frenchmen delivered her to him. Wartime made returning home difficult, so she ended up instead at Dwight Mission among the Arkansas Cherokees, becoming known as Maria and eventually marrying a Cherokee man. Tossed by war and commerce, Maria crossed borders of region and culture and eventually made a new life for herself, as generations of captive women had before her.[45]

Another Osage girl similarly found herself in the fissures of the era's military and culture wars. When Cherokees attacked her Arkansas Osage town, she and her mother hid in some bushes. When the raiders discovered them, they shot her mother, captured the young girl, carried her east of the Mississippi, and sold her to another Cherokee for a horse. Christian missionary Elias Cornelius arranged for her to be bought and delivered to Brainerd, the mission to the eastern Cherokees, and christened her Lydia Carter in honor of the woman who donated the money for her release. At Brainerd, she began to learn to read English, sing hymns, and pray to the Christian god, as did three other Osage captives. One may have been the girl's brother, a boy delivered to Brainerd by Cherokee John Ross and christened "John Osage Ross."

In the summer of 1820, an Osage delegation in Washington pressed Calhoun to make the Cherokees return all Osage captives. In August 1820, John Rogers, Tolluntuskee's nephew, arrived at Brainerd to escort the captives home. Frightened, the girl known as Lydia ran into the woods and reportedly traveled nine miles before being apprehended. With Rogers, she and the other children traveled many more miles back to Arkansas; however, by that time the war had heated up again, and the Osages refused to surrender the Cherokee

Figure 11. "The Little Osage Captive." In Osage country, Cherokees captured the girl who became known as Lydia Carter and took her to the Dwight Christian Mission among the eastern Cherokees. Missionary Elias Cornelius, in the hat on the right side of the engraving, here receives Carter from her Cherokee captors, who, Cornelius claims, displayed two scalps to show what happened to her parents. Carter looks up at the scalps from between the two Cherokees. From Cornelius's *The Little Osage Captive* (Boston, 1832). Courtesy Newberry Library, Chicago.

prisoners that they held. The other captives' fate is unclear, but, perhaps believing the girl had been successfully adopted by the missionaries, the Osages acceded to Governor Miller's request to return her to her new family at Brainerd. In the meantime, she had contracted malaria and dysentery, so Persis Lovely, the widow of the Arkansas Cherokee agent, took her into her home, where the girl died in March 1821. Her burial reflected her cross-cultural life: enslaved Africans belonging to Persis Lovely and Cherokee Walter Webber laid her in a graveyard of Cherokees and Anglo-Americans.[46]

The war increased divisions among the Osage bands. Like many of the Cherokees who moved west, the Arkansas Osages prided themselves on continuing traditions that, they believed, other Osages had lost. The Arkansas bands retained leadership structures that had diminished among other Osages. The Arkansas Osages had two head chiefs, Clermont II and Tally, who each held specific, traditional responsibilities. The northern Osages had collapsed the two offices into one, held by Pawhuska. The Arkansas Osages challenged Pawhuska's right to authority, accusing him of being a tool of the Chouteau family. With these accusations flying, Pawhuska and his fellow leaders in the north were not inclined to assist Clermont's and Tally's Arkansas bands in their war against the Cherokees. Anger at Pawhuska had prompted much of the migration to the Arkansas, and the northern bands tended to see the Arkansas Osages as rebels. The northern Osages had troubles of their own, as Indian immigration from the Ohio Valley continued and Anglo-American immigrants began to arrive in Missouri in large numbers after the War of 1812.[47]

This was a bad time for the Arkansas Osages to be isolated from other Osages. Never before had they faced such a destructive war. In the past, they had usually chosen their battles, attacking small groups of hunters or traders. Even when clashes with the Shawnees and other Ohio Valley peoples accelerated, timely gifts could stop the violence. While the Osages required retribution when one of their people was murdered, goods could substitute for blood revenge. The offending parties, or the Spanish or United States in their place, could cover the homicide with a payment. Having outsiders pay worked particularly well, because they usually gave presents to both parties to ensure that the violence stopped.

Cherokee war practices disrupted the long-standing custom of quelling violence with goods. In contrast to other native people in the Arkansas Valley, Cherokee custom nearly always required blood revenge by the victim's clan. If the culprit was not Cherokee, the clan would organize a war party, which other Cherokee men could join. Gifts could rarely substitute. Since the

Figure 12. *Tal-lee, a Warrior of Distinction*, by George Catlin. 1834. Tally was an Arkansas Osage chief. Here he holds a lance and shield and carries a bow and arrows, demonstrating his military leadership. Catlin painted Tally and other Osages during an 1834 visit to Fort Gibson in Indian Territory. The Osages clearly impressed Catlin, who referred to them as "graceful and quick" and called Tally a nobleman. Courtesy Smithsonian American Art Museum, Washington, D.C. For Catlin's comments, see his *Letters and Notes on the Manners, Customs, and Conditions of the North American Indians* (New York, 1973), 2: 40–42.

1780s, Cherokee agents in the East had been attempting to erode the Cherokee law of blood. Chiefs there had agreed to limit blood revenge to acts of
intentional murder, and not killings committed accidentally or in self-
defense, but many Cherokee common people resented this interference in
Cherokee justice. Because many Cherokees who moved to the Arkansas Valley intended to reinvigorate Cherokee traditions, they were the least likely to
overlook the mandate to retaliate. A Cherokee death required an Osage
death, and often garnered more than one. War parties against the Osages
probably helped Cherokee men to feel that they were following in the paths
of their ancestors and not giving in to white men's dictates to live and work
like women. Furthermore, Osage losses forwarded Cherokee goals of land
acquisition and political dominance.[48]

Thus, the raids that had created the Osage reputation as a fearsome enemy and thereby dissuaded retaliation now backfired. The flexibility of
Osage revenge demands had served them well in the past, stemming retalia-
tory violence and providing goods. But when faced with a people eager for a
fight, Osage methods did not work. Every Cherokee death brought another
Cherokee war party. And Cherokees exploited Osage notoriety to portray
themselves as the victims.

*   *   *

Both sides urged the United States and other Indian nations to come to their
aid, portraying their people as innocent victims defending themselves
against an aggressive rival. The Cherokees would have an easier time shaping
potential allies' interpretations. Most Cherokees who moved to the Arkansas
River Valley intended to continue traditional roles—hunting for men and
farming for women—but most of their spokesmen were deposed or dis-
graced chiefs who had fled west less voluntarily. Most of these leaders lived
differently from average Cherokees, running plantations, living in frame
houses surrounded by livestock, and conforming to Anglo-American gender
roles. Cherokee warriors seeking game and an occasional skirmish and
Cherokee chiefs dressed in European clothes and living in European style
made a powerful combination. The chiefs made treaties to legitimate their
land claims with the United States, while the warriors (often accompanied by
the chiefs) instituted a military conquest of the region.

The people who finally proved able to build an anti-Osage alliance were
Cherokees, skillful diplomats able to negotiate with both the United States
and western Indians and not reluctant to engage the Osages. The Cherokees

worked to isolate the Osages by persuading their neighbors, Indian and white, that they were the enemy of all. Other Indians were not difficult to convince. The Quapaws had invited the first Cherokees to settle on the Arkansas River in 1805 to serve as an Osage barrier. Once there, the Cherokees recruited additional enemies of the Osages. Around the turn of the century, a Caddo party had killed a Cherokee. Desire for revenge had kept the killing on the minds of the Cherokees, but the need for allies against the Osages prompted a Cherokee party to travel to the Caddo towns on the Red River in 1807 to extend forgiveness and friendship. The Cherokees probably negotiated peace between the Quapaws and Caddos, whose longstanding conflicts ceased in these years. In 1818, the Cherokees and Quapaws invited Shawnee and Delaware bands that had settled in Missouri but were being troubled by white neighbors, declining game, and disease to settle near them on the Arkansas River.[49]

The Cherokees assumed the old French and Spanish role for the Quapaws and others better than the United States had. By befriending and mediating among the various Osage enemies, the Cherokees worked their way into older networks. They impressed these longtime victims of Osage violence and expansion with unprecedented military challenges to Osage dominance. Using native idioms, the Cherokees portrayed themselves as friends and the Osages as the common enemy. Where the Spanish had failed to organize Osage enemies, the Cherokees succeeded by representing themselves as fighting Osage tyranny over weaker peoples. As Chief John Jolly was leaving the East for Arkansas in 1818, he wrote Calhoun that the Osages understood nothing but aggression and "have wickedly exercised it on all the small tribes of Indians in that country and on our white brothers also."[50]

For the Quapaws, the Cherokees seemed a more reliable ally than the pushy United States and the best candidate for helping them preserve their native ground. While the Quapaws had maintained fairly peaceful relations with the Osages, they had never built a strong alliance with them. Thus, when the Cherokees started a war against the Osages and offered friendship to the Quapaws, they were not tempted to defend the Osages. As usual, the Quapaws would stay out of the fighting and pursue the most advantageous relationships that they could. In turn, the Cherokees would help the Quapaws to improve relations with the Caddos and the United States.

The Osages tried to reverse their isolation by attracting Indian allies. They did patch relations with the struggling Missouris. Pushed out of their lands in 1812, half of them joined the northern Osage towns. The Osages also apparently healed old wounds with the Kansa Indians through a series of diplomatic marriages, perhaps inspired by Pike's attempts in 1806. However, with most others, history got in their way. The Osages had been the enemy of too many people for too long. Around 1819, the Arkansas Osages invited Sauk and Fox representatives to the Arkansas towns. The Osages presented their guests with 100 horses, and the Sauks and Foxes agreed to ally with the Osages against their enemies. But these promised allies did not join the war. The gift of 100 horses could not erase 100 years of Osage aggression. Osage success in dominating their neighbors left them isolated and vulnerable when the Cherokees arrived. Most people either joined the Cherokees or applauded their success from the sidelines.[51]

The Cherokees had an advantage over the Osages in recruiting the United States. From their years in the East, the Cherokees knew the assumptions and language that United States officials employed in analyzing Indian affairs, and they had a more accurate understanding of United States power and importance. Cherokee chiefs adopted the rhetorical dichotomy of "savagery" and "civilization" and portrayed the Cherokee people as a civilized people in an uncivilized place, thereby laying claim to the Arkansas Valley as their native ground. They claimed that their farming techniques and social organization were similar to those of whites and thus justified a higher position for themselves in American society relative to other Indians. In his letter to Calhoun, Chief Jolly promised, "our women will raise the cotton and the indigo & spin and weave cloth to cloath our children." He looked to a future in which Cherokee children would read and write, Cherokees would "settle more compactly on our new lands than we were here," and through "intermarriages with our white brethren" gradually become "one people."[52]

Anglo-American travelers backed up the Cherokees' claim to be the most "civilized" people in the mid-continent. Visiting the region with Stephen Long's 1819 expedition, Edwin James called the Arkansas Cherokees "almost exclusively agriculturists." The expedition stayed in the home of Cherokee Chief Thomas Graves, who raised corn, cotton, and sweet potatoes on the north bank of the Arkansas River. On his property, the welcoming host had corn cribs, sheds, "droves of swine, flocks of geese, and all the usual accompaniments of a thriving settlement."[53] Cherokee economic pursuits were similar to those of the Quapaws, but the Quapaws' multi-family bark-covered dwellings could not compare favorably in Anglo-American eyes with Graves's frame house, enclosed fields, and livestock.[54]

Cherokees were able to present this front of assimilation because most Anglo-American travelers visited the homes and farms of the Cherokee elite. While Cherokees did farm, they were no more "exclusively agriculturalists" than their neighbors. Enough elite families lived as Graves did to make the

Cherokees look different. Their numerous livestock and large plantations were more visible to visitors than the practices of the Cherokee majority. Ironically, the use of slaves made the Cherokee elite look industrious to white observers. They sidestepped the gender problems of farming by simply having neither Cherokee men nor Cherokee women farm, but black male and female slaves. Thus, the Cherokees as a whole seemed less "Indian" than even their common white neighbors.[55]

An early nineteenth-century Cherokee archaeological site from the Arkansas River reveals that, over the centuries, Cherokees had developed a way of life that combined "Indian" and "European" material culture. They used goods made by Indians and Europeans near and far. While Quapaw households probably continued to manufacture and buy Indian pottery, the Cherokee site's ceramics consisted mostly of British-made plates, platters, cups, mugs, and silverware, with prints and designs common in eastern Anglo-American (and Cherokee) households. But western Cherokees also brought some Cherokee pottery with them, perhaps using the British sets for everyday and Cherokee-made ceramics for ceremonial meals. Only these pots and some beads and brass bells, probably for costuming, distinguish Cherokee sites from Anglo ones. As Cherokee material culture changed, it retained key ceremonial goods.[56]

Downplaying their ties to the past, Cherokee leaders used their "civilized" reputation to attract United States support. Chief Tolluntuskee wrote Eastern Cherokee Agent Return J. Meigs that the Osages were "savage," "barbarous," "uncultivated," "wild Indians."[57] Cherokees argued that they were implementing United States Indian policy while the Osages were impeding it. While planning the destruction of an Osage town in 1817, Cherokee chiefs realized that federal officials would be shocked at this bloody vengeance and might withdraw their financial and moral support for the Cherokee settlements west of the Mississippi. Tolluntuskee and the other western Cherokee chiefs carefully constructed a letter to Governor William Clark, justifying the violence in the terms of the civilization policy. They alleged that for nine years "we have been trying to make friends" with the Osages, who instead insisted on fighting. The chiefs said they were simply living the way Jefferson had advised, "to raise our crops for the support of our families."[58] The Cherokees continued to claim self-defense throughout the war, claiming that only when "provoked beyond bearing" had they taken up arms in a defensive war against the aggression of wild Indians.[59] When President James Monroe urged a Cherokee delegation to make peace, they responded: "We thank our Father the President for being desirous that we should live in peace with all our neighbors; but defensive war is sometimes necessary," and they reminded him that the United States had gone to war once or twice itself. The Cherokees argued that they were not squatters but, rather, the instruments of federal policy. Those western Indians who refused to comply were the natural enemies of the United States.[60]

The Cherokee chiefs alleged that they and the United States were on the same side of a larger war for civilization. If the United States supported the peaceful civilization and incorporation of Indians, it should side with the Cherokees, who, unlike the Osages, were abiding by their treaties and adopting the ways of civilization. In 1821, Chief Jolly reminded Monroe that Jefferson had promised his people "protection in the new and unexplored wilderness," where they had moved in order to give white easterners more land. Yet since they had arrived in Louisiana, "our people have been most inhumanly murdered, butchered and plundered by a band of Savages." Defending themselves against irrational "Savages" in the place Jefferson had promised them, the Cherokee leaders argued that the United States should be on their side.[61]

Through their friendship with the United States, Cherokee leaders alleged, they had learned a better way of life. Because of their debt to their friend and their concern for unredeemed "savages," the Arkansas Cherokee chiefs offered to help persuade eastern Indians that their best interest lay in migrating west. In 1824, the Arkansas Cherokees informed Clark that the Shawnees, Delawares, Kickapoos, Peorias, and others east of the Mississippi had asked Chief Tekatoka to assist with their negotiations in Washington. Tekatoka intended to comply with their request because the Cherokee nation felt "a deep solicitude in the success of said negotiation as being in its beliefs immediately connected with the preservation and future respectability of the Red people." Like white reformers, Tekatoka and other Arkansas Cherokee chiefs declared that Indians' future in the American republic depended on moving west and becoming civilized. The Arkansas Cherokees offered to take the lead in transforming "savages." Those who did not comply, such as the Osages, would be enemies of both civilized and civilizing people.[62]

Cherokees claimed that, as a civilized people, they were a natural friend of the United States, but they also threatened to be a dangerous enemy if provoked. In 1813, Chief Graves and thirty-two other Arkansas Cherokees wrote to Upper Louisiana Governor Benjamin Howard to report incursions onto their property by white bandits. The Cherokees maintained that their own agricultural pursuits qualified them for American protection, declaring "we are indeavouring to cultivate the soil for our support." Unfortunately,

SPRING FROG

A CHEROKEE CHIEF.

PUBLISHED BY F.W. GREENOUGH, PHILAD⁴
Drawn Printed & Coloured at I.T.Bowens Lithographic Establishment N° 94 Walnut St.
Entered according to act of Congress in the Year 1836 by F Wienmough in the Clerks Office of the District Court of the Eastern District of Penn⁴

Figure 13. *Spring Frog*, attributed to Alfred M. Hoffy, copy after Charles Bird King. c. 1838. Spring Frog was an Arkansas Cherokee chief and war leader. He signed the 1817 treaty and accompanied Tekatoka to Washington on his 1824–1825 visit to negotiate land boundaries with the United States. From Thomas McKenney and James Hall, *History of the Indian Tribes of North America* (Philadelphia, 1836). Courtesy Smithsonian American Art Museum, Washington, D.C.

they continued, "there are a few bad men combined together for the purpose of stealing our . . . property; & thereby [preventing us] from persueing our Farms." As a further incentive to remove the bandits, they informed Howard that some of these "characters have solicited us to join them in killing robing & burning the Houses of the honest & industrious part of the white inhabitance." The Cherokee leaders made a distinction between the "honest & industrious" whites and the murderous, arsonous, thieving, "bad" white men.[63]

By stressing their own efforts "to cultivate the soil," the Cherokees placed themselves on the side of the industrious whites. Yet mentioning that the bandits had tried to recruit them left open the possibility that the Cherokees might enlist on the side of savagery if the United States treated them poorly. The Cherokees gained protection, gifts, and representation by portraying themselves as steadfast friends of the United States, endeavoring to become an agricultural people and to encourage other "savages" to do likewise, and by hinting at the danger that could befall those who made enemies of them. The Cherokee chiefs lined up their friends—Quapaw, Caddo, Chickasaw, Shawnee, Delaware, Anglo-American—against the obstinately "savage" Osages. At the same time, the Cherokees pursued their right to the land by conquest and certainly did not surrender their sovereignty. To white reformers, Indians should civilize in order to join the republic, but becoming United States citizens was not what most Cherokees had in mind, any more than did Osages or Quapaws. Rather, Cherokees portrayed their people as civilized Indians who could help forward United States objectives as long as they were treated as a civilized, sovereign nation of equal status with the United States. If the United States complied, the Cherokees would be the arbiters of their new native ground, teaching other Indians how to use it properly and identifying Indians and whites who would not do so.

As the Cherokees adopted and adapted federal Indian policy, the Osages directly pointed out the fallacies behind it. They accused the United States of starting the war by illegally granting Osage lands to the Cherokees. Resenting the preferential treatment that the United States gave the Cherokees, the Osages charged that, if the United States was a friend to both, as its representatives claimed, it should not allow one friend to invade another.

As they lost ground in the war, the Arkansas Osages realized the importance of courting the United States and began to use federal officials' paternalistic rhetoric to seek protection against the Cherokees. In 1821, Chief Clermont II told Major William Bradford, the commanding officer of Fort Smith: "you tell us the president looks on all the Red People as a Father looks on his Children" and "you tell us he is sorry to hear that the Cherokees & us are killing each other." The only solution, the chief insisted, was for the president to tell the Cherokees to "keep off our land and out of our Town." If the president was going to set himself up as the "Father" of all Indians, he bore the responsibility of monitoring their behavior and preventing one group from dominating. Like the Cherokee chiefs, Clermont portrayed his people's violence as simply self-defense. If the United States insisted on sending Indians west, the chief held the United States responsible for compelling those Indians to respect the rights of those already there.

The Arkansas Osages also used their non-agrarian image to justify their need for uniquely large amounts of land and game. Clermont II developed a new rhetoric of a people slowly becoming agrarian. To him, the Cherokees' hogs and cattle were their property, while the region's game was Osage property. The Cherokees should not hunt the rapidly shrinking supply of game just as Osages should not steal their cattle and hogs. The chief described to Bradford the difference between Osage and Cherokee subsistence: "We cannot farm like the Cherokees[;] we have not yet learn'd how to raise Hogs Cattle and other things like the Cherokees—When we want meat for our women and Children and clothing[,] our dependance is in the woods—If we do not get it there we must go hungry and naked—This is not the Case with the Cherokees[.] If they Can't find those things in the woods their Cattle, Hogs, Corn, and Sheep will give it to them at home." Clermont conceded that his band would eventually have to learn to "farm like the Cherokees." But since his band had "not yet learn'd" the new ways, he based his people's land and hunting rights on their (exaggerated) status as a non-agricultural people.[64]

As the war battered them, the Arkansas Osages also turned the rhetoric of civilization against the Cherokees. Osage chiefs charged that their enemy was hampering Osage attempts to civilize. When Protestant missionary William Vaill established a school for young Osages on the Arkansas River, the parents told him that, if it were not for the war, they would be eager for him to instruct their children. But past Cherokee attacks made Osage parents fear separation from their children. They blamed the Cherokees, saying: "It is owing to them that our children are not in your school."[65] Of course, the Osages had their own long-standing ways of training children to be proper Osages. As Willard H. Rollings has shown, nineteenth-century Osages had little interest in missionaries' plan of converting them to Christianity. Rather, Osages, as Rollings puts it, "sometimes feigned interest in order to use the missionaries to their advantage."[66]

While the Cherokees claimed to lead other Indians to civilization, the Osages alleged that the Cherokees were blocking their path. Arkansas Osage representatives told Governor Miller that, if he truly wanted the Osages to "civilize," he should populate the ceded lands with white settlers, who surely could train them better than Cherokees could. The Osages declared that their "object, in selling the country, was to have the White people settle it, so as to instruct them in husbandry" and to teach "their Women how to spin and weave."[67] Tally, one of the Arkansas Osage chiefs, gave a speech to his people in 1819 in which he urged them to end warfare and become partners in the international community. In Tally's rhetoric, rather than attempting to dominate trade and land as they had in the past, the Osages should "learn to do right" in their relations with other peoples. Tally explained what he meant by doing right—creating peace with neighbors by treating them with respect and generosity. Clearly, the chiefs intended to discourage Cherokee land grants, but it is also possible that Osage leaders did fear that declining game would eventually make their way of life untenable. In either case, they saw the political advantages that the Cherokee chiefs gained by portraying themselves as civilized. The Arkansas Osage chiefs promised federal officials to learn to farm and produce domestic goods in order to keep the Cherokees from getting their lands.[68]

But the Osages found it difficult to abandon the methods of intimidation that had worked to their advantage for a century. The next year, a 400-man war party, headed by an Arkansas Osage named Mad Buffalo, gathered outside the poorly-defended Fort Smith. According to newspaper accounts, the Osages were angry at the fort's neutrality in their war with the Cherokees. The officers opened the gates for the chiefs but insisted that they leave the rest of the men on the other side of the Arkansas River. The chiefs came into the fort but refused to eat, drink, or shake hands with the officers. The United States soldiers understood enough of Indian diplomacy to know that this meant trouble. The chiefs demanded ammunition and provisions, while they "minutely examined every part of the fort," including the artillery, and inquired the number of men defending it. In the meantime, according to later reports, the Osage warriors terrorized a soldier's family who lived outside the fort, holding guns against their heads and tomahawks over their scalps. French and Spanish officials would reluctantly have handed over enough ammunition to ward off the attack. Instead, as soon as the chiefs went out to check on their men, the United States soldiers aimed their cannons on the Osages. Facing this level of resistance, the Osages retreated.

Unable to punish the enclosed fort, the Osages expressed their opposition to another group they felt was showing too much friendliness to the Cherokees, the Quapaws. While in the fort, the Osage chiefs had heard that four Quapaws, a Cherokee, and a Frenchman were nearby, having just returned from the hunt. The chiefs invited this party to their camp. The Cherokee wisely headed for home, but the rest accepted the invitation. The Osages "received them in the most friendly manner." However, once they were inside the camp, the Osages fired on them, killing three. One Quapaw and the Frenchman escaped across the river. As a warning to the Quapaws against allying with Osage enemies, the warriors decapitated two of the bodies and cut off all of the scalps and ears. On their way home, they robbed several whites and Delawares whom they encountered.[69]

Osage frustration grew as it became clear that the Cherokees were winning the war. More Osages than Cherokees had been killed, and the Cherokee population steadily grew with new immigration. By 1820, the number of Cherokees nearly equaled the entire Osage population, north and south, which was spread over a greater area and politically divided. Not only did the Osages lose more people and horses than did the Cherokees, but direct attacks on their camps threatened Osage livelihood. As a result of the 1817 massacre and another in 1821, women, children, and old men now accompanied all Arkansas Osage hunts. Because Osage women did the farming, their frequent and long absence from home disrupted Osage agriculture. In turn, the presence of the children and the elderly, combined with Cherokee attacks, incapacitated the hunt. Thus, the Cherokee war cut into both agricultural and hunting production, endangering Osage subsistence.[70]

For the first time, the Osages faced deadly isolation in a world dependent on connections. The Cherokees had undermined their United States alliance, wooed the region's other Indians, and fought a successful war. By 1822, most Osages had decided that "the war has made us poor enough. We ought not to pursue it any longer."[71] Militarily defeated, economically depleted, and unable to defend their vast land claims, the Osages agreed in the late summer of 1822 to a peace that surrendered their centuries-old control of access to hunting lands on the Arkansas River.[72]

Despite repeated appeals from both sides, federal officials did not get involved in the war. Their policies had precipitated the conflict, but they had little power or desire to stop it once it began. To most Anglo-Americans, fighting was in the nature of Indians. Osages seemed to deserve their savage reputation, and Cherokees were not much more effective in convincing federal officials that their war was defensive. Most Anglo-American observers believed that, at least after the 1817 massacre, the Cherokees were aggressors who exaggerated Osage attacks to expand their own lands, an peculiar condemnation coming from white expansionists. These critics included Major Bradford, who in 1820 encountered some very-much-alive Cherokees whom Cherokee chiefs had accused the Osages of murdering. Such incidents seemed to support Anglo-American beliefs that no Indians played by civilized men's rules of war. To many white observers, Indians fought dirty: scalping their enemies, massacring women and children, and then alleging that they were the victims.[73]

Instead of entering or trying to stop the war, the United States used its limited resources to protect the growing numbers of white settlers, justifying this logic with the assumption that Indian nations had the right to fight each other. From the outbreak of the war until the 1822 treaty, civil and military officials urged the parties to make peace and at times mediated between them, but federal policy avoided direct involvement in Indian-Indian violence. In 1821, when the Osages pleaded for outside assistance, their missionary William Vaill was surprised to learn of Bradford's lack of authority to intervene. Vaill noted that "we expected that the design of the garrison was to keep peace among the Indians. We find, however, that they are not to oppose the Indians in their wars with each other."[74] Similarly, Osage chiefs repeatedly asked "whether their great Father the President has it not in his power to keep his red children from fighting." Despite their assurances of friendship and their prominent role in causing the Cherokee-Osage war, federal officials responded that Indians were independent peoples, free to make their own decisions about war against one another.[75]

Recognizing Indian independence was more a matter of expedience than conviction. While Jefferson's plans assumed the eventual dissolution of Indian nationhood, in Louisiana during the 1810s and 1820s it was convenient as well as unavoidable to see both native and settler Indians as independent peoples. Calhoun looked forward to a time when his government could "assume a full control over the tribes within our limits," but that time had not yet come. Bradford's garrison of fewer than 100 men was no match for thousands of Cherokees and Osages. Indian power and settler exuberance exceeded the federal government's ability to rationalize westward expansion. Across the West, federal officials found themselves incapable of controlling Indians or squatters, and the Cherokees were both.[76]

Federal officials had no qualms about intervening when Indian warfare endangered whites, an increasingly common situation as they moved across the Mississippi during the early 1820s. Official policy on the Osage-Cherokee war stated that "the U.States will take no part in their quarrel; but, if, in carrying on the War, either party commit outrages upon the persons or property of our citizens," Major Bradford's troops should act.[77] When a rumor circulated that an Osage band had "rudely threatened and rob[b]ed" some white settlers and that both the Osages and the Cherokees were trying to stir up other Indians in the region into "open war," Territorial Secretary Robert Crittenden persuaded President Monroe to arm a 200-man militia with swords and pistols.[78] Bradford warned both the Cherokees and the Osages, "if you shed one single drop of a White man's blood I will exterminate the Nation that does it," leaving "not a Cherokee or Osage alive on this Side of the Mississippi."[79] While certainly a bluff, this threat reflected the fact that the army's job was to protect whites, not Indians. If Indians wore each other down with constant warfare, protecting white settlers would be that much easier. The Cherokees who moved west saw themselves as the instruments of United States policy, but the white settlers beginning to arrive took precedence in the eyes of United States officials.

*   *   *

In the early 1820s, Indians still controlled the mid-continent, but the Osages no longer held the upper hand. A new Indian people, the Cherokees, had achieved what many other Indian and European newcomers had desired— the defeat of the Osages. The Cherokees had accomplished this feat due to their large numbers and their knowledge of both Indian and Anglo-American beliefs and practices, which allowed them to establish powerful connections. They shaped United States officials' interpretation of the Cherokee-Osage conflict and recruited their support by adopting the rhetoric of civilization and savagery. At the same time, the Cherokees built Indian alliances by the old means of respectful diplomacy and exchange, as well as their unprecedented ability to lead an anti-Osage war. The Cherokees thereby enabled their allies, including the Quapaws, to retain their rights in the native ground while establishing for themselves a valued position in local relationships and their own sovereignty over part of the Arkansas River Valley.

Anglo-American settlers would enter this world of diminished Osage power, rising Cherokee confidence, continuing Quapaw diplomacy, and United States government impotence. These settlers held a new understanding of their country's future and the place of Native Americans therein. Whereas the Cherokees had united Indians and whites against the Osages, and the Osages had rejected Tecumseh's call for a united Indian identity, Anglo-Americans came with a well-formed racialized view of their continent's peoples. Soon, they would have the demographic advantage to enforce their will in the Arkansas Valley.

Chapter 8
The End of the Native Ground? 1815–1828

Initially, Cherokees had little difficulty representing themselves as more "civilized" than their white neighbors. In contrast to Cherokee Chief Thomas Graves's neatly tended domestic animals, white settlers practiced traditional backwoods husbandry, setting pigs out to range and hunting them like game. In 1805, John Treat reported to the secretary of war that some white families grew wheat to sell but did not bother to rotate crops or fertilize their fields. Some grew cotton for their own consumption, but because they had no cotton gin or substantial slave labor, production for the market held little promise.[1]

Cherokee immigrants had more immediate effects on the residents of the Arkansas Valley than these isolated white settlers or the Louisiana Purchase itself. Yet both would come to have great importance for the valley. At first, Anglo-American settlers followed the Cherokee lead, settling along the lower river valley, hunting in the Ozark mountains, and distinguishing between the fearsome Osages and the more welcoming Quapaws. But after the War of 1812, these latest newcomers came in numbers large enough to overpower all of the other groups in the region. While elite white easterners advocated eventual Indian inclusion into the republic, Anglo-American settlers in the mid-continent rejected sharing the land and labeled all Indians, including Cherokees, savage. The Osages had preferred white settlers to Cherokees, but soon white settlers would define all Indians as the enemy and push them all to the margin, establishing the region as their own exclusive native ground.

*   *   *

Early Anglo-American settlers in the Arkansas Valley had little reason or means to argue against Indians' right to their lands. The few Anglo-Americans lived in isolated farms or small communities and had little access to government officials. One early settler recalled that his family lived on "buffalo, bear, deer, and elk and fish and honey." The men and boys dressed in full suits of buckskin. The family bought their occasional cloth, dishes, and coffee from French traders and paid for them in "bear skins and deer skins and coon skins and bear oil, some beaver and otter skins and bees wax." Yet neighbors addressed this settler's father as *Squire* Billingsley and elected him to the first territorial legislature.[2]

In 1808, traveler Fortescue Cuming reported that the Anglo-American settlements in the Arkansas region "raise neither grain nor cotton, except for their own consumption." A French hunters' and traders' village was even farther from the agrarian ideal than the more settled communities. It seemed to him "a poor place" because such people "never look for any thing beyond the mere necessaries of life, except whisky."[3]

Like Cuming, traveler Henry Schoolcraft described whites in Arkansas as living "beyond the pale of the civilized world." He found the region's white women particularly disturbing. The girls wore "buck-skin frocks" arranged in a "careless manner." Their clothes and bodies "were abundantly greasy and dirty." He tried to make small talk with the women of a northern Arkansas settlement but, to his horror, found that they "could only talk of bears, hunting, and the like." Having none of the social graces of civilized women, they only knew "the coarse enjoyments of the hunter state." He attributed the low birthrate among white families in Arkansas to the "savage life" that the women lived, implying that their "disgust[ing]" appearance might be an additional reason for infrequent pregnancies. Schoolcraft concluded that "the state of society is not essentially different from that which exists among the savages," and the most obvious sign of savagery was the coarse white women. Arkansas Cherokees and poor white settlers defied the simple dichotomy of savage Indians and civilized whites.[4]

Immigration to Arkansas became easier after 1820, when steamboats began to move up and down the Mississippi, Arkansas, and White rivers, transporting commercial goods, squatters, and speculators. The defeat of Tecumseh's forces and the conclusion of the War of 1812 had decreased fears of Indian uprisings. As a result, the number of non-Indian settlers rose from fewer than 400 in 1803 to over 14,000 in 1820, making them the most populous group in the Arkansas region. And their numbers kept growing, reaching 30,000 by 1830. These settlers pursued new economic goals. Regular steamboat travel provided the transportation needed for commercial agriculture on an unprecedented scale. Cotton prices were soaring due to demand from textile mills in Britain and New England. Cotton plantations rapidly grew up along the region's rivers. Between the Louisiana Purchase and 1820, slaves as a percentage of Arkansas's non-Indian population had actually declined, from fourteen percent to eleven percent. But cotton brought slaves. By 1830, slaves constituted fifteen percent of non-Indians in Arkansas, and by the Civil War they were twenty-six percent. A plantation economy had arrived.[5]

With changes in the type of settlement came new land demands. Early Anglo-American settlers came to hunt, trade furs, and raise a few crops for themselves and possibly for local sale. Their lives differed little from those of their Indian and French neighbors, and they did not disrupt older methods of land division. The Osages had been right to prefer these settlers to Cherokees. But now white settlers came to make their fortune from agriculture, and they wanted exclusive use of the land. Like the Osages, they would object to the Arkansas Valley's designated status as country for immigrant Indians. Even those without the capital for plantation agriculture dreamed of vast landholdings and feared that Indians would impair their chances. As white settlers' numbers increased, the long-term visions of both United States officials and the mid-continent's native peoples would become less tenable. When Arkansas became a territory in 1819, white Arkansans gained a voice in government. The federal government's continued efforts to move eastern Indians there suddenly seemed to threaten Arkansas's future prosperity and statehood.

Ethnocentrism was not new in the Arkansas Valley. But Indians, Europeans, and elite American easterners all believed, at least in theory, that people could change. In contrast, Anglo-American settlers cast the civilization-savage dichotomy in permanent, racialized terms. Most white immigrants came to Arkansas from Kentucky, Tennessee, Virginia, Maryland, and Pennsylvania seeking land and a better life. They believed that Indians stood in their way. Like the Arkansas Cherokees, white settlers declared that civilized farmers deserved land while "savages" wasted it. But when Cherokee settlers used the word *savages,* they meant the Osages. They envisioned a future that included the region's other Indians, as subordinate but valued allies. When white settlers disparaged "savages," they meant all Indians, including the Cherokees.[6]

These new settlers contrasted their own agricultural life with the perceived violence and inefficiency of Indian life. Despite the fact that this racial dichotomy had little reality in Arkansas, they justified Indian removal by labeling all Indians savage and undeserving of United States friendship. As their numbers grew, they persuaded Congress to move the region's native peoples farther west and make the land a white man's republic.

So many immigrants came that they quickly outnumbered the native peoples of the Arkansas Valley. Rather than fitting into older patterns of friendship and alliance, the newcomers labeled their native neighbors defeated and unwanted enemies. The settlers also doomed Jefferson's plans of a peaceful, gradual incorporation of Indian lands and Indian peoples into the United States. For his policy to succeed, Indians would have to want to change and Anglo-Americans would have to allow them to change slowly and peacefully. In reality, most Indians resisted this outside intrusion, and land-seeking settlers moved west more rapidly and more chaotically than Jefferson had wanted. In theory, the Arkansas Valley was to be a transformative place, where "wild" Indians could slowly become acceptable members of the new republic. In the real world, the theory of peaceful change and inclusion led to violence and expulsion.

*   *   *

By 1818, the Quapaws were crowded by thousands of settlers, while their population numbered around 400. While the Quapaws had generally good relations with their Indian and European neighbors, the Anglo-American settlers were less respectful of Quapaw land rights and diplomatic practices, and they were coming in larger numbers. As promising an ally as the Cherokees seemed, they proved powerless to prevent white settlement on Quapaw lands. When the United States closed the Arkansas River factory in 1810, the War Department recalled Factor and Indian Agent John Treat and did not appoint another Quapaw agent. Fearful that they would lose all their lands to the newcomers, the Quapaws offered to relinquish much of their claim in order to secure their hold on the rest. As early as 1805, they had suggested trading their claims on the White and St. Francis rivers, where others were rapidly settling, in exchange for the promise "that the powerful arm of the U.S. will defend us their children in the possession of the remainder of our hunting grounds." When the United States finally made a treaty with them in 1818, the land cession was considerably larger than the Quapaws had proposed. They sold about ninety percent of the lands they had claimed in 1803. They kept a small reservation along the lower Arkansas River, which included their towns. As with the Osages in 1808, the United States promised that the Quapaws could continue to hunt throughout the ceded territory.[7]

The cession did not provide Quapaws the security they sought. President Monroe appointed an agent for the Quapaws in 1820, but when that agent died two years later, the office remained empty for more than three years. The treaty promised the Quapaws $1,000 in goods annually, but transportation difficulties repeatedly delayed these annuities. Competition for game contin-ued to increase. White settlers squatted even on the Quapaws' greatly reduced lands, and the Arkansas Territorial Assembly petitioned Congress to seize the remaining Quapaw lands, claiming that the Quapaws were wasting "the most rich and fertile Soil in the western country." Local whites accused the govern-ment of squandering good land on "Savages" rather than giving it to "citizens" who knew how to use it.[8] Territorial Secretary Robert Crittenden added his disapproval of letting this "poor indolent, miserable, remnant, of a nation, in-significant, and inconsiderable" continue to own 250 miles of "high rich, and immensely valuable" cotton land along the navigable Arkansas River. In the past, the Quapaws had agreed to share their resources with newcomers in exchange for friendly relations, presents, and mutual protection. Anglo-American settlers and their local representatives took their land offers with-out reciprocating. Crittenden's words reflect the special contempt that they held for Indians who did not pose a military threat.[9]

White Arkansans had decided that their territory must purge itself of Indians, but the federal government had not yet come to this conclusion. In fact, lands the Osages and Quapaws had ceded were central to the plans of General Andrew Jackson and Tennessee Governor Joseph McMinn to re-move the Choctaws from the states of Tennessee and Mississippi. In October 1820, the United States made a treaty with the Choctaws much like the 1808 Cherokee agreement. Negotiated by Jackson, the Treaty of Doak's Stand en-couraged Choctaws who wanted to continue to "live by hunting" to exchange their lands in Mississippi for a large land grant on the south bank of the Arkansas River, opposite the Cherokees.[10]

The 3,000 white settlers who had already moved onto these lands re-fused to give them up. When white Arkansans heard of the Choctaw treaty, they erupted in protest. Founded as the territorial paper in 1819, the *Arkansas Gazette* voiced their complaints. The paper expressed shock that citizens were being "supplanted by the savages, through the medium of their own government." The writer condemned the civilization policy, asserting, "it is astonishing, that government can readily appropriate $10,000 per annum, to pay missionaries for civilizing their Indians, (whose business has remained in *statu quo* since its first commencement), but not one cent for the relief of 14,273 of their own citizens," referring to the territory's white population.[11] In December 1820, Governor James Miller wrote the secretary of war asking, "where is the provision made for the poor white man, who has spent many years laboring to improve this land?"[12]

An 1821 letter to the editor complained that Jackson and the other treaty commissioners "cared much less for their fellow-citizens (many of whom have fought for their country in the late war with England, and in Indian wars) than they did for the ruthless savages," despite the fact that many Choctaws had fought alongside the Americans in the Creek Wars.[13] In a letter to Secretary Calhoun, one settler living in the disputed lands declared that his and his white neighbors' pioneering efforts "should have placed them above Savages in the estimation of *their* Govt."[14] The *Gazette* declared, "you cannot take from a proprietor his soil and his home; they are sacred from violence, and beyond the reach of any treaty." To the writer, there was no irony in the settlers' own desire to remove others from their homes. A later passage reveals why: "To despoil a white man of his home, and bestow it upon a red one, is without the shadow of justice."[15] Not just any proprietorship was sacred, only white proprietorship. An 1825 settlers' petition objected that the Choctaw treaty betrayed whites "to give Place to Indians!!" In the eyes of Washington officials, the ceded lands belonged to the federal government, not to individual settlers. To the settlers, lands that their government had bought from Indians belonged to its citizens. "Citizens" were fundamentally different from "savages," and neither could become the other.[16]

Sending Indians to the Arkansas Valley appeased eastern citizens but angered western ones. Although official policy required removing settlers from Indian lands in Louisiana, the federal government was ultimately no more willing or able to control these white settlers than to refuse their eastern counterparts. Governors did order squatters to leave, and occasionally the army even forcibly removed them, but settlers got their way in the end. If forced to leave, they soon returned. Jeffersonian-Republican army officers were not likely to shoot their fellow white citizens, and sometimes they persuaded their superiors to change their orders.[17]

For example, in 1816, Governor Clark sent men to notify white settlers south of the Arkansas River that they were squatting on Indian land. The soldiers reported back that 200 families were living there, industriously improving their farms and erecting mills. The report also stated that the squatters could muster 300 armed men, who would render it "impracticable" for Clark's force to remove the families. The Governor concluded that persuading Indians to give up their title might be easier.[18] Similarly, in July 1820, an Osage delegation visited Washington and told Calhoun that whites were squatting on their lands. When Calhoun ordered General Henry Atkinson to keep out white intruders, Atkinson replied that the Osage complaints referred to lands that were not actually theirs. The secretary accepted the general's explanation.[19]

Based on their country's history with Indians, squatters suspected that if they held out long enough, the federal government would eventually obtain the land from the Indian owners. Then the squatters would have preemption rights to buy the titles from the government. In the words of General Land Office official Josiah Meigs, "occupants indulge a hope that they may hereafter obtain a pre emption right to the Same lands which they illegally occupy." In his opinion, the preemption laws and "the difficulty of preventing or punishing intruders on the Public Lands" combined to "rather *encourage*, than forbid intrusion." Indeed, white settlers' methods almost always paid off. For more than a century, Arkansas Valley locals had manipulated outside authorities to suit their own ends. However, for the first time, the most powerful locals were not Indians.[20]

By the late 1820s, officials were agreeing to white settlers' requests to classify all Indians as enemies and drive them out of the territory. In 1824, Robert Crittenden, now Acting Governor, strong-armed the Quapaws into ceding their remaining lands with full support from Washington. The United States government's solution was to move the Quapaws to Caddo lands in the state of Louisiana. Shocked at the land loss and doubtful of the welcome his people would receive from their former enemies, the Quapaw great chief in this era, Hekaton, reminded Crittenden that Indians were not all the same. "To leave my native soil, and go among red men who are aliens to our race, is throwing us like outcasts on the world. The lands you wish us to go to belong to strangers."[21] In June 1825, Hekaton and the other chiefs asked to "remain a few years longer on the land," but the secretary of war denied their petition. That December, the Quapaws unwillingly moved 150 miles south, walking and carrying their children alongside their laden horses.[22]

Quapaws had welcomed Illinois, French, Spanish, British, Chickasaws, Shawnees, Cherokees, and Anglo-Americans to their valley, as long as they abided by established ways of sharing the land. Now, the United States had expelled the Quapaws from their native ground. Once the Quapaws had surrendered their lands and gone to live with the Caddos, the government continued to disappoint them. In 1826, Chief Hekaton wrote Arkansas Territorial Governor George Izard, "I am not at all satisfied in my present situation." Rather than simply sharing the lands with the Caddos, which would have been tricky enough, "we are surrounded by *red skins* of the tribes of several nations besides the Cadeaux who threaten to steal or take from us not only our beef and other provisions, but also our land." Since the government had not sent enough supplies, the groups were stealing from one another. To save money, the government had dismissed the Quapaws' agent and interpreter.

Without an interpreter, increased misunderstandings arose between the Quapaws and the Caddos. The Caddos' agent, who was now supposed to be the agent for both tribes, made matters worse. Unlike the Quapaws' previous agent, who had respected Hekaton, the Caddo agent tried to dominate him. According to Chief Hekaton, the agent told him "that I was not *chief*" but instead under the agent's rule now.[23]

Between 1826 and 1830, fleeing starvation and hostility from other Indians, including the Caddos, most Quapaws moved back to their Arkansas homeland and requested American citizenship and individual land grants. They were willing to surrender their sovereignty and accept the civilization policy's ultimate promise. The territory tolerated them for a while but considered them squatters and in 1834 assigned them lands instead in what was to become Oklahoma. As long as European numbers were small, Quapaw hospitality mattered a great deal. But once white settlers came in larger numbers and collapsed Quapaws, Osages, and Cherokees into the general category *Indian*, the friendly hosts were recast as enemies to progress and made outcasts from their homeland.[24]

For more than a century, the Quapaws had forged alliances that were essential to their survival. But by the late 1820s, Anglo-Americans were unprecedentedly powerful, land-hungry, and uninterested in Quapaw alliance. As their French and Indian neighbors, including the Cherokees, suffered the same pressures, the Quapaws lost the connections that had sustained their position. Once they lost their allies, their lands and lives were in jeopardy. By no means viewing the colonial period as their difficult times, Quapaws today call the post-Purchase decades the saddest part of their history. While the French and Spanish had considered them valuable hosts and allies, Anglo-Americans demonstrated a disdain that the Quapaws found inexplicable.[25]

While Anglo-American settlers refused to forge connections with the region's previous occupants, they were far from isolated. Unlike the peripatetic Spaniards of the 1540s, these men and women colonized the Arkansas Valley backed by the largest and most powerful collection of outsiders ever— the federal government, nearly a score of states, and millions of people equally wedded to the ideas of white male citizenship and independence based on land ownership. The decline of the Indians' powerful alliance system, the refusal of Anglo-American settlers to be incorporated, and their connections to people and goods in the East eroded Indians' ability to control land and define the future of the mid-continent.

The expulsions continued. In January 1825, the United States adjusted the Choctaw grant of 1820. The new treaty moved the Choctaw lands west,

Figure 14. *Clermont, First Chief of the Tribe,* by George Catlin. 1834. This is probably Clermont III, the grandson of the Clermont who was Osage Great Chief before 1800 and the son of Clermont II, who became chief of the Arkansas Osages and claimed to be the rightful chief of all the Osages. Catlin noted that his subject's father had recently died. Here, Clermont III displays a peace medal, a war club and, according to Catlin, leggings fringed with scalp locks. Courtesy Smithsonian Museum of American Art, Washington, D.C.

Figure 15. *Wah-chee-te, Wife of Clermont, and Child*, by George Catlin. 1834. These are probably the daughter-in-law and grandson of Clermont II, who was chief of the Arkansas Osages. According to Catlin, Wahcheete was the only Osage dressed in manufactured cloth (rather than skins) that he saw on his 1834 trip to Fort Gibson. Of course, the Osages had been importing European cloth for more than a century. Courtesy Smithsonian Museum of American Art, Washington, D.C.

past the Arkansas border. That June, Pawhuska, Clermont II, and the other Osage chiefs ceded their last remaining lands in the state of Missouri and the territory of Arkansas. Finally, white Arkansans set their sights on the last Indian claim in Arkansas, that of the Cherokees. These Anglo-Americans maintained that no Indians could become civilized, be valuable to white men, or share the land with white farmers. To them, the Cherokees had no rights to land that whites wanted. They argued that the government could not possibly have gone to the trouble of acquiring land from the Osages and Quapaws simply to give it to other Indians. These settlers rejected their government's right to make good land a *"hunting ground* for some . . . Tribe," whatever that tribe might be. To them, the Arkansas Valley should not be Indians' ground at all. It was their own birthright, as citizens of the United States.[26]

*   *   *

The Cherokees did not believe that the United States government's only obligations were to white settlers. When Arkansas newspapers reported a rumor that Cherokees might cede some of their Arkansas lands, the Cherokees declared themselves "astonished" at the suggestion. Describing themselves as pioneers, they claimed that they had left the land of their birth to settle a land "then uninhabited," where they made improvements and raised produce. If they went farther west, they would be "strangers in a wilderness." They would have to get their living from the chase because those lands were "unfit for agricultural pursuits." Moving west would reverse the advances their people had made. Surely, they said, the government does not want to monopolize "all the *good* lands for our *white* brethren and give *us* the *worst*." They called on the United States government to remember past promises of friendship and Cherokee success in meeting expectations. Rejecting white claims that all Indians were enemies, the Cherokees asserted Cherokee-Anglo brotherhood. To them, the federal government was equally responsible to both siblings.[27]

The Cherokees had fought the Osages to stake out their place on the Arkansas River and had used their knowledge of Anglo-American political culture to lobby Indian agents, secretaries of war, and presidents to support their claims; now they employed the instruments of white settlers to argue for their place among them. In April 1828, Nu-Tah-E-Tuil, or No-Killer, wrote a letter to the *Arkansas Gazette.* He referred to a memorial of the Territorial Legislature that the *Gazette* had printed, which vehemently argued that the Cherokees had no rights to lands in Arkansas. Nu-Tah-E-Tuil called the memorial "replete with savage barbarity and injustice" and urged the *Gazette* and Governor Izard to denounce it. He countered directly the accusation that the Cherokees were too uncivilized to live among whites:

What is civilization? Is it a practical knowledge of agriculture? Then I am willing to compare the farms and gardens of this nation with those of the mass of white population in the Territory. The advantage will be on our side. Does civilization consist in good and comfortable buildings? Here, if the comparison be made, we shall have the advantage over the mass of your people. . . . Does it consist in morality and religion? Our people have built, wholly at their own expense, the only Meeting house in the Territory; and though the number of truly religious people is small, and though many immoral practices prevail, yet I believe we might compare with your very best settlements in these respects. Does it consist in schools and the education of youth? I believe a larger portion of our youths can read and write than of those in your own settlements.[28]

Nu-Tah-E-Tuil identified the flaws in Anglo-American reasoning. If the federal government wanted Indians to civilize, it should not make them leave their farms, homes, churches, and schools. If the government wanted only civilized people in its country, it should move Osages and maybe a few Anglo-Americans west. By all the standards Anglo-American leaders had cited in the past, the Cherokees deserved their place in the United States. White Arkansans should proudly claim them as neighbors and friends, not insult them in the territory's newspaper.

The Arkansas Cherokees took their case to Washington in 1828. A delegation that included Thomas Graves and Sequoyah presented documents demonstrating Jefferson's promise and subsequent assurances that they had earned their right to a place on the Arkansas River. They requested that their lands be surveyed and all squatters removed. But they were swimming against the tide. Cherokees in the East would use the same solid reasoning and poignant language to defend their right to stay in their homelands in the following decade. They would be no more successful. Sequoyah's international prestige as an educator and the inventor of a new kind of writing did not prevent congressmen from heaping unprecedented scorn on the people he was representing. The House Committee on Indian Affairs reaffirmed its belief that Indians were theoretically capable of change but concluded that "they remain, to this hour, *a miserable and degraded race*" likely destined for extinction. It was too late to forge a compromise, they reasoned, and Indians faced either extinction or removal "*from the scene of the controversy to a more peaceable and better regulated home.*" Policymakers in Washington increasingly concurred with white settlers that Indians could only be enemies to American progress.[29]

White settlers wanted good agricultural land, and their government existed to supply it. The United States was a white man's republic where white men had the power of the vote. In the early decades of the republic, their country had become what it would long remain, a multiracial society with an all-white polity. American men had fought their revolution in part to protest the British government's restrictions on western settlement, established in response to Pontiac's War. During the 1780s and 1790s, eastern states had controlled Congress and the presidency. With the exception of Georgia, white people in those states had already occupied most Indian land, and their native populations there had drastically declined due to disease, warfare, and emigration. The elected representatives of eastern states then pursued ideals of Indian transformation and incorporation. But as westerners obtained greater representation in Congress, federal policies began to reflect their fear and hatred toward Indians. Trans-Appalachian states insisted that Indians move across the Mississippi, and trans-Mississippi territories and states in turn lobbied for Indian removal beyond their borders. Federal officials acknowledged and lamented the settlers' passion for acquiring land. Secretary of War James Barbour blamed this passion for driving "in ceaseless succession, the white man on the Indian." But the officials ultimately acquiesced every time.[30]

The John Quincy Adams administration made Thomas Graves and Sequoyah wish they had never come to Washington. In response to their requests, the War Department's official in charge of Indian affairs, Thomas McKenney, made an alternative proposal. If the Cherokees would just move a bit west, the government could both meet their need for a surveyed and permanent tract and appease the white inhabitants of Arkansas, who were pressuring Indian removal from their territory. The delegation vehemently declined and asked again that the government secure Cherokee lands where they were "now located."[31] For a month, McKenney pressured the delegation and added individual grants of $1,200 for Graves and $500 plus rights to a salt spring in the new country for Sequoyah. On May 6, the delegation gave in.[32]

Federal officials felt this breach of faith more acutely than they had during previous cessions. They knew that this was a betrayal, both of proven friends following stated federal policy and of the civilization policy itself. In the midst of the negotiations, McKenney wrote a guilt-ridden letter to his superior, Secretary Barbour, stressing the obligations that the federal government bore to these people who had trusted in Jefferson's promises, left their home-lands, and built farms west of the Mississippi, which McKenney was now pressuring them to leave. Blaming white Arkansans, he asked, "What right . . . have white people to go and settle a Country, and then require for their accommodation and comfort that the Executive pledge shall be vio-lated for them?" This treaty would betray Jefferson's promises, and, by cast-ing more doubt on the government's word, "be fatal to our plan of Colonizing," all for the sake of illegal, undeserving squatters. But McKenney felt helpless to stop the cycle of illegal settlement and forced land cessions.[33]

The Cherokee delegation gained one small victory. Their new eastern boundary became the same longitude as the western border of Missouri, thus moving the western border of Arkansas Territory some fifty miles east-ward. And they persuaded McKenney to order the Arkansas governor to re-move any white settlers west of that line. But this was a minor concession to a people forced to abandon the land they had won by treaty, conquest, and settlement. In the contest between Indians who were good friends to the gov-ernment and white squatters who disobeyed the government's orders at every turn, the latter won.[34]

The delegation knew they would be in trouble back home. Secretary Barbour wrote them a note to carry home, stating that they had been sober and diligent in forwarding their people's interest and had negotiated the best deal the government would give. The Cherokees were not impressed. Rumors flew that the delegates would be killed as soon as they returned to the Arkansas Valley and that the Cherokees there had erected poles on which to place the delegates' heads. Like Doublehead and other chiefs who had ac-cepted earlier land cessions, Graves, Sequoyah, and their delegation had made themselves enemies of the Cherokee people.[35]

In October, the nation's newspaper, the *Cherokee Phoenix*, printed a let-ter from an Arkansas Cherokee called The Glass that charged the delegation with betraying their duty. Written in Sequoyah's characters and also trans-lated into English, the letter reported that the Arkansas Cherokees had called a council where the delegation members were "to be tried for not following their instructions," unless someone killed them first.[36] Another report soon followed that the delegation had been voted out of their chieftanships and "silenced forever" for their "fraud and deception." They were still alive but suffered civic death—stripped of their power to speak within or for their community. The council declared the treaty void but had to comply as their white neighbors became even bolder in their intrusions after learning that they had their government's law on their side.[37]

The eastern Cherokees responded just as negatively. As part of the treaty, the western chiefs agreed to encourage more emigration from east of the Mississippi. One delegation member, Thomas Maw, and interpreter James Rogers traveled from Washington to eastern Cherokee country with a federal agent to recruit emigrants. Even before Maw and Rogers arrived, Cherokees there pointed out the irony of the federal government's recruiting emigrants while simultaneously robbing the western Cherokees of the lands they had settled. The *Cherokee Phoenix* mocked the treaty, which offered each new emigrant "a good Rifle, a Blanket, and Kettle, and five pounds of Tobacco."[38] The newspaper explained: "a blanket has lost its former value with us, so has the rifle and the kettle, and the mention of five pounds of tobacco in a treaty, where the interest of a nation of Indians is supposed to be concerned, looks to us, too much like jesting." Perhaps in the past, the *Phoenix* admitted, Cherokees had been dazzled by rifles and kettles, but now they were a civilized nation and could not be trifled with so. In short, the article stated, "the case of these Cherokees afford[s] one proof of the uselessness of this emigrating scheme."[39]

Another article pointed to the treaty's obvious duplicity—now that "we are prospering under the exhilarating rewards of agriculture, the rifle is again put into our hands, and the brass kettle swung to our backs, and we are led into the deep forest where game is plenty, by the hands of those who would once have had us abandon the chase. Admirably consistent."[40] As the Cherokees understood, calls for their removal belied American rhetoric of transformation and inclusion. Interestingly, white Arkansans had made similar arguments against removing eastern Indians to their territory. The *Arkansas Gazette* in 1822 had asserted that "to remove Indians from a situation where they are surrounded by a white population, to a frontier where they have it in their power to practise their natural habits, implies a contradiction to that holy zeal and anxiety which the government has uniformly expressed, for reclaiming those sons of the forest to the bosom of the church and civilization."[41]

In their critiques, the Cherokees exposed the central contradiction in the civilization policy. It was designed at least as much for the purpose of freeing land for white settlement as it was for the preparation of Indians to join the republic. When those goals came into conflict, the government of and for white men always chose the former. Removal was structurally guaranteed to create conflict. First came intra-Indian strife between old inhabitants and immigrants, disrupting the lives of all the Indians in the now-embattled territory. Then, white squatters inevitably arrived, because they could reach any place that Indians could. Anglo-American settlement in turn necessitated a new solution, requiring Indians to move again. Every move was justified in the name of agriculture, but every move disrupted the stability on which agriculture depends.

*   *   *

Despite some easterners' lingering abstract belief in Indians' ability to change, the United States had developed a new policy, Indian expulsion. An 1826 treaty with the Creeks assigned them lands wedged in among the Osage, Cherokee, and Choctaw lands west of the Territory of Arkansas. The Delawares, Shawnees, Miamis, and others who had settled on Quapaw and Cherokee lands in earlier decades were pushed west with them. In the 1830s and 1840s, the government would forcibly remove Cherokees, Choctaws, Chickasaws, Creeks, Seminoles, and their black relatives, slaves, and allies from their eastern homes. Soon, Senecas, Caddos, Wichitas, Peorias, Modocs, Ottawas, Miamis, Shawnees, Delawares, Wyandots, Tonkawas, Poncas, Otos, Missouris, Pottawatomies, Kickapoos, Iowas, Sauks, Foxes, Pawnees, Kaws, Cheyennes, Arapahos, Comanches, Kiowas, and Apaches would all be added to the crowded occupants of former Osage (and before that, Wichita and Quiviran) territory along the Arkansas River in Oklahoma. The Oklahoma land rush of the late nineteenth century put most of even those lands in the hands of non-Indians.[42]

Regardless of some federal officials' hand-wringing, even elite white easterners increasingly believed that their race was inherently and permanently superior to all others. Despite blaming the land seizures on white settlers, Secretary Barbour reflected that this could all be the work of "an inscrutable destiny, whose fulfillment requires their extinction, however it may fill us with sorrow." If so, he concluded, neither the government nor the land-hungry white settlers bore the moral culpability.[43] Arkansas Governor George Izard, a South Carolinian by birth, reflected white America's growing insistence that racism was scientific. In an ethnographic report for the American Philosophical Society in 1827, the governor called the Quapaws "among the filthiest of their degraded race," ludicrously reporting that they had only ceased practicing human sacrifice a few years earlier. Izard concluded that "there is not among them the slightest approximation to a civilized state."[44] No previous official had written of the mid-continent's native peoples in such terms. To Izard, Indians were barbarians, and they showed no signs of changing. In the 1820s, Anglo-American belief in Indian transformation, always largely rhetorical, disappeared. Americans increasingly argued, in the words of historian Reginald Horsman, that "it was neither circumstances nor environment but specific, inherent physical differences that accounted for the failure of the non-Caucasian races to achieve Christianity and civilization."[45]

When and why the concept of race emerged is a long-standing debate. Most historians have come to agree that as colonialism and slavery developed, ideas about human difference became increasingly somatic and less about other kinds of distinctions. Racial ideology shifted and gradually solidified from the early colonial period through the twentieth century. Most fifteenth-century societies in Europe, Africa, and the Americas differentiated among peoples and defined their own people as superior in some way. Categorization might rest on lineage, religion, way of life, place of origin, or physical characteristics.[46]

Although ethnocentric, most societies had methods of transforming "the other" into an equal. In the case of Native American adoption ceremonies, these were actual practices that assimilated individuals in a short period of time. Envisioning a longer time period necessary for transformation, late medieval English thinkers hypothesized that changing climates or cultural practices would eventually change the body, darkening English men and women or blanching darker peoples. Over several generations, English influence might uplift heathen, savage societies, as the ancient Romans and then Roman Christianity had civilized the English. European hierarchies of Christian/heathen and civilized/savage aligned conveniently with economic motivations for seizing land and labor in Africa, the Americas, and Ireland, whose Catholicism the English defined as quasi-heathenism. Europeans built the economic structure of colonialism on inequality.[47]

Over time, when non-elites challenged inequality or sought inclusion in colonialism's benefits, categories of inequality became increasingly rigid and based on physical differences, rather than cultural ones. For example, when slaves converted to Christianity, English slaveholders in the 1660s changed whom they defined as enslaveable from non-Christians to people of black African descent. As historian Kathleen Brown puts it, non-whites "provoked English people to define themselves as white people." Spaniards developed a less dichotomized hierarchy with Iberian-born, light-skinned Catholics at the top. Throughout the Americas, these changes reified the existing structure of inequality and de-emphasized transformation. By the end of the eighteenth century, most white Americans believed that all blacks were naturally and permanently inferior to all whites, and they were rapidly extending the analysis to Indians.[48]

This ideology ignored the fact that native peoples had adapted to changing circumstances. As heavy competition in hunting diminished the fur trade, the Indians of the mid-continent adopted alternative economic and diplomatic strategies. They used their various ways of life to justify retaining their lands. They directly countered the long-standing assumption that Indians could only be hunters and that when game declined, they would have to keep moving west. They pointed out that they had compromised with countless foreign peoples in the past, working out ways of sharing the land by developing common understandings of friendship.

Why did the Arkansas Valley's native peoples not fight back? If the same Anglo-Americans had entered the region in 1541, the people of that era certainly would have. But largely peaceful and beneficial coexistence with Europeans left the valley's native peoples unprepared for racialized military conflict. The Quapaws had built their art of negotiation around avoiding violence. The Cherokees and Osages found themselves fighting the wrong enemy, each other. Only once the Osages were weakened did Anglo-Americans move in.

Unlike all previous newcomers, Anglo-Americans came in large enough numbers that they did not have to compromise. To them, the land was theirs to take, their own self-proclaimed native ground, cultivated not through diplomacy and incorporation but through violence and exclusion. Consequently, anyone who opposed them was an enemy. In the 1820s, Congress acceded to their vision, which foreshadowed Indian policy in the Jacksonian era. In 1828, the same year that the Cherokees left Arkansas, the country elected its first western president, Andrew Jackson. Jackson embodied white settlers' belief that, in his words, Indians had "neither the intelligence, the industry, the moral habits, nor the desire of improvement" to co-exist with Anglo-Americans. American Indian policy until the Civil War would rest on the assumption that Indians could not become part of a civilized, agrarian, white man's democracy. Inevitably enemies, they could only die off or remove farther west.[49]

Conclusion

In Andrew Jackson's annual message to Congress in 1830, the president reflected on the continent's Mississippian past. According to Jackson, "in the monuments and fortresses of an unknown people, spread over the extensive regions of the West, we behold the memorials of a once powerful race, which was exterminated or has disappeared to make room for the existing savage tribes." He concluded that, because the "savage tribes" of the colonial era and early republic took the mound-builders' place, Anglo-Americans should not lament that these Indians were in turn disappearing.[1]

Jackson had both his history and his present wrong. Colonial-era Indians had their roots in the Mississippian past and beyond. By no means a break with the past or a wholly different kind of people, they adapted to sixteenth-century changes in ways that demonstrate exactly what Jackson denied—Indians' ability to change. The past was not a series of conquest and extermination but of adaptations. Over the centuries, native North Americans had developed agriculture, adjusted their spiritual and diplomatic practices to changing circumstances, established new kinds of trade and trade networks, dealt with climatic and demographic changes, incorporated newcomers, and written constitutions and newspapers. The Arkansas Valley's residents incorporated wave after wave of Indian and European newcomers into local customs of diplomacy and land use. But in the 1820s, Anglo-Americans labeled them incapable of change, doomed to extinction, savage.

As their numbers grew, white Arkansans called on their powerful eastern connections. They persuaded their Congress to honor their metaphoric border with a geographic border between "savage" and "civilized" lands and to push the region's native peoples west. At the same time, they constructed a revised history of the place and its peoples, which obliterated past waves of immigrants and legitimized exclusive right to their native ground. The French, Spanish, and British had adopted local customs, calling the river the *Arkansas* after the people living there. They also came to recognize less-obvious geographic markers such as *Osage lands*, even as they overlaid them with colonial names such as *French Louisiana*. In contrast, Anglo-Americans coopted the name *Arkansas* for the lower valley and called the far reaches *Indian Territory*. No one in the past had established exclusive domain. Connections with other peoples had been crucial to native survival strategies long before the 1500s. Native links with Europeans had simply continued age-old strategies.

Locals had long directed the workings of empire on this borderland. For centuries, Indian and white newcomers had arrived with plans to change the locals, but locals had instead fit newcomers into their own concepts of friendship and land use and their own desires for the region. In the 1540s, when Hernando de Soto and Francisco de Vázquez Coronado proved more destructive than useful, the region's peoples expelled them. Beginning in the 1670s, Indians and Europeans found one another advantageous. Thinking in purely racial terms would have been illogical and counter-productive. The Osages could not have become the most powerful people in the eighteenth-century mid-continent if they had shunned the French. Yet even as Indians contested with one another, they controlled the form and content of their relations with the smaller numbers of Europeans.

In the 1989 book *The Indians' New World*, James Merrell described the waves of invasions that dramatically changed the existence of colonial-era Indians—microbes, trade, missionaries, and settlers. In the North American mid-continent, there were few missionaries or settlers until the 1810s and 1820s, a circumstance that gave native peoples plenty of time to respond to the changes borne by disease and new trade goods. Without a huge influx of foreign people, Indians retained control. They adopted European goods, but they set the terms of exchange, informed by a long history of trade with foreign peoples. Their world did change, but native peoples had the most influence over what form that change would take, and they negotiated and fought with one another over it. As historians have come to realize that Europeans "never had complete power" over those that they colonized or enslaved, this study of the Arkansas Valley illuminates a place where they had almost no power, where Europeans were peripheral to a Native American core.[2]

Although European empires never shaped colonies in exactly the ways that they intended, their intrusion mattered a great deal. But mattering and dominating are not the same. Europeans dominated some places. In others, they had to operate on middle grounds. In the Arkansas Valley, Indians dominated. Rather than being either "retained" or "destroyed," cultures and identities shifted to fit changing circumstances as they had for centuries before the arrival of Europeans. Arkansas Valley identities often incorporated aspects of European economies and cultures, but they remained Indian-centered and Indian-determined.[3]

People on the ground had great cultural and political influence on the European experience in the Americas. Colonialism was seldom if ever imposed but instead built through interaction. In their homelands, some African and Native American peoples set the terms of trade and diplomacy with Europeans. Even slaves and truly subject Indians played a role in shaping the institutions of slavery and colonialism. When we recognize that colonizers often exaggerated their mastery over their "colonies," it becomes clear that core regions were not safe and separate either. Native peoples had a steady and powerful influence over most parts of the Americas until at least the nineteenth century. None of this absolves Europeans of the horrors of colonialism and slavery but instead demonstrates the complicated and contingent colonial history of North America, which was not pre-determined to end in domination by European peoples, much less by an Anglo-American republic.[4]

But the United States did take over the heart of the continent in the early nineteenth century. Only Anglo-Americans decided their group could survive without the help of any others. While the residents of Quivira and Quigaltam had jettisoned a few roving strangers, Anglo-Americans expelled thousands of people who had made the valley their native ground. Unlike all previous newcomers, these latest settlers successfully rebuffed local ties because of military and economic support from the East and because they removed the problem. Even the Osages had needed to cultivate some allies. Unwilling to find ways of living with other groups in this diverse place, Anglo-Americans emptied the land of its former complexity, making it their own exclusive and uncontested native ground. They had the power to expel Indians forcibly, an easier task than keeping them nearby as subjugated people. The fact that for centuries Indians and Europeans had relied on one another to achieve what they wanted from their world makes nineteenth-century racism, dispossession, and exclusion all the more tragic and unjustifiable.[5]

But to end this story with Anglo-American triumph would privilege Jackson's myopic nineteenth-century construct. Just as underneath the teleological story of colonialism lies the Arkansas Valley where Indians dominated for centuries, so too, behind Anglo-Americans' victory is a more complicated cultural, political, and economic reality. Indians still live in the heart of the continent and still function culturally and politically as Osages, Quapaws, Cherokees, Caddos, and Wichitas. The states of Arkansas, Kansas, and Missouri still bear the names of the region's nations, as do smaller places—Wichita, Osage Gap, Pawhuska, the Quapaw Quarter. Since the nineteenth century, Indians have regained some sovereignty. Federally recognized tribes remain "distinct, independent political communities." In many ways self-governing, these tribes deal with states, and even the United States, as independent governments.[6]

Despite many Americans' tendency to seek their country's roots in the Pilgrims' landing, in many ways colonial Louisiana better foreshadowed the twenty-first-century United States than colonial Plymouth or Jamestown did. The Louisiana Purchase introduced exactly the *"Gallo-Hispano-Indian ominium gatherum"* that opponent Congressman Fisher Ames warned against in 1803, a multicultural reality that constitutes a major part of American identity today.[7] And populations of particular mid-continental tribes have risen in Oklahoma and other parts of the nation. The 2000 census reported over 15,000 Osages, more than 2,000 Quapaws, nearly 2,000 Wichitas, over 4,000 Caddos, and over 700,000 Cherokees.[8]

These Indians' histories did not end in the 1820s any more than they began in 1492. As before, they changed with the times. Even today, tendencies to romanticize pre-colonial Native Americans as twenty-first-century environmentalists reveal that old nineteenth-century assumption of Indian stagnancy. In reality, two more centuries have passed in which Indians have adapted to changing times: more land rushes, repeated attempts at forced assimilation, waves of repressing native languages and spiritual practices, the Red Power movement's calls for a united Indian identity, and the opportunities of multiculturalism and changing ideas about tribal sovereignty.

Indians have continued to assert self-determination and agency as individuals and as peoples through good and bad times, wars, depressions, oil booms, lawsuits, living, dying, and remembering. Even after the United States extinguished the last Indian land claim on the lower Arkansas River and created the state of "Arkansas" as a white man's land, most of the valley remained Indian Territory, running right through the heart of Oklahoma. For another 200 years, these Indians have shifted but not abandoned their past views of themselves and their world, while adapting to opportunities in tourism, gaming, and the courts. In the nineteenth century, Native Americans lost their dominance over the continent, but their histories, identities, and cultures continued to adjust as they had in the past.

Abbreviations

BLC	*Before Lewis and Clark: Documents Illustrating the History of the Missouri, 1785–1804,* ed. and trans. A. P. Nasatir (St. Louis, 1952)
LBATH	Letter Book of the Arkansas Trading House, 1805–10, M142, Record Group 75, National Archives, Washington, D.C.
LCRP	Louisiana Colonial Records Project, Historic New Orleans Collection, New Orleans, microfilmed from the Archives Nationales, Colonies, Paris
MPAFD	*Mississippi Provincial Archives: French Dominion,* ed. and trans. Dunbar Rowland and A. G. Sanders (vols. 1–3: Jackson, Miss., 1927; vols. 4–5: ed. Patricia Kay Galloway, Baton Rouge, La., 1984)
NCE	*Narratives of the Coronado Expedition,* 1540–1542, ed. George P. Hammond and Agapito Rey (Albuquerque, 1940)
PC	Papeles de Cuba, Archivo General de Indias, Seville, Spain
SLS	St. Louis Superintendency, Field Records, 1813–53, U.S. Office of Indian Affairs, Kansas State Historical Society, Topeka, Kans.
SMV	*Spain in the Mississippi Valley, 1765–1794,* ed. and trans. Lawrence Kinnaird (Washington, D.C., 1946–49)
TP	*The Territorial Papers of the United States,* ed. Clarence E. Carter (Washington, D.C., 1934–62)
VL	Vaudreuil Letterbook, Loudoun Collection, Huntington Library, San Marino, Calif.
VP	Vaudreuil Papers, Loudoun Collection, Huntington Library
WMQ	*William and Mary Quarterly,* 3rd ser.

Notes

Introduction

1. The introductory vignette comes from Jacques Marquette, "Of the first Voyage made by Father Marquette toward new Mexico," in *The Jesuit Relations and Allied Documents: Travels and Explorations of the Jesuit Missionaries in New France, 1610–1791*, ed. Reuben Gold Thwaites (Cleveland, 1896–1901), 59: 153–59.

2. For various interpretations of Quapaw pre-seventeenth-century history, see the discussion in Chapter 3.

3. Richard White, *The Middle Ground: Indians, Empires, and Republics in the Great Lakes Region, 1650–1815* (New York, 1991). Another influential model, James H. Merrell's "the Indians' new world," also describes a broken-apart place. James H. Merrell, *The Indians' New World: Catawbas and Their Neighbors from European Contact Through the Era of Removal* (New York, 1989).

4. For a wide-angle view of dependency and world capitalist systems, see Eric Wolf, *Europe and the People Without History* (Berkeley, Calif., 1982). For an argument that Native Americans very early became "prisoners of an implacable process that led to impoverishment and dependency," see Denys Delâge, *Bitter Feast: Amerindians and Europeans in Northeastern North America, 1600–64*, trans. Jane Brierley (Vancouver, 1993), 78. The most sophisticated application of dependency theory to Native American relations with Europeans is Richard White, *The Roots of Dependency: Subsistence, Environment, and Social Change Among the Choctaws, Pawnees, and Navajos* (Lincoln, Neb., 1983). See his explication of dependency theory on pages xvi–xvii. But also see White, *Middle Ground*, especially pages 94–96, 128–40, 482–85, in which White argues that the native peoples of the Great Lakes region did not fit the dependency model, at least not until the nineteenth century. For critiques of over-emphasizing European-imposed change, see Lauren Benton, *Law and Colonial Cultures: Legal Regimes in World History, 1400–1900* (New York, 2002); Gary Clayton Anderson, *The Indian Southwest, 1580–1830: Ethnogenesis and Reinvention* (Norman, Okla., 1999); John Thornton, *Africa and Africans in the Making of the Atlantic World, 1400–1680* (New York, 1992), 2–5. For Mill Creek, see Charles R. Cobb, *From Quarry to Cornfield: The Political Economy of Mississippian Hoe Production* (Tuscaloosa, Ala., 2000). Theda Perdue provides an example of eighteenth-century southeastern Indian communities as cosmopolitan places, vibrantly full of new goods and ideas. Theda Perdue, *"Mixed Blood" Indians: Racial Construction in the Early South* (Athens, Ga., 2003), 3.

5. On the purposes of empire, see John Robert McNeill, *Atlantic Empires of France and Spain: Louisbourg and Havana, 1700–1763* (Chapel Hill, N.C., 1985), 3; Eric

Hinderaker, *Elusive Empires: Constructing Colonialism in the Ohio Valley, 1673–1800* (New York, 1997), xi. On the role of non-Spaniards in creating the Spanish empire, see Henry Kamen, *Spain's Road to Empire: The Making of a World Power, 1492–1763* (London, 2002). For an argument against assumptions of thorough and immediate Spanish "conquest," see Stephanie Wood, *Transcending Conquest: Nahua Views of Spanish Colonial Mexico* (Norman, Okla., 2003). For the North American West, see Colin G. Calloway, *One Vast Winter Count: The Native American West Before Lewis and Clark* (Lincoln, Neb., 2003).

6. For European views of sovereignty, see Patricia Seed, *Ceremonies of Possession in Europe's Conquest of the New World, 1492–1640* (New York, 1995); David Armitage, *The Ideological Origins of the British Empire* (New York, 2000); Martin van Gelderen, "The State and Its Rivals in Early-Modern Europe," in *States and Citizens: History, Theory, Prospects*, ed. Quentin Skinner and Bo Stråth (New York, 2003); *The Cambridge History of Political Thought, 1450–1700*, ed. J. H. Burns (New York, 1991); Kenneth Pennington, *The Prince and the Law, 1200–1600: Sovereignty and Rights in the Western Legal Tradition* (Berkeley, Calif., 1993).

7. Nancy Shoemaker, *A Strange Likeness: Becoming Red and White in Eighteenth-Century North America* (New York, 2004), 15–23; Alan Ryan, "Property," in *The Foundations of Modern Political Thought*, ed. Quentin Skinner (New York, 1978), 1: 322; Daniel W. Bromley, "The Commons, Property, and Common-Property Regimes," in *Making the Commons Work: Theory, Practice, and Policy*, ed. Daniel W. Bromley et al. (San Francisco, 1992), 3–15; Elinor Ostrom, *Governing the Commons: The Evolution of Institutions for Collective Action* (New York, 1991); Anthony Pagden, *Lords of All the World: Ideologies of Empire in Spain, Britain and France c.1500–c.1800* (New Haven, Conn., 1995); R. Douglas Hurt, *Indian Agriculture in America: Prehistory to the Present* (Lawrence, Kan., 1987), 74–75.

8. See April Lee Hatfield, "Spanish Colonization Literature, Powhatan Geographies, and English Perceptions of Tsenacommacah/Virginia," *Journal of Southern History* 69 (2003), 245–82.

9. For discussions of the perception of Indian timelessness and the difficulties of rooting it out of colonial history, see James H. Merrell, "Some Thoughts on Colonial Historians and American Indians," *WMQ* 46 (1989), 94–119; Daniel K. Richter, "Whose Indian History?" *WMQ* 50 (1993), 379–93. For a defense of a more essential Indian nature, see Calvin Martin, "The Metaphysics of Writing Indian-White History" and "Time and the American Indian," in *The American Indian and the Problem of History*, ed. Calvin Martin (New York, 1987). For the argument that disease doomed Indian occupation, see Alfred W. Crosby, "Virgin Soil Epidemics as a Factor in the Aboriginal Depopulation in America," *WMQ* 33 (1976), 289–99. For warnings against assuming the totality of diseases' power, see Paul Kelton, "Avoiding the Smallpox Spirits: Colonial Epidemics and Southeastern Indian Survival," *Ethnohistory* 51 (2004), 45–71; David S. Jones, "Virgin Soils Revisited," *WMQ* 60 (2003), 703–42.

10. On borders, see Jeremy Adelman and Stephen Aron, "From Borderlands to Borders: Empires, Nation-States, and the Peoples in Between in North American History," *American Historical Review*, 104 (1999), 814–41; Alan Taylor, "The Divided Ground: Upper Canada, New York, and the Iroquois Six Nations, 1783–1815"; Andrés Reséndez, "Getting Cured and Getting Drunk: State Versus Market in Texas and New

Mexico, 1800–1850"; Andrew R. L. Cayton, "Comment: Writing North American History"; all in "Symposium: Understanding Boundaries in the Early Republic," *Journal of the Early Republic* 22 (2002), 55–111. For the Casqui-Pacaha border, see Rodrigo Rangel, "Account of the Northern Conquest and Discovery of Hernando De Soto," trans. John E. Worth, *The De Soto Chronicles: The Expedition of Hernando de Soto to North America in* 1539–1543, ed. Lawrence A. Clayton, Vernon James Knight, Jr., and Edward C. Moore (Tuscaloosa, Ala., 1993), 303.

11. For a recent example of the old narrative, see Bernard Bailyn, *Voyagers to the West: A Passage in the Peopling of America on the Eve of the Revolution* (New York, 1986). In his work analyzing European conquest from colonial Native American perspectives, Daniel Richter writes that "the 'master narrative' of early America remains essentially European-focused." Daniel K. Richter, *Facing East from Indian Country: A Native History of Early America* (Cambridge, Mass., 2001), 8. Neal Salisbury traces these narratives of inevitability back to early English colonial accounts. Neal Salisbury, *Manitou and Providence: Indians, Europeans, and the Making of New England, 1500–1643* (New York, 1982), 3–6.

12. Zenon Trudeau to Manuel Gayoso de Lemos, Jan. 15, 1798, *BLC,* 2: 538.

Chapter 1. *A Bordered Land, to* 1540

1. George Sabo III, "Native American Prehistory," in Jeannie M. Whayne, Thomas A. Deblack, George Sabo III, and Morris S. Arnold, *Arkansas: A Narrative History* (Fayetteville, Ark., 2002), 1–2; J. Christopher Gillam, "Paleoindian Settlement in Northeastern Arkansas," in *Arkansas Archaeology: Essays in Honor of Dan and Phyllis Morse,* ed. Robert C. Mainfort, Jr., and Marvin D. Jeter (Fayetteville, Ark., 1999), 100–101; Dan F. Morse and Phyllis A. Morse, *Archaeology of the Central Mississippi Valley* (New York, 1983), 41, 71–72; Dan F. Morse and Phyllis A. Morse, "Northeast Arkansas," in *Prehistory of the Central Mississippi Valley,* ed. Charles H. McNutt (Tuscaloosa, Ala., 1996), 119–22; Robert H. Lafferty III and James E. Price, "Southeast Missouri," in *Prehistory of the Central Mississippi Valley,* 2–3; John H. House, "East-Central Arkansas," in *Prehistory of the Central Mississippi Valley,* 140; Waldo R. Wedel, "The Prehistoric Plains," in *Ancient North Americans,* ed. Jesse D. Jennings (San Francisco, 1983), 215.

2. Bruce D. Smith, "The Archaeology of the Southeastern United States: From Dalton to De Soto, 10,500–500 B.P.," *Advances in World Archaeology* 5 (1986), 11–13; George Sabo III and Anne M. Early, "Prehistoric Culture History," in George Sabo III et al., *Human Adaptation in the Ozark and Ouachita Mountains* (Fayetteville, Ark., 1990), 40, 53–57.

3. Neal Salisbury, "The Indians' Old World: Native Americans and the Coming of Europeans," *WMQ* 53 (1996), 437; James F. Brooks, *Captives and Cousins: Slavery, Kinship, and Community in the Southwest Borderlands* (Chapel Hill, N.C., 2002), 17–18, 88; Richard White, *The Middle Ground: Indians, Empires, and Republics in the Great Lakes Region, 1650–1815* (New York, 1991), 80.

4. Jon Muller, *Mississippian Political Economy* (New York, 1997), 248, 327; Daniel K. Richter, *Facing East from Indian Country: A Native History of Early America*

(Cambridge, Mass., 2001), 29; Marshall Sahlins, *Stone Age Economics* (Chicago, 1972), 215. For European first contacts in the Arkansas Valley, see Chapters 2 and 3.

5. Smith, "Archaeology of the Southeastern United States," 30–31; William A. Turnbaugh, "Wide-Area Connections in Native North America," *American Indian Culture and Research Journal* 1 (1976), 23–24.

6. James A. Brown, Richard A. Kerber, and Howard D. Winters, "Trade and the Evolution of Exchange Relations at the Beginning of the Mississippian Period," in *The Mississippian Emergence*, ed. Bruce D. Smith (Washington, D.C., 1990), 273; Morse and Morse, "Northeast Arkansas," 125; James B. Griffin, "Comments on the Late Prehistoric Societies in the Southeast," in *Towns and Temples Along the Mississippi*, ed. David H. Dye and Cheryl Anne Cox (Tuscaloosa, Ala., 1990), 6.

7. Morse and Morse, *Archaeology of the Central Mississippi Valley*, 116, 120–25, 163–66; Lynda Norene Shaffer, *Native Americans Before 1492: The Moundbuilding Centers of the Eastern Woodlands* (Armonk, N.Y., 1992), 21, 42; Muller, *Mississippian Political Economy*, 135, 327, 366–67; Turnbaugh, "Wide-Area Connections," 22–28; Smith, "Archaeology of the Southeastern United States," 30–31, 41–42; Martha Ann Rolingson, "The Toltec Mounds Site: A Ceremonial Center in the Arkansas River Lowland," in *Mississippian Emergence*, 27.

8. Sabo, "Native American Prehistory," 8; Smith, "Archaeology of the Southeastern United States," 32–33; Shaffer, *Native Americans Before 1492*, 22, 36, 42; Marvin D. Jeter and Ann M. Early, "Prehistory of the Saline River Drainage Basin, Central to Southeast Arkansas," in *Arkansas Archaeology*, 35–36; Dan F. Morse and Phyllis A. Morse, "Changes in Interpretation in the Archaeology of the Central Mississippi Valley Since 1983," *North American Archaeologist* 17 (1996), 11; Collections at University of Arkansas Museum, Fayetteville, Ark.

9. Brian M. Fagan, *Ancient North America: The Archaeology of a Continent* (London, 2000), 170; Morse and Morse, "Changes in Interpretation," 14; Morse and Morse, *Archaeology of the Central Mississippi Valley*, 130.

10. Stuart J. Fiedel, *Prehistory of the Americas* (New York, 1992), 109; Morse and Morse, *Archaeology of the Central Mississippi Valley*, 137–42; Phyllis Morse and Dan F. Morse, "The Zebree Site: An Emerged Early Mississippian Expression in Northeast Arkansas," in *Mississippian Emergence*, 56.

11. I use R. Douglas Hurt's definition of agriculture, "raising things on purpose." It is possible that people grew gourds several thousand years earlier, possibly as fishing net floats. Written and oral records from across North America reveal that women were responsible for plant cultivation and food preparation. Artifacts that portray corn, hoes, and corn-grinding equipment show women using them, and farming and cooking tools have been found buried with women. R. Douglas Hurt, *Indian Agriculture in America: Prehistory to the Present* (Lawrence, Kans., 1987), 1, 11–12; Gayle J. Fritz, "Gender and the Early Cultivation of Gourds in Eastern North America," *American Antiquity* 64 (1999), 417–29; Gayle J. Fritz, "A Three-Thousand-Year-Old Cache of Crop Seeds from Marble Bluff, Arkansas," in *People, Plants, and Landscapes: Studies in Paleoethnobotany*, ed. Kristen J. Gremillion (Tuscaloosa, Ala., 1997), 42–62; Morse and Morse, *Archaeology of the Central Mississippi Valley*, 95, 137, 143; Shaffer, *Native Americans Before* 1492, 24, figures 26, 27; Fiedel, *Prehistory of the Americas*, 112–13.

12. Morse and Morse, "Changes in Interpretation," 6, 11; Smith, "Archaeology of the Southeastern United States," 44, 50–51, 61; Fagan, *Ancient North America*, 306–8, 446; A Gentleman of Elvas, "True Relation of the Hardships Suffered by Governor Don Hernando de Soto," trans. James Alexander Robertson, *The De Soto Chronicles: The Expedition of Hernando de Soto to North America in* 1539–1543, ed. Lawrence A. Clayton, Vernon James Knight, Jr., and Edward C. Moore (Tuscaloosa, Ala., 1993), 1: 169.

13. Morse and Morse, *Archaeology of the Central Mississippi Valley*, 205, 210, 255; Frank F. Schambach, "Spiro and the Tunica: A New Interpretation of the Role of the Tunica in the Culture History of the Southeast and the Southern Plains, A.D. 1100–1750," in *Arkansas Archaeology*, 170–71; Charles R. Cobb, *From Quarry to Cornfield: The Political Economy of Mississippian Hoe Production* (Tuscaloosa, Ala., 2000), 1–3, 190; Neal H. Lopinot, "Cahokian Food Production Reconsidered," in *Cahokia: Domination and Ideology in the Mississippian World*, ed. Timothy R. Pauketat and Thomas E. Emerson (Lincoln, Neb., 1997), 54; Fagan, *Ancient North America*, 308; Richter, *Facing East*, 55–56; David W. Benn, "Moon: A Fortified Mississippian-Period Village in Poinsett Country, Arkansas," in *Changing Perspectives on the Archaeology of the Central Mississippi River Valley*, ed. Michael J. O'Brien and Robert C. Dunnell (Tuscaloosa, Ala., 1998), 257.

14. Henry W. Hamilton, "The Spiro Mound," *Missouri Archaeologist* 14 (1952), 38, plate 20; Ian W. Brown, "The Calumet Ceremony in the Southeast as Observed Archaeologically," *Powhatan's Mantle*, 2nd ed., forthcoming; Donald J. Blakeslee, "The Origin and Spread of the Calumet Ceremony," *American Antiquity* 46 (1981), 759–68.

15. Smith, "Archaeology of the Southeastern United States," 52; David G. Anderson, "The Role of Cahokia in the Evolution of Southeastern Mississippian Society," in *Cahokia: Domination and Ideology*, 254; Morse and Morse, *Archaeology of the Central Mississippi Valley*, 181, 186; Brown, Kerber, and Winters, "Trade and the Evolution of Exchange Relations," 264–65.

16. For the prominence of goods exchange in first encounters between Indians and Europeans, see, besides examples throughout this book, Daniel H. Usner, Jr., *Indians, Settlers, and Slaves in a Frontier Exchange Economy: The Lower Mississippi Valley Before* 1783 (Chapel Hill, N.C., 1992), 26; Robert A. Williams, Jr., *Linking Arms Together: American Indian Treaty Visions of Law and Peace, 1600–1800* (New York, 1997), 62, 76–81; Cornelius J. Jaenen, "The Role of Presents in French-Amerindian Trade," in *Explorations in Canadian Economic History: Essays in Honour of Irene M. Spry*, ed. Duncan Cameron (Ottawa, 1985), 231. See also Marcel Mauss, *The Gift: The Form and Reason for Exchange in Archaic Societies*, trans. W. D. Halls (New York, 1990); Lewis Hyde, *The Gift: Imagination and the Erotic Life of Property* (New York, 1983).

17. This gendered nature of diplomacy pervaded North America. See, for example, the pre-colonial Iroquois in Daniel K. Richter, *The Ordeal of the Longhouse: The Peoples of the Iroquois League in the Era of European Colonization* (Chapel Hill, N.C., 1992), 23. Thanks to Kathleen Bragdon for her thoughts on Mississippian women and diplomacy in her comment on "A Bordered Land: Mississippian Foreign Relations, 700–1600" panel, The Atlantic World and Virginia, 1550–1624, Conference, Williamsburg, Va., Mar. 2004.

18. Fagan, *Ancient North America*, 53; Rodrigo Rangel, "Account of the Northern Conquest," 1: 301–3; Luis Hernández de Biedma, "Relation of the Island of Florida," 1: 241–42; both trans. John E. Worth, *De Soto Chronicles*; Elvas, "True Relation," 1: 119–20, 125; Garcilaso de la Vega, the Inca, "La Florida," trans. Charmion Shelby, *De Soto Chronicles*, 2: 402–3; Shaffer, *Native Americans Before* 1492, 58, figure 25.

19. Smith, "Archaeology of the Southeastern United States," 41; Elvas, "True Relation," 1: 117.

20. Morse and Morse, *Archaeology of the Central Mississippi Valley*, 202–3; Charles M. Hudson, *The Southeastern Indians* (Knoxville, Tenn., 1976), 95–96.

21. Robert L. Hall, "Cahokia Identity and Interaction Models of Cahokia Mississippian," in *Cahokia and the Hinterlands: Middle Mississippian Cultures of the Midwest*, ed. Thomas E. Emerson and R. Barry Lewis (Urbana, Ill., 1991), 11; Morse and Morse, "Zebree Site," 56; Sabo, "Native American Prehistory," 18–19; James A. Brown, Robert E. Bell, and Don G. Wyckoff, "Caddoan Settlement Patterns in the Arkansas River Drainage," in *Mississippian Settlement Patterns*, ed. Bruce D. Smith (New York, 1978), 169–200; Bruce D. Smith, "Variation in Mississippian Settlement Patterns," in *Mississippian Settlement Patterns*, 479–503; Sabo and Early, "Prehistoric Culture History," 82–99; James A. Brown, *Prehistoric Southern Ozark Marginality: A Myth Exposed* (Columbia, Mo., 1984).

22. Rolingson, "Toltec Mounds," 37–46; Sabo, "Native American Prehistory," 12.

23. J. Daniel Rogers, "Dispersed Communities and Integrated Households: A Perspective from Spiro and the Arkansas Basin," in *Mississippian Communities and Households*, ed. J. Daniel Rogers and Bruce D. Smith (Tuscaloosa, Ala., 1995), 93; Brown, Kerber, and Winters, "Trade and the Evolution of Exchange Relations," 264–65, 274; James A. Brown, *The Spiro Ceremonial Center: The Archaeology of Arkansas Valley Caddoan Culture in Eastern Oklahoma* (Ann Arbor, Mich., 1996), 199; John E. Kelly, "The Evidence for Prehistoric Exchange and Its Implications for the Development of Cahokia," in *New Perspectives on Cahokia: Views from the Periphery*, ed. James B. Stoltman (Madison, Wisc., 1991), 82–85; J. Daniel Rogers, "Markers of Social Integration: The Development of Centralized Authority in the Spiro Region," in *Political Structure and Change in the Prehistoric Southeastern United States*, ed. John F. Scarry (Gainesville, Fla., 1996), 64–68; Schambach, "Spiro and the Tunica," 170–75; Hamilton, "Spiro Mound," 30–41, 44–45, 48–50, 55–57; Charles C. Willoughby, "Textile Fabrics from the Spiro Mound," *Missouri Archaeologist* 14 (1952), 107–8; J. Daniel Rogers, Carla J. Dove, Marcy Heacker, and Gary R. Graves, "Identification of Feathers in Textiles from the Craig Mound at Spiro, Oklahoma," *Southeastern Archaeology* 21 (2002), 245–51; Spiro Mounds Archaeological Center, Spiro, Okla.

24. Anderson, "Role of Cahokia," 254.

25. Shaffer, *Native Americans Before* 1492, figure 18; Brown, *Spiro Ceremonial Center*, 196; Hamilton, "Spiro Mound," 30, 36, 42; Hudson, *Southeastern Indians*, 245–47; Rita Fisher-Carroll and Robert C. Mainfort, Jr., "Late Prehistoric Mortuary Behavior at Upper Nodena," *Southeastern Archaeology* 19 (2000), 105–19; Dan F. Morse, "The Nodena Phase," in *Towns and Temples*, 86–87; Muller, *Mississippian Political Economy*, 380–81; Vincas P. Steponaitis, "Prehistoric Archaeology in the Southeastern United States, 1970–1985," *Annual Review of Anthropology* 15 (1986), 392; Karl

T. Steinen, "Ambushes, Raids, and Palisades: Mississippian Warfare in the Interior Southeast," *Southeastern Archaeology* 11 (1992), 132–39.

26. George Sabo III, "Indians and Spaniards in Arkansas: Symbolic Action in the Sixteenth Century," in *The Expedition of Hernando de Soto West of the Mississippi, 1541–1543: Proceedings of the De Soto Symposia, 1988 and 1990*, ed. Gloria A. Young and Michael P. Hoffman (Fayetteville, Ark., 1993), 195–98, 206–7.

27. Richter, *Facing East*, 14, 84; James Axtell, *The Invasion Within: The Contest of Cultures in Colonial North America* (New York, 1985), 285; Eric Hinderaker, *Elusive Empires: Constructing Colonialism in the Ohio Valley, 1673–1800* (New York, 1997), 55–66.

28. Pauketat and Emerson, *Cahokia: Domination and Ideology*, 22; Michael J. O'Brien, "The General Physical and Cultural Environment," in *Mississippian Community Organization: The Powers Phase in Southeastern Missouri*, ed. Michael J. O'Brien (New York, 2001), 48–49; Patricia Galloway, "Colonial Period Transformations in the Mississippi Valley: Dis-integration, Alliance, Confederation, Playoff," in *The Transformation of the Southeastern Indians, 1540–1760*, ed. Robbie Ethridge and Charles Hudson (Jackson, Miss., 2002), 230–31; Morse and Morse, *Archaeology of the Central Mississippi Valley*, 237, 259, 266–67, 271, 280–84, 290–93; Phyllis A. Morse, "The Parkin Site and the Parkin Phase," in *Towns and Temples*, 121–23.

29. Rangel's account of the expedition credited Casqui and Pacaha with the "best towns that they had seen" in their three years of travel across the Southeast. Rangel, "Account of the Northern Conquest," 1: 301.

30. J. Daniel Rogers, "The Archaeological Analysis of Domestic Organization," in *Mississippian Communities and Households*, 25; Rogers, "Dispersed Communities and Integrated Households, 81, 85, 89–93; Spiro Mounds Archaeological Center. For similar reactions in the East, see Richter, *Facing East*, 5.

31. The French called these peoples by many names, including the Panis, the Mentos (probably referring to the Tawakonis or an additional group who lived amongst the Tawakonis), and the Panis Piqués (referring to the Taovayas, Guichitas, and Iscanis). David La Vere, *The Caddo Chiefdoms: Caddo Economics and Politics, 700–1835* (Lincoln, Neb., 1998); James B. Griffin, "An Interpretation of the Place of Spiro in Southeastern Archaeology," *Missouri Archaeologist* 14 (1952), 106; Francisco Vázquez de Coronado to His Majesty, Oct. 20, 1541, *NCE*, 186, 188–89; F. Todd Smith, *The Wichita Indians: Traders of Texas and the Southern Plains, 1540–1845* (College Station, Tex., 2000), xi, 3–4, 8; George E. Hyde, *The Pawnee Indians* (Norman, Okla., 1974), 13–14; Elizabeth A. H. John, *Storms Brewed in Other Men's Worlds: The Confrontation of Indians, Spanish, and French in the Southwest, 1540–1795* (Norman, Okla., 1996), 214–15; Mildred Mott Wedel, "The Wichita Indians in the Arkansas River Basin," in *Plains Indian Studies: A Collection of Essays in Honor of John C. Ewers and Waldo R. Wedel*, ed. Douglas H. Ubelaker and Herman J. Viola (Washington, D.C., 1982), 119; Wedel, "Prehistoric Plains," 233; Pedro de Castañeda de Náxera, "Narrative of the Expedition to Cíbola, Undertaken in 1540," *NCE*, 261.

32. The Teyas may instead have been ancestors of the Jumanos, or both. Coronado to His Majesty, Oct. 20, 1541, *NCE*, 188–89; David La Vere, *Contrary Neighbors: Southern Plains and Removed Indians in Indian Territory* (Norman, Okla., 2000), 10, 32; Brooks, *Captives and Cousins*, 83–88; Salisbury, "The Indians' Old World," 448;

Smith, *Wichita Indians*, 3–9; Carroll L. Riley, "The Teya Indians of the Southwestern Plains," in *The Coronado Expedition to Tierra Nueva: The 1540–1542 Route Across the Southwest*, ed. Richard Flint and Shirley Cushing Flint (Niwot, Colo., 1997), 320–43; Juan Jaramillo, "Narrative Given by Captain Juan Jaramillo of His Journey to the New Land in New Spain and to the Discovery of Cíbola Under General Francisco Vázquez Coronado," *NCE*, 300–301; "Relación postrera de Cíbola," *NCE*, 311; Elvas, "True Relation," 1: 123–24; Biedma, "Relation of the Island of Florida," 1: 241; Schambach, "Spiro and the Tunica," 169–224; Jack D. Forbes, *Apache, Navaho, and Spaniard* (Norman, Okla., 1960), 15; John, *Storms Brewed in Other Men's Worlds*, 20–21.

33. See, for example, Quivira and the Great Settlement in Chapter 2. On the importance of the sixteenth-century South and why it is little-studied, see Charles Hudson, "An Unknown South: Spanish Explorers and Southeastern Chiefdoms," in *Visions and Revisions: Ethnohistoric Perspectives on Southern Cultures*, ed. George Sabo III and William M. Schneider (Athens, Ga., 1987), 6–24.

34. Richard White, *The Roots of Dependency: Subsistence, Environment, and Social Change among the Choctaws, Pawnees, and Navajos* (Lincoln, Neb., 1983), 7–9.

Chapter 2. Hosting Strangers, 1541–1650

1. I have followed the most recent consensus that the Bradley archaeological site is the main town of Pacaha province and the Parkin site is the main town of the Casqui province, but nearby potential sites are reasonably similar. Information about life in Pacaha comes from accounts of de Soto's visit to the town (cited later in the chapter) and from excellent archaeological research over the past two decades, including Dan F. Morse and Phyllis A. Morse, "Northeast Arkansas," in *Prehistory of the Central Mississippi Valley*, ed. Charles H. McNutt (Tuscaloosa, Ala., 1996), 128–32; Dan F. Morse and Phyllis A. Morse, "Changes in Interpretation in the Archaeology of the Central Mississippi Valley Since 1983," *North American Archaeologist* 17 (1996), 1–35; Rita Fisher-Carroll and Robert C. Mainfort, Jr., "Late Prehistoric Mortuary Behavior at Upper Nodena," *Southeastern Archaeology* 19 (2000), 105–19; and sources cited elsewhere in this chapter. For the most recent interpretation of de Soto's route, see Charles Hudson, "Reconstructing the de Soto Expedition Route West of the Mississippi River: Summary and Contents," 143–54; David H. Dye, "Reconstruction of the de Soto Expedition Route in Arkansas: The Mississippi Alluvial Plain," 47–49; both in *The Expedition of Hernando de Soto West of the Mississippi, 1541–1543: Proceedings of the De Soto Symposia 1988 and 1990*, ed. Gloria A. Young and Michael P. Hoffman (Fayetteville, Ark., 1993).

2. Luis Hernández de Biedma, "Relation," trans. John E. Worth, *The De Soto Chronicles: The Expedition of Hernando de Soto to North America in 1539–1543*, ed. Lawrence A. Clayton, Vernon James Knight, Jr., and Edward C. Moore (Tuscaloosa, Ala., 1993), 1: 239–40. For archaeological evidence of Pacahan expansion, see Dan F. Morse and Phyllis A. Morse, *Archaeology of the Central Mississippi Valley* (New York, 1983), 296, 301; Dan F. Morse, "The Nodena Phase," in *Towns and Temples Along the Mississippi*, ed. David H. Dye and Cheryl Anne Cox (Tuscaloosa, Ala., 1990), 80. For

Native American accounts of seeing the Spanish for the first time, see Bernardino de Sahagún, *Florentine Codex*, trans. Lysander Kemp, *The Broken Spears: The Aztec Account of the Conquest of Mexico*, ed. Miguel Leon-Portilla (Boston, 1992), 25–31, 33–34. For a narrative account of the de Soto expedition, see Charles Hudson, *Knights of Spain, Warriors of the Sun* (Athens, Ga., 1997).

3. Christopher L. Miller and George R. Hamell, "A New Perspective on Indian-White Contact: Cultural Symbols and Colonial Trade," *Journal of American History* 73 (1986), 320–21; Daniel K. Richter, *Facing East from Indian Country: A Native History of Early America* (Cambridge, Mass., 2001), 11–40; James Axtell, *Natives and Newcomers: The Cultural Origins of Early America* (New York, 2001), 21. Gananath Obeyesekere, *The Apotheosis of Captain Cook: European Mythmaking in the Pacific* (Princeton, N.J., 1992), argues that Pacific Islanders did not see Europeans as gods but rather that Europeans created this idea as part of their own myth-making.

4. For the de Soto accounts, see the essays in *The Hernando de Soto Expedition: History, Historiography, and "Discovery"*, ed. Patricia Galloway (Lincoln, Neb., 1997); David Henige, "Proxy Data, Historical Method, and the de Soto Expedition," in *Expedition of Hernando de Soto West of the Mississippi*, 155–72; George E. Lankford, "Legends of the Adelantado," in *Expedition of Hernando de Soto West of the Mississippi*, 173–91. For the Coronado accounts, see Charles W. Polzer, "The Coronado Documents: Their Limitations," in *The Coronado Expedition to Tierra Nueva: The 1540–1542 Route Across the Southwest*, ed. Richard Flint and Shirley Cushing Flint (Niwot, Co., 1997), 36–43; Carroll L. Riley, introduction, *Coronado Expedition to Tierra Nueva*, 11–12; Jane MacLaren Walsh, "Myth and Imagination in the American Story: The Coronado Expedition, 1540–1542" (Ph.D. diss., Catholic University, 1993).

5. Pedro Castañeda de Náxera, "Narrative of the Expedition to Cíbola, Undertaken in 1540," *NCE*, 243; Garcilaso de la Vega, the Inca, "La Florida," trans. Charmion Shelby, *De Soto Chronicles*, 2: 503; James F. Brooks, *Captives and Cousins: Slavery, Kinship, and Community in the Southwest Borderlands* (Chapel Hill, N.C., 2002), 47–48.

6. Biedma, "Relation," 1: 235, 237; Rodrigo Rangel, "Account of the Northern Conquest," trans. John E. Worth, *De Soto Chronicles*, 1: 269, 270, 279, 293–94, 298; A Gentleman of Elvas, "True Relation of the Hardships Suffered by Governor Don Hernando de Soto," trans. James Alexander Robertson, *De Soto Chronicles*, 1: 75, 99, 101, 104, 108, 110.

7. Mark A. Burkholder and Lyman L. Johnson, *Colonial Latin America* (New York, 1998), 50–56; John L. Kessell, *Spain in the Southwest: A Narrative History of Colonial New Mexico, Arizona, Texas, and California* (Norman, Okla., 2002), 23.

8. Biedma, "Relation," 1: 240; Hernán Cortés, "The Second Letter," *Letters from Mexico*, trans. and ed. Anthony R. Pagden (New York, 1971), 50–51, 133, 153, 159; Tlatelolca account, 135; Tezcoco account, 124; Miguel Leon-Portilla, introduction, xli; all in *Broken Spears*.

9. Elvas, "True Relation," 1: 122–23; Biedma, "Relation," 1: 241; Garcilaso, "La Florida," 2: 410. For archaeological sites that may be the remains of Quiguate and Coligua, see Phyllis A. Morse, "The Parkin Archaeological Site and Its Role in Determining the Route of the de Soto Expedition," in *Expedition of Hernando de Soto West of the Mississippi*, 65–66.

10. Elvas, "True Relation," 1: 131.

11. Elvas, "True Relation," 1: 127–28.

12. Elvas, "True Relation," 1: 130. For more on interpreters and language, see James Axtell, "Babel of Tongues: Communicating with the Indians in Eastern North America," in *The Language Encounter in the Americas*, ed. Edward G. Gray and Norman Fiering (New York, 2000), 15–60.

13. Garcilaso, "La Florida," 2: 438–39.

14. Elvas, "True Relation," 1: 115; Biedma, "Relation," 1: 239; Rangel, "Account," 1: 300; Garcilaso, "La Florida," 2: 390–91. On Burgos's role in the narrative, see Patricia Galloway, "The Incestuous Soto Narratives," in *Hernando de Soto Expedition: History, Historiography, and "Discovery"*, 18–27.

15. Alan Taylor, *American Colonies* (New York, 2001), 33; Felipe Fernández-Armesto, *Columbus* (New York, 1991), 49–50; Rangel, "Account," 1: 301–2; Elvas, "True Relation," 1: 114–16, 120; Garcilaso, "La Florida," 2: 393–95.

16. Biedma, "Relation," 1: 239–40; Elvas, "True Relation," 1: 116–18; Rangel, "Account," 1: 301. Garcilaso says the Casquis wreaked havoc on the fields and scalped Pacahan men, but the other accounts do not include such descriptions. "La Florida," 2: 395–98, 400.

17. Elvas, "True Relation," 1: 118–20; Rangel, "Account," 1: 301–3; Biedma, "Relation," 1: 241; Garcilaso, "La Florida," 2: 400–404.

18. Hudson, "Reconstructing the de Soto Expedition Route West of the Mississippi," 26, 148; Elvas, "True Relation," 1: 131–33; Garcilaso, "La Florida," 2: 437–42; Biedma, "Relation," 1: 243.

19. Biedma, "Relation," 1: 242; Elvas, "True Relation," 1: 125. For possible locations of Cayas and Tula, see Hudson, "Reconstructing the de Soto Expedition Route West of the Mississippi," 146–47; Ann M. Early, "Finding the Middle Passage: The Spanish Journey from the Swamplands to Caddo Country," in *Expedition of Hernando de Soto West of the Mississippi*, 70–75.

20. Biedma, "Relation," 1: 242; Garcilaso, "La Florida," 2: 411–13, 420–21; Rangel, "Account," 1: 305; Elvas, "True Relation," 1: 125–27.

21. Richter, *Facing East*, 14–15. Historians have debated whether European goods served utilitarian or nonutilitarian purposes in Native American societies. I agree with Bruce M. White's conclusions that European goods served many purposes—religious, ceremonial, decorative, protective, subsistence, political—for various peoples, places, and times. Usefulness is, after all, in the eye of the consumer. Bruce M. White, "Encounters with Spirits: Ojibwa and Dakota Theories about the French and Their Merchandise," *Ethnohistory* 41 (1994), 369–405. For early exchange between Europeans and Native Americans on the Atlantic coast, see Neal Salisbury, *Manitou and Providence: Indians, Europeans, and the Making of New England, 1500–1643* (New York, 1982), 52–54. Thanks to George Sabo III for his assistance with Mississippian symbolism here and elsewhere in this chapter.

22. Garcilaso, "La Florida," 2: 510; Castañeda, "Narrative," 282. For more on horses in early contacts, see Ian K. Steele, *Warpaths: Invasions of North America* (New York, 1994), 14; Inga Clendinnen, "'Fierce and Unnatural Cruelty': Cortés and the Conquest of Mexico," *Representations* 33 (1991), 65–100.

23. Elvas, "True Relation," 1: 119; Bernal Díaz del Castillo, *The Discovery and Conquest of Mexico, 1517–1521*, ed. Genaro García, trans. A. P. Maudslay (New York,

1956), 59, 61–62; Alvar Núñez Cabeza de Vaca, *Castaways*, ed. Enrique Pupo-Walker, trans. Frances M. López-Morillas (Berkeley, Calif., 1993), 71.

24. Elvas, "True Relation," 1: 116; Rangel, "Account," 1: 302; Garcilaso, "La Florida," 2: 391–92. Archaeologists have found remains of what may be this cross. Morse and Morse, *Archaeology of the Central Mississippi Valley*, 293.

25. Biedma, "Relation," 1: 240; Rangel, "Account," 1: 302; Garcilaso, "La Florida," 2: 391; Charles M. Hudson, *The Southeastern Indians* (Knoxville, Tenn., 1976), 122.

26. Garcilaso, "La Florida," 2: 397–98, 400; George Sabo III, "Indians and Spaniards in Arkansas: Symbolic Action in the Sixteenth Century," in *Expedition of Hernando de Soto West of the Mississippi*, 202.

27. Rangel, "Account," 1: 301–2.

28. Rangel, "Account," 1: 301–3; Biedma, "Relation," 1: 241; Elvas, "True Relation," 1: 119–20; Garcilaso, "La Florida," 2: 402–3.

29. Elvas, "True Relation," 1: 119–21, 124; Rangel, "Account," 1: 303; Castañeda, "Narrative," 219, 237–38; Francisco Vázquez de Coronado, "Testimony of Francisco Vázquez de Coronado On the Management of the Expedition," Sept. 3, 1544, *NCE*, 325, 329; Natalie Zemon Davis, *The Gift in Sixteenth-Century France* (Madison, Wisc., 2000). Similarly, colonies used gifts to ease relations with other colonies. For example, in 1732, the South Carolina Assembly gave one hundred head of cattle, five bulls, twenty breeding sows, four boars, and twenty barrels of rice to Georgia to welcome the new colony. Charles Jones, *The History of Georgia* (Boston, 1883), 1: 124–25. Thanks to Timothy Birnbaum for this example.

30. For the importance of friendship between western leaders, see Martha Elena Rojas, " 'Insults Unpunished': Barbary Captives, American Slaves, and the Negotiation of Liberty," *Early American Studies* 1 (2003), 159–86. For the personal nature of Mississippian diplomacy, see Sabo, "Indians and Spaniards in Arkansas," 206.

31. Elvas, "True Relation," 1: 121–23, 128–29, 131–32. For possible location of Utiangue (called Autiamque and Autianque by Elvas and Viranque by Biedma), see Charles Hudson and Associates, map of "The Hernando de Soto Expedition, 1539–1543," illustration 26 in *Expedition of Hernando de Soto West of the Mississippi*.

32. Juliana Barr, "A Diplomacy of Gender: Rituals of First Contact in the 'Land of the Tejas,' " *WMQ* 61 (2004), 428–31.

33. Biedma, "Relation," 1: 243; Elvas, "True Relation," 1: 130; Sabo, "Indians and Spaniards in Arkansas," 204.

34. Elvas, "True Relation," 1: 134–35.

35. Elvas, "True Relation," 1: 133–34; Biedma, "Relation," 1: 243.

36. Elvas, "True Relation," 1: 137–38; Garcilaso, "La Florida," 2: 449–50.

37. Biedma, "Relation," 1: 243–45; Elvas, "True Relation," 1: 138–40, 147–48; Garcilaso, "La Florida," 2: 458.

38. Elvas, "True Relation," 1: 151–52.

39. Garcilaso, "La Florida," 2: 445, 478–79; Elvas, "True Relation," 1: 134.

40. Elvas, "True Relation," 1: 151–52.

41. Elvas, "True Relation," 1: 152–53; Garcilaso, "La Florida," 2: 498.

42. Elvas, "True Relation," 1: 155.

43. Biedma, "Relation," 1: 245; Elvas, "True Relation," 1: 155–58; Garcilaso, "La Florida," 2: 507–18; Steele, *Warpaths*, 16.

44. Castañeda, "Narrative," 239–41; "Relation of the Events on the Expedition That Francisco Vázquez Made to the Discovery of Cíbola," *NCE*, 290–92; Juan Jaramillo, "Narrative Given by Captain Juan Jaramillo of His Journey to the New Land in New Spain and to the Discovery of Cíbola Under General Francisco Vázquez Coronado," *NCE*, 302; Mildred Mott Wedel, "The Indian They Called *Turco*," in *Pathways to Plains Prehistory*, ed. Don G. Wyckoff and Jack L. Hofman (Duncan, Okla., 1982), 157; Walsh, "Myth and Imagination," 201–3, 207–9.

45. Joseph P. Sánchez, "A Historiography of the Route of the Expedition of Francisco Vázquez de Coronado: Río de Cicúye to Quivira," 294, 297–98; Carroll L. Riley, "The Teya Indians of the Southwestern Plains," 320, 335; David H. Snow, " 'Por alli no ay losa ni se hace': Gilded Men and Glazed Pottery on the Southern Plains," 354; all in *Coronado Expedition to Tierra Nueva*; questioning of the Indian Miguel Brought from New Mexico, *Don Juan de Oñate: Colonizer of New Mexico, 1595–1628*, ed. George P. Hammond and Agapito Rey (Albuquerque, 1953), 874; F. Todd Smith, *The Wichita Indians: Traders of Texas and the Southern Plains, 1540–1845* (College Station, Tex., 2000), 9; Brooks, *Captives and Cousins*, 46; Walsh, "Myth and Imagination," 175–76.

46. Coronado to the King, Oct. 20, 1541, *NCE*, 185–86; Castañeda, "Narrative," 219, 221; Jaramillo, "Narrative," 301–2; "A Transcription of the Testimony, 8th de Oficio Witness (Juan Troyano)," in Richard Flint, "Great Cruelties Have Been Reported: The 1544 Investigation of the Coronado Expedition" (Ph.D. diss., University of New Mexico, 1999), 184–85. For discussions of El Turco's history and motives, see Wedel, "The Indian They Called *Turco*," 153–62; Riley, Introduction, *Coronado Expedition to Tierra Nueva*, 26–27; Donald J. Blakeslee, Richard Flint, and Jack T. Hughes, "Una Barranca Grande: Recent Archeological Evidence and a Discussion of Its Place in the Coronado Route," *Coronado Expedition to Tierra Nueva*, 379–80.

47. Castañeda, "Narrative," 217; "Testimony of Francisco Vázquez de Coronado," 326–28; "A Transcription of the Testimony, 8th de Oficio Witness," 186–87; Kessell, *Spain in the Southwest*, 40–41; Riley, introduction, *Coronado Expedition to Tierra Nueva*, 8.

48. "A Transcription of the Testimony, 8th de Oficio Witness," 189; George P. Hammond and Agapito Rey, introduction, *NCE*, 23–25; Walsh, "Myth and Imagination," 205–6.

49. Castañeda, "Narrative," 261, 278–79; Coronado to the King, Oct. 20, 1541, *NCE*, 186; Riley, introduction, *Coronado Expedition to Tierra Nueva*, 5–8; Richard Flint, "Armas de la Tierra: The Mexican Indian Component of Coronado Expedition Material Culture," in *Coronado Expedition to Tierra Nueva*, 60; Flint, "Great Cruelties," 43–47.

50. Castañeda, "Narrative," 241, 280; "Relation of the Events on the Expedition That Francisco Vázquez Made," 289, 292; "Relación postrera de Cíbola," *NCE*, 310–11.

51. Castañeda, "Narrative," 219, 235–37.

52. García López de Cárdenas, "Deposition of Don García Before Licentiate Cianca," 362–63.

53. Coronado to the King, Oct. 20, 1541, *NCE*, 189; "A Transcription of the Testimony, 8th de Oficio Witness," 190; Jaramillo, "Narrative," 301; Castañeda, "Narrative," 241–42.

54. Coronado to the King, Oct. 20, 1541, *NCE*, 187; Castañeda, "Narrative," 237, 242; "Relation of the Events on the Expedition That Francisco Vázquez Made," 291; Jaramillo, "Narrative," 301–2. "Ysopete" is Spanish for Aesop, a teller of tales. Walsh, "Myth and Imagination," 202.

55. Coronado to the King, Oct. 20, 1541, *NCE*, 186–88; Castañeda, "Narrative," 239, 241–42, 262–63; Jaramillo, "Narrative," 303; "Relation of the Events on the Expedition That Francisco Vázquez Made," 292.

56. Coronado to the King, Oct. 20, 1541, *NCE*, 188; "Relation of the Events on the Expedition That Francisco Vázquez Made," 292; Jaramillo, "Narrative," 303–4; "Testimony of Francisco Vázquez de Coronado," 336; "A Transcription of the Testimony, 8th de Oficio Witness," 190.

57. Castañeda, "Narrative," 234.

58. "Relation of the Events on the Expedition That Francisco Vázquez Made," 290.

59. The Teya guides arose in the morning to see where the sun was rising, used it to determine their direction, shot an arrow in that direction, then shot one after another over previous ones to ensure that they were following a straight course. Jaramillo, "Narrative," 304–5; Castañeda, "Narrative," 242.

60. Coronado to the King, Oct. 20, 1541, *NCE*, 189.

61. Castañeda, "Narrative," 245–46, 261.

62. Castañeda, "Narrative," 246.

63. Jaramillo, "Narrative," 304; John, *Storms Brewed*, 21.

64. Garcilaso, "La Florida," 2: 423.

65. Castañeda, "Narrative," 221–31, 241.

66. Castañeda, "Narrative," 263, 281; "Relation of the Events on the Expedition That Francisco Vázquez Made," 294; Jaramillo, "Narrative," 306–7. For the 1593 expedition, see Jusepe Gutiérrez, "Account by an Indian of the Flight of Umaña and Leyba from New Mexico," Feb. 16, 1599, 416–18; Vicente de Zaldívar's inquiry before the Audiencia, Apr. 1602, 784; testimony of Juan Rodríguez, Apr. 26, 1602, 871; George P. Hammond and Agapito Rey, introduction, 6; all in *Don Juan de Oñate*.

67. Information on Oñate's expedition comes from "Faithful and True Report of the Events that took Place on the Entrada Made by the Adelantado and Governor, Don Juan de Oñate," Dec. 14, 1601, 746–47, 751–58; Vicente de Zaldívar et al., addendum to Oñate report, Dec. 14, 1601, 759; Gaspar de Zúñiga y Acevedo, Count of Monterrey, to the King, Mar. 8, 1602, 770; Zaldívar's Inquiry, 785–86, 793, 797, 800, 804, 807; testimony of Juan Rodríguez, 865, 868; testimony by Baltasar Martínez Coxedor, Apr. 23, 1602, 841–44, 848; testimony of Juan de Léon, Apr. 24, 1602, 854–59; testimony of Miguel Montero de Castro, Apr. 22, 1602, 880–82; testimony of Diego de Ayarde, Apr. 23, 1602, 884–85; testimony of Juan Gutiérrez Bocanegra, Apr. 26, 1602, 889–91; all in *Don Juan de Oñate*; Gary Clayton Anderson, *The Indian Southwest, 1580–1830: Ethnogenesis and Reinvention* (Norman, Okla., 1999), 148–49.

68. Testimony by Baltasar Martínez Coxedor, 849; testimony of Juan de Léon, 860–61; testimony of Juan Rodríguez, 869–70; questioning of the Indian Miguel, 873–76. For evidence that the Great Settlement was in the same location as Coronado's Quivira, see Hammond and Rey, *Don Juan de Oñate*, 754n15, 754n17, 919n20; Herbert Eugene Bolton, *Coronado: Knight of Pueblos and Plains* (New York, 1949),

294; Herbert Eugene Bolton, *Spanish Exploration in the Southwest,* 1542–1706 (New York, 1916), 260n2. For Tanico, see Biedma, "Relation," 1: 241; Rangel, "Account," 1: 304–5; Elvas, "True Relation," 1: 123–24. For Aguacay, see Biedma, "Relation," 1: 243; Elvas, "True Relation," 1: 141–42.

69. Jacques Marquette, "Of the first Voyage made by Father Marquette toward new Mexico," *The Jesuit Relations and Allied Documents: Travels and Explorations of the Jesuit Missionaries in New France,* 1610–1791, ed. Reuben Gold Thwaites (Cleveland, 1896–1901), 59: 87; "The Expedition of Juan de Archuleta to El Cuartelejo, 1664–1680 (ca.)," *After Coronado: Spanish Exploration Northeast of New Mexico, 1696–1727, Documents from the Archives of Spain, Mexico, and New Mexico,* trans. and ed. Alfred Barnaby Thomas (Norman, Okla., 1935), 53; John, *Storms Brewed,* 78–79, 162, 176; Brooks, *Captives and Cousins,* 50.

70. Lynda Norene Shaffer, *Native Americans Before 1492: The Moundbuilding Centers of the Eastern Woodlands* (Armonk, N.Y., 1992), 82, 87; Ann F. Ramenofsky and Patricia Galloway, "Disease and the Soto Entrada," in *Hernando de Soto Expedition: History, Historiography, and "Discovery,"* 259–79; Alfred W. Crosby, *Ecological Imperialism: The Biological Expansion of Europe,* 900–1900 (New York, 1986), 197–201.

71. Barbara A. Burnett and Katherine A. Murray, "Death, Drought, and de Soto: The Bioarcheology of Depopulation," in *Expedition of Hernando de Soto West of the Mississippi,* 232–35; Ramenofsky and Galloway, "Disease and the Soto Entrada," 266; John, *Storms Brewed,* 83, 86; Alfred W. Crosby, "Virgin Soil Epidemics as a Factor in the Aboriginal Depopulation in America," *WMQ* 33 (1976), 290; Kessell, *Spain in the Southwest,* 297. For the role of continental connections in spreading an eighteenth-century smallpox epidemic, see Elizabeth A. Fenn, *Pox Americana: The Great Smallpox Epidemic of* 1775–82 (New York, 2001). For an argument that a region-wide smallpox epidemic did not strike the Southeast until later, see Paul Kelton, "The Great Southeastern Smallpox Epidemic, 1696–1700: The Region's First Major Epidemic?," in *The Transformation of the Southeastern Indians, 1540–1760,* ed. Robbie Ethridge and Charles Hudson (Jackson, Miss., 2002), 21–37.

72. Burnett and Murray, "Death, Drought, and de Soto," 228–29; Shaffer, *Native Americans before* 1492, 87–90; David Sloan, "The Expedition of Hernando de Soto: A Post-mortem Report," in *Cultural Encounters in the Early South: Indians and Europeans in Arkansas,* ed. Jeannie Whayne (Fayetteville, Ark., 1995), 36; Russell Thornton, *American Indian Holocaust and Survival: A Population History since* 1492 (Norman, Okla., 1987); Timothy K. Perttula, "The Long-Term Effects of the de Soto Entrada on Aboriginal Caddoan Populations," in *Expedition of Hernando de Soto West of the Mississippi,* 244–50; Raymond D. Fogelson, "The Ethnohistory of Events and Nonevents," *Ethnohistory* 36 (1989), 143–44.

73. Elvas, "True Relation," 1: 168.

74. Estimating pre-colonial and early colonial Native American populations with a reasonable degree of accuracy is impossible. Still, archeological, oral, and documentary evidence suggest substantial change in population and living arrangements in the Mississippi Valley between 1540 and 1673. My compilations come from the accounts of the de Soto and Coronado expeditions and archeological sources cited throughout the chapter. For discussions of pre-colonial population estimates across North America, see Richter, *Facing East,* 258n9; Nancy Shoemaker, *American*

Indian Population Recovery in the Twentieth Century (Albuquerque, 1999), 1–3; David P. Henige, *Numbers from Nowhere: The American Indian Contact Population Debate* (Norman, Okla., 1998); Shaffer, *Native Americans Before 1492*, 4, 87–90; Sloan, "Expedition of Hernando de Soto," 36.

75. Paul Kelton, "Avoiding the Smallpox Spirits: Colonial Epidemics and Southeastern Indian Survival," *Ethnohistory* 51 (2004), 45–71.

76. Richter, *Facing East*, 34–39; Hudson, *Southeastern Indians*, 205–6; Tristram R. Kidder, "Excavations at the Jordan Site (16MO1), Morehouse Parish, Louisiana," *Southeastern Archaeology* 11 (1992), 109–31.

77. John, *Storms Brewed*, 155–56; Luis Granillo to Diego de Vargas Zapata Lujan Ponze de Leon, Sept. 29, 1695; report by Diego de Vargas Zapata Lujan Ponze de Leon, Oct. 2, 1695; report by Luis Granillo, Oct. 4, 1695; all in "French Intrusion Toward New Mexico in 1695," ed. and trans. F. W. Hodge, *New Mexico Historical Review* 4 (1929), 72–76.

78. Richter, *Facing East*, 39.

Chapter 3. Negotiators of a New Land, 1650–1740

1. John H. House, "Wallace Bottom: A Colonial-Era Archaeological Site in the Menard Locality, Eastern Arkansas," *Southeastern Archaeology* 21 (2002), 257–68. On the changing environment of the region, see Joseph Patrick Key, " 'Masters of This Country': The Quapaws and Environmental Change in Arkansas, 1673–1833" (Ph.D. diss., University of Arkansas, 2001).

2. On French immigrants' desire to return home, see Peter N. Moogk, "Reluctant Exiles: Emigrants from France in Canada Before 1760," *WMQ* 46 (1989), 463–505.

3. Daniel K. Richter, *Facing East from Indian Country: A Native History of Early America* (Cambridge, Mass., 2001), 34–39; Tristram R. Kidder, "Excavations at the Jordan Site (16MO1), Morehouse Parish, Louisiana," *Southeastern Archaeology* 11 (1992), 109–31; Patricia K. Galloway, *Choctaw Genesis, 1500–1700* (Lincoln, Neb., 1995). Catherine M. Desbarats argues persuasively that Indian alliances and services were worth the cost. Catherine M. Desbarats, "The Cost of Early Canada's Native Alliances: Reality and Scarcity's Rhetoric," *WMQ* 52 (1995), 609–30.

4. For the Ohio Valley theory, see Henri de Tonti to his brother, Mar. 4, 1700, "Tonti Letters," *Mid-America: An Historical Review* 21 (1939), 230; Jacques Gravier, "Relation or Journal of the voyage of Father Gravier, of the Society of Jesus, in 1700," Feb. 16, 1701, in *The Jesuit Relations and Allied Documents: Travels and Explorations of the Jesuit Missionaries in New France, 1610–1791*, ed. Reuben Gold Thwaites (Cleveland, 1896–1901), 65: 107; Anastasius Douay, Relation, *First Establishment of the Faith in New France*, ed. Christian Le Clerq, trans. John Gilmary Shea (New York, 1881), 2: 272; George Izard, "Notes Respecting the Arkansa Territory," Jan. 1827, "A Report on the Quapaw: The Letters of Governor George Izard to the American Philosophical Society, 1825–1827," ed. David W. Bizzell, *Pulaski County Historical Review* 29 (1981), 72; Richard J. Allan and Carrie V. Wilson, Official Quapaw Tribal Website, http://www.geocities.com/Athens/Aegean/1388/index.html; Susan C. Vehik, "Dhegiha

Origins and Plains Archaeology," *Plains Anthropologist* 38 (1993), 231–52; Michael P. Hoffman, "The Terminal Mississippian Period in the Arkansas River Valley and Quapaw Ethnogenesis," in *Towns and Temples Along the Mississippi*, ed. David H. Dye and Cheryl Anne Cox (Tuscaloosa, Ala., 1990), 208–26; George Sabo III, "The Quapaw Indians of Arkansas, 1673–1803," in *Indians of the Greater Southeast: Historical Archaeology and Ethnohistory*, ed. Bonnie G. McEwan (Gainesville, Fla., 2000), 185–86; Marvin D. Jeter, "From Prehistory through Protohistory to Ethnohistory in and near the Northern Lower Mississippi Valley," in *The Transformation of the Southeastern Indians, 1540–1760*, ed. Robbie Ethridge and Charles Hudson (Jackson, Miss., 2002), 177–223; J. Owen Dorsey, "Migrations of Siouan Tribes," *American Naturalist* 20 (1886), 215. John Berrey, Chair of the Quapaw Tribe of Oklahoma, mentioned the oral history about de Soto in "Quapaw History: Yesterday and Today," Colonial Arkansas Conference and Powwow, Little Rock, Ark., Oct. 10, 2003. Garcilaso called "Pacaha" "Capaha." Jacques de la Métairie called Kappa "Kapaha." Garcilaso de la Vega, the Inca, "La Florida," trans. Charmion Shelby, *The De Soto Chronicles: The Expedition of Hernando de Soto to North America in 1539–1543*, ed. Lawrence A. Clayton, Vernon James Knight, Jr., and Edward C. Moore (Tuscaloosa, Ala., 1993), 2: 394–404; Jacques de la Métairie, "Narrative of the Expedition of M. Cavalier de la Salle," *Historical Collections of Louisiana and Florida*, ed. and trans. B. F. French (New York, 1875), 7: 21. For connections to Pacaha, see Dan F. Morse and Phyllis A. Morse, *Archaeology of the Central Mississippi Valley* (New York, 1983), 318–21. For the interpretation of the Quapaws as later immigrants, see Ian W. Brown, "Historic Indians of the Lower Mississippi Valley: An Archaeologist's View," in *Towns and Temples*, 231; Marvin D. Jeter and Ann M. Early, "Prehistory of the Saline River Drainage Basin, Central to Southeast Arkansas," in *Arkansas Archaeology: Essays in Honor of Dan and Phyllis Morse*, ed. Robert C. Mainfort, Jr., and Marvin D. Jeter (Fayetteville, Ark., 1999), 59–60; Robert L. Rankin, "Language Affiliations of Some de Soto Place Names in Arkansas," in *The Expedition of Hernando de Soto West of the Mississippi, 1541–1543: Proceedings of the De Soto Symposia 1988 and 1990*, ed. Gloria A. Young and Michael P. Hoffman (Fayetteville, Ark., 1993), 213–17. For possible Cahokia connections, see Timothy R. Pauketat and Thomas E. Emerson, introduction, *Cahokia: Domination and Ideology in the Mississippian World* (Lincoln, Neb., 1997), 24–26.

    5. Some historians have assumed that *Arkansas* was the Illinois name for the Quapaws, not their name for themselves, but Alan Gallay points out that the French were too eager for the Quapaws' friendship to get their name wrong. Gradually, all of the "Arkansas" Indians were incorporated into the town, and name, of Kappa, or Quapaw. Because the Quapaws today and most historians use *Quapaw*, I follow that convention. Alan Gallay, *The Indian Slave Trade: The Rise of the English Empire in the American South, 1670–1717* (New Haven, Conn., 2002), 112–13.

    6. The French called the future Wichitas and Pawnees by many names, including the Panis, the Mentos (probably referring to the Tawakonis or an additional group who lived among the Tawakonis), and the Panis Piqués (referring to the Taovayas, Guichitas, and Iscanis). Some names probably came from the Michigamea interpreters, who may have used those words simply to mean any Caddoan-speaking group. Michael P. Hoffman, "Identification of Ethnic Groups Contacted by the de Soto Expedition in Arkansas," in *Expedition of Hernando de Soto West of the Mississippi*,

133–34, 140–41; George E. Hyde, *The Pawnee Indians* (Norman, Okla., 1974), 13–14; F. Todd Smith, *The Wichita Indians: Traders of Texas and the Southern Plains, 1540–1845* (College Station, Tex., 2000), xi, 6; Elizabeth A. H. John, *Storms Brewed in Other Men's Worlds: The Confrontation of Indians, Spanish, and French in the Southwest, 1540–1795* (Norman, Okla., 1996), 214–15; Wallace Chafe, "Caddo Names in the de Soto Documents," in *Expedition of Hernando de Soto West of the Mississippi,* 222–25; Timothy K. Perttula, "The Long-Term Consequences and Effects of the de Soto Entrada on Aboriginal Caddoan Populations," in *Expedition of Hernando de Soto West of the Mississippi,* 237; Gary Clayton Anderson, *The Indian Southwest, 1580–1830: Ethnogenesis and Reinvention* (Norman, Okla., 1999), 148–51; Jeffrey P. Brain, *Tunica Archaeology* (Cambridge, Mass., 1988), 21–25; Ann M. Early, "The Caddos of the Trans-Mississippi South," in *Indians of the Greater Southeast,* 123; George Sabo III, "Indians and Spaniards in Arkansas: Symbolic Action in the Sixteenth Century," in *Expedition of Hernando de Soto West of the Mississippi,* 205–6; Rankin, "Language Affiliations of Some de Soto Place Names," 217–19. Frank Schambach hypothesizes that the Tulas may have moved east and become the Tunicas. Frank F. Schambach, "Spiro and the Tunica: A New Interpretation of the Role of the Tunica in the Culture History of the Southeast and the Southern Plains, A.D. 1100–1750," in *Arkansas Archaeology,* 189–90.

7. Dan F. Morse, "The Nodena Phase," in *Towns and Temples,* 81–82; Dan F. Morse and Phyllis A. Morse, "Northeast Arkansas," in *Prehistory of the Central Mississippi Valley,* ed. Charles H. McNutt (Tuscaloosa, Ala., 1996), 134; Karl G. Lorenz, "The Natchez of Southwest Mississippi," in *Indians of the Greater Southeast,* 147–61; Ian W. Brown, "An Archaeological Study of Culture Contact and Change in the Natchez Bluffs Region," in *La Salle and His Legacy: Frenchmen and Indians in the Lower Mississippi Valley,* ed. Patricia K. Galloway (Jackson, Miss., 1982), 178–79; Jeffrey P. Brain, "La Salle at The Natchez: An Archaeological and Historical Perspective," in *La Salle and His Legacy,* 58; Jervis Cutler, *A Topographical Description of the State of Ohio, Indiana Territory, and Louisiana* (Boston, 1812), 115.

8. Métairie, "Narrative of the Expedition," 7: 22; W. David Baird, *The Quapaw Indians: A History of the Downstream People* (Norman, Okla., 1980), 8; Michael P. Hoffman, "Protohistoric Tunican Indians in Arkansas," in *Cultural Encounters in the Early South: Indians and Europeans in Arkansas,* ed. Jeannie Whayne (Fayetteville, Ark., 1995), 66–67, 72–73; Hoffman, "Identification of Ethnic Groups Contacted by the de Soto Expedition," 134–35; Henri Joutel, *Journal historique du Dernier voyage que feu M. de la Sale fit dans le golfe de Mexique* (Paris, 1713), 319; Jean-Baptiste Bénard de La Harpe, "Exploration of the Arkansas River by Benard de la Harpe, 1721–1722: Extracts from His Journal and Instructions," ed. and trans. Ralph A. Smith, *Arkansas Historical Quarterly* 10 (1951), 348; Minet, "Voyage Made From Canada Inland Going Southward during the Year 1682," trans. Ann Linda Bell, *La Salle, the Mississippi, and the Gulf,* ed. Robert S. Weddle, Mary Christine Morkovsky, and Patricia K. Galloway (College Station, Tex., 1987), 68; W. J. Eccles, *The French in North America, 1500–1783* (East Lansing, Mich., 1998), 96, 102–3; Gallay, *Indian Slave Trade,* 296–99.

9. R. P. Louis Hennepin, *Nouvelle découverte d'un très grand pays situé dans l'Amérique* (Utrecht, 1697), 260; Gallay, *Indian Slave Trade,* 106–11. Guns probably provided a psychological advantage and bullets, while generally less accurate than

arrows, were more fatal when they hit and could not be dodged. Wayne Lee, "State of the Art: Seventeenth-Century American Military History," paper presented at the annual meeting of the Organization of American Historians, Washington, D.C., Apr. 2002. See also Richter, *Facing East*, 49–50.

10. For similar uses of presents, see Richard White, *The Middle Ground: Indians, Empires, and Republics in the Great Lakes Region, 1650–1815* (New York, 1991), 100–101; Marshall Sahlins, *Stone Age Economics* (Chicago, 1972), 205; James Axtell, *Natives and Newcomers: The Cultural Origins of North America* (New York, 2001), 40.

11. Richter, *Facing East*, 34–39; Patricia Galloway, " 'The Chief Who Is Your Father': Choctaw and French Views of the Diplomatic Relation," in *Powhatan's Mantle: Indians in the Colonial Southeast*, ed. Peter H. Wood, Gregory A. Waselkov, and M. Thomas Hatley (Lincoln, Neb., 1989), 257–58.

12. Axtell, *Natives and Newcomers*, 22–24; George Sabo III, "Rituals of Encounter: Interpreting Native American Views of European Explorers," in *Cultural Encounters in the Early South*, 79; Sabo, "Quapaw Indians," 179.

13. Kenneth Pennington, *The Prince and the Law, 1200–1600: Sovereignty and Rights in the Western Legal Tradition* (Berkeley, Calif., 1993), 4; Cornelius J. Jaenen, "The Role of Presents in French-Amerindian Trade," in *Explorations in Canadian Economic History: Essays in Honour of Irene M. Spry*, ed. Duncan Cameron (Ottawa, 1985), 235, 239, 249; James Axtell, *The Invasion Within: The Contest of Cultures in Colonial North America* (New York, 1985), 89–90.

14. W. David Baird, *The Quapaw People* (Phoenix, 1975), 6–7, 27; Denombrement du Poste des Akanzas, Aug. 3, 1777, folio 111, legajo 190, PC; d'Orgon to Vaudreuil, Oct. 7, 1752, LO 399, box 8, VP. On gender and diplomacy in other Native American societies, see Bruce M. White, "The Woman Who Married a Beaver: Trade Patterns and Gender Roles in the Ojibwa Fur Trade," *Ethnohistory* 46 (1999), 109–47; Juliana Barr, "A Diplomacy of Gender: Rituals of First Contact in the 'Land of the Tejas,' " *WMQ* 61 (2004), 393–434.

15. Patricia Seed, *Ceremonies of Possession in Europe's Conquest of the New World, 1492–1640* (New York, 1995), 41–68.

16. Antoine Simon Le Page Du Pratz, *Histoire de la Louisiane* (Paris, 1758), 1: map following 138; Tonti to Cabart de Villermont, Sept. 11, 1694, *Découvertes et établissements des Francais dans l'ouest et dans le sud de l'Amérique septentrionale, 1614–1698*, ed. Pierre Margry (New York, 1974), 4: 4.

17. Berrey, "Quapaw History"; author's conversations with Quapaw Tribal Chief John Berrey, Oct. 2003; author's telephone interview with Carrie Wilson, July 1999.

18. R. P. Louis Hennepin, *Description de la Louisiane, nouvellement découverte au sud'oüest de la nouvelle France* (Paris, 1683), 180–81.

19. Henri de Tonti, "Entreprises de M. De La Salle, de 1678 a 1683," *Découvertes*, 1: 599; Jacques de la Métairie, "Procès-verbal de cette prise de possession au pays des Akansas," Mar. 13 and 14, 1682, *Découvertes*, 2: 182–83, 189; Zenobius Membré, Relation, *First Establishment of the Faith*, 2: 166–70; Minet, "Voyage Made From Canada," 46–49.

20. Jacques Marquette, "Of the first Voyage made by Father Marquette toward new Mexico," *Jesuit Relations*, 59: 157–59; Hennepin, *Nouvelle découverte*, 258–59; Henri de Tonti, "Memoir on La Salle's Discoveries, by Tonty, 1678–1690," *Early Narratives of*

the Northwest, 1634–1699, ed. Louise Phelps Kellogg (New York, 1917), 298, 313; Joutel, *Journal Historique*, 298, 304–7; Gravier, "Relation," 65: 117–21; Carl O. Sauer, *Seventeenth Century North America* (Berkeley, Calif., 1980), 241–42; Baird, *Quapaw Indians*, 9–10.

21. Joutel, *Journal historique*, 308–10.

22. Tanis C. Thorne, *The Many Hands of My Relations: French and Indians on the Lower Missouri* (Columbia, Mo., 1996), 42–43, 54–57, 60–62; Mary Druke Becker, "Linking Arms: The Structure of Iroquois Intertribal Diplomacy," in *Beyond the Covenant Chain: The Iroquois and Their Neighbors in Indian North America, 1600–1800*, ed. Daniel K. Richter and James H. Merrell (University Park, Pa., 2003), 29–39; Robert A. Williams, Jr., *Linking Arms Together: American Indian Treaty Visions of Law and Peace, 1600–1800* (New York, 1997), 62.

23. Stanley Faye, "The Arkansas Post of Louisiana: French Domination," *Louisiana Historical Quarterly* 26 (1943), 638.

24. Tonti, "Memoir on La Salle's Discoveries," 308, 313; Edmund Robert Murphy, *Henry de Tonty: Fur Trader of the Mississippi* (Baltimore, 1941), 37–38; Robert S. Weddle, *The Wreck of the* Belle, *the Ruin of La Salle* (College Station, Tex., 2001), 48, 240–41; Joutel, *Journal Historique*, 300, 305.

25. Faye, "Arkansas Post of Louisiana: French Domination," 638.

26. Philip Pittman, *The Present State of the European Settlements on the Mississippi* (London, 1770), 40.

27. Etienne Veniard de Bourgmont, "Etienne Veniard De Bourgmont's 'Exact Description of Louisiana,'" c. 1714, trans. Mrs. Max W. Myer, ed. Marcel Giraud, *Missouri Historical Society Bulletin* 15 (1958), 13; *The Present State of the Country and Inhabitants, Europeans and Indians, of Louisiana, On the North Continent of America. By an Officer at New Orleans to his Friend at Paris* (London, 1744); "Translated Excerpts from Declarations Made in Santa Fé, New Mexico, in 1749 and 1750," Appendix A, Mildred Mott Wedel, *The Deer Creek Site, Oklahoma: A Wichita Village Sometimes Called Ferdinandina, An Ethnohistorian's View* (Oklahoma City, 1981), 68–69; Henri Folmer, "Contraband Trade Between Louisiana and New Mexico in the Eighteenth Century," *New Mexico Historical Review* 16 (1941), 259–67; Morris S. Arnold, "Indians and Immigrants in the Arkansas Colonial Era," in Jeannie M. Whayne, Thomas A. Deblack, George Sabo III, and Morris S. Arnold, *Arkansas: A Narrative History* (Fayetteville, Ark., 2002), 54; Key, "Masters of This Country," 70–71, 77.

28. Eric Hinderaker, *Elusive Empires: Constructing Colonialism in the Ohio Valley, 1673–1800* (New York, 1997), 66–72. For a more extreme view, see Calvin Martin, *Keepers of the Game: Indian-Animal Relationships and the Fur Trade* (Berkeley, Calif., 1978).

29. Dan F. Morse, "The Seventeenth-Century Michigamea Village Location in Arkansas," in *Calumet and Fleur-de-lys: Archaeology of Indian and French Contact in the Midcontinent*, ed. John A. Walthall and Thomas E. Emerson (Washington, D.C., 1992), 55–74; Marquette, "Of the first Voyage," 59: 151–53; Gravier, "Relation," 65: 105, 119.

30. Jean François Buisson de St. Cosme to the Bishop of Quebec, [1699], *Early Voyages Up and Down the Mississippi by Cavelier, St. Cosme, Le Sueur, Gravier, and Guignas*, ed. and trans. John Gilmary Shea (Albany, N.Y., 1861), 72–74.

31. Francis Jolliet de Montigny to—, May 6, 1699, "Tonti Letters," 229n; Tonti to his brother, Mar. 4, 1700, "Tonti Letters," 229; François Le Maire, "M. Le Maire on Louisiana," Jan. 15, 1714, ed. and trans. Jean Delanglez, *Mid-America: An Historical Review* 19 (1937), 147.

32. "Relation de la Louisianne ou Mississippi, écrite à une dame, par un officier de marine," *Relations de la Louisiane, et du Fleuve Mississippi*, ed. Jean Frederic Bernard (Amsterdam, 1720), 30; Jean-Baptiste Bénard de La Harpe to the Directors of the Compagnie des Indes, Dec. 25, 1720, fol. 99, roll 9, C13A6, LCRP; John Anthony Caruso, *The Mississippi Valley Frontier: The Age of French Exploration and Settlement* (New York, 1966), 259.

33. Wedel, *Deer Creek Site*, 37; La Harpe, "Exploration of the Arkansas River," 362; Du Poisson to Patouillet, [1726], *Jesuit Relations*, 67: 259–61; Jean Baptiste Le Moyne, Sieur de Bienville, order, Nov. 26, 1721, fol. 148, roll 9, C13A6, LCRP; Bienville, order, Dec. 12, 1721, fol. 148, roll 9, C13A6, LCRP; Caruso, *Mississippi Valley Frontier*, 268.

34. Jean-Baptiste Bénard de La Harpe, *The Historical Journal of the Establishment of the French in Louisiana*, trans. Joan Cain and Virginia Koenig, ed. Glenn R. Conrad (Lafayette, La., 1971), 202; Pierre François Xavier de Charlevoix, *Histoire et Description Generale de la Nouvelle France* (Paris, 1744), 3: 411; André Pénicaut, *Fleur de Lys and Calumet, Being the Pénicaut Narrative of French Adventure in Louisiana*, trans. and ed. Richebourg Gaillard McWilliams (Baton Rouge, La., 1953), 241–42; *The Census Tables for the French Colony of Louisiana from 1699 Through 1732*, comp. and trans. Charles R. Maduell, Jr. (Baltimore, 1972), 30, 60; Faye, "Arkansas Post of Louisiana: French Domination," 665, 668–69; Morris S. Arnold, *Colonial Arkansas, 1686–1804: A Social and Cultural History* (Fayetteville, Ark., 1991), 11–17; Arnold, "Indians and Immigrants," 49; Clarence Walworth Alvord, *The Illinois Country, 1673–1818* (Springfield, Ill., 1920), 151–52, 158–59; Diron d'Artaguiette, journal, 1722–23, *Travels in the American Colonies*, ed. Newton D. Mereness (New York, 1916), 56; "Recensement general des habitans establys a sotébouy Arkansas," Feb. 18, 1723, ed. Dorothy Core, no. 6a, box I, Small Manuscripts Collection, Arkansas Historical Commission, Little Rock, Ark.

35. Louis Xavier Martin de Lino de Chalmette, Recensements, 1749, LO 200, oversize box, VP; Vaudreuil to Antoine Louis Rouillé, Comte de Jouy, Feb. 1, 1750, LO 203, box 5, VP; Le Page Du Pratz, *Histoire de la Louisiane*, 1: 319; Pittman, *State of the European Settlements*, 40; Norman Ward Caldwell, *The French in the Mississippi Valley, 1740–1750* (Urbana, Ill., 1941), 35.

36. Harry Gordon, "Journal of Captain Harry Gordon, 1766," *Travels in the American Colonies*, 480; Etienne de Périer to Jean Frédéric Phélypeaux, Compte de Maurepas, Dec. 10, 1731, *MPAFD*, 4: 107; Hubert de St. Malo to the Council, [1717?], *MPAFD*, 2: 232.

37. "Translated Excerpts from Declarations Made in Santa Fé," 68, 70–72; Vaudreuil to the Court, July 20, 1751, 2: 152, LO 9, VL; Macarty Mactique to Vaudreuil, Sept. 2, 1752, LO 376, box 7, VP; Caldwell, *French in the Mississippi Valley*, 13; Faye, "Arkansas Post of Louisiana: French Domination," 700.

38. Vaudreuil to Maurepas, Dec. 20, 1744, 1: 42v, LO 9, VL; Paul Augustin Le Pelletier de La Houssaye to Vaudreuil, Dec. 1, 1752, LO 410, box 8, VP.

39. Guedelonguay, Speech, June 20, 1756, *MPAFD*, 5: 173–75; Arnold, *Colonial Arkansas*, 132–34.

40. Alexandre de Clouet to Alejandro O'Reilly, Aug. 4, 1769, fol. 14, leg. 107, PC. For instances of the Quapaws' returning runaways, see Fernando de Leyba to Luis de Unzaga y Amezaga, July 19, 1771, fol. 253, leg. 107, PC; M. Carmen González López-Briones, "Spain in the Mississippi Valley: Spanish Arkansas, 1762–1804" (Ph.D. diss., Purdue University, 1983), Chapter 3.

41. 1785 census tables list 31 free people of color, 17 slaves, and 148 whites. See Daniel H. Usner, Jr., *Indians, Settlers, and Slaves in a Frontier Exchange Economy: The Lower Mississippi Valley Before 1783* (Chapel Hill, N.C., 1992), 114 for the census and throughout for the "frontier exchange economy."

42. Le Page du Pratz, *Histoire de la Louisiane*, 2: 243–44; Alvord, *Illinois Country*, 222–23; Josef Orieta to Unzaga, May 1, 1775, fol. 222, leg. 107, PC.

43. La Harpe, *Historical Journal*, 199, 202; d'Artaguiette, journal, 56; House, "Wallace Bottom," 261, 263; Charlevoix to Lesoiguieres, Dec. 2, 1721, in Charlevoix, *Histoire et Description*, 3: 410; Du Poisson to Father—, Oct. 3, 1727, *Jesuit Relations*, 67: 319; Balthazár de Villiers, Denombrement du Poste des Akanzas et de la Nation Sauvages de ce nom, Aug. 3, 1777, fol. 111, leg. 190, PC.

44. Le Page du Pratz, *Histoire de la Louisiane*, 2: 291.

45. Morris S. Arnold, *The Rumble of a Distant Drum: The Quapaws and Old World Newcomers, 1673–1804* (Fayetteville, Ark., 2000), 63–76; Gregory A. Waselkov, "French Colonial Archeology in the South," Colonial Arkansas Conference and Pow-wow, Oct. 9, 2003.

46. Dorothy Jones Core, comp. and ed., *Abstract of Catholic Register of Arkansas (1764–1858)*, trans. Nicole Wable Hatfield (DeWitt, Ark., 1976), especially 13–14, 18–19, 23, 32–34, 37; Dave Wallis and Frank Williamson, *A Baptismal Record of the Parishes Along the Arkansas River, August 5, 1796 to July 16, 1802* (n.p., 1977), esp. 25.

47. D'Artaguiette, journal, 58; Theda Perdue, "Race and Culture: Writing the Ethnohistory of the Early South," *Ethnohistory* 51 (2004), 703. In contrast, matrilineal peoples more often incorporated European men into their wives' households and considered the children of these unions as Indian rather than European. Theda Perdue, *"Mixed Blood" Indians: Racial Construction in the Early South* (Athens, Ga., 2003); Sylvia Van Kirk, *Many Tender Ties: Women in Fur-Trade Society, 1670–1870* (Norman, Okla., 1980); Susan Sleeper-Smith, *Indian Women and French Men: Rethinking Cultural Encounter in the Western Great Lakes* (Amherst, Mass., 2001).

48. Jennifer M. Spear, "Colonial Intimacies: Legislating Sex in French Louisiana," *WMQ* 60 (2003), 75–98; Jennifer M. Spear, " 'Whiteness and the Purity of Blood': Race, Sexuality, and Social Order in Colonial Louisiana" (Ph.D. diss., University of Minnesota, 1999).

49. Marquette, "Of the first Voyage," 59: 155. On Indian views of Catholicism, see Axtell, *Invasion Within*, 278; Richter, *Facing East*, 85–88.

50. Du Poisson to Patouillet, [1726], *Jesuit Relations*, 67: 255–57.

51. Du Poisson to Patouillet, [1726], *Jesuit Relations*, 67: 255.

52. Hennepin, *Nouvelle découverte*, 260. Hennepin was largely discredited in his own time because his 1683 and 1697 accounts of the same trip had major discrepancies, particularly in their chronology. Catherine Broué persuasively argues that political concerns prompted elisions in Hennepin's first account and that there is no

reason to suspect deceit in the second. Catherine Broué, "En filigrane des récits du Père Louis Hennepin 'trous noirs' de l'exploration Louisianaise, 1679–1681," *Revue d'histoire de l'Amérique française* 53 (2000), 339–66.

53. Thwaites, *Jesuit Relations,* 66: 339n12; Le Maire, "M. Le Maire on Louisiana," 147; Shea, *Early Voyages Up and Down the Mississippi,* 46n1.

54. Perier to La Chaise, Mar. 30, 1728, fol. 66, roll 17, C13A11, LCRP; François Philibert Watrin, "Banishment of the Jesuits from Louisiana," Sept. 3, 1764, *Jesuit Relations,* 70: 241–43; Axtell, *Invasion Within,* 54–70; Arnold, "Indians and Immigrants," 66; Arnold, *Colonial Arkansas,* 136.

55. George Sabo III, "New Traditions for a New World: Seventeenth- and Eighteenth-Century Native Americans in Arkansas," in *Arkansas: A Narrative History,* 33.

56. La Harpe to the Directors of the Compagnie des Indes, Dec. 25, 1720, fol. 99, roll 9, C13A6, LCRP; Bienville to Jérôme de Pontchartrain, Oct. 12, 1708, *MPAFD,* 2: 39–40; Périer to La Houssaye, Apr. 1, 1729, fol. 7, roll 18, C13A12, LCRP; David J. Weber, *The Spanish Frontier in North America* (New Haven, Conn., 1992), 152–68. The Bourbon alliance mitigated French-Spanish tension during and immediately after the War of Spanish Succession (1702–1713). For English beliefs that Spanish cruelty would drive Indians into English hands, see Edmund S. Morgan, *American Slavery, American Freedom: The Ordeal of Colonial Virginia* (New York, 1975), 6–18.

57. Hubert, Mémoire au sujet de l'etablissement de la colonie de la Louisianne, 1723, fol. 228, roll 11, C13A7, LCRP.

58. Périer to La Houssaye, Apr. 1, 1729, fol. 7, roll 18, C13A12, LCRP; Périer to Maurepas, Apr. 10, 1730, fol. 300, roll 19, C13A12, LCRP; Bienville and Edme Gatien Salmon to Maurepas, Apr. 8, 1734, *MPAFD,* 3: 666; Troops in Louisiana, Sept. 10, 1754, *MPAFD,* 5: 142; "Translated Excerpts from Declarations Made in Santa Fé," 68; Louis Billouart, Chevalier de Kerlérec, to Minister, Oct. 1, 1755, fol. 35, roll 46, C13A39, LCRP; Etats de Révue de la garrison du Poste des Akanças, Jan. 1, 1758, fol. 360, roll 47, C13A40, LCRP; Conseil de Marine, Oct. 9, 1716, fol. 401, roll 6, C13A4, LCRP; Pittman, *State of the European Settlements,* 40; Caldwell, *French in the Mississippi Valley,* 12–13.

59. Vaudreuil to Rouillé, Feb. 1, 1750, LO 203, box 5, VP; Alan Taylor, *American Colonies* (New York, 2001), 49.

60. Jean Baptiste Le Moyne, Sieur de Bienville, Memoir on Louisiana, 1725, *MPAFD,* 3: 513–14.

61. Caldwell, *French in the Mississippi Valley,* 14; Arnold, *Colonial Arkansas,* 55–56.

62. Weddle, *Wreck of the* Belle, 215–16.

63. Joutel, *Journal Historique,* 300–309.

64. See, for example, Pénicaut, *Fleur de Lys,* 34, 239.

65. John C. Ewers, "Symbols of Chiefly Authority in Spanish Louisiana," in *The Spanish in the Mississippi Valley, 1762–1804,* ed. John Francis McDermott (Urbana, Ill., 1974), 280; James H. Merrell, *The Indians' New World: Catawbas and Their Neighbors from European Contact through the Era of Removal* (New York, 1989), 150–55. On the importance of public ratification, see Richter, *Facing East,* 139.

66. Leyba to Unzaga, June 6, 1771, fol. 247, leg. 107, PC. As late as 1777, the Arkansas commandant complained of too many Quapaw chiefs. Balthazár de Villiers to Bernardo de Gálvez, Oct. 12, 1777, fol. 117, leg. 190, PC.

67. D'Orgon to Vaudreuil, Oct. 7, 1752, LO 399, box 8, VP; Baird, *Quapaw Indians*, 37.

68. Thomas W. Kavanagh, *Comanche Political History: An Ethnohistorical Perspective*, 1706–1875 (Lincoln, Neb., 1996), 478–79.

69. Métairie, "Procès-verbal," 2: 181–85.

70. Bienville to Pontchartrain, Sept. 6, 1704, *MPAFD*, 3: 22–23.

71. Métairie, "Procès-verbal," 2: 182–83, 189; Marquette, "Of the first Voyage," 59: 155; Tonti, "Entreprises de M. De La Salle," 1: 599; Membré, Relation, 2: 169; Minet, "Voyage Made From Canada," 46–51.

72. Jean-Baptiste Bénard de la Harpe, "Relation du voyage de Bénard de la Harpe," *Découvertes*, 6: 289–93; La Harpe to the Directors of the Compagnie des Indes, Dec. 25, 1720, fol. 99, roll 9, C13A6, LCRP; George H. Odell, *La Harpe's Post: A Tale of French-Wichita Contact on the Eastern Plains* (Tuscaloosa, Ala., 2002); Jack D. Forbes, *Apache, Navaho, and Spaniard* (Norman, Okla., 1960), 19.

73. Gravier, "Relation," 65: 115; La Harpe, *Historical Journal*, 202–9; La Harpe, "Exploration of the Arkansas River," 348–51, 360. Osages had attacked the missing Frenchmen, but they had survived and made it to their destination, although presumably stripped of their trade goods.

74. Joseph C. de Lusser to Maurepas, Mar. 16, 1730, *MPAFD*, 1: 92.

75. Jeffrey P. Brain, "The Natchez 'Paradox,'" *Ethnology* 10 (1971), 215–22; Brain, "La Salle at The Natchez," 53–55; Ian W. Brown, "Natchez Indians and the Remains of a Proud Past," in *Natchez Before* 1830, ed. Noel Polk (Jackson, Miss., 1989), 8–28; Brian M. Fagan, *Ancient North America: The Archaeology of a Continent* (London, 2000), 467; Pénicaut, *Fleur de Lys*, 28–30, 83, 85, 89–96, 159–63, 167–77, 180–82; "Memoir Sent in 1693, on the Discovery of the Mississippi and the Neighboring Nations by M. de La Salle, from the Year 1678 to the time of his death, and by the Sieur de Tonty to the Year 1691," *Historical Collections of Louisiana*, ed. B. F. French (Baton Rouge, La., 1994), 1: 62–65; Le Page Du Pratz, *Histoire de la Louisiane*, 1: 177–87, 197–200; Bienville to Raudot, Jan. 20, 1716, *MPAFD*, 3: 198; Périer to Maurepas, Mar. 18, 1730, *MPAFD*, 1: 63–64; d'Artaguette to Maurepas, Mar. 20, 1730, *MPAFD*, 1: 76; Gwendolyn Midlo Hall, *Africans in Colonial Louisiana: The Development of Afro-Creole Culture in the Eighteenth Century* (Baton Rouge, La., 1992), 100–101; Daniel H. Usner, Jr., *American Indians in the Lower Mississippi Valley: Social and Economic Histories* (Lincoln, Neb., 1998), 15–32.

76. D'Artaguette to Maurepas, Feb. 9, 1730, *MPAFD*, 1: 57–58; Lusser to Maurepas, Mar. 9, 1730, *MPAFD*, 1: 99–100; Périer to Maurepas, Mar. 18, 1730, *MPAFD*, 1: 62–63, 71; d'Artaguette to Maurepas, Mar. 20, 1730, *MPAFD*, 1: 76–77; Father Philibert, Register of those massacred at Natchez, June 9, 1730, *MPAFD*, 1: 122–26; Le Page Du Pratz, *Histoire de la Louisiane*, 3: 230–61; Patricia Dillon Woods, *French-Indian Relations on the Southern Frontier*, 1699–1762 (Ann Arbor, Mich., 1979), 96. On historians' tendency to label Indian wars uprisings or massacres, see Frederic W. Gleach, *Powhatan's World and Colonial Virginia: A Conflict of Cultures* (Lincoln, Neb., 1997), 4.

77. Mathurin Le Petit to Louis d'Avaugour, July 12, 1730, *Jesuit Relations*, 67: 217; Watrin, "Banishment of the Jesuits," 70: 247. For Quapaw war ceremonies, see Key, "Masters of This Country," 79–83.

78. Périer to Maurepas, Apr. 10, 1730, fol. 300, roll 19, C13A12, LCRP; Synopsis of letters from Bienville, May 15–20, 1733, fol. 206, roll 23, C13A16, LCRP; Usner, *American Indians in the Lower Mississippi Valley*, 30–31.

79. Alexandre de Batz, tracing and explanation of Mingo Ouma's map, Sept. 7, 1737, *MPAFD*, 1: 355–56, 4: page facing 142; Gregory A. Waselkov, "Indian Maps of the Colonial Southeast," in *Powhatan's Mantle*, 329–32; Le Petit to d'Avaugour, July 12, 1730, *Jesuit Relations*, 67: 217; Périer to Maurepas, Aug. 1, 1730, *MPAFD*, 4: 35; Périer to Maurepas, Dec. 10, 1731, *MPAFD*, 4: 105; Bienville to Maurepas, May 18, 1733, *MPAFD*, 3: 622; Vaudreuil to La Houssaye, Nov. 2, 1743, 3: 16, LO 9, VL; Périer to Maurepas, Jan. 25, 1733, *MPAFD*, 1: 168; Faye, "Arkansas Post of Louisiana: French Domination," 673.

80. Bienville to Maurepas, Feb. 28, 1737, *MPAFD*, 3: 693–94; Bienville and Salmon to Maurepas, Dec. 22, 1737, *MPAFD*, 1: 358–60; Usner, *Indians, Settlers, and Slaves*, 84.

81. Gaspard-Joseph Chaussegros de Léry, "Memorandum to be used for capturing an Indian fort," June 1739, *Letters from New France: The Upper Country, 1686–1783*, ed. and trans. Joseph L. Peyser (Urbana, Ill., 1992), 167–76; Salmon to Maurepas, May 4, 1740, *MPAFD*, 1: 442–45; Bienville to Maurepas, May 6, 1740, *MPAFD*, 1: 449–61; Le Page Du Pratz, *Histoire de la Louisiane*, 3: 419–24; Usner, *Indians, Settlers, and Slaves*, 84.

82. Vaudreuil to Maurepas, Nov. 5, 1748, LO 147, box 3, VP; Vaudreuil to Pierre Henri d'Erneville, Nov. 11, 1744, 3: 144, LO 9, VL; Vaudreuil to Maurepas, Dec. 24, 1744, 1: 44v, LO 9, VL; Vaudreuil to Maurepas, Oct. 30, 1745, 1: 65, LO 9, VL; Vaudreuil to Maurepas, Mar. 15, 1747, LO 89, box 2, VP; Vaudreuil to Rouillé, Sept. 22, 1749, LO 185, box 4, VP; Brett Rushforth, "'A Little Flesh We Offer You': The Origins of Indian Slavery in New France," *WMQ* 60 (2003), 777–808. For evidence that scalping was a precolonial practice, see Charles M. Hudson, *The Southeastern Indians* (Knoxville, Tenn., 1976), 251; James Axtell and William C. Sturtevant, "The Unkindest Cut, or Who Invented Scalping," *WMQ* 37 (1980), 451–72.

83. La Houssaye to Vaudreuil, Dec. 1, 1752, LO 410, box 8, VP; Layssard to Minister, Oct. 11, 1758, fol. 325, roll 47, C13A40, LCRP; Kavanagh, *Comanche Political History*, 131–32, 184. For similar trends in New France, see Jaenen, "Role of Presents in French-Amerindian Trade," 231; White, *Middle Ground*.

84. Vaudreuil to Maurepas, Mar. 20, 1748, LO 120, box 3, VP; Marcel Giraud, *A History of French Louisiana* (Baton Rouge, La., 1974), 5: 118; Caldwell, *French in the Mississippi Valley*, 26–27; Woods, *French-Indian Relations*, 11.

85. Vaudreuil to Maurepas, Oct. 30, 1745, 1: 65, LO 9, VL; Pierre Le Moyne, Sieur d'Iberville, "Journal du voyage du chevalier d'Iberville sur le vaisseau du Roi la *Renommée*, en 1699," *Découvertes*, 4: 430; Bienville to Pontchartrain, Oct. 12, 1708, *MPAFD*, 2: 39–40; Pénicaut, *Fleur de Lys*, 35; Verner W. Crane, "The Tennessee River as the Road to Carolina: The Beginnings of Exploration and Trade," *Mississippi Valley Historical Review* 3 (1916), 6–13; Verner W. Crane, "The Southern Frontier in Queen Anne's War," *American Historical Review* 24 (1919), 382, 390.

86. Vaudreuil to Rouillé, Sept. 22, 1749, LO 185, box 4, VP; Louis Vivier to Father—, Nov. 17, 1750, *Jesuit Relations*, 69: 217; Roger E. Coleman, *The Arkansas Post Story: Arkansas Post National Monument* (Santa Fe, N.M., 1987), 39–40.

87. Vaudreuil to Rouillé, Apr. 28, 1751, LO 281, box 6, VP; Vaudreuil to Rouillé, Feb. 1, 1750, LO 203, box 5, VP; Vaudreuil to the Court, June 24, 1750, 2: 80, LO 9, VL; Vaudreuil to Rouillé, May 10, 1751, *MPAFD*, 5: 76; Coleman, *Arkansas Post Story*, 43.

88. La Houssaye to Vaudreuil, Dec. 1, 1752, LO 410, box 8, VP.

89. Kerlérec to Rouillé, Aug. 20, 1753, *MPAFD*, 5: 131. On rumors, see Gregory Evans Dowd, "The Panic of 1751: The Significance of Rumors on the South Carolina-Cherokee Frontier," *WMQ* 53 (1996), 527–60.

90. Kerlérec to Jean-Baptiste Machault d'Arnouville, Sept. 15, 1754, *MPAFD*, 5: 144–48.

91. Pierre de la Rue, Abbé de l'Isle Dieu, to Machault, Oct. 12, 1754, *Illinois on the Eve of the Seven Years' War*, 1747–1755, ed. and trans. Theodore Calvin Pease and Ernestine Jenison (Springfield, Ill., 1940), 907; Vaudreuil to Maurepas, July 18, 1743, 1: 3v, LO 9, VL.

92. Jean-Bernard Bossu, *Noveaux voyages aux Indes Occidentales* (Paris, 1768), 1: 80; Le Page du Pratz, *Histoire de la Louisiane*, 2: 291; Le Petit to D'Avaugour, July 12, 1730, *Jesuit Relations*, 68: 217–19.

93. Louis Billouart, Chevalier de Kerlérec, Memoir on Indians, Dec. 12, 1758, *MPAFD*, 5: 210–11.

94. Jean-Jacques-Blaise D'Abbadie, journal, *A Comparative View of French Louisiana, 1699 and 1762: The Journals of Pierre Le Moyne d'Iberville and Jean-Jacques-Blaise d'Abbadie*, trans. and ed. Carl A. Brasseaux (Lafayette, La., 1981), 122.

95. Synopsis of letters from Bienville, May 15–20, 1733, fol. 206, roll 23, C13A16, LCRP.

Chapter 4. An Empire in the West, 1700–1777

1. Claude-Charles Du Tisné to Jean Baptiste Le Moyne, Sieur de Bienville, Nov. 22, 1719, in Phil E. Chappell, "A History of the Missouri River," *Transactions of the Kansas State Historical Society* 9 (1906), 252; F. Todd Smith, *The Wichita Indians: Traders of Texas and the Southern Plains, 1540–1845* (College Station, Tex., 2000), 21.

2. Osage Tribal Council and Osage Tribe, Official Website of the Osage Nation, http://www.osagetribe.com; Louis F. Burns, *A History of the Osage People* (Fallbrook, Calif., 1989), 49–52, 58; George P. Hammond and Agapito Rey, *Don Juan de Oñate: Colonizer of New Mexico, 1595–1628* (Albuquerque, 1953), 752n11; Willard H. Rollings, *The Osage: An Ethnohistorical Study of Hegemony on the Prairie-Plains* (Columbia, Mo., 1992), 5; John Joseph Mathews, *The Osages, Children of the Middle Waters* (Norman, Okla., 1961), 28–29; Carl Haley Chapman, *The Origin of the Osage Indian Tribe* (New York, 1974), 11; William E. Unrau, *The Kansa Indians: A History of the Wind People, 1673–1873* (Norman, Okla., 1971), 12.

3. George Sabo III, "New Traditions for a New World: Seventeenth- and Eighteenth-Century Native Americans in Arkansas," in Jeannie M. Whayne, Thomas A. Deblack, George Sabo III, and Morris S. Arnold, *Arkansas: A Narrative History* (Fayetteville, Ark., 2002), 39; Smith, *Wichita Indians*, 8; J. Frederick Fausz, "Becoming 'a Nation of Quakers': The Removal of the Osage Indians from Missouri," *Gateway*

Heritage 20 (2000), 29–30; George Catlin, *Episodes from Life Among the Indians and Last Rambles, with* 152 *Scenes and Portraits by the Artist*, ed. Marvin C. Ross (Norman, Okla., 1959), 66.

4. Jacques Gravier to Reverend Father in Quebec, Feb. 15, 1694, *The Jesuit Relations and Allied Documents: Travels and Explorations of the Jesuit Missionaries in New France, 1610–1791*, ed. Reuben Gold Thwaites (Cleveland, 1896–1901), 64: 161, 169–71; David La Vere, *Contrary Neighbors: Southern Plains and Removed Indians in Indian Territory* (Norman, Okla., 2000), 32.

5. Mildred Mott Wedel, "Claude-Charles Dutisné: A Review of His 1719 Journeys," *Great Plains Journal* 12 (1973), 150; Rollings, *The Osage*, 8. For similarly uneven effects of disease, see Richard White, "The Winning of the West: The Expansion of the Western Sioux in the Eighteenth and Nineteenth Centuries," *Journal of American History* 65 (1978), 319–43.

6. Mathews, *The Osages*, 341. For more on Mathews, see Robert Allen Warrior, *Tribal Secrets: Recovering American Indian Intellectual Traditions* (Minneapolis, 1995).

7. Noni Athashudse Wigie, Ritual of the Four Symbolic Animals, appendix, Francis La Flesche, *A Dictionary of the Osage Language* (Washington, D.C., 1932), 363–64.

8. Francis La Flesche, "The Osage Tribe: Rite of the Chiefs; Sayings of the Ancient Men," *Annual Report of the Bureau of American Ethnology to the Secretary of the Smithsonian Institution, 1914–1915* (Washington, D.C., 1921), 36: 59–60, 67–58; Louis F. Burns, *Osage Indian Customs and Myths* (Fallbrook, Calif., 1984), 3–4, 29; Mathews, *The Osages*, 31–52, 103–8, 141–48; W. David Baird, *The Osage People* (Phoenix, 1972), 6.

9. Osage Tribal Council and Osage Tribe, Official Website of the Osage Nation, http://www.osagetribe.com.

10. W. J. Eccles, *The French in North America, 1500–1783* (East Lansing, Mich., 1998), 185; Rollings, *The Osage*, 88–89; R. P. Louis Hennepin, *Description de la Louisiane, Nouvellement Découverte au Sud'Oüest de la nouvelle France* (Paris, 1683), 180–81; Joseph Guyon Dubuisson to Philippe de Rigault, Marquis de Vaudreuil, June 15, 1712, *The French Regime in Wisconsin, 1634-1760*, ed. and trans. Reuben Gold Thwaites (Madison, Wis., 1902–8), 1: 272–84; Brett Rushforth, " 'A Little Flesh We Offer You': The Origins of Indian Slavery in New France," *WMQ* 60 (2003), 788–89, 799; Mathews, *The Osages*, 253–54. For more on the battle at Fort Detroit, see Richard White, *The Middle Ground: Indians, Empires, and Republics in the Great Lakes Region, 1650–1815* (New York, 1991), 154–58.

11. Sieur Chassin to —, July 1, 1722, folio 297, roll 10, C13A6, LCRP; White, *Middle Ground*.

12. Superior Counsel Minutes, Jan. 10, 1725, fol. 171v, roll 12, C13A8, LCRP; John Anthony Caruso, *The Mississippi Valley Frontier: The Age of French Exploration and Settlement* (New York, 1966), 263; Bienville to the Navy Council, July 20, 1721, *MPAFD*, 3: 305–6; Bienville to the Navy Council, Apr. 25, 1722, *MPAFD*, 3: 320; Bienville to the Navy Council, Feb. 1, 1723, *MPAFD*, 3: 343. Some New Mexican officials were certain that the French had not only approved of but also joined in the attack. The few who escaped were less sure. *After Coronado: Spanish Exploration Northeast of New Mexico, 1696-1727, Documents from the Archives of Spain, Mexico, and New Mexico*, trans. and ed. Alfred Barnaby Thomas (Norman, Okla., 1935), 164–65, 171–74, 183–87, 227–30;

David J. Weber, *The Spanish Frontier in North America* (New Haven, Conn., 1992), 170–71; Unrau, *Kansa Indians*, 57. The Padoucas were probably Plains Apaches. Frank R. Secoy, "The Identity of the 'Paduca': An Ethnohistorical Analysis," *American Anthropologist* 53 (1951), 525–42.

13. "An Indian Delegation in France, 1725," ed. Richard N. Ellis and Charlie R. Steen, trans. Steen, *Journal of the Illinois State Historical Society* 67 (1974), 385–405; Caruso, *Mississippi Valley Frontier*, 268, 275; "Instructions Données au Sieur Bourgmont," Jan. 17, 1722, *Découvertes et établissements des Français dans l'ouest et dans le sud de l'Amérique septentrionale, 1614–1698: mémoires et documents inédits*, ed. Pierre Margry (New York, 1974), 6: 390–91.

14. Saint-Ange, "Relation du voyage du Sieur de Bourgmont, Chevalier de l'ordre militaire de Saint-Louis, Commandant de la Rivière du Missouri, sur le haut de celle des Arkansas," *Découvertes*, 6: 398–449; Antoine Simon Le Page du Pratz, *Histoire de la Louisiane* (Paris, 1758), 2: 214, 251, 255, 3: 141–214.

15. Etienne de Périer to La Chaise, Mar. 30, 1728, fol. 66, roll 17, C13A11, LCRP; Caruso, *Mississippi Valley Frontier*, 269–70, 277.

16. Vaudreuil to Jean Jacques de Macarty Mactique, Aug. 8, 1751, *Illinois on the Eve of the Seven Years' War, 1747-1755*, ed. and trans. Theodore Calvin Pease and Ernestine Jenison (Springfield, Ill., 1940), 313; Louis Billouart, Chevalier de Kerlérec, Memoir on Indians, Dec. 12, 1758, *MPAFD*, 5: 206; Fabry de la Bruyère, "Extrait des letters du sieur Fabry, à l'occasion du voyage projeté à Santa-Fé," 1742, *Découvertes*, 6: 474; Mathews, *The Osages*, 156–58; Rollings, *The Osage*, 109; Smith, *Wichita Indians*, 18; Colin G. Calloway, ed., *Our Hearts Fell to the Ground: Plains Indian Views of How the West Was Lost* (Boston, 1996), 38; W. J. Eccles, "The Fur Trade and Eighteenth-Century Imperialism," *WMQ* 40 (1983), 341–62; Fausz, "Becoming 'a Nation of Quakers,'" 31.

17. Fabry de la Bruyère, "Extrait des lettres," 6: 474–75; Smith, *Wichita Indians*, 17, 19–20; La Vere, *Contrary Neighbors*, 32–34.

18. Fabry de la Bruyère, "Extrait des lettres," 6: 474–77; Smith, *Wichita Indians*, 16, 25; Bienville, Report, May 15, 1733, *MPAFD*, 1: 201; Bienville and Edme Gatien Salmon to Minister, May 20, 1733, fol. 110, roll 23, C13A16, LCRP; Henri, Chevalier de Louboey, to Jean Frédéric Phélypeaux, Compte de Maurepas, May 20, 1733, *MPAFD*, 1: 221; Joseph Patrick Key, "The Quapaws and Their Neighbors in Arkansas Before 1803," Colonial Arkansas Conference and Powwow, Little Rock, Ark., Oct. 9, 2003.

19. Kerlérec, Memoir on Indians, 5: 207; Unrau, *Kansa Indians*, 23–24.

20. Victor Collot, "State of the Indian Nations," *BLC*, 2: 384; Anastasius Douay, Relation, *First Establishment of the Faith in New France*, ed. Christian Le Clercq, trans. John Gilmary Shea (New York, 1881), 2: 271–72; "Summary of the Indian Tribes of the Misuri River," 1777, *French Regime in Wisconsin*, 3: 358–63; Périer to Maurepas, Apr. 1, 1730, fol. 352, roll 19, C13A12, LCRP; Cezard de Blanc to Vaudreuil, Nov. 14, 1752, LO 405, box 8, VP.

21. Fabry de la Bruyère, "Extrait des lettres," 6: 474.

22. George Dorsey and Carl Chapman both assert that Osage expansion was in part a mourning war, but I believe this interpretation is too inflexible to describe Osage retributive practices. Victor Tixier observed a mourning ceremony in 1840 that apparently did not include a scalp sacrifice, and I have not found mourning-war

references in any of the eighteenth-century sources. George A. Dorsey, "The Osage Mourning-War Ceremony," *American Anthropologist* 4 (1902), 404; Chapman, *Origin of the Osage Indian Tribe*, 90–91; Victor Tixier, *Tixier's "Travels on the Osage Prairies,"* ed. John Francis McDermott, trans. Albert J. Salvan (Norman, Okla., 1940), 256. Also see Burns, *Osage Indian Customs and Myths*, 125–26; Henry Leavitt Ellsworth, *Washington Irving on the Prairie, or a Narrative of a Tour of the Southwest in the Year* 1832, ed. Stanley T. Williams and Barbara D. Simison (New York, 1937), 115–16. For examples of Osage ceremonies, see Union Mission Journal, in W. W. Graves, *The First Protestant Osage Missions, 1820–1837* (Oswego, Kans., 1949), 63–64. For more on clashes between European and Indian views of justice and attempts to reconcile the two, see White, *Middle Ground*, 76–81, 343–51. For another native people's efforts to curb the demands of blood revenge, see Bruce G. Trigger, "Order and Freedom in Huron Society," *Anthropologica* 5 (1963), 161–62. For mourning wars, see Daniel K. Richter, "War and Culture: The Iroquois Experience," *WMQ* 40 (1983), 528–59.

23. Osages continued these practices through the end of the nineteenth century. See, for example, Philip Jackson Dickerson, *History of the Osage Nation: Its People, Resources and Prospects* (Pawhuska, Okla., 1906), 25–27. Patricia Galloway explores this kind of understanding for the Choctaws. Patricia K. Galloway, "Choctaw Factionalism and Civil War, 1746–1750," *Journal of Mississippi History* 44 (1982), 299–300.

24. Henri de Tonti to his brother, Mar. 4, 1700, "Tonti Letters," *Mid-America: An Historical Review* 21 (1939), 232; Jean François Buisson de St. Cosme to the Bishop of Quebec, (1699), *Early Voyages Up and Down the Mississippi by Cavelier, St. Cosme, Le Sueur, Gravier, and Guignas*, ed. and trans. John Gilmary Shea (Albany, N.Y., 1861), 74; Périer to Maurepas, Apr. 10, 1730, *MPAFD*, 1: 120.

25. Stuart Banner, *Legal Systems in Conflict: Property and Sovereignty in Missouri, 1750–1860* (Norman, Okla., 2000), 90–94; Morris S. Arnold, *Unequal Laws Unto a Savage Race: European Legal Traditions in Arkansas, 1686–1836* (Fayetteville, Ark., 1985), 146–47, 164.

26. Vaudreuil to Maurepas, Aug. 26, 1749, LO 187, box 4, VP.

27. Vaudreuil to Antoine Louis Rouillé, Comte de Jouy, Aug. 6, 1749, *Illinois on the Eve*, 103; Pierre Jacques de Taffanel, Marquis de La Jonquière, to Jean Baptiste Benoist, Sieur de St. Claire, June 10, 1750, LO 213, box 5, VP; Jouy to Vaudreuil, Sept. 26, 1750, LO 230, box 5, VP.

28. Jean Baptiste Bénard de la Harpe, "Relation du voyage," *Découvertes*, 6: 284; St. Claire to Charles de Raymond, Feb. 11, 1750, *Illinois on the Eve*, 165; La Jonquière to Jouy, Oct. 15, 1750, *Illinois on the Eve*, 241.

29. La Jonquière to Jouy, Sept. 25, 1751, *Illinois on the Eve*, 356–57.

30. White, *Middle Ground*, x.

31. Burns, *Osage Indian Customs and Myths*, 31–32; Burns, *History of the Osage People*, 64; J. Owen Dorsey, "An Account of the War Customs of the Osages," *American Naturalist* 18 (1884), 113–33.

32. Macarty to Vaudreuil, Jan. 20, 1752, LO 328, oversize box, VP.

33. White, *Middle Ground*, 33.

34. Burns, *History of the Osage People*, 66; Garrick Alan Bailey, *Changes in Osage Social Organization: 1673–1906* (Eugene, Oreg., 1973), 43–44.

35. Carl H. Chapman, *A Preliminary Survey of Missouri Archaeology* (New York, 1974), 19–24; George Catlin, *Letters and Notes on the Manners, Customs, and Conditions of North American Indians* (New York, 1973), 2: 40.

36. Bienville to the Navy Council, Dec. 15, 1721, *MPAFD*, 3: 315; Vaudreuil to Maurepas, Mar. 15, 1747, LO 89, box 2, VP; Smith, *Wichita Indians*, 25–26.

37. Gary Clayton Anderson, *The Indian Southwest, 1580–1830: Ethnogenesis and Reinvention* (Norman, Okla., 1999), 156–58; La Jonquière to Jouy, Sept. 25, 1751, *Illinois on the Eve*, 358–59.

38. Vaudreuil to Macarty, Aug. 8, 1751, LO 325, box 6, VP.

39. St. Claire to Raymond, Feb. 11, 1750, *Illinois on the Eve*, 164; Vaudreuil to Macarty, Sept. 1, 1751, LO 309, box 6, VP; Vaudreuil to the Court, Oct. 10, 1751, 2: 156, LO 9, VL; Charles le Moyne, baron de Longueuil, to Minister, Apr. 21, 1752, *French Regime in Wisconsin*, 3: 111; Macarty to Vaudreuil, Sept. 2, 1752, LO 376, box 7, VP; Henri d'Orgon to Vaudreuil, Oct. 7, 1752, LO 399, box 8, VP; Clarence Walworth Alvord, *The Illinois Country, 1673–1818* (Springfield, Ill., 1920), 187–89.

40. Kerlérec, Memoir on Indians, 5: 206; Smith, *Wichita Indians*, 27, 33; Rollings, *The Osage*, 127–28; George E. Hyde, *The Pawnee Indians* (Norman, Okla., 1974), 14, 97–99; Le Page Du Pratz, *Histoire de la Louisiane*, 2: 245.

41. Jean-Jacques-Blaise d'Abbadie, journal, *A Comparative View of French Louisiana, 1699 and 1762: The Journals of Pierre Le Moyne d'Iberville and Jean-Jacques-Blaise d'Abbadie*, trans. and ed. Carl A. Brasseaux (Lafayette, La., 1981), 111.

42. Kerlérec to Nicolas René Berryer, Nov. 25, 1758, *MPAFD*, 5: 196–97.

43. Gilbert C. Din, "Protecting the 'Barrera': Spain's Defenses in Louisiana, 1763–1779," *Louisiana History* 19 (1978), 183–211.

44. Weber, *Spanish Frontier*, 158–59, 200–203. For more on various European Indian policies, see Patricia Seed, *American Pentimento: The Invention of Indians and the Pursuit of Riches* (Minneapolis, 2001).

45. Jack D. L. Holmes, "Alexander O'Reilly," in *The Louisiana Governors: From Iberville to Edwards*, ed. Joseph G. Dawson III (Baton Rouge, La., 1990), 49. On Irish involvement in Louisiana, see Irene D. Neu, "From Kilkenny to Louisiana: Notes on Eighteenth-Century Irish Emigration," *Mid-America* 49 (1967), 101–14. On the New Orleans rebellion, see David Ker Texada, *Alejandro O'Reilly and the New Orleans Rebels* (Lafayette, La., 1970); Marc de Villiers Du Terrage, *The Last Years of French Louisiana*, trans. Hosea Phillips, ed. Carl A. Brasseaux and Glenn R. Conrad (Lafayette, La., 1982), 324–77; John P. Moore, *Revolt in Louisiana: The Spanish Occupation, 1766–1770* (Baton Rouge, La., 1976).

46. Edward H. Spicer, *Cycles of Conquest: The Impact of Spain, Mexico, and the United States on the Indians of the Southwest, 1533–1960* (Tucson, 1962), 282–84. See also George Foster, *Culture and Conquest: America's Spanish Heritage* (New York, 1960).

47. Weber, *Spanish Frontier*, 213–20. For more on Spanish relations in the Southwest, see Jack D. Forbes, *Apache, Navaho, and Spaniard* (Norman, Okla., 1960); Elizabeth A. H. John, *Storms Brewed in Other Men's Worlds: The Confrontation of Indians, Spanish, and French in the Southwest, 1540–1795* (Norman, Okla., 1996); Max L. Moorhead, *The Apache Frontier: Jacobo Ugarte and Spanish-Indian Relations in Northern New Spain, 1769–1791* (Norman, Okla., 1968).

48. Alejandro O'Reilly, proclamation, Dec. 7, 1769, *SMV*, 1: 125–26; *Athanase de Mézières and the Louisiana-Texas Frontier, 1768–1780*, ed. Herbert Eugene Bolton (Cleveland, 1914), 1: 70–71; Holmes, "Alexander O'Reilly," 50; Francisco Cruzat, "Report of the Indian Tribes Who Receive Presents at St. Louis," Nov. 15, 1777, *The Spanish Régime in Missouri: A Collection of Papers and Documents Relating to Upper Louisiana*, ed. Louis Houck (New York, 1971), 1: 144; Collot, "State of the Indian Nations," 2: 384; Balthazár de Villiers to Bernardo de Gálvez, July 11, 1781, folder 83, box 1, Louisiana Collection, Bancroft Library, Berkeley, Calif.; Jacobo Du Breuil to Esteban Miró, May 5, 1783, folio 403, legajo 107, PC; Alexandre de Clouet to O'Reilly, Nov. 14, 1769, fol. 23, leg. 107, PC; Quapaw census, Apr. 17, 1784, fol. 510, leg. 107, PC; Stanley Faye, "The Arkansas Post of Louisiana: Spanish Domination," *Louisiana Historical Quarterly* 27 (1944), 637; Morris S. Arnold, *Colonial Arkansas, 1686–1804: A Social and Cultural History* (Fayetteville, Ark., 1991), 63; Morris S. Arnold, *The Rumble of a Distant Drum: The Quapaws and Old World Newcomers, 1673–1804* (Fayetteville, Ark., 2000), 157–60.

49. Gilbert C. Din and A. P. Nasatir, *The Imperial Osages: Spanish-Indian Diplomacy in the Mississippi Valley* (Norman, Okla., 1983), 56.

50. Tanis C. Thorne, *The Many Hands of My Relations: French and Indians on the Lower Missouri* (Columbia, Mo., 1996), 68–96; Jennifer Turner, "Being Creole, Becoming American: St. Louis after the Louisiana Purchase," paper given at McNeil Center for Early American Studies, Philadelphia, Apr. 9, 2003. Also see Turner's forthcoming dissertation, University of Wisconsin.

51. J. Gaignard, "Journal of an Expedition up the Red River, 1773–1774," *Athanase de Mézières*, 2: 85; Smith, *Wichita Indians*, 33–36, 46; Cecile Elkins Carter, *Caddo Indians: Where We Come From* (Norman, Okla., 1995), 58–59, 181.

52. Josef Orieta to Luis de Unzaga y Amezaga, Oct. 30, [1774], fol. 205, leg. 107, PC.

53. Pedro Piernas, trade report, May 19, 1775, *SMV*, 1: 228. The Great Osages had seven traders and 15,000 pounds; the Little Osages had two traders and 7,200 pounds. The second largest trade volume belonged to the Kansas with two traders and 7,500 pounds of furs.

54. Athanase de Mézières to Unzaga, Nov. 29, 1770, *Athanase de Mézières*, 1: 193; Din and Nasatir, *Imperial Osages*, 89, 93; Gaignard to Unzaga, Jan. 6, 1774, *Athanase de Mézières*, 2: 81–82; Antonio de Ulloa to Clouet, June 5, 1768, fol. 3, leg. 107, PC; François Desmazellières to Unzaga, May 15, 1770, fol. 89, leg. 107, PC; Fernando de Leyba to Unzaga, Oct. 9, 1772, fol. 326, leg. 107, PC.

55. William E. Foley and C. David Rice, *The First Chouteaus: River Barons of Early St. Louis* (Urbana, Ill., 1983), 17–18; Unrau, *Kansa Indians*, 73.

56. Pedro Piernas to Unzaga, July 4, 1772, *SMV*, 1: 204–5.

57. Piernas to Unzaga, July 30, 1772, *SMV*, 1: 206–7; Din and Nasatir, *Imperial Osages*, 81.

58. Unzaga to Piernas, draft, Aug. 21, 1772, qtd. in Din and Nasatir, *Imperial Osages*, 82; Cruzat, "Report of the Indian Tribes," 1: 144; Collot, "State of the Indian Nations," 2: 384; Zenon Trudeau to Manuel Gayoso de Lemos, Jan. 15, 1798, *BLC*, 2: 539; Louis de Vilemont to French Minister, July 3, 1802, *BLC*, 2: 694; Pierre Chouteau to Henry Dearborn, Nov. 19, 1804, *BLC*, 2: 759–60; Faye, "Arkansas Post of Louisiana: Spanish Domination," 637.

59. Unzaga to Leyba, Oct. 26, 1773, fol. 368, leg. 107, PC; Leyba to Gálvez, Jan. 13, 1779, *Spanish Régime*, 1: 163.

60. Din and Nasatir, *Imperial Osages*, 89; Carter, *Caddo Indians*, 210, 213–14.

61. Mézières, "Plan for a campaign against the Osages," Sept. 14, 1777, *Athanase de Mézières*, 2: 143–44; Mézières to Gálvez, Sept. 14, 1777, *Athanase de Mézières*, 2: 141–42.

62. Miró to the Marquis de Sonora, Feb. 1, 1781, *Spanish Régime*, 1: 256–57; Du Breuil to Miró, Mar. 18, 1785, fol. 560, leg. 107, PC; Terry P. Wilson, "Claremore, the Osage, and the Intrusion of Other Indians, 1800–1824," *Indian Leaders: Oklahoma's First Statesmen*, ed. H. Glenn Jordan and Thomas M. Holm (Oklahoma City, 1979), 142. Cashesegra was also called Cuchechire, Big Track, La Peste, and Makes-Tracks-Far-Away.

63. Pedro Piernas, trade report, May 19, 1775, *SMV*, 1: 228.

64. Mathews, *The Osages*, 138.

Chapter 5. New Alliances, 1765–1800

1. Fernando de Leyba to Luis de Unzaga y Amezaga, Nov. 26, 1773, fol. 377, leg. 107, PC; Pierre François de Rigaud, Marquis de Vaudreuil, "Ordre de commandement pour M. de Macarty," Aug. 8, 1751, LO 325, box 6, VP; Alexandre de Clouet to Alejandro O'Reilly, Sept. 20, 1769, folio 18, legajo 107, PC; Philip Pittman, *The Present State of the European Settlements on the Missisippi* (London, 1770), 40; Quapaw census, Apr. 17, 1784, fol. 510, leg. 107, PC.

2. Jean-Jacques-Blaise D'Abbadie, journal, *A Comparative View of French Louisiana, 1699 and 1762: The Journals of Pierre Le Moyne d'Iberville and Jean-Jacques-Blaise d'Abbadie*, trans. and ed. Carl A. Brasseaux (Lafayette, La., 1981), 96–97, 106, 121–22.

3. Le Gros de la Grandcour to Antonio de Ulloa, Apr. 21, 1766, fol. 606, leg. 107, PC.

4. Clouet to Ulloa, Feb. 27, 1768, fol. 36, leg. 107, PC; Ulloa to Grandcour, July 15, 1766, fol. 607, leg. 107, PC.

5. Marc de Villiers Du Terrage, *The Last Years of French Louisiana*, trans. Hosea Phillips, ed. Carl A. Brasseaux and Glenn R. Conrad (Lafayette, La., 1982), 264, 269; Ulloa to Clouet, Mar. 21, 1768, fol. 1, leg. 107, PC.

6. Clouet to Ulloa, Feb. 27, 1768, fol. 36, leg. 107, PC; Clouet to Ulloa, Mar. 30, 1768, fol. 41, leg. 107, PC.

7. Clouet to Ulloa, May 10, 1768, fol. 45, leg. 107, PC; Ulloa to Clouet, May 3, 1768, fol. 3, leg. 107, PC.

8. Clouet to O'Reilly, July 14, 1769, fol. 11, leg. 107, PC.

9. O'Reilly to François Desmazellières, Nov. 14, 1769, "The First Spanish Instructions for Arkansas Post," ed. and trans. Gilbert C. Din, *Arkansas Historical Quarterly* 53 (1994), 317.

10. Desmazellières to O'Reilly, Jan. 15, 1770, fol. 76, leg. 107, PC; Desmazellières to O'Reilly, Feb. 15, 1770, fol. 78, leg. 107, PC; Winston De Ville, *Louisiana Troops,*

1720–1770 (Fort Worth, Tex., 1965), 129; Villiers Du Terrage, *Last Years of French Louisiana*, 62–63

11. Desmazellières to Unzaga, Oct. 7, 1770, fol. 134, leg. 107, PC.

12. Jean Frédéric Phélypeaux, Compte de Maurepas, to Vaudreuil, Aug. 11, 1746, LO 83, box 2, VP; Roland Michel Barrin, Compte de La Gallissonière, to Vaudreuil, June 17, 1749, LO 175, box 4, VP; Norman Ward Caldwell, *The French in the Mississippi Valley*, 1740–1750 (Urbana, Ill., 1941), 26; Navarro, statement of payment for Indian presents, Jan. 9, 1770, *SMV*, 1: 154–55; Caldwell, *French in the Mississippi Valley*, 26–27; statement of expenses of the Province of Louisiana, 1766 through 1785, *SMV*, 2: 209. Vaudreuil to Maurepas, Mar. 20, 1748, LO 120, box 3, VP; Vaudreuil to the Court, July 20, 1751, 2: 152, LO 9, VL; Paul Augustin Le Pelletier de La Houssaye to Vaudreuil, Dec. 1, 1752, LO 410, box 8, VP. Exchange rates are from Derek N. Kerr, *Petty Felony, Slave Defiance, and Frontier Villainy: Crime and Criminal Justice in Spanish Louisiana, 1770–1803* (New York, 1993), 70–71; Nancy Maria Miller Surrey, *The Commerce of Louisiana During the French Regime, 1699–1763* (New York, 1916), 106.

13. *The Present State of the Country and Inhabitants, Europeans and Indians, of Louisiana, On the North Continent of America. By an Officer at New Orleans to his Friend at Paris* (London, 1744), 10–11; Henri Folmer, "Contraband Trade Between Louisiana and New Mexico in the Eighteenth-Century," *New Mexico Historical Review* 16 (1941), 250, 259; Vaudreuil, "Ordre de commandement pour M. de Macarty"; Vaudreuil to Maurepas, July 18, 1743, 1: 3v; LO 9, VL.

14. "David Taitt's Journal," Mar. 12, 1772, *Documents of the American Revolution, 1770–1783*, ed. K. G. Davies (Shannon and Dublin, 1972–1981), 5: 262; W. David Baird, *The Quapaw Indians: A History of the Downstream People* (Norman, Okla., 1980), 28–40; Arrell M. Gibson, *The Chickasaws* (Norman, Okla., 1971), 53–56, 74; Peter Chester to the Earl of Dartmouth, June 4, 1774, *Documents of the American Revolution*, 8: 127; Desmazellières to O'Reilly, June 7, 1770, fol. 98, leg. 107, PC.

15. *South Carolina Gazette*, Feb. 2, 1765; Dan Rea to Colonel Taylor, June 2, 1767, *Early American Indian Documents: Treaties and Laws, 1607–1789, Georgia and Florida Treaties, 1763–1776*, ed. John T. Juricek (Bethesda, Md., 2002), 12: 337; John Richard Alden, *John Stuart and the Southern Colonial Frontier: A Study of Indian Relations, War, Trade, and Land Problems in the Southern Wilderness, 1754–1775* (New York, 1966), 201, 239; James Lovell, account of provisions delivered to the different tribes resorting to the post at Natchez, 1767–68, B-11, Haldimand Papers, British Library, London, England. Many thanks to Wendy St. Jean for copies of the Haldimand Papers.

16. Clouet to Ulloa, May 10, 1768, fol. 45, leg. 107, PC.

17. Clouet to Ulloa, July 26, 1768, fol. 50, leg. 107, PC.

18. Clouet to Charles Philippe Aubry, Feb. 25, 1769, fol. 9, leg. 107, PC; Clouet to Aubry, Feb. 14, 1769, fol. 7, leg. 107, PC; John Fitzpatrick to John McGillivray and William Struthers, Feb. 1771, *The Merchant of Manchac: The Letterbooks of John Fitzpatrick, 1768–1790*, ed. Margaret Fisher Dalrymple (Baton Rouge, La., 1978), 102–3; David J. Weber, *The Spanish Frontier in North America* (New Haven, Conn., 1992), 175.

19. Clouet to O'Reilly, Sept. 20, 1769, fol. 18, leg. 107, PC.

20. Clouet to O'Reilly, Sept. 1, 1769, fol. 16, leg. 107, PC; Alden, *John Stuart*.

21. Clouet to O'Reilly, Sept. 1, 1769, fol. 16, leg. 107, PC.

22. Clouet to O'Reilly, Sept. 20, 1769, fol. 18, leg. 107, PC.

23. Wendy Barbara St. Jean, "Trading Paths: Chickasaw Diplomacy in the Greater Southeast, 1690s–1790s" (Ph.D. diss., University of Connecticut, 2004), Chapter 8; Esteban Miró to Francisco Bouligny, Dec. 21, 1785, "Papers from the Spanish Archives Relating to Tennessee and the Old Southwest, 1783–1800," trans. and ed. D. C. Corbitt and Roberta Corbitt, *East Tennessee Historical Society's Publications* 9 (1937), 142.

24. *The Pennsylvania Gazette,* July 16, 1772.

25. John Thomas to John Stuart, Mar. 11, 1772, *Documents of the American Revolution,* 5: 48–49.

26. John McIntosh to Charles Stuart, Sept. 3, 1772, *Documents of the American Revolution,* 5: 186.

27. Thomas to Thomas Gage, Mar. 8, 1773, *Early American Indian Documents,* 12: 436; J. Stuart to Earl of Dartmouth, June 21, 1773, *Documents of the American Revolution,* 6: 158–59.

28. J. Stuart to Earl of Hillsborough, Dec. 2, 1770, 2: 282; Thomas to J. Stuart, Oct. 5, 1771, 3: 207; Thomas to J. Stuart, Dec. 12, 1771, 3: 263; all in *Documents of the American Revolution*; Desmazellières to O'Reilly, Oct. 7, 1770, fol. 134, leg. 107, PC; Unzaga to Leyba, July 23, 1771, fol. 255, leg. 107, PC.

29. Thomas Nairne, *Nairne's Muskhogean Journals: The 1708 Expedition to the Mississippi River* (Jackson, Miss., 1988), 40–41; Nancy Shoemaker, *A Strange Likeness: Becoming Red and White in Eighteenth-Century North America* (New York, 2004), 40; St. Jean, "Trading Paths," introduction and Chapter 8; Thomas to Hillsborough, Dec. 1, 1770, summary, *Documents of the American Revolution,* 1: 216; Alden, *John Stuart,* 330–31; C. Stuart to J. Stuart, abstract, Aug. 26, 1770, *Documents of the American Revolution,* 2: 175.

30. "Congress of the Principal Chiefs and Warriors of the Chickasaw and Choctaw Nations," Jan. 1, 1772, *Publications of the Mississippi Historical Society,* centenary series, ed. Dunbar Rowland (Jackson, Miss., 1925), 5: 142; Chester to Captain Dickson, May 5, 1771, B-13, Haldimand Papers; Frederick Haldimand to Gage, June 11, 1771, B-5, Haldimand Papers; Bernard Romans, *A Concise Natural History of East and West Florida,* ed. Kathryn E. Holland Braund (Tuscaloosa, Ala., 1999), 123–24; Colin G. Calloway, *The American Revolution in Indian Country: Crisis and Diversity in Native American Communities* (New York, 1995), 222–23.

31. Thomas to J. Stuart, Mar. 12, 1772, *Documents of the American Revolution,* 5: 49–51.

32. Thomas to J. Stuart, Mar. 11, 1772, *Documents of the American Revolution,* 5: 48–49; Henry Le Fleur, deposition, Feb. 21, 1772, *Early American Indian Documents,* 12: 426.

33. Thomas to Gage, Mar. 8, 1773, *Early American Indian Documents,* 12: 435–36; J. Stuart to Hillsborough, June 12, 1772, *Documents of the American Revolution,* 5: 117; C. Stuart to J. Stuart, Aug. 12, 1772, *Early American Indian Documents,* 12: 430; Robert R. Rea, "Redcoats and Redskins on the Lower Mississippi, 1763–1776: The Career of Lt. John Thomas," *Louisiana History* 11 (1970), 25. Thomas had a history of difficulty with his superiors, including a previous dismissal. J. Russell Snapp, *John Stuart and the Struggle for Empire on the Southern Frontier* (Baton Rouge, La., 1996), 99–101.

34. Thomas to Gage, Mar. 8, 1773, *Early American Indian Documents*, 12: 436; Josef Orieta to Unzaga, May 1, 1775, fol. 222, leg. 107, PC; Orieta to Unzaga, May 31, 1775, fol. 226, leg. 107, PC; Balthazár de Villiers to Bernardo de Gálvez, Apr. 13, 1778, fol. 231, leg. 191, PC.

35. Desmazellières to Unzaga, Aug. 18, 1770, fol. 124, leg. 107, PC; Desmazellières to O'Reilly, Mar. 4, 1770, fol. 80, leg. 107, PC.

36. Unzaga to Orieta, July 20, 1770, fol. 150, leg. 107, PC.

37. John W. Caughey, "Bernardo de Gálvez and the English Smugglers on the Mississippi, 1777," *Hispanic American Historical Review* 12 (1932), 48; Jack D. L. Holmes, *Honor and Fidelity: The Louisiana Infantry Regiment and the Louisiana Militia Companies, 1766–1821* (Birmingham, Ala., 1965), 17–18, 160; Charles Gayarré, *History of Louisiana: The French Domination* (New York, 1854), 2: 293; John P. Moore, *Revolt in Louisiana: The Spanish Occupation, 1766–1770* (Baton Rouge, La., 1976), 194.

38. Leyba to Unzaga, June 6, 1771, fol. 247, leg. 107, PC; John C. Ewers, "Symbols of Chiefly Authority in Spanish Louisiana," in *The Spanish in the Mississippi Valley, 1762–1804*, ed. John Francis McDermott (Urbana, Ill., 1974), 280.

39. Leyba to Unzaga, June 6, 1771, fol. 247, leg. 107, PC.

40. Leyba to Unzaga, June 6, 1771, fol. 247, leg. 107, PC.

41. Leyba to Unzaga, July 27, 1771, fol. 256, leg. 107, PC.

42. Leyba to Unzaga, Nov. 22, 1771, fol. 267, leg. 107, PC.

43. Unzaga to Leyba, Mar. 14, 1772, fol. 282, leg. 107, PC.

44. Leyba to Unzaga, July 27, 1771, fol. 256, leg. 107, PC; Kerr, *Petty Felony*, 79; Stanley Faye, "The Arkansas Post of Louisiana: Spanish Domination," *Louisiana Historical Quarterly* 27 (1944), 641.

45. Leyba to Unzaga, Apr. 13, 1772, fol. 286, leg. 107, PC.

46. Leyba to Unzaga, June 15, 1772, fol. 310, leg. 107, PC; Leyba to Unzaga, June 24, 1772, fol. 312, leg. 107, PC.

47. Leyba to Unzaga, June 12, 1772, fol. 307, leg. 107, PC.

48. Leyba to Unzaga, Apr. 30, 1773, fol. 357, leg. 107, PC. The governor sent Labucière to Spain for trial, where he was sentenced to life imprisonment in a Spanish prison in North Africa. Morris S. Arnold, *The Rumble of a Distant Drum: The Quapaws and Old World Newcomers, 1673–1804* (Fayetteville, Ark., 2000), 153; Kerr, *Petty Felony*, 79.

49. Unzaga to Leyba, Jan. 26, 1772, fol. 284, leg. 107, PC; Leyba to Unzaga, Apr. 13, 1772, fol. 286, leg. 107, PC; Leyba to Unzaga, May 26, 1772, fol. 301, leg. 107, PC; Leyba to Unzaga, Oct. 9, 1772, fol. 326, leg. 107, PC; Leyba to Unzaga, Nov. 26, 1773, fol. 374, leg. 107, PC; Alden, *John Stuart*, 329; Chester to Earl of Dartmouth, June 4, 1774, *Documents of the American Revolution*, 8: 126–28; Orieta to Unzaga, Dec. 26, 1775, fol. 35, leg. 189B, PC.

50. Leyba to Unzaga, May 25, 1773, fol. 359, leg. 107, PC; Leyba to Unzaga, June 18, 1773, fol. 360, leg. 107, PC.

51. Faye, "Arkansas Post of Louisiana: Spanish Domination," 629–30; Villiers Du Terrage, *Last Years of French Louisiana*, 112; Unzaga to Leyba, Aug. 21, 1772, fol. 321, leg. 107, PC.

52. Report of Quapaw presents, Apr. 17, 1784, fol. 512, leg. 107, PC.

53. Villiers to Galvez, June 11, 1778, fol. 184, leg. 191, PC.

54. Leyba to Unzaga, Sept. 11, 1771, fol. 261, leg. 107, PC; Desmazellières to O'Reilly, Oct. 6, 1770, fol. 133, leg. 107, PC; Leyba to Unzaga, Apr. 27, 1772, fol. 291, leg. 107, PC; Leyba to Unzaga, June 12, 1772, fol. 307, leg. 107, PC; Leyba to Unzaga, Apr. 6, 1773, fol. 348, leg. 107, PC.

55. Leyba to Unzaga, Apr. 30, 1773, fol. 355, leg. 107, PC.

56. Unzaga to Leyba, Sept. 22, 1771, fol. 263, leg. 107, PC; Unzaga to Cazenon-point, Sept. 22, 1771, fol. 265, leg. 107, PC.

57. Leyba to Unzaga, Jan. 4, 1772, fol. 279, leg. 107, PC; Unzaga to Leyba, Jan. 26, 1772, fol. 284, leg. 107, PC.

58. Orieta to Unzaga, May 31, 1775, fol. 226, leg. 107, PC; Leyba to Unzaga, Apr. 27, 1772, fol. 291, leg. 107, PC; Gilbert C. Din and A. P. Nasatir, *The Imperial Osages: Spanish-Indian Diplomacy in the Mississippi Valley* (Norman, Okla., 1983), 88; Orieta to Unzaga, Oct. 17, 1774, fol. 200, leg. 107, PC; Orieta to Unzaga, Dec. 14, 1774, fol. 209, leg. 107, PC; Orieta to Unzaga, May 1, 1775, fol. 222, leg. 107, PC.

59. St. Jean, "Trading Paths," Chapter 8.

60. Villiers to Gálvez, Mar. 4, 1777, fol. 84, leg. 190, PC.

61. Athanase de Mézières to Unzaga, May 2, 1777, *Athanase de Mézières and the Louisiana-Texas Frontier, 1768–1780*, ed. Herbert Eugene Bolton (Cleveland, 1914), 2: 131.

62. Villiers to Gálvez, July 14, 1777, fol. 109, leg. 190, PC; Gálvez to Villiers, Aug. 11, 1777, fol. 108, leg. 190, PC; Francisco Cruzat to Gálvez, Dec. 6, 1777, *The Spanish Régime in Missouri: A Collection of Papers and Documents Relating to Upper Louisiana*, ed. Louis Houck (New York, 1971), 1: 149–51; Villiers to Gálvez, Sept. 14, 1777, fol. 116, leg. 190, PC.

63. Villiers to Gálvez, Jan. 26, 1778, fol. 199, leg. 191, PC.

64. Villiers to Gálvez, Apr. 13, 1778, fol. 231, leg. 191, PC; Din and Nasatir, *Imperial Osages*, 125.

65. Dalrymple, *Merchant of Manchac*, 24. For an analysis of the relationship of British Indian policies to the American Revolution, see Snapp, *John Stuart and the Struggle for Empire*.

66. Orieta to Unzaga, July 14, 1774, fol. 191, leg. 107, PC; Orieta to Unzaga, Apr. 18, 1776, fol. 48, leg. 189B, PC; Villiers to Gálvez, May 28, 1777, fol. 100, leg. 190, PC; Villiers to Gálvez, Aug. 14, 1777, fol. 115, leg. 190, PC.

67. Denombrement du Poste des Akanzas, Aug. 3, 1777, fol. 111, leg. 190, PC; Villiers to Pedro Piernas, Dec. 1, 1781, fol. 76, leg. 194, PC.

68. Leyba to Unzaga, June 18, 1773, fol. 360, leg. 107, PC; report of Quapaw presents, Apr. 17, 1784, fol. 511, leg. 107, PC; Jacobo Du Breuil to Miró, Jan. 17, 1783, fol. 387, leg. 107, PC.

69. John Campbell to George Germain, Sept. 22, 1780, *Documents of the American Revolution*, 18: 175; Alexander Cameron to Germain, July 18, 1780, *Documents of the American Revolution*, 18: 121; Hopoiyamuttahah to Cameron, n.d., abstract, *Documents of the American Revolution*, 16: 367; Gálvez to Opaye Mathaa, Dec. 17, 1779, abstract, *Documents of the American Revolution*, 16: 367. On the difficulties of neutrality, see Calloway, *American Revolution*.

70. Gibson, *The Chickasaws*, 65, 80; James R. Atkinson, *Splendid Land, Splendid People: The Chickasaw Indians to Removal* (Tuscaloosa, Ala., 2004), 93, 102; Testimony

of Madame Cruzat to Miró, May 30, 1782, *Spanish Régime*, 1: 221–31; Calloway, *American Revolution*, 229; C. Stuart to J. Stuart, Dec. 26, 1770, *Documents of the American Revolution*, 2: 303. For exaggerations of Colbert's leadership, see Guy B. Braden, "The Colberts and the Chickasaw Nation," *Tennessee Historical Quarterly* 17 (1958), 222–49, 318–35; D. C. Corbitt, "James Colbert and the Spanish Claims to the East Bank of the Mississippi," *Mississippi Valley Historical Review* 24 (1938), 457–72.

71. Calloway, *American Revolution*, 226–30.

72. Miró to Gálvez, June 5, 1782, *Spanish Régime*, 1: 214–15; Calloway, *American Revolution*, 229–30.

73. Du Breuil to Miró, Feb. 18, 1783, fol. 393, leg. 107, PC; Du Breuil to Miró, Mar. 1, 1783, fol. 396, leg. 107, PC; Du Breuil to Miró, Mar. 26, 1783, fol. 399, leg. 107, PC. For a parallel case, see Karim M. Tiro, "A 'Civil' War? Rethinking Iroquois Participation in the American Revolution," *Explorations in Early American Culture* 4 (2000), 148–65.

74. Du Breuil to Miró, May 5, 1783, fol. 403, leg. 107, PC; Corbitt, "James Colbert," 466. The Quapaw with a hatchet returned to the post a hero and is still a legend in Arkansas as a hero of the Revolution. It is generally forgotten that the "Americans" he saved were Spanish, French, and African and that the "British" over whom he triumphed were Scottish, Chickasaw, and African. Arnold, *Rumble of a Distant Drum*, 146–48.

75. Du Breuil to Miró, Aug. 7, 1786, fol. 38, leg. 13, PC.

76. Du Breuil to Miró, May 5, 1783, fol. 403, leg. 107, PC. Food was short that year. Du Breuil to Miró, Mar. 26, 1783, fol. 398, leg. 107, PC. After Angaska's death, the Quapaws blamed him for their inaction during the battle. Du Breuil to Miró, Apr. 14, 1785, fol. 565, leg. 107, PC.

77. Du Breuil to Miró, May 5, 1783, fol. 403, leg. 107, PC; Du Breuil to Miró, May 22, 1783, fol. 433, leg. 107, PC; Joseph Valliere, "Estado de los servicios de Don Josef Valliere Dauterire," Mar. 30, 1788, fols. 214–16, leg. 14, PC, photostat in folder 4, box 26, Core Family Papers, Special Collections, University of Arkansas Library, Fayetteville, Ark.

78. Du Breuil to Miró, May 22, 1783, fol. 433, leg. 107, PC.

79. Du Breuil, "Relacion de la artilleria, pertrechos, y municiones de guerra," Feb. 1, 1784, fol. 491, leg. 107, PC. The entire annual allotment of gunpowder for a Spanish soldier in North America was only three pounds. Odie B. Faulk, "The Presidio: Fortress or Farce?," in *New Spain's Far Northern Frontier: Essays on Spain in the American West, 1540–1821*, ed. David J. Weber (Albuquerque, 1979), 74.

80. Du Breuil to Miró, Aug. 26, 1783, fol. 464, leg. 107, PC; Gilbert C. Din, "Loyalist Resistance after Pensacola: The Case of James Colbert," in *Anglo-Spanish Confrontation on the Gulf Coast During the American Revolution*, ed. William S. Coker and Robert R. Rea (Pensacola, Fla., 1982), 166.

81. "Tratado de Paz celebrado entre la Nacion Española y la Nacion Chicacha," June 23, 1784, Transcripts of Selected Manuscript Documents Pertaining to Arkansas, reel 1, film 663, Library of Congress, held at University of Arkansas.

82. Dale Van Every, *Ark of Empire: The American Frontier, 1784–1803* (New York, 1963), 16–17; William G. McLoughlin, *Cherokee Renascence in the New Republic* (Princeton, N.J., 1986), 25; Robert S. Cotterill, "The Virginia-Chickasaw Treaty of

1783," *Journal of Southern History* 8 (1942), 494–95; Gibson, *The Chickasaws*, 75–79; Calloway, *American Revolution*, 235–39; "Treaty with the Chickasaw, 1786," *Indian Affairs: Laws and Treaties*, ed. Charles J. Kappler (Washington, D.C., 1904–41), 2: 14–16.

83. Gálvez to José de Gálvez, Oct. 24, 1778, qtd. in Elizabeth Howard West, "The Indian Policy of Bernardo de Galvez," *Proceedings of the Mississippi Valley Historical Association* 8 (1914–15), 100–101.

84. Daniel Clark, "An Account of the Indian Tribes in Louisiana," Sept. 29, 1803, *TP*, 9: 63–64; C. A. Weslager, *The Delaware Indians: A History* (New Brunswick, N.J., 1972), 319, 331; Louis Lorimier, journal, *Spanish Régime*, 2: 72–73, 81, 88, 95, 97, 99.

85. Joseph Valliere, "Investigation Concerning Sale of Liquor at Arkansas Post to the Abenaquis," May 19, 1787, *SMV*, 2: 203–4; Joseph Patrick Key, "'Masters of This Country': The Quapaws and Environmental Change in Arkansas, 1673–1833" (Ph.D. diss., University of Arkansas, 2001), 139–40.

86. Valliere, "Investigation Concerning Sale of Liquor," 2: 204–8.

87. Valliere to Jean Filhiol, Sept. 10, 1789, *SMV*, 2: 280–81; Valliere to Miró, June 3, 1787, fol. 429, leg. 13, PC.

88. Valliere to Miró, Jan. 12, 1790, *SMV*, 2: 292–93. For more on Pacane, see Richard White, *The Middle Ground: Indians, Empires, and Republics in the Great Lakes Region, 1650–1815* (New York, 1991), 427–29.

89. Delino to Miró, Aug. 2, 1790, *SMV*, 2: 368–69; De Blanc to Miró, Mar. 27, 1790, *SMV*, 2: 316; De Blanc to Miró, May 4, 1790, *SMV*, 2: 335.

Chapter 6. Better at Making Peace Than War, 1790–1808

1. Carl J. Ekberg, *Colonial Ste. Genevieve: An Adventure on the Mississippi Frontier* (Gerald, Mo., 1985), 98–100; John Pope, *A Tour through the Southern and Western Territories of the United States of North-America; the Spanish Dominions on the River Mississippi, and the Floridas* (Richmond, Va., 1792), 26; Louis Lorimier, journal, *The Spanish Régime in Missouri: A Collection of Papers and Documents Relating to Upper Louisiana*, ed. Louis Houck (New York, 1971), 2: 88, 95, 97; Daniel Clark, "An Account of the Indian Tribes in Louisiana," Sept. 29, 1803, *TP*, 9: 63; Morris S. Arnold, "Cultural Imperialism and the Legal System: The Application of European Law to Indians in Colonial Louisiana," *Loyola Law Review* 42 (1997), 739; C. A. Weslager, *The Delaware Indians: A History* (New Brunswick, N.J., 1972), 319.

2. Ekberg, *Colonial Ste. Genevieve*, 98–100.

3. François Luis Hector, Barón de Carondelet, to Ignacio Delino, June 29, 1792, *SMV*, 3: 56; Juan de la Villebeuvre to Carondelet, Feb. 7, 1793, "Papers from the Spanish Archives Relating to Tennessee and the Old Southwest," trans. and ed. D. C. Corbitt and Roberta Corbitt, *East Tennessee Historical Society's Publications* 29 (1957), 152.

4. Carondelet to Zenon Trudeau, Dec. 22, 1792, *SMV*, 3: 107.

5. Carondelet, draft order, (1793), *SMV*, 3: 144; Carondelet to Trudeau, May 6, 1793, *SMV*, 3: 155; Jack D. L. Holmes, *Gayoso: The Life of a Spanish Governor in the Mississippi Valley, 1789–1799* (Baton Rouge, La., 1965), 156–57; Arthur Preston

Whitaker, *The Spanish-American Frontier, 1783–1795: The Westward Movement and the Spanish Retreat in the Mississippi Valley* (Gloucester, Mass., 1962), 153–54.

6. St. Louis Merchants to Carondelet, June 22, 1793, *BLC*, 1: 181–84; Trudeau to Carondelet, Apr. 10, 1793, *SMV*, 3: 148.

7. Zenon Trudeau, trade report, entries for 1793 and 1794, *BLC*, 2: 530; *La Fleche* Log, *SMV*, 3: 119; Morris S. Arnold, *Colonial Arkansas, 1686–1804: A Social and Cultural History* (Fayetteville, Ark., 1991), 62; Morris S. Arnold and Dorothy Jones Core, eds., *Arkansas Colonials, 1686–1804: A Collection of French and Spanish Records Listing Early Europeans in the Arkansas* (Dewitt, Ark., 1986), 47–91; John B. Treat to Henry Dearborn, Mar. 27, 1806, LBATH; Manuel Perez to Esteban Miró, Aug. 23, 1790, *BLC*, 1: 134–35; St. Louis Merchants, petition, Oct. 15, 1793, *SMV*, 3: 195–98; Zenon Trudeau, minutes of merchants' meeting, May 3, 1794, *SMV*, 3: 278–79.

8. Perez to Miró, Oct. 5, 1791, *SMV*, 2: 416; Perez to Miró, Nov. 8, 1791, *BLC*, 1: 150; St. Louis Merchants to Carondelet, June 22, 1793, *BLC*, 1: 182; Marqués de Casa Calvo to Ramón de Lopez y Angulo, May 8, 1801, *Spanish Régime*, 2: 309–10; Francisco Cruzat, "Report of the Indian Tribes Who Receive Presents at St. Louis," Nov. 15, 1777, *Spanish Régime*, 1: 144–45; Stanley Faye, "The Arkansas Post of Louisiana: Spanish Domination," *Louisiana Historical Quarterly* 27 (1944), 637.

9. *La Fleche* Log, 3: 119.

10. Miró to Bernardo de Gálvez, Aug. 1, 1780, qtd. in Miró to Marqués de Sonora, Feb. 1, 1781, *Spanish Régime*, 1: 255; Lorimier, journal, 2: 94; Ekberg, *Colonial Ste. Genevieve*, 92.

11. Trudeau to Carondelet, Sept. 28, 1793, *BLC*, 1: 197.

12. Trudeau to Carondelet, Sept. 28, 1793, *SMV*, 3: 206–7.

13. Jacobo Du Breuil to Miró, Dec. 29, 1786, *SMV*, 2: 196.

14. Miró to Du Breuil, Jan. 25, 1787, *SMV*, 2: 197.

15. Miró to Joseph Valliere, Feb. 4, 1790, fol. 219, leg. 7, PC; Pierre Rousseau and Luis de Blanc to Miró, Mar. 20, 1787, *SMV*, 2: 199.

16. Gilbert C. Din and A. P. Nasatir, *The Imperial Osages: Spanish-Indian Diplomacy in the Mississippi Valley* (Norman, Okla., 1983), 193, 234–35; Villebeuvre to Carondelet, Feb. 9, 1793, "Papers from the Spanish Archives Relating to Tennessee," 29: 154; Villebeuvre to Carondelet, Feb. 1793, "Papers from the Spanish Archives Relating to Tennessee," 29: 160; Villebeuvre to Carondelet, Apr. 21, 1794, *SMV*, 3: 270; Carondelet to Trudeau, June 10, 1794, *SMV*, 3: 299.

17. Lorimier to Carondelet, Sept. 17, 1793, *SMV*, 3: 204–5.

18. Trudeau to Carondelet, Apr. 10, 1793, *BLC*, 1: 171–73.

19. Ste. Geneviève Inhabitants to Miró, Apr. 9, 1790, fol. 338, leg. 7, PC.

20. Trudeau to Carondelet, Sept. 28, 1793, *BLC*, 1: 199; Ekberg, *Colonial Ste. Genevieve*; David J. Weber, *The Spanish Frontier in North America* (New Haven, Conn., 1992), 284–85.

21. Richard White, *The Roots of Dependency: Subsistence, Environment, and Social Change among the Choctaws, Pawnees, and Navajos* (Lincoln, Neb., 1983), 152–53.

22. Bernardo de Gálvez, *Instructions for Governing the Interior Provinces of New Spain, 1786*, ed. and trans. Donald E. Worcester (Berkeley, Calif., 1951), 43.

23. Trudeau to Carondelet, July 25, 1792, *BLC*, 1: 156–57.

24. Trudeau to Carondelet, Sept. 28, 1793, *BLC*, 1: 200.

25. Francisco Cruzat, "Investigation of Benito Vasquez' Activities Among the Great Osage," June 22, 1787, *SMV*, 2: 214–15.

26. Rollings, *The Osage*, 160; Carl H. Chapman, "The Indomitable Osage in Spanish Illinois (Upper Louisiana) 1763–1804," in *The Spanish in the Mississippi Valley, 1762–1804*, ed. John Francis McDermott (Urbana, Ill., 1974), 293–94.

27. While Osage chieftanships were not strictly patrilineal, the new chief apparently always came from the family and clan of the deceased. Chapman, "Indomitable Osage," 293–94; Garrick Alan Bailey, *Changes in Osage Social Organization: 1673–1906* (Eugene, Oreg., 1973), 22, 45, 59; Du Breuil to Miró, Mar. 18, 1785, fol. 560, leg.107, PC; Miró to Sonora, Feb. 1, 1781, *Spanish Régime*, 1: 254–55; Rollings, *The Osage*, 167; Trudeau to Carondelet, July 25, 1792, *BLC*, 1: 156–57; Miró to Alange, Aug. 7 [or 11], 1792, *Documentos inéditos para la historia de la Luisiana, 1792–1810*, ed. Jack D. L. Holmes (Madrid, 1963), 61.

28. Auguste Chouteau and Carondelet, contract, May 18, 1794, *Spanish Régime*, 2: 106–8; Rollings, *The Osage*, 191.

29. Trudeau to Carondelet, Apr. 18, 1795, *BLC*, 1: 320.

30. Trudeau to Carondelet, Aug. 30, 1795, *BLC*, 1: 346; Ekberg, *Colonial Ste. Genevieve*, 103.

31. Chapman, "Indomitable Osage," 294; William E. Foley and C. David Rice, *The First Chouteaus: River Barons of Early St. Louis* (Urbana, Ill., 1983), 53; J. Frederick Fausz, "Becoming 'a Nation of Quakers': The Removal of the Osage Indians from Missouri," *Gateway Heritage* 21 (2000), 31. Many thanks to J. Frederick Fausz for his generous and knowledgeable answers to my questions about trade goods here and elsewhere in this chapter.

32. Carondelet to Trudeau, June 10, 1794, *SMV*, 3: 299–300; Din and Nasatir, *Imperial Osages*, 261; Carondelet to Villebeuvre, June 4, 1794, "Papers from the Spanish Archives Relating to Tennessee," 39: 101–2; Trudeau to Carondelet, Aug. 30, 1795, *BLC*, 1: 346; Rollings, *The Osage*, 200, 211; Carlos DeHault de Lassus to Casa Calvo, Sept. 25, 1800, *Spanish Régime*, 2: 301; Casa Calvo to Lopez y Angulo, May 8, 1801, *Spanish Régime*, 2: 309; Carondelet to Trudeau, Jan. 26, 1797, folder 260, box 3, Correspondence and Papers of Francisco Luis Hector Carondelet: Outgoing and Incoming A-L, Louisiana Collection, Bancroft Library, Berkeley, Calif.; Foley and Rice, *First Chouteaus*, 56.

33. Trudeau to Manuel Gayoso de Lemos, Jan. 15, 1798, *BLC*, 2: 538.

34. Timothy Flint, *Recollections of the Last Ten Years, Passed in Occasional Residences and Journeyings in the Valley of the Mississippi* (New York, 1968), 155; Casa Calvo to Lopez y Angulo, May 8, 1801, *Spanish Régime*, 2: 310.

35. De Lassus to Casa Calvo, Sept. 25, 1800, *Spanish Régime*, 2: 301–5; Rollings, *The Osage*, 202; Terry P. Wilson, "Claremore, the Osage, and the Intrusion of other Indians, 1800–1824," in *Indian Leaders: Oklahoma's First Statesmen*, ed. H. Glenn Jordan and Thomas M. Holm (Oklahoma City, 1979), 142.

36. Carondelet, military report on Louisiana and West Florida, Nov. 24, 1794, *Louisiana Under the Rule of Spain, France, and the United States, 1785–1807*, ed. and trans. James Alexander Robertson (Cleveland, 1911), 1: 297.

37. Stephen Aron, *How the West Was Lost: The Transformation of Kentucky from Daniel Boone to Henry Clay* (Baltimore, 1996), 58; Elise Marienstras, "Liberty," in

A Companion to the American Revolution, ed. Jack P. Greene and J. R. Pole (Malden, Mass., 2000), 629; Alan Taylor, *Liberty Men and Great Proprietors: The Revolutionary Settlement on the Maine Frontier, 1760–1820* (Chapel Hill, N.C., 1990).

38. Carondelet, military report on Louisiana and West Florida, 1: 300, 302, 309; Carondelet to Luis de las Casas, Dec. 2, 1795, *Spanish Régime*, 2: 100.

39. Lorimier, journal, 2: 73.

40. Lorimier, journal, 2: 95–96.

41. Minister Alvarez to Captain-General of Cuba, June 26, 1798, *Louisiana Under the Rule of Spain, France, and the United States*, 1: 349; de Lassus to Casa Calvo, Sept. 25, 1800, *Spanish Régime*, 2: 303; Jonathan Daniels, *Ordeal of Ambition: Jefferson, Hamilton, Burr* (Garden City, N.Y., 1970), 114; Thomas Perkins Abernathy, *The South in the New Nation, 1789–1819* (Baton Rouge, La., 1961), 46–48, 61, 176–216; Thomas Robson Hay and M. R. Werner, *The Admirable Trumpeter: A Biography of General James Wilkinson* (Garden City, N.Y., 1941), 134, 138; Thomas Perkins Abernathy, *The Burr Conspiracy* (New York, 1954), 4–5; Weber, *Spanish Frontier*, 282; Anthony F. C. Wallace, *Jefferson and the Indians: The Tragic Fate of the First Americans* (Cambridge, Mass., 1999), 260; Meade Minnigerode, *Jefferson, Friend of France, 1793* (New York, 1928), 245, 258, 261; Harry Ammon, *The Genet Mission* (New York, 1973), 31.

42. Trudeau to Gayoso de Lemos, Jan. 15, 1798, *BLC*, 2: 538.

43. Carondelet, military report on Louisiana and West Florida, 1: 337.

44. Barthélemi Tardiveau to Carondelet, July 17, 1792, *SMV*, 3: 61–62; Ekberg, *Colonial Ste. Genevieve*, 352; minutas de las actas del Supremo Consejo de Estado, Nov. 13, 1795, "Materials Relating to the History of the Mississippi Valley," ed. A. P. Nasatir and Ernest R. Liljegren, *Louisiana Historical Quarterly* 21 (1938), 59–60.

45. Trudeau to Carondelet, May 27, 1794, *BLC*, 1: 214.

46. Daniel H. Usner, Jr., *Indians, Settlers, and Slaves in a Frontier Exchange Economy: The Lower Mississippi Valley Before 1783* (Chapel Hill, N.C., 1992), 106, 109–15; census [1791 or 1795], *Spanish Régime*, 1: 324–25; De Blanc to Carondelet, Feb. 18, 1792, *SMV*, 3: 9; Manuel Gayoso de Lemos, political condition of the province of Louisiana, July 5, 1792, *Louisiana Under the Rule of Spain, France, and the United States*, 1: 284; Tardiveau to Carondelet, July 17, 1792, *SMV*, 3: 61–62; James MacKay, "Table of Distances Along the Missouri," 1797, *BLC*, 2: 485–86; Trudeau to Gayoso de Lemos, Jan. 15, 1798, *BLC*, 2: 543.

47. Miró to Alange, Aug. 7, 1792, *BLC*, 1: 158–59; Carondelet to Jacques Clamorgan, May 11, 1796, *BLC*, 2: 421n.

48. Cruzat to Miró, Aug. 23, 1784, *SMV*, 2: 117–18.

49. Carondelet to Las Casas, Dec. 2, 1795, *Spanish Régime*, 2: 102.

50. Gayoso de Lemos, political condition of the province of Louisiana, 1: 275; Carondelet to Gayoso de Lemos, Dec. 18, 1792, *SMV*, 3: 104, 106; A. P. Nasatir, *Spanish War Vessels on the Mississippi, 1792–1796* (New Haven, Conn., 1968), 331n.

51. De Lassus, yearly summary of trade licenses, 1799–1804, *BLC*, 2: 590–92. On the Purchase and its effects, see Jon Kukla, *A Wilderness So Immense: The Louisiana Purchase and the Destiny of America* (New York, 2003); Peter J. Kastor, *The Nation's Crucible: The Louisiana Purchase and the Creation of America* (New Haven, Conn., 2004).

52. Jedidiah Morse, *A Report to the Secretary of War of the United States, on Indian Affairs, Comprising a Narrative of a Tour Performed in the Summer of* 1820 (New Haven, Conn., 1822), 79; Thomas Jefferson to John Breckenridge, Aug. 12, 1803, *State Papers and Correspondence Bearing upon the Purchase of the Territory of Louisiana* (Washington, D.C., 1903), 234–35; Jefferson to Pierre Samuel Dupont de Nemours, Nov. 1, 1803, *State Papers and Correspondence Bearing upon the Purchase*, 261–62; Jefferson to Dearborn, Apr. 8, 1804, *TP*, 13: 19; Wilkinson to Jefferson, Nov. 6, 1805, *TP*, 13: 266; Jennifer M. Spear, "Colonial Intimacies: Legislating Sex in French Louisiana," *WMQ* 60 (2003), 85–86.

53. Berkhofer, *White Man's Indian*, 47; Wallace, *Jefferson and the Indians*; Bernard W. Sheehan, *Seeds of Extinction: Jeffersonian Philanthropy and the American Indian* (Chapel Hill, N.C., 1973); Horsman, "Indian Policy of an 'Empire for Liberty,'" 48–52. For similar desires to assimilate "miserable Germans," in John Adams's words, see Birte Pfleger, "'Miserable Germans' and Fries's Rebellion: Language, Ethnicity, and Citizenship in the Early Republic," *Early American Studies* 2 (2004), 343–61.

54. Fausz, "Becoming 'a Nation of Quakers,'" 34.

55. Daniel K. Richter, "'Believing That Many of the Red People Suffer Much for the Want of Food': Hunting, Agriculture, and a Quaker Construction of Indianness in the Early Republic," *Journal of the Early Republic* 19 (1999), 601–28; Wallace, *Jefferson and the Indians*, 216; Francis Paul Prucha, *A Guide to the Military Posts of the United States*, 1789–1895 (Madison, Wisc., 1964), 143; Dearborn to George W. Carmichael, Nov. 7, 1803, *TP*, 13: 10; Treat to William Davy, Apr. 15, 1806, LBATH; Roger E. Coleman, *The Arkansas Post Story: Arkansas Post National Monument* (Santa Fe, N.M., 1987), 147; Dearborn to Daniel Bissell, Nov. 7, 1803, *TP*, 13: 10; Elijius Fromentin and Richard Waters to James Bruff, Sept. 19, 1804, *TP*, 13: 61; *Annals of St. Louis in Its Territorial Days from 1804 to 1821*, ed. Frederic L. Billon (New York, 1971), 23–24, 92; James Neal Primm, *Lion of the Valley: St. Louis, Missouri* (Boulder, 1990), 105–6, 137; Bruff to Wilkinson, Nov. 5, 1804, *TP*, 13: 79–80; Wilkinson to Dearborn, Aug. 10, 1805, *TP*, 13: 180; Meriwether Lewis to Dearborn, Aug. 20, 1808, *TP*, 14: 212; Dearborn to Lewis, July 2, 1808, *TP*, 14: 204; Wilkinson to Dearborn, Aug. 10, 1805, *TP*, 13: 182.

56. Jefferson to Lewis, Jan. 22, 1804, *TP*, 13: 15–16.

57. William Dunbar to Jefferson, Sept. 30, 1803, *TP*, 9: 68; Wilkinson to James Madison, July 28, 1805, *TP*, 13: 173; Wilkinson to Madison, Aug. 24, 1805, *TP*, 13: 190–91; Wilkinson to Dearborn, Dec. 10, 1805, *TP*, 13: 299; William Clark to Dearborn, May 18, 1807, *TP*, 14: 124; Lewis to Dearborn, July 1, 1808, *TP*, 14: 202; Villiers du Terrage, *Last Years of French Louisiana*, 436, 456–57; Weber, *Spanish Frontier*, 291; Colin G. Calloway, *Crown and Calumet: British-Indian Relations*, 1783–1815 (Norman, Okla., 1987), 13, 131–35.

58. In reality, Burr assembled fewer than one hundred men. Joseph Browne to Dearborn, Jan. 6, 1807, *TP*, 14: 72–73; Donald Barr Chidsey, *The Great Conspiracy: Aaron Burr and His Strange Doings in the West* (New York, 1967), 60; Abernethy, *Burr Conspiracy*, 176; Dearborn to Wilkinson, May 6, 1806, *TP*, 13: 505; Nemesio Salcedo to Joaquín del Real Alencaster, Sept. 9, 1805, *The Journals of Zebulon Montgomery Pike, with Letters and Related Documents*, ed. Donald Jackson (Norman, Okla., 1966), 2:

104–5; Zebulon Pike to Wilkinson, Aug. 28, 1806, *Journals of Zebulon Montgomery Pike*, 2: 144; "George C. Sibley Journal," *Journals of Zebulon Montgomery Pike*, 2: 371.

59. Salcedo to Alencaster, Sept. 9, 1805, *Journals of Zebulon Montgomery Pike*, 2: 104–5.

60. Wilkinson to Madison, Aug. 24, 1805, *TP*, 13: 190–91; Wilkinson to the Officers of the Territory, Aug. 22, 1805, *TP*, 13: 188.

61. John Sibley to Dearborn, Aug. 18, 1807, Roll 1, M271, Letters Received by the Office of the Secretary of War Relating to Indian Affairs, 1800–24, Record Group 75, National Archives, Washington, D.C.

62. Jefferson to Chiefs and Warriors of the Osage Nation, July 18, 1804, Roll 2, M15, RG 75, NA.

63. See, for example, James B. Wilkinson to Wilkinson, Apr. 6, 1807, *Journals of Zebulon Montgomery Pike*, 2: 12; Clark to Dearborn, May 18, 1807, *TP*, 14: 122; Lewis to Dearborn, July 1, 1808, *TP*, 14: 198–99.

64. Wilkinson to Dearborn, Sept. 22, 1805, *TP*, 13: 230.

65. Jefferson to Chiefs and Warriors of the Osage Nation, July 18, 1804, Roll 2, M15, RG 75, NA; Zebulon Pike, "Diary of an Expedition Made under the Orders of the War Department," *Journals of Zebulon Montgomery Pike*, 1: 305n; Dearborn to P. Chouteau, July 17, 1804, Roll 2, M15, RG 75, NA; Hezekiah Rogers to Jefferson, Aug. 21, 1804, *Letters of the Lewis and Clark Expedition, with Related Documents, 1783–1854*, ed. Donald Jackson (Urbana, Ill., 1962), 208–9; Din and Nasatir, *Imperial Osages*, 359–61.

66. Bruff to Wilkinson, Nov. 5, 1804, *TP*, 13: 80.

67. Dearborn to Harrison, June 20, 1805, Roll 2, M15, RG 75, NA; Bruff to Wilkinson, Mar. 12, 1805, *TP*, 13: 102.

68. Wallace, *Jefferson and the Indians*, 248–51.

69. William Clark, journal, *The Journals of Lewis and Clark*, ed. Bernard DeVoto (Boston, 1953), 7, 8; Jean Baptiste Du Coigne [Macouissa] to Como'l, Mar. 2, 1805, *TP*, 13: 104; Wallace, *Jefferson and the Indians*, 227–34.

70. William Dunbar, "The Exploration of the *Red*, the *Black*, and the *Washita* Rivers," *Documents Relating to the Purchase and Exploration of Louisiana* (Boston, 1904), 74; George Hunter, *The Western Journals of Dr. George Hunter, 1796–1805*, ed. John Francis McDermott, *Transactions of the American Philosophical Society* 53 (1963), 98; Du Coigne to Como'l, Mar. 2, 1805, *TP*, 13: 103–4; Wilkinson to Dearborn, Sept. 22, 1805, *TP*, 13: 228; Wilkinson to Dearborn, Oct. 8, 1805, *TP*, 13: 235; "A Treaty Between the Tribes of Indians Called the Delawares, Miamis, Patawatimis, Kickapoos, Sacks, Foxes, Kaskaskias, Scioux of the River Demoin & Iowas, of the one part and the Great and Little Osages of the Other part," Oct. 18, 1805, *TP*, 13: 245–47; Zebulon Pike, "Dissertation on Louisiana," 1810, *Journals of Zebulon Montgomery Pike*, 2: 29, 33; Onothe (James Rogers) and Noma (Fish) to James Madison, Mar. 29, 1811, Roll 1, M271, RG 75, NA.

71. Wilkinson to Dearborn, Nov. 26, 1805, *Journals of Zebulon Montgomery Pike*, 1: 253; Jefferson to Harrison, Jan. 16, 1806, *Messages and Letters of William Henry Harrison*, ed. Logan Esarey (New York, 1975), 1: 186; Pike, "Dissertation on Louisiana," 2: 33; Rollings, *The Osage*, 221; Wilkinson to Dearborn, Dec. 23, 1805, *Journals of Zebulon Montgomery Pike*, 1: 287n.

72. "The Speech of an Osage Indian Enclosed to the Secretary of War," May 1807, *The Life and Papers of Frederick Bates*, ed. Thomas Maitland Marshall (St. Louis, 1926), 1: 124; Dearborn to Wilkinson, Feb. 10, 1806, *TP*, 13: 442.

73. Pike, "Diary of an Expedition," 1: 290–91, 304–5; Wilkinson to Chiefs of the Sauk Nation, Dec. 10, 1805, *TP*, 13: 301–2; James B. Many to Wilkinson, May 20, 1806, *TP*, 13: 512–13; Pike, "Dissertation on Louisiana," 2: 33; Dearborn to Wilkinson, Apr. 9, 1806, *TP*, 13: 487; Jackson, *Journals of Zebulon Montgomery Pike*, 1: 287–88n. Efforts continued in the following years. See Browne to Dearborn, Mar. 23, 1807, *TP*, 14: 110; Dearborn to Frederick Bates, July 3, 1807, Roll 2, M15, RG 75, NA; Dearborn to Bates, Aug. 18, 1807, Roll 2, M15, RG 75, NA; Dearborn to P. Chouteau, Aug. 18, 1807, Roll 2, M15, RG 75, NA; Bates to Dearborn, Sept. 28, 1807, *Life and Papers of Frederick Bates*, 1: 199.

74. Pike, "Diary of an Expedition," 1: 308; James B. Wilkinson to Wilkinson, Apr. 6, 1807, *Journals of Zebulon Montgomery Pike*, 2: 5; Pike, "Dissertation on Louisiana," 2: 31.

75. Pike to Wilkinson, Aug. 14, 1806, *Journals of Zebulon Montgomery Pike*, 2: 137–38; Pike to Wilkinson, Aug. 28, 1806, *Journals of Zebulon Montgomery Pike*, 2: 142; Pike, "Diary of an Expedition," 1: 310, 312, 314, 316; William E. Unrau, *The Kansa Indians: A History of the Wind People*, 1673–1873 (Norman, Okla., 1971), 83, 86, 91.

76. Treat to Dearborn, Nov. 15, 1805, LBATH; Wilkinson to Dearborn, July 27, 1805, *TP*, 13: 170. For a history of Indian trade in the early republic, see Ora Brooks Peake, *A History of the United States Indian Factory System, 1795–1822* (Denver, 1954).

77. "Jacob Bright's Journal of a Trip to the Osage Indians," ed. Harold W. Ryan, *Journal of Southern History* 15 (1949), 516–19; Treat to Dearborn, July 13, 1806, LBATH; Treat to Dearborn, Nov. 18, 1806, LBATH; Treat to Dearborn, Dec. 31, 1806, *TP*, 14: 57; Treat to John Mason, Mar. 31, 1808, LBATH.

78. "Jacob Bright's Journal," 517–19. For Osage raids, see, for example, Sibley to Dearborn, Mar. 20, 1807, Roll 1, M271, RG 75, NA; Treat to John Shee, Sept. 30, 1807, LBATH.

79. Bright to Dearborn, Dec. 20, 1806, "Jacob Bright's Journal," 512; Perly Wallis to Bates, Dec. 18, 1808, *Life and Papers of Frederick Bates*, 2: 46; Rollings, *The Osage*, 167–68; Louis F. Burns, *Osage Indian Customs and Myths* (Fallbrook, Calif., 1984), 34–35; Louis F. Burns, *A History of the Osage People* (Fallbrook, Calif., 1989), 57; John Joseph Mathews, *The Osages, Children of the Middle Waters* (Norman, Okla., 1961), 299; Bailey, *Changes in Osage Social Organization*, 59; Lewis to Dearborn, July 1, 1808, *TP*, 14: 196. Clermont II was also known as Arrow-Going-Home.

80. Dunbar to Dearborn, Feb. 25, 1806, *Life, Letters and Papers of William Dunbar of Elgin, Morayshire, Scotland, and Natchez, Mississippi*, ed. Mrs. Dunbar Rowland (Jackson, Miss., 1930), 330.

81. Bruff to Wilkinson, Mar. 12, 1805, *TP*, 13: 102; Bruff to Wilkinson, Nov. 5, 1804, *TP*, 13: 76; "Jacob Bright's Journal," 521–23; Treat to Dearborn, Nov. 18, 1806, LBATH; Pike, "Diary of an Expedition," 1: 307; "Petition of Joseph Bogy, Praying compensation for spoliations on his property by a numerous party of Choctaw Indians," Dec. 24, 1835, 24th Congress, 1st Session (Washington, D.C., 1835), Graff Collection 337, Newberry Library, Chicago.

82. Dunbar, "Dunbar on Indians of Louisiana," c. 1806, *Life, Letters and Papers of William Dunbar*, 211; Hunter, *Western Journals*, 110.

83. Balthazár de Villiers to Luis de Unzaga y Amezaga, Mar. 4, 1777, fol. 84, leg. 190, PC; Treat to Dearborn, Mar. 27, 1806, LBATH.

84. George Peter to Wilkinson, Sept. 8, 1805, *TP*, 13: 231; Treat to Dearborn, Nov. 15, 1805, LBATH; Dunbar, "Exploration of the *Red*, the *Black*, and the *Washita* Rivers," 167; Nicholas Biddle, notes, *Letters of the Lewis and Clark Expedition*, 2: 522; Treat to Dearborn, Dec. 31, 1806, LBATH; Dunbar, *Life, Letters and Papers of William Dunbar*, 210–11.

85. Treat to Dearborn, Mar. 27, 1806, LBATH; Treat to Dearborn, Jan. 7, 1808, *TP*, 14: 164.

86. Treat to Davy, Nov. 15, 1805, LBATH.

87. Treat to Dearborn, May 20, 1806, LBATH.

88. Treat to Dearborn, Nov. 18, 1806, LBATH.

89. Treat to Dearborn, Mar. 27, 1806, LBATH.

90. Dearborn to Treat, June 23, 1807, *TP*, 14: 129.

91. Treat to Dearborn, Mar. 27, 1806, LBATH.

92. Treat to Dearborn, Nov. 15, 1805, LBATH.

93. Morse, *Report*, 79, 233; Mary Young, "Review Essay: Indian Policy in the Age of Jefferson," *Journal of the Early Republic* 20 (2000), 299; Drew R. McCoy, *The Elusive Republic: Political Economy in Jeffersonian America* (Chapel Hill, N.C., 1980); Theda Perdue, *Cherokee Women: Gender and Culture Change*, 1700–1835 (Lincoln, Neb., 1998), 111–12.

94. Dearborn to Treat, Mar. 29, 1808, Roll 2, M15, RG 75, NA; William Eustis to Samuel Treat, Jan. 9, 1811, Roll 3, M15, RG 75, NA; Treat to Dearborn, Apr. 1, 1807, LBATH; Dwight to Treat, May 8, 1807, LBATH.

95. *Arkansas Gazette*, June 28, 1825.

96. Pike, "Speech to the Osages," Aug. 22, 1806, *Journals of Zebulon Montgomery Pike*, 2: 139–41; Dearborn to P. Chouteau, July 17, 1806, Roll 2, M15, RG 75, NA; Wilkinson to Dearborn, Oct. 17, 1806, *Journals of Zebulon Montgomery Pike*, 2: 154.

97. Dearborn to Sibley, July 8, 1805, Roll 2, M15, RG 75, NA; Davy to Treat, May 10, 1805, LBATH; Davy to Treat, Mar. 3, 1806, LBATH; Treat to Davy, July 13, 1806, LBATH; "Articles recommended to be delivered to Indian Chiefs and party on a visit to the President of the United States," [between 1812 and 1816], Roll 1, M271, RG 75, NA; Treat to Dearborn, Nov. 15, 1805, LBATH.

98. Eustis to Clark, Aug. 7, 1809, Roll 3, M15, RG 75, NA; P. Chouteau to Albert Gallatin, Nov. 7, 1804, *BLC*, 2: 759.

99. William Clark estimated that nine out of ten traders paid no attention to trade regulations. Clark to Madison, Apr. 10, 1811, Roll 1, M271, RG 75, NA; Wallace, *Jefferson and the Indians*, 211–12; Dearborn to Treat, Apr. 29, 1806, LBATH; Little Turtle to Jefferson, Jan. 4, 1802, *The New American State Papers, Indian Affairs* (Wilmington, Del., 1972), 3: 150; Treat to Dearborn, Mar. 27, 1806, LBATH; Wright to Treat, May 8, 1807, LBATH; Dearborn to Commanding Officer, May 8, 1804, *TP*, 13: 21–22; Dearborn to Bissell, May 9, 1804, *TP*, 13: 22; Wilkinson to Dearborn, July 27, 1805, *TP*, 13: 169–70; Wilkinson to Dearborn, Aug. 10, 1805, *TP*, 13: 181. For effects of alcohol on Native American communities, see Peter C. Mancall, *Deadly Medicine: Indians and Alcohol in Early America* (Ithaca, N.Y., 1995); William E. Unrau, *White Man's Wicked Water: The Alcohol Trade and Prohibition in Indian Country*, 1802–1892 (Lawrence, Kans., 1996).

100. St. Louis Merchants to Wilkinson, Aug. 24, 1805, *TP*, 13: 202–3.

101. Jefferson to Dearborn, Apr. 8, 1804, *TP*, 13: 19; Wilkinson to Jefferson, Nov. 6, 1805, *TP*, 13: 266; Lewis, Proclamation, Apr. 6, 1809, *TP*, 14: 261; George Graham to Clark, Nov. 10, 1815, Roll 3, M15, RG 75, NA.

Chapter 7. *A New Order, 1808–1822*

1. Arrell Morgan Gibson, *The American Indian: Prehistory to the Present* (Lexington, Mass., 1980), 299–300; Gilbert Imlay, *A Topographical Description of the Western Territory of North America* (New York, 1792); Dianna Everett, *The Texas Cherokees: A People Between Two Fires, 1819–1840* (Norman, Okla., 1990), 9–10.

2. Theda Perdue, *Cherokee Women: Gender and Culture Change, 1700–1835* (Lincoln, Neb., 1998), 25, 36, 40; Tom Hatley, *The Dividing Paths: Cherokees and South Carolinians Through the Era of Revolution* (New York, 1993), 9; William G. McLoughlin, *Cherokee Renascence in the New Republic* (Princeton, N.J., 1986), 26, 43–44; Robert A. Myers, "Cherokee Pioneers in Arkansas: The St. Francis Years, 1785–1813," *Arkansas Historical Quarterly* 56 (1997), 127–57.

3. McLoughlin, *Cherokee Renascence*, 30, 92, 94, 267; Hatley, *Dividing Paths*, 9; Charles M. Hudson, *The Southeastern Indians* (Knoxville, Tenn., 1976), 240–41, 320–27; Perdue, *Cherokee Women*, 37.

4. Dixie Ray Haggard, "Anigaduwagi and the Sacred Fire: Religious Foundations for the Arkansas Cherokees, 1700–1830," Annual Meeting of the Society for Ethnohistory, Riverside, Calif., Nov. 8, 2003.

5. James Wilkinson to Henry Dearborn, Sept. 22, 1805, *TP*, 13: 228–29; William Dunbar, "Dunbar on Indians of Louisiana," c. 1806, *Life, Letters and Papers of William Dunbar of Elgin, Morayshire, Scotland, and Natchez, Mississippi*, ed. Mrs. Dunbar Rowland (Jackson, Miss., 1930), 210–11; John Treat to Dearborn, Dec. 31, 1806, *TP*, 14: 57; Treat to Dearborn, Apr. 1, 1807, LBATH.

6. Thomas Jefferson to the Upper Cherokees, May 5, 1808, Roll 2, M15, Record Group 75, National Archives, Washington, D.C.

7. Jefferson to the Cherokees, Jan. 9, 1809, Letters Sent by the Office of the Secretary of War Relating to Indian Affairs, 1800–24, Roll 2, M15, RG 75, NA; "Treaty with the Cherokee," July 8, 1817, *Indian Treaties, 1778–1883*, ed. Charles J. Kappler (Mattituck, N.Y., 1972), 140–44; McLoughlin, *Cherokee Renascence*, 109, 145–60, 164; Everett, *Texas Cherokees*, 10–11.

8. Robert Paul Markham, "The Arkansas Cherokees, 1817–1828" (Ph.D. diss., University of Oklahoma, 1972), 34–36.

9. Wilkinson to Dearborn, Oct. 8, 1805, *TP*, 13: 235.

10. "Deposition of William T. Lamme," Jan. 17, 1807, *The Journals of Zebulon Montgomery Pike, with Letters and Related Documents*, ed. Donald Jackson (Norman, Okla., 1966), 2: 163; Wilkinson to Dearborn, Aug. 2, 1806, *Journals of Zebulon Montgomery Pike*, 2: 128.

11. There were 20,000 whites in Louisiana, not counting New Orleans and its environs, by 1810. *Annals of St. Louis in Its Territorial Days from 1804 to 1821*, ed. Frederic

L. Billon (St. Louis, 1888), 66; Dearborn to William Clark, Mar. 24, 1807, Roll 2, M15, RG 75, NA; Frederick Bates to Meriwether Lewis, Apr. 28, 1807, *The Life and Papers of Frederick Bates*, ed. Thomas Maitland Marshall (St. Louis, 1926), 1: 106; Bates to Richard Bates, Mar. 24, 1808, *Life and Papers of Frederick Bates*, 1: 316–17; Bates to Treat, May 26, 1808, *Life and Papers of Frederick Bates*, 1: 344; Lewis to Dearborn, July 1, 1808, *TP*, 14: 196–98; Treat to Dearborn, July 26, 1808, *TP*, 14: 206.

12. Lewis to Dearborn, July 1, 1808, *TP*, 14: 196–98; William Henry Harrison to Dearborn, July 12, 1808, *Messages and Letters of William Henry Harrison*, ed. Logan Esarey (New York, 1975), 1: 296; Tommaqua Beaver, Wenavakhenon Killbuck, Woquickguckhomman, and Phkoakhug to Harrison, Sept. 9, 1808, *Messages and Letters of William Henry Harrison*, 1: 303–4; Pierre Chouteau, Jr., to William Eustis, Sept. 1, 1809, *TP*, 14: 316.

13. Clark to Dearborn, Sept. 23, 1808, *TP*, 14: 224–25. The final treaty, with minor changes, is printed as "Treaty with the Osage," Nov. 10, 1808, *Indian Treaties*, 95–99.

14. Clark to Dearborn, Sept. 23, 1808, *TP*, 14: 225–26; *Westward with Dragoons: The Journal of William Clark on His Expedition to Establish Fort Osage, August 25 to September 2, 1808*, ed. Kate L. Gregg (Fulton, Mo., 1937), 38–41.

15. Clark to Jonathan Clark, Oct. 5, 1808, *Dear Brother: Letters of William Clark to Jonathan Clark*, ed. James J. Holmberg (New Haven, Conn., 2002), 154.

16. Lewis to Jefferson, Dec. 15, 1808, *American State Papers, Indian Affairs* (Washington, D.C., 1832–61), 1: 766; Gilbert C. Din and A. P. Nasatir, *The Imperial Osages: Spanish-Indian Diplomacy in the Mississippi Valley* (Norman, Okla., 1983), 361.

17. Lewis to Jefferson, Dec. 15, 1808, *American State Papers, Indian Affairs*, 1: 766; Clark to Dearborn, Dec. 2, 1808, *TP*, 14: 243; P. Chouteau, Jr., to Eustis, Sept. 1, 1809, *TP*, 14: 316.

18. Daniel K. Richter, *Facing East from Indian Country: A Native History of Early America* (Cambridge, Mass., 2001), 134–40.

19. See, for example, Couzichequeday (Cashesegra), speech, Aug. 8, 1806, "Jacob Bright's Journal of a Trip to the Osage Indians," ed. Harold W. Ryan, *Journal of Southern History* 15 (1949), 520; James B. Wilkinson to Wilkinson, Apr. 6, 1807, *Journals of Zebulon Montgomery Pike*, 2: 15–16. For a discussion of views of land rights, see William Cronon, *Changes in the Land: Indians, Colonists, and the Ecology of New England* (New York, 1983), 62–68.

20. Lewis to P. Chouteau, Oct. 3, 1808, *American State Papers, Indian Affairs*, 1: 766; "Treaty with the Osage," Nov. 10, 1808, 96; Lewis to Jefferson, Dec. 15, 1808, *American State Papers, Indian Affairs*, 1: 766; P. Chouteau, Jr., to Eustis, Sept. 1, 1809, *TP*, 14: 316; Son of White Hair to P. Chouteau, Mar. 4, 1811, *TP*, 14: 467; Willard H. Rollings, *The Osage: An Ethnohistorical Study of Hegemony on the Prairie-Plains* (Columbia, Mo., 1992), 226–27.

21. Dunbar, "Dunbar on Indians of Louisiana," 211; Din and Nasatir, *Imperial Osages*, 359; Couzichequeday, speech, Aug. 4, 1806, 515; Bright to Dearborn, Dec. 20, 1806, "Jacob Bright's Journal," 512; Rollings, *The Osage*, 167–68; Louis F. Burns, *Osage Indian Customs and Myths* (Fallbrook, Calif., 1984), 34–35; Louis F. Burns, *A History of the Osage People* (Fallbrook, Calif., 1989), 57, 65–66; John Joseph Mathews, *The Osages, Children of the Middle Waters* (Norman, Okla., 1961), 299; Garrick Alan Bailey,

Changes in Osage Social Organization: 1673–1906 (Eugene, Oreg., 1973), 59; Treat to John Shee, Dec. 31, 1807, LBATH.

22. James McFarlane to Lewis, Dec. 11, 1808, *TP*, 14: 266–67; Perly Wallis to Bates, Dec. 18, 1808, *Life and Papers of Frederick Bates*, 2: 46.

23. Zebulon Pike, "Dissertation on Louisiana," 1810, *Journals of Zebulon Montgomery Pike*, 2: 32–33; Treat to Dearborn, Dec. 27, 1805, LBATH; Pike to Wilkinson, Aug. 30, 1806, *Journals of Zebulon Montgomery Pike*, 2: 146; P. Chouteau to Clark, July 29, 1813, SLS; Edwin James, "Account of an Expedition from Pittsburgh to the Rocky Mountains Performed in the Years 1819, 1820," *Early Western Travels*, ed. Reuben Gold Thwaites (Cleveland, 1904–7), 16: 274; Richard Graham to James Miller, Jan. 14, 1822, *TP*, 19: map opposite 392; Jedidiah Morse, *A Report to the Secretary of War of the United States, on Indian Affairs, Comprising a Narrative of a Tour Performed in the Summer of* 1820 (New Haven, Conn., 1822), appendix, 203–4, 219.

24. Addendum to "Treaty with the Osage," Aug. 31, 1809, *Indian Treaties*, 99; P. Chouteau, Jr., to Eustis, Sept. 1, 1809, *TP*, 14: 315–19; Clark to Eustis, Feb. 20, 1810, *American State Papers, Indian Affairs*, 1: 765.

25. Bates to Thomas Hunt, Sept. 4, 1807, *Life and Papers of Frederick Bates*, 1: 179; Clark to Dearborn, Apr. 29, 1809, *TP*, 14: 265; Harrison to Eustis, Aug. 6, 1811, *Messages and Letters of William Henry Harrison*, 1: 545; P. Chouteau to John Armstrong, Mar. 5, 1813, *TP*, 14: 640; Clark to Armstrong, Sept. 18, 1814, *TP*, 14: 787; John Dunn Hunter, *Manners and Customs of Several Indian Tribes Located West of the Mississippi* (Philadelphia, 1823), 51–56. On unity and nativism in the pan-Indian movements of the eighteenth and early nineteenth centuries, see Gregory Evans Dowd, *A Spirited Resistance: The North American Indian Struggle for Unity*, 1745–1815 (Baltimore, 1992); R. David Edmunds, *Tecumseh and the Quest for Indian Leadership* (Boston, 1984); Richard White, *The Middle Ground: Indians, Empires, and Republics in the Great Lakes Region*, 1650–1815 (New York, 1991), 502–17.

26. John Bradbury, "Travels in the Interior of America In the Years 1809, 1810, and 1811," *Early Western Travels*, 5: 48–49, 52; Bates to Clark, Sept. 15, 1807, *Life and Papers of Frederick Bates*, 1: 188; John Sugden, *Tecumseh: A Life* (New York, 1998), 351.

27. Qtd. in H. B. Cushman, *History of the Choctaw, Chickasaw and Natchez Indians* (Norman, Okla., 1999), 254–55. Thanks to David Nichols for this comparison.

28. Sugden, *Tecumseh*, 252.

29. Bates to Hunt, Sept. 4, 1807, *Life and Papers of Frederick Bates*, 1: 179; P. Chouteau to Armstrong, May 20, 1813, *TP*, 14: 671–72; Benjamin Howard to Armstrong, Mar. 6, 1813, *TP*, 14: 641.

30. Eustis to Indian Agents, Apr. 15, 1811, Roll 3, M15, RG 75, NA; Eustis to Clark, Dec. 23, 1811, Roll 3, M15, RG 75, NA; Eustis to Indian Agents, June 19, 1812, Roll 3, M15, RG 75, NA; Bates to Howard, Feb. 27, 1813, *TP*, 14: 638; Bates to P. Chouteau, Mar. 4, 1813, *TP*, 14: 673–74.

31. P. Chouteau to Armstrong, Mar. 5, 1813, *TP*, 14: 640.

32. Edward Hempstead to Armstrong, June 14, 1813, *TP*, 14: 676; Howard to P. Chouteau, Apr. 1813, *TP*, 14: 674; P. Chouteau to Armstrong, May 20, 1813, *TP*, 14: 671.

33. Clark to Armstrong, Aug. 20, 1814, *TP*, 14: 786–87; Clark to Armstrong, Sept. 18, 1814, *TP*, 14: 787.

34. David J. Weber, *The Spanish Frontier in North America* (New Haven, Conn., 1992), 296.

35. John Norton, *The Journal of Major John Norton, 1816*, ed. Carl F. Klink and James J. Talman (Toronto, 1970), 54–55; William L. Lovely to Armstrong, Oct. 1, 1813, *TP*, 14: 705–6; Esteban Miró to Francisco Cruzat, Mar. 24, 1786, *SMV*, 2: 171–73; Markham, "Arkansas Cherokees," 15.

36. James, "Account of an Expedition," 17: 19–20; Alpheus H. Favour, *Old Bill Williams, Mountain Man* (Norman, Okla., 1962), 55; Rollings, *The Osage*, 239; Mathews, *Osages*, 422–24; Tillie Karns Newman, *The Black Dog Trail* (Boston, 1957), 54; "The Journals of Jules De Mun," ed. Thomas Maitland Marshall, trans. Nettie H. Beauregard, *Missouri Historical Society Collections* 5 (1928), 167–208; Pekka Hämäläinen, "The Rise and Fall of Plains Indian Horse Cultures," *Journal of American History* 90 (2003), 857.

37. Charles C. Royce, *Indian Land Cessions in the United States* (New York, 1971), Plates 5 and 21; Lovely to Clark, May 27, 1815, *TP*, 15: 57; Lovely to Alexander Dallas, May 27, 1815, *TP*, 15: 49; Lovely to Clermont and all the Chiefs of the Osage Nation, July 9, 1816, Document E, *Report of the Secretary of War Relative to Settlement of Lovely's Purchase*, Apr. 30, 1828, House Document No. 263, 20th Congress, 1st Session, *The United States and the Indians*, vol. 5, Ayer Collection, Newberry Library, Chicago; Clark to John C. Calhoun, Oct. 1818, Letters Received by the Office of the Secretary of War Relating to Indian Affairs, 1800–24, Roll 2, M271, RG 75, NA; Clark-Osage Treaty, Dec. 25, 1818, U.S. Office of Indian Affairs, SLS; "Treaty with the Osage," Sept. 25, 1818, 167–68.

38. Calhoun to Clark, May 8, 1818, Roll 4, M15, RG 75, NA.

39. Miller to Calhoun, Mar. 24, 1820, *TP*, 19: 153–54; Stephen H. Long to Thomas A. Smith, Jan. 30, 1818, *TP*, 19: 7.

40. Union Mission Journal, in W. W. Graves, *The First Protestant Osage Missions, 1820–1837* (Oswego, Kans., 1949), 41.

41. Clermont II, speech, Sept. 15, 1821, *TP*, 19: 321.

42. Calhoun to W. Clark, May 8, 1818, Roll 4, M15, RG 75, NA.

43. Clark, Ninian Edwards, and Auguste Chouteau to William H. Crawford, June 30, 1816, *TP*, 15: 151–52. For more on relations between Cherokees and western Indians throughout the nineteenth century, see David La Vere, *Contrary Neighbors: Southern Plains and Removed Indians in Indian Territory* (Norman, Okla., 2000).

44. A. H. Abney, *Life and Adventures of L. D. Lafferty* (New York, 1875), 23; James, "Account of an Expedition," 17: 21; Bradford to Calhoun, Feb. 4, 1819, *TP*, 19: 33–34; *Arkansas Gazette*, July 21, 1821.

45. Althea Bass, *Maria, The Osage Captive* (Norman, Okla., 1978), 25.

46. Brent Gary Bergherm, "The Little Osage Captive: The Tragic Saga of Lydia Carter," *Arkansas Historical Quarterly* 62 (2003), 123–52; Elias Cornelius, *The Little Osage Captive* (New York, 1977); Calhoun to Clark, July 20, 1820, *TP* 15: 628.

47. Rollings, *The Osage*, 243; Clark, "A Report of the Names and Probable Number of the Tribes of Indians in the Missouri Territory," Nov. 4, 1816, Roll 1, M271, RG 75, NA; S. Charles Bolton, *Arkansas, 1800–1860: Remote and Restless* (Fayetteville, Ark., 1998), 5.

48. John Phillip Reid, *A Better Kind of Hatchet: Law, Trade, and Diplomacy in the Cherokee Nation During the Early Years of European Contact* (University Park, Pa.,

1976), 9; Rennard Strickland, *Fire and the Spirits: Cherokee Law from Clan to Court* (Norman, Okla., 1975), 27–28, 54; McLoughlin, *Cherokee Renascence*, 12–13, 21, 44, 50; Perdue, *Cherokee Women*, 49–52; Hudson, *Southeastern Indians*, 229–32; Rollings, *The Osage*, 237.

49. John Sibley to Dearborn, Mar. 20, 1807, Roll 1, M271, RG 75, NA; Calhoun to Clark, May 8, 1818, Roll 4, M15, RG 75, NA; C. A. Weslager, *The Delaware Indians: A History* (New Brunswick, N.J., 1972), 353–55; Sugden, *Tecumseh*, 208.

50. John Jolly to Calhoun, Jan. 28, 1818, Letters Received by the Office of the Secretary of War Relating to Indian Affairs, 1800–24, Roll 2.

51. Rollings, *The Osage*, 240; Burns, *Osage Indian Customs and Myths*, xi; William E. Unrau, *The Kansa Indians: A History of the Wind People* 1673–1873 (Norman, Okla., 1971), 33, 83, 86, 91; Thomas Nuttall, *A Journal of Travels into the Arkansas Territory During the Year* 1819, ed. Savoie Lottinville (Norman, Okla., 1980), 207.

52. Jolly to Calhoun, Jan. 28, 1818, Letters Received by the Office of the Secretary of War Relating to Indian Affairs, 1800–24, Roll 2.

53. James, "Account of an Expedition," 17: 17–18.

54. W. David Baird, *The Quapaw Indians: A History of the Downstream People* (Norman, Okla., 1980), 11.

55. McLoughlin, *Cherokee Renascence*, 217; Nathaniel Sheidley, "Origins of the First New South: Manhood, Capital, and the Making of a Native American Elite in the Post-Revolutionary Southeast," unpublished article.

56. Leslie C. Stewart-Abernathy, "Some Archeological Perspectives on the Arkansas Cherokee," *Arkansas Archeologist* 37 (1996), 39–54.

57. Tolluntuskee to Return J. Meigs, June 28, 1812, qtd. in McLoughlin, *Cherokee Renascence*, 217.

58. Arkansas Cherokee Chiefs to Clark, July 11, 1817, *TP*, 15: 304.

59. Chiefs of the Arkansaw Cherokees to James Monroe, Mar. 17, 1821, Roll 3, M271, RG 75, NA. In turn, Cherokees in the East pointed to the Osage war as a reason why they should not be forced to move west. *Cherokee Phoenix*, July 9, 1828, Huntington Library Collections, San Marino, Calif.

60. Cherokee Delegation to Calhoun, Feb. 26, 1823, Roll 4, M271, RG 75, NA.

61. Chiefs of the Arkansaw Cherokees to Monroe, Mar. 17, 1821, Roll 3, M271, RG 75, NA.

62. Cherokee Chiefs to Clark, Oct. 27, 1824, SLS.

63. Cherokees to Howard, Apr. 27, 1813, *Life and Papers of Frederick Bates*, 2: 239–41.

64. Clermont II, speech, Sept. 15, 1821, *TP*, 19: 320–21.

65. Union Mission Journal, 55.

66. Willard H. Rollings, *Unaffected by the Gospel: Osage Resistance to the Christian Invasion* 1673–1906: *A Cultural Victory* (Albuquerque, 2004), 6.

67. Miller to Calhoun, Mar. 24, 1820, *TP*, 19: 153–54.

68. Nuttall, *Journal*, 212–13. For references to declining game, see Arkansas Cherokees to Monroe, Mar. 17, 1821, *TP*, 19: 273; Clermont II, speech, Sept. 15, 1821, *TP*, 19: 321; Clark to Osage Nation, n.d., SLS.

69. *Arkansas Gazette*, May 12, 1821; *Niles' Weekly Register*, June 30, 1821; Grant Foreman, *Pioneer Days in the Early Southwest* (Lincoln, Neb., 1994), 58–59.

70. George Peter to Wilkinson, Sept. 8, 1805, *TP*, 13: 231; Pike, *The Expeditions of Zebulon Montgomery Pike, To Headwaters of the Mississippi River, Through Louisiana Territory, and in New Spain, during the years* 1805–6–7, ed. Elliott Coues (New York, 1895), 2: 590; Meigs to Crawford, Feb. 17, 1816, *TP*, 15: 121; "A List of Indian Tribes under the Superintendence of the Governor of Missouri Territory," Aug. 24, 1817, *TP*, 15: 305; Morse, *Report*, appendix, 152; Henry Rowe Schoolcraft, *Rude Pursuits and Rugged Peaks: Schoolcraft's Ozark Journal*, 1818–1819, ed. Milton D. Rafferty (Fayetteville, Ark., 1996), 48; Thomas McKenney to James Barbour, Jan. 10, 1825, *Message from the President of the United States, Transmitting Sundry Documents in Relation to the Various Tribes of Indians within the United States*, Jan. 27, 1825, Senate Document No. 21, 18th Congress, 2nd Session, *The United States and the Indians*, vol. 1. Observers described the Osages as "very poor." Union Mission Journal, 54.

71. Union Mission Journal, 53.

72. "Treaty with the Osage," Aug. 31, 1822, *Indian Treaties*, 201–2.

73. Bradford to Calhoun, Mar. 4, 1820, *TP*, 19: 151; James, "Account of an Expedition," 17: 19; Union Mission Journal, 41; Andrew Jackson to Calhoun, Apr. 30, 1820, *TP*, 19: 169; Bradford to Jackson, Mar. 4, 1820, *TP*, 19: 169.

74. Union Mission Journal, 49; Bradford to Calhoun, Mar. 28, 1819, *TP*, 19: 58; Foreman, *Pioneer Days*, 58–59.

75. William Vaill to Calhoun, Oct. 30, 1821, Roll 3, M271, RG 75, NA.

76. Calhoun to Matthew Lyon, July 21, 1821, *TP*, 19: 304–5.

77. Calhoun to Miller, June 29, 1820, *TP*, 19: 199.

78. Robert Crittenden to Calhoun, May 17, 1821, *TP*, 19: 288–89; Calhoun to Crittenden, July 7, 1821, *TP*, 19: 299.

79. Bradford to Calhoun, Aug. 10, 1821, *TP*, 19: 309.

Chapter 8. The End of the Native Ground? 1815–1828

1. Edwin James, "Account of an Expedition from Pittsburgh to the Rocky Mountains, Performed in the Years 1819, 1820," *Early Western Travels*, ed. Reuben Gold Thwaites (Cleveland, 1904–7), 17: 31–33; John Treat to Henry Dearborn, Nov. 15, 1805, LBATH; Stephen Aron, "Pigs and Hunters: 'Rights in the Woods' on the Trans-Appalachian Frontier," in *Contact Points: American Frontiers from the Mohawk Valley to the Mississippi, 1750–1830*, ed. Andrew R. L. Cayton and Fredrika J. Teute (Chapel Hill, N.C., 1998), 175–204.

2. John Billingsley, "Letters from an Early Arkansas Settler," ed. Ted R. Worley, *Arkansas Historical Quarterly* 11 (1952), 327–29; James, "Account of an Expedition," 17: 13.

3. Fortescue Cuming, "Sketches of a Tour to the Western Country," *Early Western Travels*, 4: 298–99.

4. Henry Rowe Schoolcraft, *Rude Pursuits and Rugged Peaks: Schoolcraft's Ozark Journal*, 1818–1819, ed. Milton D. Rafferty (Fayetteville, Ark., 1996), 52–55, 74, 63.

5. S. Charles Bolton, introduction, *A Documentary History of Arkansas*, ed. C. Fred Williams, S. Charles Bolton, Carl H. Moneyhon, and LeRoy T. Williams

(Fayetteville, Ark., 1984), 25; S. Charles Bolton, *Arkansas, 1800–1860: Remote and Restless* (Fayetteville, Ark., 1998), 17, 50, 125–27; Donald P. McNeilly, *The Old South Frontier: Cotton Plantations and the Formation of Arkansas Society, 1819–1861* (Fayetteville, Ark., 2000); Joseph Patrick Key, " 'Masters of This Country': The Quapaws and Environmental Change in Arkansas, 1673–1833" (Ph.D. diss., University of Arkansas, 2001), Chapter 6; Treat to Dearborn, Nov. 15, 1805, LBATH; Daniel H. Usner, Jr., *Indians, Settlers, and Slaves in a Frontier Exchange Economy: The Lower Mississippi Valley before 1783* (Chapel Hill, N.C., 1992), 114; James Logan Morgan, 1820 *Census of the Territory of Arkansas (Reconstructed)* (Newport, Ark., 1984), 92.

6. Roy Harvey Pearce, *Savagism and Civilization: A Study of the Indian and the American Mind* (Baltimore, 1965); Robert F. Berkhofer, Jr., *The White Man's Indian: Images of the American Indian from Columbus to the Present* (New York, 1978); Reginald Horsman, *Race and Manifest Destiny: The Origins of American Racial Anglo-Saxonism* (Cambridge, Mass., 1981); Theda Perdue, *"Mixed Blood" Indians: Racial Construction in the Early South* (Athens, Ga., 2003), 81–90; Treat to Dearborn, Nov. 15, 1805, LBATH; Cuming, "Sketches," 4: 298; Billingsley, "Letters," 327; Walter N. Vernon, "Beginnings of Methodism in Arkansas," *Arkansas Historical Quarterly* 31 (1972), 359, 367. On slim opportunities east of the Mississippi, see Alan Taylor, "Land and Liberty on the Post-Revolutionary Frontier," in *Devising Liberty: Preserving and Creating Freedom in the New American Republic,* ed. David Thomas Konig (Stanford, Calif., 1995), 87.

7. William Dunbar, Jan. 10, 1805, "The Exploration of the *Red*, the *Black*, and the *Washita* Rivers," *Documents Relating to the Purchase and Exploration of Louisiana* (Boston, 1904), 167; Stephen H. Long to Thomas A. Smith, Jan. 30, 1818, *TP*, 19: 5; petition to the president by the Territorial Assembly, Feb. 11, 1820, *TP*, 19: 144; Memorial to Congress by the Territorial Assembly, Oct. 17, 1821, *TP*, 19: 328; Charles C. Royce, *Indian Land Cessions in the United States* (New York, 1971), Plate 5; "Treaty with the Quapaw," Aug. 24, 1818, *Indian Treaties, 1778–1883,* ed. Charles J. Kappler (New York, 1972), 160–61.

8. Petition to Congress by Inhabitants of Arkansas County, Nov. 2, 1818, *TP*, 19: 11–12; Reuben Lewis to John C. Calhoun, Jan. 21, 1820, *TP*, 19: 137; James Miller to Calhoun, Feb. 15, 1820, *TP*, 19: 149–50; Miller to Calhoun, Mar. 24, 1820, *TP*, 19: 154; Miller to Calhoun, June 20, 1820, *TP*, 19: 194; Calhoun to David Brearley, May 3, 1822, *TP*, 19: 430; "Executive Register for the Arkansas Territory, 1819–1836," *TP*, 19: 801.

9. Robert Crittenden to Calhoun, Sept. 28, 1823, *TP*, 19: 549.

10. "Treaty with the Choctaw," Oct. 18, 1820, *Indian Treaties*, 191.

11. *Arkansas Gazette*, Oct. 15, 1822; Clayborn Wright, "Census of West Portion of Miller County," July 10, 1825, *TP*, 20: 92–93; Henry Conway to Calhoun, Oct. 19, 1821, *TP*, 19: 329; William Woodward to Calhoun, Dec. 15, 1821, *TP*, 19: 380–81; Morgan, 1820 *Census.*

12. Miller to Calhoun, Dec. 11, 1820, *TP*, 19: 244–46.

13. *Arkansas Gazette*, Feb. 17, 1821.

14. Woodward to Calhoun, Dec. 15, 1821, *TP*, 19: 381.

15. *Arkansas Gazette*, Jan. 27, 1821.

16. "Petition to the President by Citizens of Miller County," 1825, *TP*, 20: 138–39.

17. Thomas Jefferson to Dearborn, Apr. 8, 1804, *TP*, 13: 19; James Wilkinson to Jefferson, Nov. 6, 1805, *TP*, 13: 266; Treat to Dearborn, Dec. 31, 1806, *TP*, 14: 56; Frederick Bates, "Writ issued to Henry Dodge for the Removal of John Henry," Nov. 5, 1807, *TP*, 14: 174–76; Meriwether Lewis, proclamation, Apr. 6, 1809, *TP*, 14: 261; George Graham to William Clark, Nov. 10, 1815, Roll 3, M15, RG 75, NA; John Jamison to Graham, Mar. 31, 1817, *TP*, 15: 257–58; Thomas McKenney to Clark, Jan. 10, 1828, Letters Sent by the Office of Indian Affairs, 1824–69, Roll 4, M21, RG 75, NA; Anthony F. C. Wallace, *Jefferson and the Indians: The Tragic Fate of the First Americans* (Cambridge, Mass., 1999), 217.

18. Clark to William Crawford, Sept. 30, 1816, *TP*, 15: 177.

19. Calhoun to Clark, July 20, 1820, *TP*, 15: 627–28; Calhoun to Henry Atkinson, July 21, 1820, *TP*, 15: 629; Atkinson to Calhoun, Nov. 23, 1820, *TP*, 15: 671; Calhoun to Atkinson, Dec. 19, 1820, *TP*, 15: 684.

20. Josiah Meigs to Crawford, May 14, 1821, *TP*, 15: 726.

21. *Arkansas Gazette*, Nov. 30, 1824.

22. George Izard to James Barbour, July 2, 1825, George Izard Letterbook No. 1, "Official Correspondence with the Department of War, Arkansa Territory Executive," No. 12, Box 9, Small Manuscripts Collection, Arkansas History Commission, Little Rock, Ark.; McKenney to Izard, Aug. 5, 1825, *Report of the Secretary of War in Relation to the Present Condition of the Quapaw Nation of Indians*, Jan. 10, 1827, 19th Congress, 2nd Session, House Document No. 43 (Washington, D.C., 1827), *The United States and the Indians*, supplement, Ayer Collection, Newberry Library, Chicago; *Arkansas Gazette*, Dec. 27, 1825; Antoine Barraque, "Historical Translation of Antoine Barraque Manuscript," ed. and trans. Laura Hinderks Thompson, *Arkansas Historical Quarterly* 40 (1981), 220–24; W. David Baird, *The Quapaw Indians: A History of the Downstream People* (Norman, Okla., 1980), 67–68.

23. Hekatton to Izard, Apr. 17, 1826, Izard Letterbook.

24. Baird, *Quapaw Indians*, 71–77.

25. John Berrey, Chair of the Quapaw Tribe of Oklahoma, "Quapaw History: Yesterday and Today," Colonial Arkansas Conference and Powwow, Little Rock, Ark., Oct. 10, 2003.

26. Crittenden to Calhoun, Sept. 28, 1823, *TP*, 19: 548; "Treaty with the Choctaw," Jan. 20, 1825, *Indian Treaties*, 211–14; "Treaty with the Osage," June 2, 1825, *Indian Treaties*, 217–21.

27. Cherokee Delegation to Barbour, Mar. 12, 1825, *TP*, 20: 4–5.

28. *Arkansas Gazette*, Apr. 23, 1828.

29. *Report of the House Committee on Indian Affairs, Regarding Indians Removing Westward*, Jan. 7, 1828, House Document No. 56, 20th Congress, 1st Session, *The United States and the Indians*, vol. 5; McKenney to William McLean, Mar. 7, 1828, Roll 4, M21, RG 75, NA.

30. Barbour, report to the Committee on Indian Affairs, Feb. 3, 1826, U.S. Congress Register of Debates, 19th Congress, 1st Session, vol. 2, part 2, appendix, 40; John Wood Sweet, *Bodies Politic: Negotiating Race in the American North, 1730–1830* (Baltimore, 2003), 10, 63; Alan Taylor, *Liberty Men and Great Proprietors: The Revolutionary Settlement on the Maine Frontier, 1760–1820* (Chapel Hill, N.C., 1990); Woody Holton, *Forced Founders: Indians, Debtors, Slaves, and the Making of the American Revolution*

in Virginia (Chapel Hill, N.C., 1999); Reginald Horsman, "The Indian Policy of an 'Empire for Liberty,'" in *Native Americans and the Early Republic*, ed. Frederick E. Hoxie, Ronald Hoffman, and Peter J. Albert (Charlottesville, Va., 1999), 54–55. Of course, there were still Indians in all the eastern states, but they no longer seemed threatening. See, for example, *After King Philip's War: Presence and Persistence in Indian New England*, ed. Colin G. Calloway (Hanover, N.H., 1997).

31. McKenney to the Arkansas Cherokee Deputation, Apr. 3, 1828, Roll 4, M21, RG 75, NA; McKenney to the Arkansas Cherokee Deputation, Mar. 27, 1828, Roll 4, M21, RG 75, NA.

32. "Treaty with the Western Cherokee," May 6, 1828, *Indian Treaties*, 288–91.

33. McKenney to Barbour, Apr. 12, 1828, Roll 4, M21, RG 75, NA. For more on McKenney, see Herman J. Viola, *Thomas McKenney: Architect of America's Early Indian Policy, 1816–1830* (Chicago, 1974).

34. McKenney to Izard, May 28, 1828, Roll 4, M21, RG 75, NA.

35. Barbour to the Arkansas Cherokee Deputation, May 17, 1828, Roll 4, M21, RG 75, NA; *Cherokee Phoenix*, Aug. 13, 1828; *Cherokee Phoenix*, Oct. 15, 1828.

36. *Cherokee Phoenix*, Oct. 29, 1828.

37. *Cherokee Phoenix*, Nov. 12, 1828.

38. "Treaty with the Western Cherokee," May 6, 1828, 290.

39. *Cherokee Phoenix*, July 9, 1828; *Cherokee Phoenix*, Oct. 22, 1828.

40. *Cherokee Phoenix*, Sept. 17, 1828.

41. *Arkansas Gazette*, Oct. 15, 1822.

42. "Treaty with the Creeks," Jan. 24, 1826, *Indian Treaties*, 264–68; John W. Morris, Charles R. Goins, and Edwin C. McReynolds, *Historical Atlas of Oklahoma* (Norman, Okla., 1986), Maps 26, 33, 34.

43. Barbour, report to the Committee on Indian Affairs, Feb. 3, 1826, 43; Reginald Horsman, *Race and Manifest Destiny: The Origins of American Racial Anglo-Saxonism* (Cambridge, Mass., 1981), 122.

44. George Izard, "Notes Respecting the Arkansa Territory," "A Report on the Quapaw: The Letters of Governor George Izard to the American Philosophical Society, 1825–1827," ed. David W. Bizzell, *Pulaski County Historical Review* 29 (1981), 72–73.

45. Horsman, *Race and Manifest Destiny*, 122.

46. Alden T. Vaughan, *Roots of American Racism: Essays on the Colonial Experience* (New York, 1995), especially viii-x, 3–33. For an introduction to the debates over the origins of race, see David Brion Davis, "Constructing Race: A Reflection," *WMQ* 54 (1997), 7–18.

47. Daniel K. Richter, *The Ordeal of the Longhouse: The Peoples of the Iroquois League in the Era of European Colonization* (Chapel Hill, N.C., 1992), 32–33, 68–70; Perdue, "*Mixed Blood*" *Indians*, 7–11; James Axtell, "The White Indians of Colonial America," *WMQ* 32 (1975), 55–88; Winthrop D. Jordan, *White over Black: American Attitudes Toward the Negro, 1550–1812* (Chapel Hill, N.C., 1968), 3–43; Nicholas P. Canny, "The Ideology of English Colonization: From Ireland to America," *WMQ* 30 (1973), 588–95.

48. Edmund S. Morgan, *American Slavery, American Freedom: The Ordeal of Colonial Virginia* (New York, 1975), 331–32; Kathleen Brown, "Native Americans and Early Modern Concepts of Race," in *Empire and Others: British Encounters with*

Indigenous Peoples, 1600–1850, ed. Martin Daunton and Rick Halpern (Philadelphia, 1999), 95; Kirsten Fischer, *Suspect Relations: Sex, Race, and Resistance in Colonial North Carolina* (Ithaca, N.Y., 2002), 1–2; Jorge Cañizares Esguerra, "New World, New Stars: Patriotic Astrology and the Invention of Indian and Creole Bodies in Colonial Spanish America, 1600–1650," *American Historical Review* 104 (1999), 34; Mia Bay, *The White Image in the Black Mind: African-American Ideas about White People,* 1830–1925 (New York, 2000), 13–14; George M. Fredrickson, *The Black Image in the White Mind: The Debate on Afro-American Character and Destiny,* 1817–1914 (New York, 1971); Ira Berlin, *Many Thousands Gone: The First Two Centuries of Slavery in North America* (Cambridge, Mass, 1998), 358, 363; Jane T. Merritt, *At the Crossroads: Indians and Empires on a Mid-Atlantic Frontier,* 1700–1763 (Chapel Hill, N.C., 2003).

49. Andrew Jackson, Fifth Annual Message to Congress, Dec. 3, 1833, *A Compilation of the Messages and Papers of the Presidents* (New York, 1897), 3: 1252.

Conclusion

1. Andrew Jackson, Second Annual Message to Congress, Dec. 6, 1830, *A Compilation of the Messages and Papers of the Presidents* (New York, 1897), 3: 1084.

2. Alan Taylor, *American Colonies* (New York, 2001), xii; James H. Merrell, *The Indians' New World: Catawbas and Their Neighbors from European Contact Through the Era of Removal* (New York, 1989).

3. On the frustrations and power of empires, see John Robert McNeill, *Atlantic Empires of France and Spain: Louisbourg and Havana,* 1700–1763 (Chapel Hill, N.C., 1985).

4. For Indians' and Africans' power in their homelands, see Daniel K. Richter, *Facing East from Indian Country: A Native History of Early America* (Cambridge, Mass., 2001); John Thornton, *Africa and Africans in the Making of the Atlantic World,* 1400–1680 (New York, 1992). For slaves' influence over their lives and the institution of slavery, see Philip D. Morgan, *Slave Counterpoint: Black Culture in the Eighteenth-Century Chesapeake and Lowcountry* (Chapel Hill, N.C., 1998); Ira Berlin, *Many Thousands Gone: The First Two Centuries of Slavery in North America* (Cambridge, Mass., 1998). For Indians' impact on colonial New England, see Mary Beth Norton, *In the Devil's Snare: The Salem Witchcraft Crisis of 1692* (New York, 2002); Ann Marie Plane, *Colonial Intimacies: Indian Marriage in Early New England* (Ithaca, N.Y., 2000); Jean M. O'Brien, *Dispossession by Degrees: Indian Land and Identity in Natick, Massachusetts,* 1650–1790 (New York, 1997).

5. The British set a precedent for removal with the Acadians in the 1750s. In that case, because the Acadians were of European descent, British officials moved them deeper into British settlements rather than farther away, in hopes of assimilating them. Geoffrey Plank, *An Unsettled Conquest: The British Campaign against the Peoples of Acadia* (Philadelphia, 2001), 140–67.

6. *Worcester v. Georgia,* 31 U.S. 515 (1832).

7. Fisher Ames to Thomas Dwight, Oct. 31, 1803, *Works of Fisher Ames, with a Selection from His Speeches and Correspondence,* ed. Seth Ames (Boston, 1854), 1: 329.

8. United States Census Bureau, "American Indian and Alaska Native Alone and Alone or in Combination Population by Tribe for the United States: 2000," http://www.census.gov/population/www/cen2000/phc-t18.html. Also see Nancy Shoemaker, *American Indian Population Recovery in the Twentieth Century* (Albuquerque, 1999).

Index

Acknowledgments

I am grateful for helpful suggestions and encouragement all along the way. Alan Taylor and Daniel Richter read the manuscript more times than I had any right to ask. Colin Calloway, Steven Crum, John DuVal, Kay DuVal, Evan Haefli, Karen Halttunen, Bob Lockhart, Andrés Reséndez, Marty Smith, Christina Snyder, Jennifer Turner, and an anonymous reader read the entire manuscript and gave me invaluable comments. David Nichols read several key chapters, and Bethel Saler helped my introduction enormously. Stephen Aron, Ned Blackhawk, Charles Bolton, George Boudreau, Michelle Craig, Bridget Ford, Phil Garone, Michael Green, Dallet Hemphill, Don Higginbotham, Eric Hinderaker, Michael Hoffman, Ronald Hoffman, Benjamin Irvin, George Jarrett, Roderick McDonald, Bob Moore, Michael Morrison, Sherri Patton, Theda Perdue, Birte Phleger, Mark Pingree, Jack Rakove, Seth Rockman, Martha Rojas, Brett Rushforth, Nancy Shoemaker, Wendy St. Jean, John Sweet, Fredrika Teute, Karim Tiro, Clarence Walker, Gregory Waselkov, Jeannie Whayne, Patrick Williams, Stephanie Wolf, and Michael Zuckerman improved certain chapters. For stimulating conversations on the Arkansas Valley, I thank Morris Arnold, John Berry, Frederick Fausz, Joseph Key, and George Sabo III. Paul Longmore got me interested in early American history to begin with. James O'Rourke corrected many errors in my notes, and John DuVal improved my translations. Many thanks to Cynthia Franco, Leslie Green, David Miller, Kathleen Moenster, John Pollack, Jill Reichenbach, Richard Sorenson, Lou Stancari, Andy Steadham, Mary Suter, and Ron Tyler for helping me track down the illustrations and to Erik Moore for indexing.

The American Philosophical Society, the Huntington Library, the Newberry Library, and the University of California, Davis, provided invaluable assistance in the initial stage, as did an Alfred M. Landon Historical Research Grant administered by the Kansas State Historical Society. The McNeil Center for Early American Studies and its director, Daniel Richter, gave me two heavenly postdoctoral years at the University of Pennsylvania, funded by the Andrew W. Mellon Foundation. The University of North Carolina, Chapel Hill, funded the finishing touches. I particularly want to thank the staffs of the Historic New Orleans Collection and of Special Collections at the University of Arkansas, the University of California, Davis, the University of North Carolina, and Duke University for their great help and good humor. Without all of this assistance, this book would be thinner in every way.

Without my friends and colleagues at Davis, the McNeil Center, and now here at Chapel Hill, my work would be less good and less fun. I particularly want to thank Alan Taylor for his mentorship and friendship. I dedicate the book to my family, especially Marty, Kay, John, Niell, Anne, Steve, Carol, and Dan. It is also for Mary, Hélène, and Erin, who were here when I started all this. And for Quentin, who has come.